T0282918

Also by James Polchin

Indecent Advances: A Hidden History of True Crime and Prejudice Before Stonewall

Shadow Men

The Tangled Story of Murder, Media, *and* Privilege *That Scandalized Jazz Age America*

James Polchin

COUNTERPOINT
CALIFORNIA

Shadow Men

First Counterpoint edition: 2024

Library of Congress Cataloging-in-Publication Data
Names: Polchin, James, author.
Title: Shadow men : the tangled story of murder, media, and privilege that scandalized jazz age America / James Polchin.
Description: Berkeley, California : Counterpoint, [2024] | Includes bibliographical references.
Identifiers: LCCN 2023052627 | ISBN 9781640096004 (hardcover) | ISBN 9781640096011 (ebook)
Subjects: LCSH: Murder—United States. | Crime and the press—United States.
Classification: LCC HV6529 .P65 2024 | DDC 364.152/30973—dc23/eng/20240112
LC record available at https://lccn.loc.gov/2023052627

Jacket design by Farjana Yasmin
Jacket image © iStock / ysbrandcosijn
Book design by Laura Berry
Shadow photograph © Adobe Stock / tomertu

COUNTERPOINT
Los Angeles and San Francisco, CA
www.counterpointpress.com

Printed in the United States of America

10 9 8 7 6 5 4 3 2 1

For Greg

there remains a mystery that always remains there
even after you know who did it

—GERTRUDE STEIN,
"American Crimes and How They Matter"

Contents

AN UNCERTAIN JUSTICE

Shadow Men

Prologue

A Lonely Road

We don't know why Duncan Rose was late to work that May morning in 1922. But there he was at around 7:45 a.m. on May 16 speeding down King Street, a concrete thoroughfare tunneled by red oaks and sweet birch trees in Westchester County, New York. The morning was unusually warm, the air damp and hazy. Rose encountered little traffic as he made his way to Rhoemer's Pharmacy on Main Street in White Plains. Thirty-year-old Rose started as a pharmacist apprentice in the years before World War I. After the war, he and his wife, Betty, settled in the town of Chappaqua, just twelve miles north from White Plains and about thirty miles from New York City. While the two would eventually have four children and raise them in the changing suburbs of Westchester, Rose was most likely not thinking about the path his life might take as he drove along King Street, rounding the northern edge of the Kensico Reservoir. His only concern was getting to the store before a small crowd of customers simmered with impatience as they found the pharmacy door locked and the CLOSED sign still hanging in the front window.[1]

As often happens when one is rushing to work, Rose soon encountered a roadblock: two Packard trucks, standing side by side, faced him as he slowed his car to a stop. Waiting for the trucks to move, he took note that one carried three or four men, and the other looked empty. The driver of the one truck stood in the middle of the road, talking and laughing with the others, animated in his hand gestures.

Rose wondered what might have motivated the man's excitement at that early-morning hour. He would later describe how the men "looked like foreigners and laborers."[2] After one of the trucks pulled to the side, Rose resumed his commute.

But not for long.

About mile or so later he encountered Clarence Eckhardt standing on the narrow, sandy shoulder, waving his arms wildly in the air. Eckhardt owned Ardson Farm adjacent to King Street, just up the hill, through a thicket of trees from where he stood. Worried about the time, Rose ignored the farmer, thinking he was just a lonely hitchhiker, or worse, some bootlegging bandit. But as he got closer, the farmer persisted in his shouting, forcing Rose to stop. Parking along the narrow shoulder, Rose walked back toward Eckhardt. He noticed three other men standing in the distance near a small clearing. William Burke, one of Eckhardt's farmhands, stood nearest the scene. Next to him was Richard Short, who worked at a neighboring farm. And farther off from the group was Frank Taxter, a twenty-year veteran of the Westchester County Light Company who was casually searching the edges of the woods. The men were all somber faced as they watched Rose approach.[3]

That's when Rose noticed the body of a young man on the ground. Dressed in a dark-brown suit with thin red stripes and wearing a white shirt, unbuttoned at the neck and absent a collar, he lay on his back, looking perfectly composed. His blond hair was slightly disheveled, a cap wedged between the back of his head and the ground's sandy gravel, his arms tight by his sides with his hands resting on his hips—both palms appeared dusty with sand—and his legs extended stiffly in front of him a few inches apart. Rose noticed how the tips of the man's shabby and worn shoes pointed skyward. It's "about the way an undertaker would do it," Rose thought.[4] But the mysterious man's eyes betrayed his fate: half-open in a frozen stare looking at the hazy morning sky.

The men were confused by the body's neat position along the road. Taxter explained how he first came upon the body around 7:00 a.m. while riding with other linemen to a jobsite near the reservoir. He made clear that neither he nor any linemen had touched or moved the body. Taxter stayed behind to find help for the man, walking up to Ardson Farm and calling on Eckhardt, who was also perplexed by how the man could have ended up along the side of the road. He hadn't heard anything unusual in the early-morning hours that could explain the man's demise. This stretch of road was fairly isolated, and Burke, his farmhand, lived not more than two hundred feet up the hill, and he said he hadn't heard any noises that morning except the usual traffic. They thought the man might have been hit by a passing car, though that didn't explain how his body could be so perfectly composed. It must have been a strange scene along King Street as those five strangers gathered around a corpse as if attending a funeral for a man they did not know.

Being a pharmacist, Rose might have felt a duty to make sure the man was dead. "I reached over and felt his pulse," he later told authorities. "There was no sign of life. The body was cold," he remembered.[5] Both Rose and Eckhardt took notice of the man's frayed and soiled suit and how his shoes were badly worn. While the suit was of a good quality, well tailored, double-breasted, it had seen better days. Underneath his jacket he wore a tattered vest. Looking into the man's jacket pocket, Rose noticed a tin cigarette case, but he thought better than to rummage through the man's possessions or explore any further. You might leave fingerprints on the body, Taxter warned. Fingerprinting was a relatively new practice for crime investigations. Lawyers often debated the reliability of such evidence in courts. It was more common to find such evidence in the era's popular crime novels, which might have been where Taxter learned of it and why he was so concerned.[6] They all noticed the one set of tire tracks in the gravel near the body. The heavy indention of the tracks indicated the car had stopped abruptly, as if the driver sped along and suddenly for some reason picked that spot to brake at the last minute. Nothing indicated a fight or a struggle. They saw no evidence the body might have been dragged or dropped there. Rose got back into his car and told Eckhardt he would call the police once he arrived at the pharmacy in White Plains.

We can imagine how torn Rose might have been, caught between anxious thoughts of his customers pressing their faces against the darkened pharmacy windows and his unease with the scene in front of him. Rose had taken King Street most mornings and could practically drive the route from Chappaqua to White Plains blindfolded. He knew every turn and curve and rough patch. At that moment though, the road seemed completely new and strange, as if he had never passed that spot before, never noticed Ardson Farm, and certainly had never met nor spoken a word to Clarence Eckhardt. But what unsettled the pharmacist the most was the mysterious man's expression. Rose knew it would be a while before he would forget the image of this young man's half-open eyes and their lifeless, empty stare into the beautiful May morning.

The Crime

Kensico

The Kensico Reservoir got its name from the small hamlet submerged within its waters. A rural outpost founded in the eighteenth century, Kensico had been in the heart of the Siwanoy lands that stretched across current-day Westchester County far into Connecticut and along the northern shores of Long Island Sound. It's believed the town was named after their tribal chief Coken-se-co. Sitting in a valley near the Bronx River proved an unfortunate place to be as New York City bulged in population and ambition in the late nineteenth century. In its need to supply the city with fresh water, in the 1880s the state planned to construct a reservoir contained by a small earthen dam that would flood the valley and sink the hamlet. The state purchased every property in Kensico, and fearing that the buildings would contaminate the reservoir, city health officials directed a team of men to take each of the town's buildings—its houses, hotel, the Methodist church, several saloons, one school, and a number of mills—and burn them to the ground.[1]

Not long after completion, the project already proved too small. Between 1900 and 1920, New York City's population grew nearly 60 percent, to over 5 million residents. The wealthy built ornate mansions on the Upper East Side or along Riverside Drive. Middle-class families bought narrow brownstones or rented sprawling apartments in brick high-rises on the Upper West Side or northward into Harlem. Immigrant families crammed into cold-water tenements on the Lower

East Side or in Greenwich Village or Manhattan's Tenderloin just west of Times Square. Along the city's waterfront a forest of stone and brick factories and warehouses grew. Manhattan streets were increasingly shadowed by iron-framed office towers and luxury hotels with such names as the Pennsylvania, Knickerbocker, and McAlpin, each one competing for the title of largest in the world. As the city expanded, reservoirs would eat up more and more land upstate. The state continued to seize towns. Homes and businesses were vacated; bodies were exhumed from cemeteries and moved to higher ground. The expanded Kensico Reservoir would become part of a vast network of rivers and basins supplying a thirsty city that was growing at a phenomenal pace.

By 1922, Kensico had become a 3-billion-gallon "architectural showpiece," as one contemporary described it, with three-hundred-foot-high rusticated stone walls supported by smooth, sculptural buttresses. On its southern edge locals could enjoy a sprawling park with fountains and picnic areas. The more adventurous could find pleasures in the isolated areas around the reservoir, well-known for the late-night outings by young couples who parked their Model Ts, roadsters, and coupes along secluded dirt roads, escaping their parents' moralities. Some innovative couples even installed curtains across their car windows for privacy from the occasional police raids.[2] Kensico was a great place for secrets.

As the men stood along King Street, they could smell the reservoir, its fresh scent mixing with the humid morning air. One thing became certain: whoever left the body along the side of the road wished for the man to be found. He could have been left in the woods, out of sight from passing motorists. There were any number of back roads on the north side of the Kensico Reservoir keen for hiding a body. With over 2,000 acres of deep water, the reservoir itself would have been perfect for anyone looking to clean up a murder. But if you wanted a body to be found, laying it along King Street in a composed manner would have been a good option.

New York state troopers Harry Green and Ralph Collins arrived at the crime scene around 8:15 a.m. They knew the area around Kensico quite well. Thirty-year-old Green looked much younger than his age with his round face and short, flat hair parted in the middle. Neither he nor Collins wished to move the body before the coroner arrived. While they gathered statements from Taxter and Eckhardt, they also examined the area around the body. Green diagramed its position and the ways the hands and feet were arranged. He noticed the man's shoes and what he would later describe as "a light coat of mud" on the soles, "the soft leather part of the shoe," he said. He then went through the man's pockets trying to determine his identity. He took the man's cap, wedged behind his head, and used it as a bag, gathering everything that he found in his pockets. In his report he included a list of all the items recovered:

a pair of dice
a pack of playing cards
four cuff buttons
a stickpin
a pipe
a box of matches
a "cheap cigarette case" with five unlit cigarettes
a new pack of Chesterfield cigarettes
a broken piece of comb
a khaki handkerchief
a ladies' handkerchief
and an assortment of coins that totaled $1.32[3]

Each object suggested a story, and together they might form some kind of picture of the victim. While they did reveal something about the man—his smoking habits, his love of card games and chance, and most acutely, his poverty—they couldn't tell Green much about the man's identity. One thing to note: the ladies' handkerchief was embroidered with two small lavender pansies in the corner and bordered in lavender thread. "Dainty" is how one newspaper described it, speculating "it may be the clew that will solve the mystery."[4] Could it have been a gift from a female friend? Or perhaps it was the man's own handkerchief, suggesting a small cotton transgression of gender or sexual norms. Green continued on, unbuttoning the man's vest. At that moment he saw the dried bloodstain blooming across his white cotton shirt.

"Up to then," Green would later state, "we didn't know what killed him."[5] The bullet had hit him in the middle of his chest, a bit to the right of his heart. Green wondered why the bullet only pierced the man's shirt and not his suit coat or vest. Did someone button them back up? Perhaps he wasn't wearing them when he was shot, and his coat and vest were put on after he was dead.

Unable to find anything to identify the man, Green and Collins began to investigate the area around the body. They inspected the gravel shoulder for signs of a struggle and the wooded area in the near distance for bullet scrapes on the tree trunks or metal smudges from where the bullet might have hit the granite rocks embedded in the hill behind the body. Green considered the single set of tire tracks but couldn't determine the nature of the tread. Collins spotted a shining metal bullet casing about sixteen feet from the body in the damp gravel. He picked it up and marked the spot with a small twig. Green knew the shell was from a .38 automatic pistol, which ejected each casing out the right side of the gun with a force that propelled it several feet. Could it have been the bullet that killed this man? Both Collins and Green got down on their hands and knees and searched through the sand and soil for more casings but found nothing.

Eventually Westchester County coroner Edward Fitzgerald arrived, along with state trooper Lieutenant Eugene Roberts and deputy sheriff Frank Cherico. Fitzgerald was a slight man, all angles and bones inside his baggy suit. He had a protruding chin and deep-set eyes, softened only slightly by a thin mustache. Looking at him you could almost see precisely the shape of his skull. Fitzgerald was barely five months on the job, having been elected on the Republican ticket the previous fall. He had no medical training whatsoever—a fact that was not uncommon at the time. His experience on the police force and in real estate probably didn't prepare him for the tasks of coroner.

In 1925, the state eliminated the elected coroner position, replacing it with an appointed medical examiner, a position that required a medical degree. Fitzgerald would eventually be known as the "last coroner of Westchester County."[6]

Fitzgerald determined that the man was about five feet eight inches tall, weighed about 130 or 140 pounds, and estimated his age around thirty years old. Green believed him to be much younger, around twenty or so. Fitzgerald also surmised the murder happened about four or five hours earlier, as rigor mortis had only just begun to set in. That would have placed the killing around three or four o'clock in the morning.[7]

Trooper Green handed Roberts, his commanding officer, the bullet casing he'd found and the contents of the man's pockets still pooled in the cap, each just a fragment of a clue, an uncertainty more than an answer. Roberts was the first to move the body. He noticed the dirt that had caked underneath the man's fingernails. As the body was still somewhat flexible, Roberts rolled him on his side from right to left, pulling the right arm out of the coat and vest so he could inspect the other side of the body. He saw clearly the exit wound on the man's lower back and the small pool of dried blood that had soaked through the shirt and into the vest and suit coat. It was clear the bullet had cut through the man's torso from upper chest to lower back, causing internal bleeding. Whoever shot this man, Roberts and Fitzgerald speculated, must have been taller, or perhaps stood above him pointing the .38 automatic downward at the victim. Roberts felt the man was shot on-site. "The bullet of that type," he would later testify, "passing through the spot that it did, has shocking power," adding that he believed the man was "shot down where he stood, and fell and never rose." It was an opinion that Fitzgerald shared. "He looked to me," he later claimed, "as though he was dropped immediately in his tracks, because the imprint of his two feet, of his heels, was right in the road, as a man going down in this position," adding, "The dirt of the road was on his shoes."

Green took exception with such conclusions. He speculated that the man was shot somewhere else and brought to this spot, laid out "the way an undertaker would do it," as Rose had described. Green noted that "there were no marks of a struggle, nothing to indicate there had been any trouble there" and found there were only slight shoe prints in the soil, suggesting the victim did not stand there for long.[8]

Lieutenant Roberts took black-and-white photographs of the crime scene, two of which still exist today. In one image, Roberts set the camera low and at a distance, giving us the wide-angle view of the scene, one that Rose might have had that morning, as he rounded a bend and saw Eckhardt waving him down. The scene stretches out to the horizon, the mysterious man lying in the small clearing off the concrete roadway. The body had clearly already been inspected: the victim's legs were spread apart, his head tilted to the left side.

In the second photograph, Fitzgerald and Green attempt to prop up the body for the camera. Fitzgerald, on the man's right side, pushed his hand against the victim's back and stared at the camera. Trooper Green placed one hand behind the victim's head and the other on the top of his left arm as if pushing and pulling against the weight of the body. He kept his gaze on the victim, whose large, distinctive ears framed his gaunt face. The man's right arm had been taken out of his jacket sleeve when Roberts inspected him, and the double-breasted coat had been pulled awkwardly over his torso and buttoned at the top, making the victim look as if he had only one arm. The holes and frayed edges of the jacket are clearly visible. It's a haunting pose, and perhaps the last image we have of this man, his mouth slightly open as if in the middle of a sentence as the force of the .38 bullet pierced his body.

Penniless Sailor

FINDING A BODY ALONG A WESTCHESTER ROADSIDE CONJURED a growing paradox about the most modern of inventions: the automobile. The open road, that powerful American myth with its associations of freedom and individualism, was just taking shape in the early decades of the twentieth century. "Be Independent With a Chevrolet" announced an ad in 1923, reflecting and encouraging an idea about car ownership. Newspapers published weekend travel excursions for city dwellers, detailing day trips to the New Jersey shore or Long Island countryside or north into the farmlands of Westchester complete with maps of the best roads to take and places to stop for lunch or dinner. One motoring guidebook about Westchester County in the 1920s described how "nature and road builder have joined together to create a motoring paradise." Increasingly the automobile allowed not only for a weekend escape but offered a solution to the ills of urban life. "We shall solve the city problem," Henry Ford predicted, "by leaving the city." It was a dream we would embrace for years to come.[1]

In Westchester, the automobile was both virtue and vice. For those so-called regionalist politicians who wished to transform the county into a bucolic suburb and curtail the encroaching evils of the city, such as crime, overcrowding, and of course, an influx of immigrants, the automobile was key to their vision. William Ward, the powerful and long-serving chair of the county's Republican Party, was keen on blocking the urbanization of Westchester. He would be instrumental in creating wide, well-maintained roads and parkways, restricting the expansion of the New York City subway into the county, and limiting development to exclusive, middle-class enclaves.

But Ward could little control the ways that people used the roads. During Prohibition, late-night bootleggers found the network of county roads useful in moving Canadian whiskey to New York and Connecticut, or hauling Caribbean-made rum from the Long Island Sound into New England. Speakeasies were turning up around the county much to the dismay and at times approval of local authorities, causing some to worry if the county was becoming a hub for underworld criminals—and if the automobile was the prime cause. "The speed of the motor car," one syndicated editorial complained, "baffles the detective. It permits the criminal to strike long distances from his rendezvous and to speed away from the scene of his crime. That is one of the unfortunate misuses of the automobile."[2]

So it was not surprising that speculation in the press about the mysterious man's murder involved bootleggers and gangsters. The playing cards and dice led some to believe that the killing had to do with a gambling dispute. Others speculated he may have been the victim of a gang or mistaken for a federal agent searching for bootlegged liquor. Calluses on his hands, one theory held, were perhaps evidence he was a laborer or truck driver. Others suggested he may have been a "high-jacker," or rather a bootlegger turned robber, and met his fate as he attempted to hold up one of the many trucks that rambled along the secluded roads.[3]

The press described the man as dressed in a dark suit of fairly good material who possessed an "expensive gold lined cigarette case" and an "expensive pipe"—the last two details exaggerations to add more intrigue to the case. From the very start, the facts of the crime would be difficult to pin down, leading to false claims and speculations that conjured any number of stories. Some reports noted the "police were certain that the man was murdered where the body was found" as there were "no signs of the corpse being thrown from a passing car or of having been dragged from another spot in the vicinity." Privately investigators debated exactly how the body ended up on King Street. Any claims of certainty had to be taken with a great deal of skepticism.

BY MIDAFTERNOON, UNDERTAKERS from the Lyon and Harnett Funeral Home in White Plains took possession of the body. At their morgue, Ray Hill, deputy sheriff for identification and investigation, examined the body. He stripped off the clothing—the suit jacket, the vest, the white cotton dress shirt with the bullet hole and bloodstains, the wool pants and the worn, thin-soled shoes, his silk socks, and undershirt and underwear. Hill inked each finger and made a complete set of prints. He surmised the man had been dead for about eight or ten hours—again placing the time of death in the predawn hours of May 16. "The fingers were not as stiff as those taken of a man dead 24 hours," Hill noted.

Once removed, the man's clothes betrayed how tattered and worn they were, their shabby thinness evident as they lay in a deflated pile. The small clue of an underwear label, issued by the U.S. Navy, would prove crucial. Hill sent the fingerprints and a photograph to the Office of Naval Intelligence in Washington, D.C. Within a day, the department confirmed a match. The body was that of nineteen-year-old Clarence Peters of Haverhill, Massachusetts.[4] Peters had served for a brief time as an apprentice seaman in the navy in 1919, but after just two months he was dishonorably discharged for stealing. Given these details, the press would sometimes refer to Peters as the "penniless sailor." Westchester County sheriff George Werner sent a telegram to the Haverhill police chief, asking them to notify Peters's parents, Inez and Elbridge, of their son's death.

Haverhill sat along the Merrimack River, forty miles north of Boston. Since the mid-nineteenth century, the industrial town of about 50,000 people had become a hub of shoemaking. The Haverhill Chamber of Commerce boasted it had more shoe factories than any city in the world, dubbing the town Slipper City and declaring that "Haverhill shoes tread the carpets of the world." Clarence spent a few months working in a shoe factory, a seeming rite of passage for many young men in Slipper City, after his ill-fated enlistment in the navy. Back in April he had attempted to join the marines, a fact that made Inez and Elbridge dubious of the telegram from Westchester County about the murder of their eldest son. They believed Clarence was still on Parris Island, South Carolina, at the marine training camp. They had recently received a letter from Peters describing his time there. Elbridge Peters told reporters, "I am at a loss how Clarence came to be in White Plains New York."[5]

LEONARD TILTON, A Haverhill undertaker, sent a telegram to the coroner's office:

> Identify body of Clarence Peters by large scars on the back of neck and back, and large mole on the chest. If correct, undertaker is to ship body in cheap casket, untrimmed, to Haverhill.[6]

In a return telegram, the coroner's office confirmed the scars—markings from the removal of boils some years earlier—and the mole on his chest. Still dubious of the victim's bodily marks, Peters's uncle Earl Hardy, only twenty-five years old himself, took a midnight train from Haverhill to White Plains to identify the body firsthand. At the Lyon and Harnett morgue, Hardy confronted the fact of his nephew's body, ending the family's doubt. Westchester police also took Hardy to King Street to see the spot where the body was found.

"The mystery about the death of my nephew, who had not been home in over a month," Hardy told reporters, "is that his Government discharge papers were missing." He added, "His mother received a letter from him dated last week, which was written from Parris Island. He said he was going to re-enlist, but he told her not to write to that address as he might not be there."[7] Confirming Clarence's identity only deepened the mystery of his murder. Inez and Elbridge could offer few answers as to how their son met his fate.

As Coroner Fitzgerald had no medical training, he directed Dr. John Black to conduct an autopsy. Black concluded Peters was shot at close range, the bullet entering just above his heart and cutting downward, exiting his lower back near his spine, just as the state troopers speculated. Black also determined that with this arc of the bullet, the person who shot him would have had to be standing above him, shooting downward at the victim's chest. Eager to capitalize on a scandal, William Randolph Hearst's *New York American* published a cartoonish illustration of the bullet's sweep through Peters's torso, an arrow marking its path to help its readers visualize the coroner's description.

The nature of the bullet's track would be a crucial fact for the ongoing investigation and prompt several initial theories about the cause of the murder. Fitzgerald speculated that Peters tried to stop a passing car for a ride when those in the car (what the press called "autoists") suspected he was a bandit. The downward path of the bullet, Fitzgerald told reporters, "makes me think that a person standing in an automobile fired the shot, which would give the range to cover the route of the bullet. The fact that no revolver was found or any signs of a struggle near the body also confirms my theory to some extent."[8]

It was an oddly specific explanation to share with the press even before completing an inquest. The idea that Peters was murdered from a passing automobile, we might speculate, could have been one of any number of possibilities for the "downward course" of the bullet. But believing for a moment the coroner's theory of how Peters was shot, reporters still might have wondered how the scene unfolded. Did the person step out of the car to compose Peters's body on the side of the road? And what of the fact that the bullet pierced only his shirt, but not his vest and coat, which were buttoned up when lineman Taxter came upon the young man on that Tuesday morning?

Such speculations created a bigger mystery about Peters's murder in the press. "Crime on lonely road is baffling to officials," *The Boston Globe* announced. "The murder is one of the most mysterious and baffling that the Westchester authorities have had to deal with in some time," *The New York Times* declared. "Haverhill Boy Victim of Mysterious Murder" read a front-page article of the *Haverhill Evening Gazette*, which considered the timing and location of the murder. "It is believed," the newspaper informed its Slipper City readers

> that the crime was committed within a radius of 25 miles from the spot where the body was found. The body to all appearances had been lying on the roadside for several hours which would have only permitted an hour or two for the transportation of the corpse. Unless the driver of the car was thoroughly familiar with the roads of that section not more than this distance could have been covered by taking back roads to avoid the vigilance of the police who have been stopping cars along the highways at night for some time in quest of liquor cases.[9]

Given the many theories that simmered in the press, Sherriff Werner gathered reporters in his office on Saturday morning, May 20, to reveal a possible break in the case. The forty-three-year-old sheriff was a very practical man. Tall and broad shouldered, he resembled a heavyweight boxer. While he had little formal education, he did have years of experience in Westchester politics. The son of a blacksmith, he also apprenticed in the profession before opening a garage in Rye, New York, servicing automobiles. His move into public service included several positions in Rye as commissioner of the poor, parks commissioner, and later as town supervisor. As a dutiful member of the county's Republican Party in the years before World War I, he eventually won election to the board of supervisors, a post that led to his election as county sheriff in 1920. Rumors swirled that Werner had little interest in the post of sheriff until the party bosses handpicked him for the ballot.[10] Few questioned his integrity for public service. His experience in police and detective work, on the other hand, was dubious.

However Werner ascended into his position as sheriff mattered little to reporters as they crowded into his office, eager for information about the growing mystery of Peters's murder. "I am forming a theory fairly well founded," he told them, "which, if it proves to be correct, might be a surprise to many people." The reporters were less than impressed by Werner's vague statement. "Reporters left the county official with not an inkling of the course being traced," one newspaper complained.[11] What Werner kept secret was the fact that twenty-four hours earlier a man had already come forward to confess to the crime.

Majestic

As the RMS *Majestic* sailed into New York Harbor just hours after Peters's body was found on May 16, large crowds along Battery Park on Manhattan's southern tip jostled for a view of the ship rounding the island. Onlookers waved small British and American flags that fluttered in the sunny afternoon breeze. Some in the crowd were armed with binoculars eager to get a closer look at the ship as it sailed north into the Hudson River escorted by two tugboats and seaplanes circling above. Nearby ships "saluted with long, hoarse blasts of whistles and wails of sirens," *The Evening World* described, adding how the entire harbor succumbed to the "deafening tumult from every noise-making device afloat or ashore."

George Ward, president of the Ward Bakery Company, watched the fanfare and excitement from his first-class cabin. George and his young wife Donna were sailing home after a five-month grand tour through Europe, north Africa, and the Middle East. The Wards joined 4,000 passengers on the *Majestic*'s maiden voyage, launching from Southampton, England, on May 11 to cheering crowds and a brass band.

The *Majestic* certainly lived up to its name. At 995 feet long, it was the largest passenger ship in the world and easily eclipsed the more infamous RMS *Titanic*, which only stretched to a mere 883 feet. Commissioned in Kaiser Wilhelm II's Germany in the months before the onset of World War I and christened the *Bismarck* after the nineteenth-century Prussian leader who created the modern German state, the ship would linger unfinished until 1919, when the defeated Germans handed the vessel over to Britain as part of the reparation treaties. The White Star Line moved it to Southampton and refurbished it in the style of Edwardian elegance and excess. Few symbols so acutely demonstrated Germany's defeat in the Great War than transforming the *Bismarck* into the "crown jewel" of British passenger ships, proudly flying the Union Jack.[1]

During their voyage, George and Donna Ward enjoyed nine decks and several outdoor promenades that gave them nearly seven and half acres of sea air strolling. First-class passengers could linger in the Grand Lounge with its hand-carved oak paneling and twenty-foot-high ceiling inlaid with crystal. Or they could dine in the Palm Court dining room ringed in Corinthian columns and potted palm trees and flooded with natural light from large French windows that gave passengers views of the open sea. This "floating town," as one report called it, held an astonishing list of supplies, including seventy-five tons of meat, twenty-eight tons of fish, 6,000 head of game, 80,000 eggs, and 16,000 pounds of tomatoes. When the Wards felt thirsty, the ship stocked 1,000 quarts of champagne and 4,000 bottles of whiskey, brandy, and gin. And to compliment the liquor, the ship had a hearty supply of tobacco, including 250,000 cigarettes and, we might expect, a much larger number of matches.[2]

The ship encountered good weather and relatively calms seas, allowing it to practically skate across the Atlantic, averaging about twenty-four knots. "We just let the *Majestic* loaf along," captain Sir Bertram Hayes told reporters, offering an unusual note of modesty amid the press hyperbole that surrounded the ship's maiden voyage. "We are after no speed records," Hayes said, adding, "Our job is to carry passengers safely across the Atlantic."[3] Despite Hayes's claims, accented as they were with a distinct British reserve, the ship arrived in New York in record time, completing the journey in five days, fourteen hours, and forty-five minutes.

As it maneuvered along the Chelsea waterfront on Manhattan's West Side, the ship's size challenged Pier 59, the city's longest mooring, built to accommodate the *Titanic*. The pier had been waiting for a decade for a ship to make proper use of it. But as the *Majestic* approached, Captain Hayes underestimated the ship's size and cut through the bulkhead, making a fifteen-foot gash in the wall of a dockside shed before retreating slightly. The incident, what the press called a "miscalculation," scattered the excited crowds standing along the pier, shifting the joyful cheers into shrieks of panic. There were no reported injuries, though the incident did delay the deboarding by nearly an hour. The ship would sit awkwardly along the pier for the next two days before returning to Southampton. With the stern sticking out into the Hudson River well past the end of the pier, each evening the crew set red lights along the decks to alert passing boats.[4]

George Ward might not have noticed the forceful jolt as the ship rammed the bulkhead. The pleasure of the sea voyage and the fanfare on its arrival were somewhat eclipsed by a smoldering scandal involving his son Walter. Not long after George left Southampton, Walter sent him a cablegram. In his message, Walter requested $40,000 to pay off a gang of blackmailers who, according to Walter, had been threatening him for weeks. George must have heard such a request before, as his response was one of exasperation: "Not one cent for blackmailers, but I would pay $100,000 to put them in jail." There were more cablegrams throughout the five-day voyage from his other son Ralph intervening on Walter's behalf, but George was little moved by his sons' pleas for cash.[5]

Hewed from the ruthless Gilded Age, George and his older brother, Robert, had built the Ward Bakery Company into an industrial empire over the previous three decades. Their father, an Irish immigrant, started a one-oven storefront bakery in New York before the U.S. Civil War, eventually moving the family and the business to Pittsburgh. But the Ward brothers had a much bigger plan for the family business. Their company would do for bread baking what Henry Ford had done for the manufacture of cars: create an industrialized assembly line where machines completed each stage of the baking. It was the dream of the modern era that transformed the domestic chore of bread making into the convenience and profitability of mass production. With specially designed machines, their factories churned out thousands of uniform loaves of white bread every hour. In 1911, the company expanded beyond Pittsburgh, returning to New York and building two new modern factories: one in the Bronx and one in Brooklyn. By the 1920s, the company had become one of largest bakeries in the country, with profits in excess of $5 million a year.[6]

Walter Ward joined the family business after only two years of study at the Wharton School at the University of Pennsylvania. In his early twenties he managed the Brooklyn factory while also overseeing the construction of the Newark, New Jersey, factory. A profile of young Walter in 1915 described him as "likable and approachable and carries none of the exaggerated ego so likely to be found in a young man who has the wherewithal to back himself and has been given responsibilities far above those usually accorded a person at his age," adding, "Ward looks on life seriously."

Seven years later at the age of thirty, Walter epitomized the era's New Man, a figure who could easily have walked out of a Jay Gatsby party. Handsome, square jawed, and clean-shaven, he had a fastidiousness about his appearance, spending on tailored suits, silk ties, diamond tiepins, and handmade straw hats (or lids, as they were often called). From all appearances Walter had a charmed life. Each morning he commuted in his red roadster to his top-floor office at the Bronx factory, where he was the head of purchasing. And each evening he drove back to his home in Sutton Manor, an exclusive and quiet community in New Rochelle, where he lived with his charming, socialite wife, Beryl, their two children—Willard, age five, and Betty, age four—and two servants—Amy Mild, a Finnish maid and cook, and Lulu Barrows, a full-time caretaker of the Wards' children.[7]

There is another fact of Walter's life that is important here. While a senior manager at the family company, he was also the head of the New Rochelle Police Commissioners, a post he'd held since 1919. It must have seemed strange to some in New Rochelle to have the mayor appoint Ward to the post when he was only twenty-seven and had no training in policing nor experience in public office. At the monthly meetings, Ward, one of three commissioners, showed little interest in police matters, rarely engaging in conversation or asking questions.

He often was the first to leave when the meeting adjourned. The New Rochelle police chief Frank Cody described Ward as a "man of few words." It seemed that Ward was as much distinguished by his taciturn demeanor as his good looks and likability. The unpaid and largely political commissioner position, however, did provide Ward with a weighty police badge and the authority to use it.

We don't know what George said to his son once he and Donna, Ward's stepmother, disembarked the *Majestic* and met Walter on the dock. The three of them chauffeured back to George Ward's home in Spuyten Duyvil, a wealthy neighborhood on the western edge of the Bronx. Was Walter annoyed by his father's refusal to give him money? Had George become tired of his son's inability to stand up to those who would feed off of their wealth? Or perhaps the two were devising a strategy to protect them from a public scandal that would surely erupt. What we do know is that on the morning of May 22, Walter Ward, "scion of the House of Ward," as one newspaper described him, arrived at the Westchester County Courthouse in White Plains, dressed in one of his well-tailored suits and silk ties and accompanied by several lawyers, to explain how he shot Clarence Peters.[8]

A Dime-Store Novel

In 1915 the old courthouse in White Plains, New York, expanded from a two-story Romanesque-style building into a seven-story neoclassical temple. Constructed of marble and granite, with twelve Corinthian columns stretching along the building's facade, the renovated courthouse made for an imposing landmark on Main Street in the middle of town. Like many in that era, the building housed a number of offices, those of everyone from county and state court judges to the district attorney and the county sheriff. Adjacent to the courthouse was the large county jail, with its cafeteria and infirmary. The Republican-led county's board of supervisors commissioned the building's expansion, which was completed in little over of a year. Coming in on time and on budget, the renovation evidenced "Republican efficiency."[1]

Ironically, while the speed of the renovations received high praise, the results appeared confusing. In expanding the old building with a modern addition, the new courthouse became, according to one observer at the time, a labyrinth of secret passages and concealed staircases, often hidden behind wooden panels that made for "the wildest maze conceivable to the human mind." These architectural details allowed staff and visitors to appear and disappear like "magic, as though they were vanishing into thin air."[2] On the building's frieze high above the marbled entrance, visitors could read a simple motto about the justice system carved into stone: TO NONE WILL WE SELL TO NONE WILL WE DELAY TO NONE WILL WE DENY RIGHT AND JUSTICE.

Walter Ward arrived at the courthouse on that Monday morning accompanied by his three attorneys. His lead attorney, Allan Campbell, had arranged the meeting the previous Friday. "I have a client of mine involved in a homicide," Campbell told Sheriff Werner, while making clear it was a "case of self-defense." Campbell, a forty-one-year-old Harvard-educated lawyer, was a partner at Rabenold & Scribner, a Wall Street firm with spacious offices on Broadway and a long list of wealthy clients. Elwood Rabenold, the firm's founding partner and Ward's personal attorney, was not in attendance, though he would soon be standing by Ward's side. Rabenold also studied at Harvard and had built one of the more respected firms in the city. But the forty-two-year-old aspired to public office. On that May morning in 1922, he was not only Walter Ward's attorney but also the Democratic Party candidate for the state senate in the November elections. Ward's third attorney commanded the most respect among those at the courthouse: Isaac N. Mills had only recently retired from the appellate division of the state supreme court and had a distinguished legal and political career. At seventy-one, Mills continued to practice criminal law and still commanded a courtroom with his deep voice and dramatic presence.[3]

Once inside Sheriff Werner's office, Campbell, Mills, and their legal assistants "surrounded" their client, according to Werner, as if shielding him from inquiries.[4] The men had all arrived on time and had clearly worked out a plan for this meeting. They came with a single sheet of paper that contained a 331-word statement about the events on King Street in the early morning hours of May 16:

> We have appeared this morning before District Attorney Weeks to make complaint on behalf of our client Mr. W.S. Ward, against a gang of blackmailers.
>
> The known members of the gang now at large are "Charlie Ross" and a man known as "Jack." A third member of the gang, known as "Pete," now dead, has since been identified as Clarence Peters, and has, we have

> learned, a criminal record and a bad conduct discharge from the Navy. It is not known whether they had other confederates.
>
> These men sought to extort money from Mr. Ward by threats in various forms, including threats of death to himself and his family.
>
> Mr. Ward at first tried to quiet them by payments but finally they demanded a lump sum of $75,000. They set the night of Monday, May 15, as the time for this clean-up and getaway.
>
> Mr. Ward met them, hoping to temporize and put them off. He was in his own car but covered by the gun of Peters who sat alongside. Ross and Jack were in a red Stutz. At the command of Peters backed by the drawn gun Mr. Ward's automobile was brought to a standstill at a lonely spot above Kensico Reservoir and the other two, Ross and Jack, planted their car in front of the Ward car, partially blocking it in the narrow road. The order of Peters that Mr. Ward leave his car resulted in a grab for the revolver in Peters' hand, thereby deflecting the shot from Peters' gun and giving opportunity to Mr. Ward to return fire. Charlie Ross opened fire on Mr. Ward from the Stutz car. Mr. Ward returned this fire and the Stutz car took flight toward Chappaqua. Peters was left at the side of the road.
>
> Mr. Ward promptly told the story to his attorneys and laid the fact before the District Attorney and the Sheriff of Westchester County.
>
> We are now directing our efforts to finding Charlie Ross and Jack.[5]

As confessions go, it was a curious one. Less a statement by a single defendant, and more a collective complaint by Ward's attorneys, carefully crafted by the men who now stood as a barrier between Ward and the authorities. The statement directed attention away from the body of Peters, toward the blackmailers, who allegedly had been victimizing

Ward for several weeks with violent threats. Ward's actions, the reasoning followed, were the inevitable result of this blackmailing gang. The implications were clear: the real crime had been committed not by Ward but rather by the mysterious men who had targeted Ward and who gave him no choice but to protect himself by shooting and killing Peters.

According to his notes about the meeting, Sheriff Werner, after reading the statement, "immediately" took Walter Ward and his legal team to the district attorney's office. Holding the single sheet of paper in his hand, Werner led the men through a maze of back stairwells and narrow hallways, the clack of their leather shoes on the marble floors echoing along the corridors.

FIFTY-ONE-YEAR-OLD FREDERICK WEEKS was no stranger to the prosecutor's office. Weeks had served for fifteen years as assistant DA before being elected for the three-year post of district attorney in 1913. In January 1922, with the resignation of district attorney Lee Parsons Davis, the governor appointed Weeks to the post for the twelve months remaining in Davis's term. By an odd coincidence, Weeks also served as the Republican mayor of White Plains, a possible conflict that seemed not to concern the governor when he asked Weeks to return to the prosecutor's office, nor did it seem to give Weeks any concern about managing two demanding public positions. He was respected in the county for his experience and years of service to Westchester and the country. A veteran of the Spanish-American War (rumor had it he rode with Theodore Roosevelt up San Juan Hill and was cited for bravery), Weeks also served in the First World War and, even in his fifties, exhibited the striking posture of a soldier. Known for his reserved manner, his round, wire-rimmed glasses, and stiff, high-collared shirts, Weeks looked more like a college professor than a public servant. While he started out as a reporter for a local newspaper in his early twenties, after his many decades as a prosecutor, he grew to dislike the intrusions of the press into the work of the DA's office.[6]

Sheriff Werner, Walter Ward, and his lawyers filed into Weeks's spacious office. Its wide windows filled one wall, giving views of Main Street and the marble steps of the courthouse entrance. They all took seats around a dark wooden conference table, heavy and sturdy, that filled one end of the rectangular room. Weeks's desk sat at the other end, as if to keep the room in balance. Coroner Fitzgerald had also been summoned. Throughout this short meeting, Ward said little, allowing his lawyers to respond for him. They explained how Ward asked his father, George Ward, for money in the days before the killing, that his father refused to pay blackmailers, quoting his response to his son that would soon become a refrain in the press: "Not one cent for blackmailers, but $100,000 to put them in jail."[7]

They offered few other facts beyond the statement, elaborating with only muted details. They described how Ward had already paid the blackmailers $30,000 and how they sent threatening letters to Ward. One letter allegedly stated: "Meet us or you will never meet the Majestic"—a reference to George Ward's arrival.[8] These letters, which were only described by the attorneys and never shown, allegedly pointed to the dire demands Walter had endured. They also described how Ward, hoping to reason with the men, met with Peters on a road near Port Chester, about halfway between New Rochelle and the murder scene. How he drove to King Street while Peters pushed his .32 Smith & Wesson against Ward's ribs. How he feared for his life and the lives of his family as Peters ordered him to pull to the side of the road. How this fear only grew when he saw the red Stutz speed past him and park at an angle in front of Ward's Peerless coupe, blocking him in. How Peters ordered him out of the car, his pistol still pointed at him. And how, as Peters backed out of the car, Ward's reactions were quick and calculated. He lunged at Peters's pistol with his right hand, at the same moment pulling his .38 Colt automatic from his side pocket with his left hand.

The two guns fired at the same time, according to Ward, with Peters shooting off to the side, smashing through a side window of Ward's car, and Ward firing the deadly shot into Peters's chest. The exchange prompted Charlie Ross and Jack to open fire on Ward, who ran behind his Peerless coupe, the heavy automobile protecting him from the barrage of bullets. There were about eight or nine shots fired between the men, and Ward might have hit one of the two other men, before they jumped back into the Stutz and accelerated with violent speed northward along King Street, one of the men still firing as they drove away. Ward had been uninjured in the dramatic gunfight and found the strength to drive himself in a fevered state of panic back to his home in New Rochelle, arriving around 4:30 in the morning.

Few in the room could have ignored the way Ward's statement echoed the heroic escapades one might have found in the popular silent films of Tom Mix Westerns or the swashbuckling antics of Douglas Fairbanks. Or, as one newspaper noted, the entire tale of blackmail and murder read "like a thriller in a dime store novel."[9] Such stories made clear and simple lines between villains and heroes. Their moral certainties were much of their appeal. But however much the story echoed the era's heroic plots, it was also a keenly developed legal defense that turned Peters's murder into a case of self-defense with the only two living witnesses—the supposed blackmailers Charlie Ross and Jack—nowhere to be found. It had been a week since the murder, allowing both men plenty of time to escape. And besides, blackmailers don't have a habit of wanting to talk with police. Their targets would be even more reticent to make public the nature of the blackmail scheme. Without finding those two men there was absolutely no one to dispute or confirm Ward's claims, which, if you wished for your story of events to prevail, made it highly unlikely that Ward would want them found at all.

Despite the fantastic nature of the attorneys' statement, few in the DA's office questioned Ward about the facts of his story. They asked nothing about the nature of the blackmail that led Ward to pay the gang so much money while he continued to suffer from their threats. Coroner Fitzgerald was the only man in that room besides Ward who had been at the crime scene and who had observed the state of Peters's body. Given what he had seen, it seemed likely he would have been dubious about Ward's story of the late-night meeting and shooting, as the details contradicted a number of facts he and the state troopers had found along the roadside. Whatever questions he might have had, Fitzgerald kept them to himself. Though at one point, near the end of the meeting, he did reveal his doubts.

"You made a pretty good shot on Peters," Fitzgerald told Ward.

"I might not be so lucky the next time," Ward responded, spoken with what would become his signature relaxed smile.[10]

As the words came out of Ward's mouth, Campbell interrupted, insisting that if anyone had any questions for their client to speak only to the attorneys. Ward appeared like some 1920s Hollywood film star: handsome, well-dressed, but silent.

Throughout the entire meeting the Westchester officials showed a pronounced cordiality toward Ward, which continued through the next necessary legal formalities. A warrant was issued. Sheriff Werner formally arrested Ward. Weeks charged him with manslaughter pending an investigation. Ward and his attorneys then stood in front of supreme court justice A. H. Seeger, who granted Ward bail of $10,000, an amount agreed upon beforehand by Weeks. The son of German immigrants, sixty-one-year-old Seeger had been a supreme court justice for five years, after a career as a prosecutor. He had a love of horse racing and was a respected member of the court.[11] Some might have questioned Seeger's granting bail to a confessed murderer, one with plenty of means to leave the state, particularly since the investigation of Ward's self-defense claims had not even begun. But allowing Ward bail appeared another act of accommodation for the son of a respected family, who also happened to be a police commissioner.

In the clerk's office, Ward pulled out a roll of bills from his pants pocket and peeled off ten $1,000 notes, laid them on the counter, and pushed them toward the clerk. He dodged a growing crowd of reporters who had gathered at the courthouse entrance, prompted no doubt by rumors of Ward's appearance. Finding a side exit, Ward left the building to an awaiting car and quickly disappeared.

The events of the entire morning seemed quite scripted, everyone playing their parts. And, in fact, they were. When Campbell and Werner met on that Friday, May 19, at the courthouse, the day before the sheriff gathered reporters in his office and hinted at his developing "theory" about the case, Campbell explained the events that had led to the homicide much as they were outlined in the statement. Werner had little interest in the nature of the blackmail. "That is a private matter," he told Campbell. "The newspapers will spread that scandal all around and we have to get after those fellows," meaning the two men in the red Stutz. Werner asked Campbell to come up with a statement to give the press. So Campbell, Elwood Rabenold, and Isaac Mills spent the weekend drafting those 331 words. It was unclear what, if any, help Walter Ward offered to his attorneys.

Not long after his Friday afternoon meeting with Campbell, Werner took a ride over to the state trooper barracks and met with Eugene Roberts, requesting the photographs of the crime scene, the items found on Peters, and any other evidence gathered along King Street. "Something big was going to break in the case," Werner told Roberts, but when asked for details, Werner remained evasive. Roberts didn't press the sheriff and simply handed over the evidence. As Werner left the barracks carrying Peters's belongings as well as the silver shell casing, Roberts might not have realized that neither he nor any of his men would have much say over the ongoing investigation.[12]

On the courthouse steps and underneath the motto about justice carved in the building's frieze, Werner and Fitzgerald faced the press.

"Ward declares," Werner announced, "that he was the victim of blackmail for six weeks before the shooting." As reporters took notes and photographers captured the scene, Werner related what happened based on the statement Ward's attorneys had provided.

"We are still working on the case," he said, "which appears to have been plainly one of blackmail. Ward confesses to having met Peters and explained to us that this man Peters was a member of a gang of blackmailers."[13] The word *plainly* might have struck some of the reporters as an odd term, given that the sheriff also indicated the investigation was ongoing. The word *plainly* had a certain conclusionary tone to it—a tone that suggested he and his colleagues believed Ward's statement unequivocally and there really was little more to be done.

At one point, as Werner described the final moments of the

gunfight, Fitzgerald, who had for the most part been silent, interrupted to correct Werner's facts.

"Ward told me he thought one man collapsed," Fitzgerald stated. Perhaps perturbed at having his recounting of the events sidetracked, Werner clarified that Ward was not sure he had hit either man.[14] This small rift between the two men signaled Fitzgerald's doubts and did not go unnoticed by reporters. It betrayed a certain pretense that Peters's murder might not be so "plainly" solved and pointed to the uncertainties about Ward's story that even the authorities had trouble getting straight.

While it was true that the mystery of who killed Clarence Peters on a lonely road apparently had been solved with Ward's statement, a new, more complicated mystery emerged. When asked if Ward revealed the cause of the blackmail, Werner said, "I cannot go into the matters at the present moment." When asked the same question a bit later he delivered a simple, terse, and emphatic, "No." None of the reporters were yet aware that Werner had no interest in pursuing the motive for the murder.[15]

In New Rochelle, police chief Frank Cody expressed disbelief.

"I cannot understand it at all," he told reporters, adding, "I have always had the utmost confidence in Commissioner Ward, a fine young man, frank and fearless." Cody described Ward as "full of grit," citing how just a few years prior when workers went on strike at the Ward Bakery Company, Ward "went to work and drove a truck to help break the strike." Cody's praise for Ward's skill at strike busting betrayed more about the police chief than Ward's character. But the example did offer an image of Ward as a fearless defender of his family's company no matter the cost.

"He never told me of any of his troubles," Cody conceded.

The mayor of New Rochelle, who had only recently reappointed Ward as police commissioner, was even more dismayed by the news of Ward's actions but expressed confidence that his police commissioner did the right thing. When the full investigation was completed, the mayor had little doubt it would reveal how Ward acted only "in a red-blooded manner."[16]

It appeared, however, that Ward's strongest defense for his actions was to do nothing. "If Walter Ward is wise enough to keep silent," Max Steuer, a well-known criminal attorney, told reporters, "there is nothing in the criminal law of New York State under which he can be punished in any way for the killing of Clarence Peters." Even if Ward's story turned out to be untrue, Steuer smugly noted, "What difference does that make?" He continued: "It is always up to the State to prove that a crime was committed. One can't be convicted of a capital offense in New York solely on a confession. His story can't be used against him."[17] All Ward needed to do was stay quiet—a skill he was well-known for.

WITH SO LITTLE information forthcoming, the questions that emerged in the press after Ward's arrest had less to do with how Peters was murdered and more with why. Speculation about the nature of the blackmail ranged from racetrack gambling debts to the suggestion of another woman to theories it might have been an act of revenge against the Ward Bakery Company by disgruntled workers. But speculation seemed all that was possible at that point. Until the Westchester authorities took seriously their investigation into claims of blackmail, all they had were the words of the killer himself.

The *New York American* summed up on its front page the essential question that many were indeed wondering: "What was the strange hold that the alleged blackmail ring seemed to have on Ward, thirty-one years old and married?" This riddle would not be easy to answer.

Shadow Men

READERS OF THE DAILY PRESS WOULD HAVE UNDERSTOOD Ward's claims of blackmail and the dire threat he might have felt in its clutches. The story of a shadowy underworld gang would have been convincing not because it seemed so outlandish and shocking, but rather because it sounded so familiar.

Blackmail had a language and a sound in the 1920s. The confidence game or just con. The shakedown or just shake. In the press, blackmailers were called lounge lizards, tango artists, or gentlemen crooks. Sometimes they were called shadow men not only for their mysterious identities but also for the ways they followed their targets, tracking their habits before the confidence game commenced. They used aliases and posed as police detectives, stockbrokers, and federal agents. One article detailed how the blackmailers put "shadowers" on the trail of Walter Ward, following him everywhere. "The shadows bobbed up at unexpected places," it said.

The schemes of blackmailers were many, their exploits splashed on the front pages. In January 1921 prominent men in Portland, Oregon, were getting threatening letters, demanding thousands of dollars, with each letter signed "The Shadow." It was a mystery that would linger for months, with two unsuccessful attempts by the police to capture the culprit. In one instance, the blackmailer spoke with police, who described the voice as "deep toned with a strong German inflection."

The echoes of World War I could still be heard in the crime pages in the 1920s.

Sex, of course, was the most compelling tactic for blackmailers. Women called vampires, or just vamps, lured men into compromising situations, often called badger games. A vamp ensnared a man in a hotel room or private apartment, what were sometimes referred to as call flats. Before long a partner appeared posing as an outraged brother or husband or sometimes a fake police officer flashing a homemade badge and broke up the party demanding money in exchange for silence. It was all a well-rehearsed performance. Sometimes, they used handsome young men to attract the attentions of queer men and draw them into hotel rooms or public bathrooms, accuse them of immoral and illegal acts, and threaten to call the police if not paid.

In Seattle, the vamps lured men into homes set up with cameras peeping out of small holes in the walls. The press called it the "house of hidden eyes." Photographs of the men's activities were then used to threaten and extort money. Even on the small scale, blackmail proved a lucrative game. In Boston four detectives, two dressed as women, played decoy spooners, a term for those engaging in sexual play in the privacy of one's car, to nab young men who had been posing as policemen, flashing fake badges, and threatening to arrest young couples in their cars unless they paid them.[1]

"It's an ugly word—blackmail," the *San Francisco Chronicle* bemoaned in 1921. "So ugly and sinister that those most familiar with it, those who profit by the practices which it defines, involuntarily shrink from its sordid syllables and say the word only when it is euphemistically glossed." The article likened blackmail to tuberculosis: "silent, insidious, treacherous." The metaphors and euphemisms were also a way of covering up the victim's plight. Phrases like *hush money* or the *price of silence*, or even, as the article noted, the rather "honest sounding and meritorious name of 'bonus' has been stretched to cover" the evils of blackmail.[2]

The confidence men had their own terms and phrases that were as lyrical and jarring as the era's jazz music. There was a vernacular to the con games, a lexicon specific to the underworld, and at times it seeped into the press and the public consciousness. Sociologist Edwin Sutherland offered a long glossary of terms he found among the underworld in the 1920s in his book *The Professional Thief.*

> BADGER GAME, *n.*—A type of extortion in which the victim is lured into a room by a woman and is there discovered in a compromising situation by a man who represents himself as a husband.
>
> . . .
>
> BLOWOFF, *n.*—The final act in the operation of a confidence game, resulting in the separation of the thieves from the victim.
>
> . . .
>
> DUKE, *n.*—A confidence game involving fraud at cards; the hand, in connection with picking pockets.
>
> DUKEMAN, *n.*—A man engaged in cheating at cards.
>
> . . .
>
> FOOT RACE, *n.*—A confidence game in which a runner enters into collusion to defraud a victim who bets on the race.
>
> . . .
>
> GLIM-DROP, *n.*—A confidence game involving the use of an artificial eye.
>
> GLIM-DROPPER, *n.*—One who plays the glim-drop.
>
> . . .
>
> GOLDBRICK, *n.*—Confidence game in which a relatively worthless brick is sold as solid gold; frauds and confidence games in general.
>
> . . .
>
> LEMON, *n.*—A confidence game involving collusion in betting.
>
> LONG-HAIR, *adj.*—Artistic.
>
> . . .
>
> KNOCKOUT DROP, *n.*—Chemicals placed in intoxicating drinks or used otherwise to render one unconscious; same

as "Mickey Finn."

. . .

MOCKEY, *adj.*—Jewish

MOLL, *n.*—Female

. . .

MOUSE, *n.*—Extortion in connection with homosexual attempts; a homosexual person.

. . .

OUTSIDE MAN, *n.*—A member of a confidence mob with whom the victim makes contact on the basis of friendship.

. . .

RAW-JAW, *adj.*—Unhampered, unafraid, without caution.

. . .

STOCK MARKET, *n.*—An elaborate confidence game; one of the methods of the pay-off.

. . .

SUCKER, *n.*—Victim; anyone who is not a thief.[3]

The sucker, of course, was eager to get something out of it. That's why they're a sucker in the first place. As Sutherland noted, "In the confidence game the principle is the same—beat a man who is trying to do something dishonest." But it's his next sentence that is more important when thinking about blackmail: "It is impossible to beat an honest man in a confidence game."

The word *sucker* was made popular at El Fey Club near Times Square. Opened in 1922 by bootlegger and gambler Larry Fay, it soon became a favorite for those in the underworld—a respectable club for the pretense of respectable people. The star of El Fey Club was a cabaret performer named Mary Louise Cecilia Guinan, known on stage at Texas Guinan after her hometown of Waco. Guinan greeted folks to each night's performance with a boisterous tone inflected with a Texas lilt: "Hello, Suckers! Leave your wallet at the bar." It was a pointed joke aimed at all those patrons who paid the newly invented entrance fees called cover charges, only to encounter the exorbitant prices for drinks once inside.

It also described New York nightlife during Prohibition where confidence schemes flourished among unsuspecting patrons who were high on the evening festivities and bootlegged alcohol but always vigilant of a police raid. New Yorkers of all classes found in Prohibition a rebellious spirit against the morality of the dry crusaders—a rebellion that played out in the transgressive thrill of the city's nightlife. Knowing where to go, how to act, what to say, and whom to avoid were part of the cosmopolitan appeal of places like El Fey Club. Prohibition only amplified the problem of confidence games. "Between blackmailing, bootlegging and home brewing, the nation is becoming honeycombed with a mess of small and contemptable crimes," one editorial complained. In the nightlife of Prohibition New York if you weren't a playing a con, you just might be the target of one.[4]

Though no glossary of the era would've included captains of industry in a list of con men, wealthy men like Ward were playing their own schemes, using their power and privilege for profit in a marketplace that was almost unregulated. This was the era that gave us the Ponzi scheme, after all, named for the infamous Charles Ponzi who bilked his Wall Street investors of $20 million with promises of getting rich quick. Throughout the twenties, there were any number of investor frauds making headlines, with the wealthy and powerful seeking to make a fortune out of almost nothing. When Ponzi's fraud was revealed in 1920, *The New York Times* argued that the investors themselves were part of the problem. The case was an "object lesson" for those seeking fortunes in such schemes, the newspaper declared, as there was an "element of misconduct on the part of those who allow themselves to be partners in such duplicity."[5] The suckers knew what they were getting into, and they hoped to come out winners. It would be an object lesson we would learn over and over again, with few results. Shadow men weren't just found among the underworld. The excesses of the Jazz Age could be seen as one big con, and the lines between wealthy men like Ward and those blackmailers and grifters were often very thin.

SEVERAL MONTHS BEFORE Clarence Peters's body appeared on King Street, *The Boston Globe* described what it called a "blackmail industry" that played on the public's more unseemly appetites. "The culprit breaks the law. But the blackmailer is a double criminal: he is a parasite on crime," the editors wrote. The real problem of blackmail, the editors claimed, was our own fascination with scandal. "If the public appetite for scandal were a trifle less keen," the editors complained, "the blackmailing industry would have a far less richly manured soil in which to thrive. A certain avidity for salacious details which prevails amongst us points to a complex of repressions and inhibitions which go to the very root of our social psychology." The editors concluded with a damning indictment of reading public: "In the final count the power of the blackmailer lies not in the law or in the breach of it, but in the unwholesome appetites of starved imagination to gloat over misfortunes of those who perhaps differ from themselves in only having been found out."[6]

If blackmail was an industry, then certainly the leader of the industry was a man known as Dapper Don Collins, whom the press described in 1922 as the "blackmailer of the century." Born Robert Arthur Tourbillon in Atlanta, Georgia, in the 1880s, Collins moved to New York just after the turn of the century. By the 1920s, Collins embodied the image of the modern thief: handsome, clean-shaven, always dressed in well-tailored suits, and always surrounded by young, beautiful women. The press referred to him as the "gilded crook," and one article described him as the "Beau Brumel of Broadway," a reference to the nineteenth-century dandy.[7] On his World War I draft registration, he used his birth name and listed his occupation as "salesman" at Smith & Haines, an auto-tire store on Broadway. While Robert Arthur Tourbillon may have been selling tires on Broadway, Dapper Don Collins was working any number of confidence games in the city. His aliases were many: Arthur David, Sir Robert, Stephen Daly, Harry Cadwell, Thomas Watson, to name a few. Just a month after he signed his draft card in 1918, he was arrested for impersonating a federal agent and extorting money from German American immigrants in upstate New York who paid Collins for fear they would be branded, as one report noted, "dangerous huns" by the government.[8]

From simple blackmail and thefts to more complex cons involving fake stock trades, racetrack betting, or impersonating federal agents, complete with official-looking badges and fake warrants, for three decades Collins and his gang bilked men out of hundreds of thousands of dollars. His exploits made for great headlines, and his appearance as a handsome, well-tailored thief would become a trope in the popular imagination.[9]

Blackmail, particularly the badger games, proved the most successful for Collins. In the years before World War I, he worked a number of badger schemes between New York and Atlantic City, using young women to lure men out of town and then having his men pose as federal agents threatening arrests under the Mann Act. Passed in 1910, the Mann Act made it a federal crime for a man to travel across state lines for sexual adventure with a woman other than his wife. Proponents defended it as necessary to stop what they erroneously described as a trade in white slavery. Detractors pointed to how the law gave rise to a hugely profitable blackmail industry.

It was Collins's highly publicized arrest for his Atlantic City extortions in 1916 that prompted a *New York Times* editorial to complain that the law encouraged "business opportunities," noting that the Mann Act gave cunning blackmailers the idea that by "enticing the partners of a drunken orgy across a boundary, they may live in comfort for the rest of their lives." It called the law an absurdity that had no effect on curbing "immoralities" in the country, but instead had the ultimate effect of "fostering and even creating crime." By the 1920s Collins had exploited the Mann Act to develop what one newspaper described as a "de Luxe Blackmailing Syndicate," earning him hundreds of thousands of dollars a year.[10]

With few exceptions, Collins avoided conviction, as victims were reluctant to go to court and face the scandal of having their indiscretions or even the suggestion of their indiscretions go public. While he did serve a few short terms in prison, it wasn't until the late thirties, after being arrested for posing as an immigration inspector and extorting two hundred dollars from an immigrant under threat of deportation, that Collins was finally convicted and sent to Sing Sing prison. He would spend the rest of his life in prison, dying in 1950 and being buried in the prison cemetery, his headstone marked only by his inmate number: 5870. It was an ignominious ending for the "gilded crook."

THE PUBLIC MIGHT have been surprised that a blackmail scheme like the one Ward described ended in murder. As Don Collins demonstrated so often, the con man was no murderer. Such schemes attacked a reputation and avoided violent harm.

But there was another element to Ward's confession that might have struck some as strange: any successful con needed a dishonest sucker. The lure of a beautiful mistress, the attentions of a handsome man, the promise of quick money from an inside stock trade or a fixed horse race all relied on an eager and ambitious target. The "slick gentry" is how a 1921 editorial in the *Miami Herald* described it. The editors complained that those who cede to blackmail and seek "riches by secret means" make it impossible that the "confidence game ever will be banished."[11] If we are to believe Ward's claims of being a victim of a gang of blackmailers, that he had already paid them thousands of dollars, we must also remember what Sutherland showed in his study of the con game: you can't con an honest man.

Slipper City

"IT'S A LIE!" THAT'S WHAT ELBRIDGE PETERS TOLD REPORTers in the days after Ward's statement made headlines. The family's private grief and confusion about Clarence's death had quickly become a front-page story. Ward's statement implicating Clarence in a violent underworld blackmailing gang cast doubt about their oldest son's character and prompted a sudden and unexpected spotlight on their family they neither wished for nor knew how to handle.

"Ward's Confession Fails to Solve Death Mystery" announced the front page of the May 23 *Haverhill Evening Gazette* on the same day Clarence's coffin arrived by train and was delivered to the family's basement apartment on Grove Street. Friends and family came by with condolences and food during the two-day wake before the funeral at Riverview Cemetery in Groveland just across the Merrimack River. Peters was a volunteer member of the 181st Infantry of the Massachusetts National Guard, which allowed for military pallbearers and a three-volley rifle salute at the grave site followed by a bugler playing taps. Inez and Elbridge must have felt it was an appropriate tribute for their oldest son, even if they had no money for a proper headstone.[1]

"All the evidence shows my son could not have been connected with such a plot," Elbridge insisted. "The boy had been in many escapades, but I have never known him to carry a gun or a knife. I doubt those statements by Ward."

Clarence was not the most innocent of Haverhill's youths. In 1917, at the age of fourteen, he dropped out of school. He had a love of poetry and particularly nineteenth-century poet and Haverhill native John Greenleaf Whittier, so his leaving school was perhaps more of a necessity to go to work and support the family, as Elbridge often struggled with his health. But work was difficult to find, and in the five years from when he stopped his studies to when he took the train to Parris Island, Clarence often made wrong choices. In 1918, he stole a bicycle. As it was his first offense, the judge sentenced him to probation. Just a month later, he stole money from a group of young girls who were collecting Red Cross donations for servicemen. Allegedly, he offered to watch their stand and donation box while the girls took a short break. When they returned, Peters and the box were gone. For that crime, the judge sentenced him to six months at Shirley Industrial School for Boys, a reformatory in Shirley, Massachusetts, born out of the Shaker belief that work was a path to a virtuous life. Whatever positive effects his time at Shirley had, they were short-lived.

Not long after leaving Shirley he was arrested for stealing two letters with checks in them from a postbox and was sent back to the reformatory. Perhaps Peters's navy enlistment at the age of sixteen was an effort to reform himself. He went to the Boston recruiting station in August 1919 and applied to be an apprentice seaman. He served on the USS *Florida V* stationed in the Boston Navy Yard. But according to navy records, just ten weeks later, Peters was court-martialed for stealing. He would continue a cycle of theft and reformatories once back in Haverhill. In 1921 Peters's proclivities took a leap when he was arrested with a group of teenagers for stealing three automobiles, taking them for a drive, and abandoning them. A few months later he stole an automobile from Charles Street in South Boston and drove it back to Haverhill, again abandoning it. The Boston police arrested him a week later, and a judge sentenced him to the Concord Reformatory. On appeal the case was dismissed.

This was the pattern for young Clarence, a series of minor and major thefts and a cycle of reformatory incarcerations that must have left Inez and Elbridge frustrated, angry, and disappointed. Details of his many arrests in the press cast doubts not only on his character but also the characters of the boy's parents. But whatever Elbridge might have felt about his son's earlier arrests, certainly nothing compared to the accusations Ward leveled at Clarence. The Peterses were genuinely at a loss to explain how Clarence might have ended up murdered on a road in New York.[2]

Elbridge and Inez were not the kind of people who were used to reporters asking them questions about their family or hanging around their home. In newspaper photos, both have a certain shocked look, a visible discomfort in front of the camera's lens. Born and raised in working-class families in Haverhill, they grew up amid the city's rapid industrial growth through the late nineteenth century. By the early 1920s the city's population had nearly tripled in size to just over 50,000 people. The growth of industrial shoe making accounted for these changes. Entering the city limits of Haverhill in the years before World War I, you might be greeted by a large sign topped with a cut-out image of a stylish man's shoe that proclaimed, HAVERHILL, THE GREAT BOOT AND SHOE CITY. The Peters home on Grove Street was just a short walk to the shoe district, a congested area of four- and five-story brick factories sitting along River Street and the Merrimack River and stretching up to the Haverhill train station. Nearly a quarter of the city's residents worked in one of those shoe factories, holding positions with such curious names as cutter, vamper, stitcher, closer-on, lining maker, doubler, turn laster, edge trimmer, and skiver. While wages always varied by position and gender, in the early 1920s, average pay was around forty-eight cents an hour, much less for those unskilled and inexperienced.[3]

The Haverhill factories paid better than many other nearby towns with big shoe industries, such as Lynn and Brockton, owing to the strength of the Shoe Workers' Protective Union. For as much as the town was known as Slipper City, it was also known as the great socialist city. Or at least for a few years at the turn of the century, when labor organizer John Chase won election to Haverhill mayor on the Socialist Party ticket, which also included a majority of the city aldermen. Chase's victory marked the first time in the country that a city elected a leader from the Socialist Party, reflecting the keen tensions between workers and owners that had flared for decades, most acutely in the 1890s with a number of citywide strikes. While Chase served only one two-year term, losing his reelection in a Republican sweep, his victory was a moment of powerful possibility for the working class in Haverhill and heralded the Progressive Era reforms across the country in the following decades, bringing new labor laws and protections for workers. Chase's unprecedent win must have lingered in conversations at meetings of the Shoe Workers' Protective Union and factory floors of Slipper City for years.[4]

The industrialized shoe factory had an order to the production process, each step atomized into particular tasks. Often soles were made on the first floor or the basement, with leather cutting and lasting on the middle floors, and finally the stitching and cleaning and buffing housed in the top floors where large windows allowed for the best light. Each part of the process required a certain level of skill and experience. When Elbridge married Inez in 1901, both just barely in their twenties, he worked as a laster, a position that entailed the stretching and fitting of leather around a wooden mold, or last, that was shaped and sized for a particular kind of shoe or boot. A laster required strength and dexterity to contour the leather into the proper size before moving the pieces upstairs to the stitching floor.

Like his grandfather and father, who worked his way from stitcher to shop foreman, Elbridge started young in factory work. Production schedules were often grueling, sometimes with factories operating around the clock and through the weekends. Workers were constantly monitored about the pace and quality of their work. It was a not an uncommon practice among different owners to share lists of workers detailing their characters and their workmanship, making it nearly impossible for those who were deemed difficult or underperforming to move from one factory to another.[5]

At some point before 1920, Elbridge left his work as a laster and began work as a housepainter. By 1917 his health had deteriorated due to lead poisoning, though claims against the painting company for compensation failed in court, leaving Elbridge with a debilitating illness that made any full-time work difficult to maintain. He took on a job as a gas fitter, working on Haverhill gas lines. That position was short-lived though, and he eventually returned to house painting, work that allowed him to be outside in the fresh air, beyond the factory fumes and noise and the constant eye of the factory foreman. But house painting was not steady work, dependent on the seasons and the weather. Elbridge's lack of a regular income weighed heavily on the family, who at times ate little more than bread soaked in milk. They often moved around Haverhill; when rent was overdue for many months, they picked up and left for a new, often cramped apartment, staying just ahead of evictions.

Like Elbridge's, Inez's family had worked in the town's industry for generations, and while women made up about 30 percent of the factory labor, particularly on those well-lit stitching floors, Inez chose work as a maid and later as a bow maker. A year after they were married, they had their first child and named her Viola May. The following year, Clarence was born. The 1910 census lists four children in the Peters household—two sons and two daughters—along with a lodger named Sarah Jones. Jones was from Maine and worked full-time in a shoe factory as what was called a closer-on, a person who stitched the lining and leather together at the top part of a shoe. It was not uncommon for residents of Haverhill to take in lodgers. Many were temporary workers who traveled from Canada or other parts of New England and worked for short periods. The town ebbed and flowed with such labor during the busier parts of the year in the fall and winter months. It was also, perhaps, a necessity to have Sarah lodge with the family, as Inez at that point was no longer working outside the house but instead focused on taking care of her young children.

But census data can be deceptive, for it records only the presence of the living, not the dead. Their son Walter died in 1907, just one year old, from gastroenteritis. Viola May, the Peters's first child, died two years later from meningitis. They lost another daughter, Sarah, in 1918 when she was only six years old. And still another, son Russell in 1920, just a month shy of his first birthday. Clarence was not the first child Elbridge and Inez had to bury.[6]

By 1920 Clarence found work as a leather cutter in one of the factories in the early part of the year, having just returned from being dishonorably discharged from the navy. Perhaps Clarence thought working as a cutter was the responsible thing to do, a required rite of passage in Slipper City, and a necessity to help out with the family expenses. After all, most of his neighbors on Grove Street worked in the industry. It was, perhaps, hard for him to imagine any other life outside of factory work. He must have been restless for some kind of adventure but also discouraged by his prospects. We can imagine his parents hoped he could find a new direction in his life, one that didn't involve theft.

His time cutting leather at the factory was short-lived though. In May, he was arrested again for stealing and again sent back to Shirley. He never returned to factory work. Between the summer of 1920 and his attempted enlistment in the marines in April 1922, Clarence pursued a series of odd jobs in between arrests for petty theft and stints in reformatories. William Smith, who owned the popular Smith Lunch Café in Haverhill, hired Clarence for a short time when his workers went on strike. He described Clarence as a "big and good looking" boy but not that smart. "He had no brains," Smith said. For a time, Clarence found part-time work loading and unloading trucks at the Carlton Fruit Company and then as a furniture mover, which took him on trips to Hartford, Connecticut, and Albany, New York. But never New York City, according to his coworkers. He would, they recalled, become nervous as they drove through wooded or mountainous areas, a behavior they found funny and strange. They related that Peters never spoke of Ward or of any wealthy friends. They mostly remembered Peters as a shy guy who didn't seem to have many friends.

In March 1922, Peters took a job as a farmhand in New Hampshire. The owners of the farm, Mr. and Mrs. Nye, remembered that Peters never got any mail or phone calls while he was working for them. He never had any money, they said, except the small amount they paid him, which he spent on candy or cigarettes or movies. The Nyes let him go after a month, unsatisfied with his work.

Similarly, the owner of Fuller Farm, where Peters worked for only one day, described how he did little of the work asked of him and often did things he was specifically told not to do. Mr. Fuller remembered how he went out into the middle of the fields and would "yell for no reason at all." He also described Peters as a moral degenerate but refused to explain why he felt this way when investigators asked. "I just didn't want him around my boys," he said.

What many remembered about Clarence Peters was how he rarely had more than a few cents in his pocket but had an abundance of wildly imagined stories about his past adventures. To the Nyes he described how he spent two years with the marines during World War I, after which he toured the world. He told them he expected to get married to a girl in Haverhill as soon as his bonus money from the marines came through. To his coworkers at the moving company, Peters claimed he was married and a father, his wife and child living with his parents in Haverhill. As he looked older than his years, perhaps Peters learned quickly that people believed his stories, and he seemed to enjoy pretending that he was something he was not.[7] After the Nyes let him go in April 1922, Clarence returned to Haverhill.

"He left the house intending to search for work on the morning of April 25th," Elbridge told reporters. "Just before noon I met him on Washington Street and Clarence told me that he had been unable to find a job and that he was on his way home. He started off up the street as though to go home and I continued on down."[8]

Clarence didn't go home but instead took the train to Boston and arrived at the marine recruitment station on the afternoon of April 26, giving his full name as Clarence Melvin Peters. Sargent Gonzales, the recruitment officer, told Peters what he told everyone who came to enlist: each recruit is fingerprinted to ensure that he has not been in another branch of service or has not been discharged from service. Fingerprinting was still a relatively new practice. During World War I, the U.S. military amassed one of the largest archives of fingerprints taken from among its recruits. Perhaps Clarence thought he could somehow dodge the military check. Or maybe he knew he would be rejected but would enjoy the journey to Parris Island nonetheless. It beat looking for a job.

The trip from Boston to Parris Island, South Carolina, was complicated. Sargent Gonzales put Clarence on a 5:10 p.m. train to Providence, Rhode Island, where he boarded an overnight boat to New York City. On April 27, he took a train from New York to South Carolina, where he boarded another boat to Parris Island, arriving in the morning on April 28. There Corporal Stearns, one of the marines who processed new recruits, fingerprinted him and issued him his uniform. Stearns remembered how Peters arrived without any baggage; his only possessions were what he had in his pockets. He was dressed in a blue-black suit that was "practically worn out," according to Stearns. He said Peters tried to sell him a ring with an imitation sapphire and bragged about how, if he needed money, he could get it. "But he didn't say how," Stearns said. As he left Parris Island after his rejection, Peters told other recruits he had plans to "hang around New York" for a while before heading back to Haverhill.[9]

INEZ AND ELBRIDGE shared two letters with the *New York American* they received from Clarence just days after he arrived at Parris Island. Boyish in tone, his letters betray a homesickness, a concern for his family, but also his own uncertainty:

> Just a few lines to let you know I have gone in the Marines to see if I pass. If I don't pass, I will let you know what I am going to do. How is all the rest of the family getting along? Tell Morton and Kenneth [Clarence's younger brothers] I hope to see them soon. You can write to me if you want to, but I don't know as I am going to get it or not. When you write to me you can put my name and the receiving barracks, Parris Island, S.C. and I will get it all right.
>
> Don't worry about me, because I will try to take care of myself all right. Tell Papa I could not wait to get work because I had waited too long already, as I got sick of looking. Is Pa and Leslie working yet? If they are let me know, because I like to know if they are working. I will try to get

> in if I can because it is the only thing there is to do. I'm not going to write very much because I can write again soon and I will tell you if I get in. Please write me and tell me how everybody is at home.

In a second letter, sent a few days later, he continued to reassure his family. "I will let you know if I pass or if I don't. Tell everybody I am thinking of them all the time. Don't worry. Your loving son, Clarence." No doubt Inez and Elbridge released these letters to dispel the image of their son as some underworld criminal. More importantly the letters cast doubt about their son's involvement in the blackmail scheme in the weeks before the murder as Ward had claimed. The timeline was important. Peters had been discharged on May 12 and left South Carolina on May 14 according to military records. For rejected marine recruits, the military provided a ticket only as far north as Philadelphia. Beyond that the men were on their own. Perhaps Peters took a train from Philadelphia to New York, but it seemed unlikely, given he had no money. It was more likely he did what other rejected recruits had done: hitchhiked their way back up north. We know that at some point on the afternoon or early evening of May 15 he found himself in New York, just hours before his murder.

Clarence's uncle Earl Hardy, the man who traveled to Westchester to identify his nephew's body, told reporters he thought Ward's story was "fishy." Hardy had visited the crime scene on King Street and had private conversations with Sheriff Werner about his investigation. He developed his own theory of the case. "It looks to me as though Ward was implicated in something unusual when he would pay over money to blackmailers. It doesn't seem to me that he, a police commissioner, would be paying over money unless they had something on him. My nephew was easily led, but it doesn't seem as if he would become a leader of a gang of blackmailers."[10]

Perhaps out of necessity or out of frustration or a genuine fear that the murderer of their son would go unpunished, Elbridge and Inez contacted Michael Sullivan, a lawyer in Salem, Massachusetts, who took on the case. Sullivan was a friend of Elbridge's deceased half brother and a well-known attorney in town. It was rumored that Sullivan had ambitions to be district attorney and, we might speculate, took on this high-profile murder for the publicity it might bring him. "If Walter S. Ward is found to have killed Clarence Peters without justification," he told reporters, "he shall pay for his act in both the criminal and civil courts."

Sullivan spoke of his own suspicions about Ward's statement, calling it an absurd "blackmail yarn." He asked, "What was the alleged blackmail threat based on? Where and when were the demands made?" adding, "Ward should be forced to give dates and names. He should be specific in this matter. It is important." Sullivan also revealed that he had reached out to a "prominent" New York attorney to help with his own investigations into the matter. "I do not wish to disclose this lawyer's identity at this time," he said.[11] It was undoubtedly a relief for Elbridge and Inez to have Sullivan represent them. Sullivan's first piece of legal advice to the Peterses: stop talking to reporters.

"Everything is in the hands of my lawyer," Elbridge told anyone asking questions. "I have nothing more to say." But, showing a sense of frustration with the press, he did add, "If anyone says that they got anything out of me it is not true. If they say anything it will be because they made it up. And interviewers had better have care about what they say."[12]

REPORTERS WEREN'T ABOUT to quit trying. The murder of Clarence Peters had moved from a local concern for Westchester authorities to a national story. The mystery of Peters's movement in the days after his discharge from Parris Island prompted the William Randolph Hearst-owned *New York American* to offer a substantial cash reward for any information—an amount more than the yearly income for most workers in one of Haverhill's shoe factories. The paper announced:

> The New York American will pay a reward of one thousand dollars to any person who supplies exclusively to The American information explaining the mystery of the killing of Clarence Peters.[13]

The emphasis on "exclusively" was important in the highly competitive wars between the New York newspapers. The announcement asked specific questions about Peters: What brought him to New York? When did he arrive in the city? When did he meet Walter Ward? Or did he renew an old acquaintance? And specifically the paper requested any information on Peters's "movements" between May 13 and the early-morning hours of May 16. The reward, published daily alongside the many articles about the case, captured the public's interest and signaled the growing potential of the story in generating newspaper sales. While the *New York American* had a reputation for indulging in scandal and half-truths, it was certainly not the only newspaper speculating about the mystery of Peters's murder. It was, however, the only newspaper offering such a huge reward for information.

As journalists pursued new leads in the case, each newspaper vying for the next big headline, Elbridge and Inez Peters's very public rejection of Ward's statement marked the beginning of the unspooling of his story.

My Man

WHEN *THE NEW YORK TIMES* SENT REPORTERS OUT TO KING Street to investigate the crime scene, it was a perfect May morning, clear and cool, much like the day a week earlier when Peters's body was found. Reporters spoke with Clarence Eckhardt, owner of Ardson Farm, and his two farmhands who had been some of the first to discover the body.

It seemed impossible, Eckhardt told the reporters, that there was some kind of gun battle in the way that Ward had described it. His farmhands were sleeping not more than two hundred yards from King Street, and none of them reported hearing any gunshots. To test the theory, Eckhardt brought his own pistol to the spot where reporters had gathered and fired it into the air. The sound cut through the sky and spread across the hilly farms that surrounded the crime scene. The gun shot "made a loud report," the journalists noted, "easily heard 200 yards away, echoing and re-echoing through the valley."

Eckhardt offered his own theory of the killing. He speculated that Peters was murdered elsewhere and his body dumped along the road in the early-morning hours. He found no blood splatter along the ground, no broken glass from a car window, and no sign of a struggle amid the gravel and sand near Peters's body. He and his workers saw only one set of tire tracks, which "had gone into the dirt off the roadway and had cut a deep impression near Peters's head." Eckhardt also described what the state troopers had discovered: there was one bullet hole in Peters's shirt but not in his vest or jacket. "If these statements prove correct," *The New York Times* reported, "they would indicate that Peters had his coat and vest off when he was shot and that he was shot at close range."[1]

Lieutenant Eugene Roberts of the state police, one of the first officers to arrive at the crime scene, told *The Evening World* he too was "convinced there was no gun battle" on King Street that night and had found only one set of tire tracks. Footprints matched Peters's shoes and appeared to be deeply set, suggesting he had been standing there for some time before he was shot, not, as Ward described, quickly stepping out of the car, with one foot on the running board and one on the ground before Ward pulled out his revolver. He suggested, based on where the tire tracks were in relation to the body, that the gun was about ten feet away from Peters when it was fired. The newspaper related how state troopers examined the deep impressions in the soil underneath Peters's shoes and determined that the "force of the impact of the .38 caliber bullet had toppled Peters over backward, and his heels dug in the sand as he fell."[2]

But one important question that remained a mystery: If the events happened as Ward described them, what had become of Peters's .32 Smith & Wesson? It was not found with the body when the linemen discovered Peters. And neither Ward's statement nor interviews with DA Weeks or Sheriff Werner indicated what happened to it after Ward shot Peters. Did someone take it, along with Peters's military papers or other identification? Or perhaps Charlie Ross and Jack returned to the roadside and removed the gun? For what reason, it was not clear. Of course we might ask if Peters even had a gun to begin with.

Doubting that Peters had a gun also cast doubt about the claim of a gun battle as Ward described. The .38 automatic Colt he used to shoot Peters and protect himself from the other two men ejected its bullet casings. If there were a barrage of gunfire, the crime scene would have been littered with shell casings, but the state troopers found only one single casing. If there was a volley of bullets as Ward's statement contends, there was certainly no evidence at the crime scene. The more investigators and journalists considered Ward's story, the more the questions kept piling up.

IN THE DAYS after Walter Ward came forward with his story and paid his bail, the Wards' neighborhood of Sutton Manor in New Rochelle, a respectable, upper-middle-class enclave on the shores of Echo Bay, was anything but quiet. Much to the displeasure of residents, journalists camped out in front of the Wards's home at 75 Decatur Road, a stone-and-stucco mansion perched on a hill looking like a medieval estate. Journalists were snooping around the neighborhood, knocking on doors, asking questions of gardeners and nannies, poking around the local boathouse trying to get information about the Wards. Detectives described how residents were "hounded" by reporters, who kept nearly twenty-four-hour watch on the comings and goings of the good people of Sutton Manor. Some reporters were bribing neighborhood children to steal photographs of the Wards from their parents' houses. One young girl had been caught by her mother absconding with such a photograph, prompting her parents to call the police to put an end to the reporters' practices. When detectives came knocking on neighbors' doors, they usually encountered silence, as residents feared they were more annoying reporters asking personal questions about the decent family on Decatur Road.[3]

Sutton Manor, or simply the Manor, as the locals called it, was an early invention of suburban living, subdivided from a large nineteenth-century estate into two-acre lots promising a unique country escape. In the years before World War I, as Westchester transformed from rural farmland into a haven for New York City elites such as John D. Rockefeller and Jay Gould, both of whom built lavish estates along the Hudson, New Rochelle gained a reputation as an artist colony, attracting set designers, painters, and illustrators. Norman Rockwell, J. C. Leyendecker, and Ernest Albert were among the more famous artists who settled in the bucolic setting.[4] Sutton Manor had been designed as a small village. Traveling along the Manor's streets, you would encounter a mixture of architectural styles—columned colonials, steeped-roofed

Tudors, red-tiled Mediterranean villas, heavy-framed Craftsman bungalows, and haunting neo-Gothic stone facades populated the neighborhood's curving streets.

From their arched stone terrace, the Wards enjoyed open views of Echo Bay that stretched out into Long Island Sound. The Wards also had a view of the Sutton Manor Boat and Club House, where locals would moor their sailboats in the summer and linger in moments of gossip about their neighbors. Many residents of the Manor worked in Manhattan. Some were company presidents or managed brokerage houses on Wall Street; many sat on charity boards. Most, however, were upper-level managers, keenly professional and reservedly middle-class. They cared about local politics, the Republican Party of Westchester, the goings-on in the society columns, and the problems with Prohibition. But mostly, they cared about privacy and privilege.

Perhaps as a rebuke to the invasion of journalists who had unsettled the Manor's suburban calm, Walter Ward made a public display of taking a stack of morning-edition newspapers to the terrace and, sitting in a wicker chair, read the front pages, laughing so loudly the reporters along the curb would take notice at just how comical he thought it all was.

While the Wards tried hard to ignore the reporters, they also saw the potential in them. Unlike her husband, Beryl appeared open to talking with the press, using her charm to distract them. "If the real facts were known," she told them, "as I believe they should be, the whole matter would be cleared up quickly and in a manner highly favorable to my husband." She told reporters she hosted a card party on the night May 15, with many of her neighbors attending. Though Walter was not there. When asked how long she had been aware of the blackmailing, she replied directly and without hesitation: "Not very long. I am standing with my husband in this ordeal and I want to do everything I can to help him."[5]

Twenty-five-year-old Beryl Ward grew up in a turreted Victorian mansion in the Cypress Hills neighborhood of Brooklyn. Her father, Willard Curtis, made a fortune in lumber, and his only child did not want for much in her life. In summers, the family stayed in a rambling seaside cottage in the exclusive Belle Harbor neighborhood along the Rockaway Peninsula in Queens. Beryl was only eighteen years old and still a student at Briarcliff College, an all-women's academy just north of New York City, when she got engaged to Walter, five years her senior. We don't know how Walter Ward met the charming Beryl Curtis, though given Beryl's age, it seemed likely their courtship was a short one. "Another Brooklyn girl of prominence is to marry a Manhattan man," the *Brooklyn Daily Eagle*'s society column announced, adding that Miss Curtis "has been the greatest of successes in society" since her debut and "among the most attractive of the girls in social life the past two years."[6]

Walter and Beryl married at Trinity Church in Brooklyn in October 1915, the pews "filled to capacity," according to press reports, and decorated "to appear like a botanical garden." Beryl walked through the garden and down the aisle in an "old fashioned style" gown, as one report described it, with a large hoopskirt made of satin, tulle, and chiffon. Orange blossoms accented the band of the tulle veil across her forehead. She also wore a large circle diamond around her neck, a gift from her fiancé. At the altar, Walter watched her procession, Ralph Ward by his side as his best man.

Three hundred people attended the reception at her parents' house just a few blocks from the church. Decorated entirely in pink roses, the house was also filled with waltz music by the well-known McKee's Society Orchestra. It was all a fairly traditional event. After a few years living with Beryl's parents, the couple would move to the stone-and-stucco house on Decatur Road. Their first child, Elizabeth, was born in 1918, followed by Willard in 1920.[7]

Walter had been living in the city for only a few years before he proposed to Beryl, his social prospects entwined with the fate of the family business. Sometime around 1911 George Ward, then vice president of the company, moved his family from Sewickley Heights, Pennsylvania, a wealthy, rural enclave just west of Pittsburgh, to New York City. He bought a house along Riverside Drive with views of the Hudson River.[8]

The chief of police in Pittsburgh remembered Walter Ward and his family well. There was "absolutely no scandal" connected with them, he told detectives who went asking about the former life of the Ward family in 1922. He described Walter and his brother Ralph as well-behaved boys. He recalled how George Ward ran an unsuccessful campaign for Pittsburgh city council, calling it a "mudslinging campaign," with his opponent criticizing the poor wages Ward paid his factory workers. A former classmate of Walter's and Ralph's said both were just "normal boys and had no degenerating habits." He added that the family was well loved by many in the community. Though in vague phrasing, he related how Walter had fallen in with a certain crowd in New York that led to his "ruination." He didn't expand on what he meant.[9]

Months after Walter and Beryl wed, his younger brother Hugh, named after his grandfather who started the storefront bakery on Broome Street before the Civil War, died at the age of twenty-two of scarlet fever in Philadelphia where he attended college. George tasked Walter with identifying the body and signing the death certificate. The grief of Hugh's loss was only compounded later that year when Walter's mother, Jessie, died after an extended illness at the age of forty-six. She was buried in the Ward family plot at the Kensico Cemetery in Westchester, not far from where Clarence Peters's body was found. George would remarry in 1919 to Donna Leslie, a wealthy widow who lived not far from the Ward home on Riverside Drive. The two eloped to Chicago and got married at the Blackstone Hotel before setting off on a monthlong honeymoon in California. George was fifty-one, and Donna was thirty.[10]

On his World War I draft card, signed in 1917, Walter is described as tall and slim, with blue eyes and blond hair. He and Beryl were living with her mother at the house on Arlington Avenue in Cypress Hills. Unlike his older brother, Ralph, who served in France from February 1918 to June 1919, Walter suffered from the unfortunate condition of pes planus, more commonly known as flat feet, a condition that could guarantee military rejection. The military believed that such men couldn't endure the long hours of marching required for service. Given this military abnormality, Ward stayed stateside, working for the family company, adjusting to being a new father, and setting up a life in New Rochelle.[11]

As more questions emerged about Ward's story of the murder and blackmail plot, his attorneys decided that Beryl should not talk to the press. The *Brooklyn Daily Eagle* took a particular interest in the story of the former Brooklyn society girl entangled in such a sensational crime. "Of course my husband has told me nothing about it all. I don't know anything," she told a reporter from the paper, taking a dramatic turn from her earlier statements. She then demurred, "I cannot discuss this case. My husband's lawyers have forbidden me. But"—she couldn't help herself—"I do want to deny the ridiculous report that Walter's extortioners had obtained a hold over him through the possession of information of his affairs with other women." When asked why she was confident that the blackmailing did not involve another woman, she replied, "Why, just on my knowledge of Mr. Ward. He is too fine a man to stoop to any such unmanly deception."

What struck the reporters the most was how little concern Beryl expressed about the murderous actions of her husband. "Mrs. Ward apparently feels no compunction over the thought that her husband and the father of her two small children shot a man to death at a mysterious midnight rendezvous," the paper noted, adding her only real concern was about the two other blackmailers. "I will never feel a moment's safety while those rats, scum of the gutter, are alive and at liberty," she said with clear rage in her eyes. "It was a blackmail plot. I cannot say more."[12]

We might think of Beryl's devotion through the hugely popular 1922 song "My Man." Originally written in French, "Mon Homme" was popularized in the U.S. by Ziegfeld Follies star Fanny Brice. "My Man," with its longing and sadness, transformed Brice from her usual comic stage characters into a "lamenting cocotte," as one reviewer noted in 1922. The song's protagonist is a young woman in love with a man who barely cares for her. "Cost me a lot / But there's one thing that I've got / It's my man," the protagonist laments. "My Man" would be performed for decades, with variations done by Billie Holiday and, later, by Barbra Streisand in the hugely successful 1964 Broadway musical *Funny Girl* based on Brice's life, which was later turned into a film. But in the spring of 1922, "My Man" might just have been the appropriate background for the image of Beryl Ward, pretty and charming and, at least in public, dedicated to her husband at all costs.

WARD'S CLAIMS ABOUT what happened that night became thinner and thinner, and the press asked more and more questions. "The investigation," the *Brooklyn Daily Eagle* announced, "has developed two camps—one under Sheriff Werner, being remarkable for its apparent willingness to accept Ward's 'confession,' and the other the State Troopers, working diligently and with grim silence." Sheriff Werner declined to answer questions about the mounting discrepancies between Ward's statement and the facts emerging from the crime scene investigation. *The New York Times* used the word *evaded* to describe Werner's response when they asked him about the absence of Peters's pistol and the fact that the state trooper found only one shell casing at the crime scene.

District Attorney Weeks also dismissed reporters' criticisms. At a brief press conference, they asked if he was in fact feeling pressure from political leaders to treat Ward with a soft hand. "I should say not!" Weeks snapped, pounding his fist on his desk. He was not a man comfortable in front of reporters, and even less so when they were questioning his ethics. He pointed out that the DA's office had only one detective, and he relied on the work of Sheriff Werner's men.

"Do not think that we have swallowed his story, hook, line and sinker, because we have not," Weeks, who was known for his love of fishing, declared. "You can say for me, in a most emphatic manner, that I am not satisfied with Ward's story of the killing," he said, clearly frustrated with the tensions building in the room. "There are many points in his story that do not sound just right to me. He must prove every point in his story to our complete satisfaction and that proof must be public property."[13]

Weeks's comments did not settle the growing concerns. They felt like little more than a half-hearted effort to convince the public that he and the sheriff were hard at work on the investigation. It seemed to many, however, that Weeks continued to leave it up to Ward to explain the discrepancies and address the many doubts about his statement, rather than a pointed and focused inquiry by Westchester authorities. For many in the press, it was unclear what, if anything, Sheriff Werner was doing to find out the truth of what happened on King Street.

Coroner Fitzgerald was more forthcoming, making public his displeasure with the way the case was being handled. If there was a divide between the state police and Werner's office, there was an even bigger one brewing within the halls of the courthouse. Rumors were circulating that a palpable rift between Werner and Fitzgerald had simmered for some time. "The conflict of views seems deeper than appears on the surface," the *New York American* told its readers, adding, "It has been apparent for some time that Sheriff Werner has not taken the Coroner entirely into his confidence and that the latter has resented this fact."

It was no surprise then that Fitzgerald told reporters that he had begun his own investigation into the evidence, delaying the inquest for over a week. "I am not going to hold an inquest until I can get sufficient evidence to make Mr. Ward talk," he said, "because he can stand on his constitutional rights and not say anything." When asked if he, like Sheriff Werner and DA Weeks, was convinced by Ward's statement, Fitzgerald snapped, "I am not convinced of anything. I intend to continue with my investigation and will hold an open hearing when I call the inquest. You can rest assured that I will do all I can to solve the mystery." He added, "Something about the case looks queer to me and I intend to get answers to several questions that have not yet been satisfactorily explained."[14]

AND THEN, A dramatic and surprising story about Walter Ward emerged. In early April, about the time that Ward claimed the blackmail had started, he arrived at his Sutton Manor home in the early-morning hours and, moving about the darkened library, drank an entire bottle of iodine. His wife Beryl found him writhing in agony on the floor of the library with severe stomach pain and a burning in his mouth and lungs. Beryl called the family doctor, eighty-six-year-old Orville Schell, who lived nearby and arrived quickly to administer a stomach pump, saving Ward's life.

"It is my personal opinion," Dr. Schell told reporters when asked about the incident from April, "that the taking of the poison was accidental. I do not know differently, and you must believe a man innocent until he is proven guilty." That last comment appeared directed to inquiries about the murder case than to potential poisoning. "Mr. Ward is subject to very severe headaches," Dr. Schell added, "and it is an easy thing to get medicines mixed in the dark." Dr. Schell also noted, in phrasing that seemed particularly pointed, that Ward had a very "narrow escape" from death. In a rare exchange, Ward took questions from reporters the day the story made headlines. Visibly nervous, clenching and unclenching his hands, his voice low and practically a whisper, he confirmed to the group of reporters that he swallowed iodine and his life was saved by Dr. Schell's treatment. He quickly retreated into silence when asked if it was an accident and refused any questions about the ongoing investigation.[15]

News of Ward's iodine poisoning cast even more doubts about his statement and the motives behind his killing of an alleged blackmailer. Was it really an accident or a desperate attempt at suicide by a man facing public scandal? Was his killing of Clarence Peters an act of self-defense or rather a carefully planned murder to rid himself of the blackmailers' demands? The *New York American* summed up much of the press opinion. "Instead of being made clear by Ward's confession," the paper announced, "the reasons and circumstance of Clarence Peters's death have been clouded in deeper mystery. And on every side is heard the question: Why is there a GREAT WARD KILLING MYSTERY?"

The day after the iodine story made headlines, Ward resigned his position as a police commissioner. His letter to mayor Harry Scott of New Rochelle was short and conciliatory.

> My dear Mr. Mayor,
>
> In order to relieve you of any possible embarrassment, I hereby tender my resignation as a Police Commissioner of the city of New Rochelle, and may I express to you my appreciation of the kindly consideration you have at all times shown me.
>
> Sincerely yours,
> Walter S. Ward

Ward had not been asked to resign, according to Charles Van Auken, counsel for the City of New Rochelle, but rather had offered his resignation in the days following his confession. "Ward indicated that he feared if he sent in the resignation voluntarily at once the community would jump to the conclusion that he was guilty," Van Auken stated. "He was afraid that people would think that he did not believe himself fit to retain his office as Police Commissioner."

It was true. There were many questions about why a police commissioner would not have immediately gone to the authorities after the murder, turned himself in, and laid out the facts. Van Auken reminded journalists that unlike the New York City police commissioner, in New Rochelle, the three panel commissioners were only "nominally" head of the police as "actual service on behalf of the police was seldom demanded." The unpaid position had little authority, he said, with commissioners tasked with choosing police officers and looking "after the morale of the department"—a curious and vague task.

In reality the commissioner post was a highly political position, appointed by the mayor, often to those loyal to the mayor's political party. It should also be noted that another police commissioner was Palmer Tubbs, appointed in 1920, whom Walter Ward then hired as his personal assistant, becoming the gatekeeper of Ward's meetings and phone calls at the Bronx factory. The relationship between the Ward Bakery Company and the New Rochelle Police Department was apparently a very strong one.[16]

Tubbs called his boss Walter, and Ward called his assistant Tubbsie. In the days after Ward's statement became public, Tubbs became an unofficial press agent for Ward, detailing Ward's movements and moods in the days surrounding Peters's murder. On May 15, Ward drove Tubbs home to New Rochelle. "I never saw him in better spirits," Tubbs said. On the morning of May 16, the Wards' maid called Tubbs requesting to know what time the *Majestic* was set to dock, as Ward planned on meeting his father at the harbor. That afternoon Ward arrived in the office. "Hello, Tubbsie," Ward greeted him. "Is everything all right?" Tubbs recalled he didn't see much of Ward in the days following the murder. When the newspapers arrived on the morning of May 22, headlines blaring Ward's confession, Tubbs and his colleagues were shocked by the news. That night, Tubbs went to Ward's home. There he spoke with Ward, "took him by the hand," and said, "Walter, I'm sorry."

"We have never spoken of the affair since," he told the press. "I am as much mystified as anyone." As to reports that Tubbs did in fact talk with Ward in the early-morning hours of May 16, just after Peters was killed, Tubbs denied such claims, protecting his boss from any speculation that deviated from Ward's statement.[17]

The day after Ward's resignation, Allan Campbell delivered to Sheriff Werner's office a .38 Colt automatic revolver and a .32 Smith & Wesson pistol, which Campbell claimed was used by Peters on the night of the murder. Ward's revolver showed three cartridges missing. The Smith & Wesson, invented in the late nineteenth century, was a more delicate weapon, easily concealed but only really effective for close-range targets. It would have been quite outmatched by Ward's more powerful .38 automatic. Some reports noted that the Smith & Wesson contained only one empty cartridge stuck under the gun's hammer, suggesting the gun had either been defective or had been broken open at some point.

The bigger question for reporters was how Ward ended up with Peters's pistol in the first place, a mystery neither the sheriff nor Weeks would explain. Did Ward pick it up from the side of the road, after Charlie Ross and Jack had sped away? King Street would have been pitch-black, the only light coming from Ward's headlights, making it difficult to imagine Ward feeling around on the sandy roadside looking for Peter's pistol. Or perhaps he returned to the crime scene and gathered up the gun and repositioned Peters in the manner he was found? Of course, why would someone, fearing for his life, return to the crime scene to fetch the gun that had just been pointed at him?

After the guns were turned over, Werner eagerly called a press conference for the first time in days. He explained to reporters how Ward's attorneys handed over both guns, answering one of the bigger mysteries of the case. It was another moment where Ward's claims about the crime were taken as fact. Werner happily declared "the case is about cleared up."[18] The entire press conference seemed a bit scripted, and as so often was the case with the sheriff, his conclusions about the case would be woefully premature.

Untouched by Human Hands

When Walter Ward confessed to the killing of Clarence Peters, the company that his family owned was worth nearly $35 million, around $600 million in today's currency. The company produced 400 million loaves of bread a year, alongside twenty-three kinds of cakes, in sixteen factories from Chicago to Providence, Boston to the Bronx, all made, as the company promotion declared, the "Ward Way," the "Clean Way." In New York City, 80 percent of the cakes sold and 20 percent of the bread consumed were made by Ward bakeries. The influence and reach of the Ward brand were unmatched.[1]

This rise to prominence began in 1910 when Robert and George Ward sought to expand their business by building two state-of-the-art bread factories, one in the Bronx and one in Brooklyn. The twin bakeries would be their glorious reentry into New York City, the place where their father first opened his one-oven shop on the Lower East Side before the Civil War. But not just any factory. The Ward brothers wished to create monuments of industrialized baking, a show of their growing influence and dominance over what was increasingly called the baking industry. They gathered a group of architects and engineers and took them to Europe. On their monthlong trip, the team explored Roman and Greek architecture looking for inspiration from classical design for their vision of a modern bread factory. On the ship back to New York, Robert kept the team busy each day drawing and revising plans for what would become the flagship factories of the Ward Bakery Company.

Within a year, both factories were completed at an astounding cost of $2 million. While the Brooklyn factory was a floor taller than the five-story Bronx factory, their designs were nearly identical. Each facade was a modern interpretation of the classical temple with arches connecting concrete columns that framed large plateglass windows. The exteriors were covered in gleaming white terra-cotta tiles, contrasting with the darker tones of red brick and granite of the surrounding warehouses and factories. Inside, the large windows created bright workrooms, light bouncing off gleaming white tiled walls and shiny steel machines. In their earliest advertisements, the company described their factories as "Snow-white Temples of Cleanliness" and as the "Brightest, Whitest, Cleanest Places in All New York."[2]

In the fall of 1911, just a few months after their New York factories opened, the Wards took out half-page ads in New York newspapers. "The Story of an American Business Success," declared the headline, looking more like a news article than a public relations pitch. The ad featured a grainy photograph of Hugh Ward's Broome Street bakery from the 1840s, the small shop sharply contrasted with the modern architectural renderings of the Brooklyn and the Bronx factories next to it. Surrounding these images was a story of the Ward Bakery from immigrant struggle to corporate success. But it was not only hard work that was behind the bakery's growth from a one-oven shop to modern factories. It was also their approach to baking that made their signature brand, Tip-Top Bread, a success. The "purity and deliciousness of their product and the sanitary excellence of their plant," the copy read, "helped to make their business one of phenomenal growth."[3]

More than taste or freshness, cleanliness and purity were the key qualities of the company's brand.[4]

When George and Robert Ward opened their first large bread factory in 1903 in Pittsburgh, they were entering an expanding marketplace of industrialized food that often was adulterated by any number of chemicals and additives. Copper salts were added to canned vegetables to enhance their color. Meats were routinely soaked in the newly invented and formaldehyde-rich Preservaline. Canned fruits contained such additives as coal-tar dye, sodium sulfite, and salicylic acid. Sodium borate, or borax, an ancient, naturally occurring mineral, was added to any number of dairy products, such as butter, to keep it from turning rancid, though it gave the butter an oddly metallic taste. In an age when refrigeration was costly, chemical preservatives were increasingly common in the American diet, developed and sold to food suppliers by such established firms as the Dow Chemical Company or the Charles Pfizer & Company pharmaceutical firm. Before 1906 when, after years of lobbying by pure-food advocates, Congress passed the Pure Food and Drug Act establishing the Food and Drug Administration, such additives had rarely been regulated as to their safety in either small or large doses. Most Americans had little idea what was in their morning jelly, their lunchtime ham, or the vegetable side dish at dinner.[5]

Factory-made bread was not immune from the pure-food movement. Aluminum sulfate, or alum, was a common additive used in baking powder to enhance the whiteness of bread, as was calcium sulfate, or gypsum, a base ingredient in plaster of paris and used to stabilize the acid in bread dough. In 1915, the Wards defended their use of calcium sulfate. Inspectors in Boston and New York charged that the company did not include this ingredient in the bread's labeling. This concern came up as the Massachusetts legislature considered a "Pure Bread" bill. George Ward claimed that gypsum was a necessary ingredient in their efforts to "standardize our loaves of bread so that the bread made in one city would be identical in quality and appearance in any other city." This goal was hampered by the differences in water mineral content, which affected the baking process. To solve this problem, the company employed chemists who found that calcium sulfate helped stabilize the baking process. When asked why the company did not list the additive on the bread packaging, lawyers for the company claimed it was not easy to educate the public about the value of calcium sulfate, but if they could, the public, as well as the state legislature, would be satisfied with its use in their bread.[6]

Concerns about the purity of bread were not only about ingredients but also the habits of those who made the bread. In an era of nativism and anti-immigrant sentiment, urban neighborhood bakeries were often owned and staffed by eastern and southern European immigrants. Work in these storefront shops was a grueling experience, as bakers were stuck in poorly ventilated basement kitchens producing hundreds of loaves a day and having to work twelve-hour shifts or more.

The same year the Wards opened their New York factories, the city health commissioner Dr. Ernst Lederle was on a crusade against those basement bakeries that dotted the neighborhoods across Manhattan and Brooklyn. One inspector, Frances Perkins, the head of the New York Consumers' League and the future secretary of labor for Franklin Roosevelt, was shocked by what she found. A progressive reformer concerned with child labor and factory conditions, Perkins toured more than one hundred small bakeries in the city. She witnessed cats sleeping in bread pans, leaking pipes, poor ventilation, and workers who lived and slept in the same rooms as they prepared bread. A particular concern rested on one common habit among many of the workers. "Tobacco chewers are not scarce among the employees," one report noted. "At times the expectoration of these chewers gets into the food they are preparing."

As more and more of these reports were published, the horrors and genuine concern for the small, one-oven shops became a public health panic. "We have got to improve conditions that surround the preparation of our food supply," Dr. Lederle told reporters. "In some places these conditions are anything but sanitary and I regret to say that in numerous cases unsanitary conditions are the rule rather than the exception." He added, "The personal conditions of the very people who are employed in them is often much as to make the distribution of the food a menace to the public health."[7]

Dirty bakeries and unclean bakers fit with the larger cultural fears of the unwashed masses filling the country's cities. In testimony before a New York State commission, one assemblyman asked if the men who worked in these bakeries were "naturally and inherently unclean" and wondered if any laws could really "counteract their natural and inherent tendencies." The state would in fact pass new laws regulating these basement bakeries and empower the city to shut down those that failed to abide by certain health codes.[8]

The Wards were keen to capitalize on these concerns and embraced two powerful sentiments of the era: optimism in the potential of science and technology to improve people's lives, and fears about germs and contamination not only in food but also in the wider culture. "Only people in perfect health work there," one of the company's ads declared. "Shower baths, uniforms, lockers, recreation rooms—every modern device to promote health and comfort." Another ad from 1911 announced, "Our Physician Guards Your Interests," promoting the in-house doctors many of the Ward factories employed. Included in the advertisement was a small article headlined "Cellar Bakeries in Shocking State." A casual reader might just miss that the article was part of the Wards' sales campaign. After a delivery-drivers' strike ended at the New York factories in July 1919, the company created a new ad campaign that simmered with nativist sentiment. The ad not only promoted the purity of its bread, but also the purity of its customers as well. "No need to accept 'other kinds,'" the ad read. "Every grocer and delicatessen dealer can now supply *your kind*."[9]

Purity campaigns were also impacting everyday life. Men shaved their beards for fear that facial hair was unsanitary. Women's hemlines rose partly for politics, and partly to avoid gathering the dirt and dust of streets and floors. Even domestic interiors were increasingly spare and open, eschewing the heavy drapes and overstuffed furnishing of the Victorians, believing they gathered germs and posed any number of health hazards in the home.

Alongside such efforts, social reformers began to ferret out urban vices as prostitution, drinking, gambling, and sexual deviancies, all under the guise of a so-called social hygiene movement. The New York Society for the Suppression of Vice and the Committee of Fourteen were powerful civic groups actively lobbying city and state leaders for increased surveillance and expanded laws regulating the morals of the city's residents. They employed undercover agents to scope out cabarets and bars, to monitor parks and public baths, actively keeping a watchful eye on private citizens' social and sexual encounters, all in a moral crusade to clean up the expanding and overcrowded city. "The consumer," a baker noted at a conference in 1916, linking a number of the era's concerns, "not only demands that the bakeshop be clean, but that the baker himself be clean in person, in morals, and in his conduct in the street."[10]

WHILE THE WARD Bakery was not the only factory bakery at the time, it was certainly one of the largest across the Northeast and upper Midwest. They built their success on technological innovations, an aggressive business expansion, and marketing campaigns that played off the sentiments of the era. Tip-Top conjured not only the benefits of bread for a healthy body, but also the conditions of the Wards' factories and the production methods. The company invited the public to visit their New York factories for guided tours. "Come and See how spick and span everything is," their ads declared.

We can get a sense of what visitors might have experienced on that Bronx factory tour from a 1915 profile of Robert Ward in *Baseball Magazine*. Robert Ward was a major investor in the short-lived Federal League and owned a Brooklyn baseball team named the Tip-Tops after their signature brand—another example of the Wards' skill at marketing. His nephew Walter was appointed as the league's treasurer.

As visitors arrived at the gleaming white factory, they were escorted up to the top floor. Unlike the making of a shoe, which started on the first floor of the factory and proceeded upward for a finished product, bread making moved from the top floor downward, using gravity at each stage of the process. On that top floor visitors watched as flour flowed from massive steel containers through cylinders into oversize vats on the lower floor. There the flour mixed with distilled water, yeast, sugar, and other additives. Once the mixture was said to be "ripe," it was "shot through" openings in the floor to a large mixing-and-kneading machine on the floor below that looked, as the reporter noted, like large "cement mixers" one might find on the street.

The next step poured the dough into huge flat troughs that were suspended high above the floor and moved along by rollers. The dough weighed nearly a ton in this elevated trough, where it was left to rise. Once it was ready, a worker would pull a lever, releasing the bottom of the trough, causing the dough to fall through openings in the floor and settle into large machines on the next level. As the reporter described, the machines tore the "groaning mass to pieces, slicing it up with the precision of clockwork into individual loaves of the proper weight."

From there, machines molded the dough into precise loaves evenly spaced along a conveyer belt. "One after another, automatically, the loaves fall from their moving platform," the reporter observed, "each into its respective pan on the moving platform beneath, and travel at the same slow pace to the fiery mouth of the oven." There large metal claws lifted sixteen loaves at a time onto a conveyor that moved them to the far end of the massive oven. For twenty minutes the loaves baked. Workers monitored the progress through small windows on the sides of the oven. Once baked, the loaves emerge crisp and steaming, moving one at a time along yet another conveyor, cooling as they made their way down to the final floor. Here a specially made machine with its "intricate mass of wheels and rods and glittering steel fixtures" wrapped each loaf in waxed paper, stamping and sealing it with the Ward Bakery logo. They appeared "properly clothed, sober, sedate," the reporter declared. From this final floor, the loaves were crated and loaded onto waiting electric trucks that carried them into the city. "Literally baked from start to finish," the reader is told, "untouched by human hands."[11]

That was the irony and the goal of large-scale factory baking: as factories shifted bread making from the home or local bakery to industrial brand, the need for a large staff of skilled bakers decreased. In Cleveland, the Wards purchased and refitted a bakery with their assembly-line approach, eliminating the work of seventy skilled bakers in the process. Of the thirty workers left, only six were trained in the art of bread making. Few of the workers who operated the machines, who staffed the shifts from morning until the late hours of the night, knew anything about the intricacies of dough or the chemistry of yeast.

The workers staffing those factories were mostly men, for as much as industrialized bread eliminated the need for expert bakers, it also shifted bread making from a domestic chore done mostly by women to a brand mostly managed by men. To get the public to trust factory-made bread required a different sensibility about the home kitchen. Like many in the baking industry, the Ward Bakery tried to convince Americans that homemade bread was a potential hazard. Housewives, the argument went, were less skilled in the chemistry of bread making and the proper balancing of ingredients for ripening and couldn't possibly achieve the proper oven temperatures in their home kitchens, risking all kinds of illness from underbaked bread.

While women's magazines offered articles on the science of the kitchen, the factory promised a more reliable approach and safer process of bread making overseen by a small army of—mostly male—chemists and master bakers. In 1920, the Wards published *Bread Facts*, a small pamphlet meant to educate on the proper scientific approach to bread baking to "help speed the coming of the day when the housewife will rely entirely on the baker for her daily supply of the 'staff of life.'"[12]

IN THE CITY, the bread, wrapped in sanitary waxed paper, was delivered by the company's electric-powered trucks ("no horses, no stables, no dirt, no odors," their ads proclaimed). In fact, the Wards owned the very company that made those trucks, as they also invested in other companies that made the machines that produced their breads and as they funded an institute in Pittsburgh to support research into better forms of yeast, which they also produced. It was a business model more familiar in such aggressive industries as steel and oil—a model that in the Gilded Age created vast amounts of wealth through monopolies and trusts, saturating entire markets, consolidating production and distribution costs, and eliminating much of the competition.[13]

In New York, the Wards mastered the art of the trust. The company would contract bakeries and grocery stores in outlying suburbs and small towns to exclusive deals, effectively eliminating smaller bakeries and the bakers they employed. One representative of the Bakery and Confectionery Workers International Union, the largest union in the industry, complained that such business tactics took "the bread and living away from hundreds of little bakers that formerly did business in a square way."[14]

Over time, such trusts became a way of price fixing bread across a vast region and gaining a monopoly over bread sales. In the years before World War I, the company faced numerous accusations of conspiracy for price fixing, threatening to remove their bread if retailers didn't lower their retail price to reduce competition for Tip-Top Bread. In 1915 the New York State attorney general began an inquiry.[15] While the company retreated on its plan, it continued to manipulate market prices through its network of trusts that stifled competition.

When the Ward Bakery delivery drivers went on strike in 1919, Walter famously donned a uniform, took the wheel of a company delivery truck, and set out to deliver bread from the Brooklyn factory to stores across Long Island. On one excursion, Walter was followed by three men in a car. When the truck stopped at a railroad crossing, the three men approached the truck, opened the doors, and began to "pummel" Walter and his assistant. The three men then jumped back into their car and sped away. Ward told police he recognized two of the men as former employees and gave descriptions of each. The attackers were eventually arrested, charged with assault, and served ten days in county jail.[16] The incident of the assault would be retold in the days after Walter made public his deadly encounter with Clarence Peters. The story showed his good character and, many thought, his bravery and commitment to the family business. It also portrayed him as standing up to the violent demands of labor unions—demands that in the years after World War I were often decried as evidence that bolshevism and radicalism were taking hold on U.S. shores. Whether brutal labor unions or a blackmailing gang, Walter, it seems, was often the victim.

But then the 1919 strike was not unusual. The Ward Bakery Company was well-known for resisting labor organizing at their factories and hiring nonunion workers. One union publication composed a parody of the company's advertisements, picturing George Ward dressed in a crown and draped in a kingly fur robe holding a scepter in one hand and pointing to a loaf of bread embossed with the words: "non union made." The headline read: "My Life's Best Work, 100% Anti-Union Bread."[17]

When Robert and George Ward began renovations on the newly leased Washington Park baseball stadium in Brooklyn in 1914, an 18,000-seat venue, many unions refused to work on the project given the Wards' habits of hiring nonunion factory workers. The workers even encouraged their members to refuse to attend games played by the Ward-owned Brooklyn Tip-Tops and often campaigned outside stadiums when the team played, passing out fliers about the anti-union Wards to the fans who attended.[18]

In response to such criticism, the company adopted a more paternal approach to their workers, establishing an aid society and even offering profit-sharing plans at some factories. But of course, this paternalism created a dependency by the workers on the company, leaving many workers vulnerable to an ever-modernizing factory where their labor was less and less in demand. While the company eventually negotiated with unions at some of its factories in the years after World War I, such concessions were hard-fought.

With the death of Robert in 1915, George Ward became company president and assumed a leadership role in the baking industry. Like Robert, George was respected for his success and also, one can imagine, feared for the company's aggressive business tactics. Robert's son William, it seems, was not that happy to see his uncle and cousins take over company management. He resigned from the company not long after his father's death to start his own bakery that, by the summer of 1922, had become a powerful rival to the Ward Bakery Company. He might have reveled in the growing scandal of the alleged blackmail and the shadow it cast over the company. As the story of the murder gained more public attention, it was not simply the character of the president's son that was an issue, but also the reputation of their entire bread empire.

We Shall Have Nothing to Say

As public interest in the "great Ward killing mystery" grew, Beryl Ward began leaving the garage doors open at the Sutton Manor home in the late afternoons so that Walter could avoid the press. Hollowed out of the rock foundation under the home, the garage had two large barn doors that had to be opened by hand. The process of having to park his car and get out to open the garage exposed Ward to questions from reporters who were camped in the front of the house. By now, almost all of Westchester knew Walter Ward's dark-red Peerless coupe.

As he drove home from work, Walter would speed along Decatur Road, ignoring the posted speed limits in the Manor, and just as the road bent toward the boathouse, he would turn quickly into his driveway and directly into the garage. Then, without the slightest gesture or glimpse toward the street, he would "make his escape," as one reporter called it, darting from his car into the house, avoiding reporters and photographers. It had become the reality for the Wards—finding strategies to avoid the constant incursion of the press, trying to keep some control over their private lives.

On the rainy, late Friday afternoon of May 26, Beryl requested that her maid, Amy Mild, open the garage door as usual. Ward had telephoned earlier in the day to say he would be home at the regular time. But as the gray skies darkened into evening, Ward had yet to arrive. When reporters told her that Walter had been rearrested for Peters's murder and taken back to the Westchester County Courthouse, she expressed a certain reserved surprise—"cooly" is how one reporter described her response. She had no word from her husband and no information about his arrest, and she saw no reason why she should go to the courthouse based on information from reporters, whom she knew could not be trusted. As evening turned into night and the reporters began to retreat, the garage doors remained open. It seemed clear that Beryl was keeping up the pretense that this was any normal evening, ignoring the possibility that Walter was sitting in the county jail and wouldn't be coming home.[1]

In fact, earlier that day, Justice Seeger, who had presided over the first bail hearing, had met with Weeks and Werner in his chambers.[2] Weeks asked for Ward's bail to be rescinded and a new arrest warrant be issued based on increasing uncertainties about Ward's statement. Seeger agreed and issued the second warrant. Werner and his deputy sheriff met Ward and his attorney near his office in the Bronx. Ward drove his own car to the Westchester County Courthouse. With him were his attorney Elwood Rabenold and Sheriff Werner. Werner directed Ward toward a side entrance away from reporters and photographers. It was not the usual way one would execute an arrest warrant for a murderer.

The three men jumped out and ran inside, avoiding the downpour and the few reporters who spotted their arrival. Dressed in a stylish raincoat over a dark-gray suit and wearing a straw hat, Ward appeared at ease, smiling even, as he entered the building. He did not look like a man facing a second arrest for murder. Once inside the building, Werner locked the doors behind them.

Publicly, Weeks suggested that new information in the case had raised concerns about the truth of Ward's statement. His attempted suicide or accidental poisoning, depending on how one viewed it, was certainly something that troubled Weeks.

"I am not satisfied with Ward's story" was his only comment about Ward's new arrest. It was four days after Ward had first come forward with his story. Whatever Weeks found not satisfactory, we can imagine his growing frustration with the uncertainties of the crime scene, with Sheriff Werner's seeming lack of interest in investigating Ward's claims, and the growing criticism in the New York press that Weeks and Werner were protecting Ward.

Why was Werner "showing Ward more leniency than the average man?" reporters later asked the sheriff. "I'm only showing him ordinary courtesy," he replied.[3]

From the street, reporters peered inside Werner's office at Ward, the sheriff, Rabenold, and Allan Campbell, who arrived a short time after Ward. The scene was one of relaxed conversation. Reporters glimpsed Ward smiling and even laughing at one point. One reporter described how he looked quite "at home." Werner ordered dinner from a local restaurant. The men dined around the conference table. Photographers gathered near the windows; their flashbulbs, burning in the damp evening air, created small puffs of steam. One eager photographer climbed a rain pipe along the side of the building and twisted himself toward the window, stretching his arm outward while holding his speed-graphic camera in one hand hoping to get a much more intimate image of the scene. Eventually, the sheriff lowered the blinds.[4]

Before dinner arrived, Werner tried a "mental test" on Ward, something physicians had suggested to the sheriff. He placed a photo of Peters on the table in front of Ward, casually and without comment. He left Ward there, alone with the photograph for a few minutes. When he returned, the photo was turned over. Werner tried the experiment again, turning the photograph face up and again leaving it on the table. Ward again flipped the photograph face down. "That won't help us solve the case," Werner said. "But it makes us believe we are on the right track." What that track was Werner did not reveal.[5]

At some point, Rabenold and Campbell left the courthouse to visit Weeks at his home in an attempt to negotiate a bail agreement for their client. It was late in the evening, and Weeks might have been annoyed to have Ward's attorneys knocking at his door. We don't know what the men discussed or how Weeks might have responded to their requests. We do know that near midnight, Sherriff Werner informed reporters that Walter Ward would be spending the night in county jail and they should all go home. Most ignored the sheriff's suggestion.

Not long after Werner's announcement, a door from his office bolted open. Werner, Ward, and a deputy sheriff ran down the hallway, out another door, and through the wet courtyard toward the entrance of the county jail. As the rain came down even heavier than before, a herd of reporters sloshed through puddles, flashbulbs popping in the heavy rain, giving off stark, shadowy illuminations as the men arrived at the jail entrance. Ward pulled his straw hat down over his forehead and clutched his raincoat collar around his neck. Werner had to pound on the locked door, while Ward and the deputy sheriff stood facing the entrance with their backs to reporters, rain running off their clothes and pooling around their feet. "I guess they don't want to let you in!" one of the reporters shouted, prompting Ward to laugh. Nearly a minute later Warden Hill opened the door and escorted Ward to his cell.

Ward's stay in the county jail was not the usual inmate experience. Warden Hill put Ward in a private room near his office, what one reporter described as a "jail apartment, a room as comfortably furnished as the usual hotel room." The *Brooklyn Daily Eagle* was keen to note that another famous criminal had stayed in the same apartment: Harry Thaw, the dissolute Gilded Age scion of a wealthy coal baron. In 1906, Thaw shot and killed architect Stanford White in front of hundreds of witnesses at the rooftop theater at Madison Square Garden. He had long been enraged by Stanford's rape of his wife, the beautiful chorus girl Evelyn Nesbit, while she was still a teenager in the years before Thaw and Nesbit were married. After two sensational trials, Thaw was found guilty by reason of insanity and sentenced to the Matteawan State Hospital for the Criminally Insane in upstate New York. In 1909, Thaw petitioned for release, which brought him to the "jail apartment" at the Westchester County Courthouse for a hearing to determine his sanity. Supreme court justice Isaac Mills, who in 1922 would be one of Ward's lead attorneys, presided over several days of testimony filled with shocking details about Thaw's proclivities to find pleasure in physically abusing young women and men. Mills refused Thaw's petition, though he was eventually released from Matteawan in 1915. A year later he was arrested again for luring a young man into a suite at the luxury Hotel McAlpin in Manhattan and spending the night whipping the nineteen-year-old against his will.

In the 1920s, the name Harry Thaw still conjured the image of a sadistic, wealthy degenerate. For some, press comparisons between Thaw and Ward may have simply evoked the dubious accommodations made by the legal system for wealthy perpetrators, no matter the nature of their crimes. But for others the connections might have been stronger.[6]

AFTER BREAKFAST, WHICH was delivered from a local restaurant and eaten in Sheriff Werner's office, Ward entered a packed courtroom in his tailored gray suit carrying his raincoat over his arm. While these were the same clothes he had worn the day before, reporters remarked how he looked immaculate and bore no signs that he'd spent a night in a jail cell—even one that resembled a hotel room. As he took his chair next to his attorneys, Ward smiled at friends in the gallery. One notable absence from the courtroom was Beryl Ward, who, according to reports, had been silent ever since Ward's arrest. There were no letters, telephone calls, or verbal messages from her, the warden told reporters.[7]

Ward's attorney Allan Campbell spoke for nearly forty minutes, making the case for the release of his client. He argued that Coroner Fitzgerald had failed to obtain a complaint against Ward that disproved his statement, and as such the state had no cause to keep him in jail. Ward had come forward and provided the state with the facts of the murder in the hope that it would be a quick investigation and resolution. This was, after all, a matter of self-defense. Campbell laid out the facts, hewing closely to the details in the statement. "We are not here explaining, excusing, or apologizing for Mr. Ward," Campbell concluded. "We are here to decide a matter of law, and I contend that the authorities have no right to hold my client."

Weeks outlined the facts of the case as well, detailing events before and after Ward's attorneys issued the statement. The district attorney's investigation had, Weeks said, raised more questions about Ward's story. He argued that there was no reason why the state should accept Ward's statement as the truth. "The statements made by Ward," he told the court, "were against his own interest when he says he shot a man in self-defense. That is a conclusion and we do not have to believe him unless we want to believe him." He continued, arguing against the primary assumption behind Ward's self-defense claims. "We are," he declared, "entitled to take as true the statement of Mr. Ward that he shot this man, and not to take as true the statement that he shot the man in self-defense."

In his argument, Weeks pointed specifically to the evasiveness of Ward and his lawyers in the investigation. "When we asked for explanation and amplifications of his version of the killing we were given to understand we could take it or leave it," he told the court. "This case is as mysterious now as it was the morning the unidentified body was found on the lonely road near the reservoir." He went on, "We are beginning to think that if the chance suggestion that Peters might be an ex-service man had not been followed and if it had not resulted in the picking of his finger prints out of 500,000 on file at Washington, so that the body was proved on May 19 to be that of Clarence Peters, that we might never have heard of Mr. Ward, whose lawyers on that day made arrangements to meet us." It was the most direct public criticism that Weeks had made of Ward. Whatever Weeks felt privately about the case, in the courtroom he showed his annoyance with Ward's evasions and the growing public distrust in his investigation. Weeks asked the court for bail of no less than $50,000.[8]

"The case is unsolved," Justice Frank Young declared after hearing both arguments,

> and there is considerable mystery so far. Whether it is a case of murder or manslaughter it is now impossible to determine satisfactorily. The only witness so far is the defendant himself, and his testimony is entitled to be considered with care. The purpose of bail is to ensure a man's appearance and not to oppress him. He is a wealthy man

> and I think it is proper to fix bail in a substantial amount. When he surrendered himself to the authorities $10,000 seemed enough, for there was then not much doubt as to the truth of his story. I now fix bail at $50,000.

After a series of court filings that concluded late in the day, Ralph Ward, Walter's brother, arrived to pay the bail, doling out forty-nine $1,000 bills and two $500 bills to the court clerk. "Throughout these proceedings," the *New-York Tribune* reported, "the prisoner had smiled, but whether from nervousness or relief could not be said with authority by anyone but Ward himself." As he left the courthouse Ward had only one response to reporters' questions: "My lawyers tell me I must not talk."

At her home in Sutton Manor, Beryl Ward was blunter with reporters. "We shall have nothing to say until this is over and perhaps not then," she declared from her front door, smiling as usual.[9]

ALL EYES TURNED to Weeks and a renewed expectation about his investigation. It was not a comfortable place for a man who disliked the spotlight. He had to prove his suspicions about Ward's story or, lacking such evidence, reconcile the discrepancies of the story with the evidence found at the crime scene.

There were numerous questions that needed answers. Was Clarence Peters murdered on King Street in the early-morning hours of May 16, or was he murdered somewhere else and brought to the spot where he was found? If so, where was Peters actually murdered? And what was the relationship between Walter Ward and Clarence Peters that it could end in such a deadly way? The more compelling question was the more difficult one: What was behind the alleged blackmail, a secret so dire Ward risked his own life to confront the men who were extorting him for thousands of dollars? A secret so scandalous Ward would rather admit to killing a man than make public the reason for such killing. Of course the motive behind any blackmail is that its victim wishes it to stay a secret, so the chances that Ward or his attorneys would reveal the secret seemed highly unlikely. If Ward was known for his taciturn ways in the past, after his second bail hearing and the growing crowds of reporters that followed him around day and night, he was hardly likely to talk now.

Weeks and others were taking at face value that the entire case rested on blackmail, but it was still only Ward's statement that made this true. Perhaps there was no blackmail at all? The pursuit of Ward's secret and the nature of the relationship between the wealthy Ward and the impoverished Peters would be the key to unlocking this mystery.

Declaring that he was "sparing no cost" with his investigation, Weeks turned to private detective agencies for assistance. In 1922, the New York City directory offered three columns of such concerns, ranging from the simple Val O'Farrell Detective Agency, to the more ambitious Lincoln International Detective Bureau. Weeks selected the well-established Pinkerton National Detective Agency. Since the late nineteenth century, the Pinkertons not only provided detective services but also, and more infamously, offered corporate security services that included infiltrating unions and breaking labor strikes.[10]

Weeks also contracted the Browne-Rykert Detective Services, a smaller outfit near Times Square with agents who had keen insights into the cabarets and nightclubs along the Great White Way and the seedier bars of the Tenderloin on Manhattan's West Side. In selecting Browne-Rykert, Weeks made clear he thought a clue to the Peters murder would be found among the haunts of Manhattan's underworld.

In the coming weeks, both agencies would produce hundreds of typed reports, each detective remaining anonymous. While the Pinkertons used initials for their reports, Browne-Rykert employed a number system for each agent, such as Operative 128 or Operative 110 to identify each investigator. "It was decided that the Agency should investigate every angle of the Ward case that would likely lead to some result," a Pinkerton supervisor told reporters just days after Ward's second bail hearing. "Mr. Weeks gave us carte-blanche to go ahead and make a thorough and complete investigation."[11]

Weeks's directive to the Pinkertons had as much to do with his duty as a district attorney as with the political realities he confronted.

It was an election year after all, and while Weeks expressed little interest in running for district attorney, the Ward case was becoming useful fodder for Democrats as a sign of the corruption of the Republican Party from Westchester all the way to the state capital and Nathan Miller, New York's Republican governor. While the New Rochelle *Standard*, a Republican mouthpiece, for example, remained all but silent about the case, the pro-Democrat *New Rochelle Daily Star* found political force in calling out the failures of the investigation. "Almost without precedent has been the handling of the Ward case by the officials sworn in their respective offices to mete out justice with an impartial hand to rich and poor alike," the editors declared. "The Ward case cannot be spoken of merely as a Westchester County case. The eyes of the entire country are today focused on us, and the questions that are being asked here are being asked from Maine to California."[12]

It was true. The mysterious case of murder and blackmail was making headlines across the country. Readers from Chicago to Los Angeles, Miami to Spokane, were aware of the strange and tragic story of the millionaire baker and the penniless sailor. This growing public interest coupled with the political pressures of an election year could make a man like Weeks desperate for a solution to the case. And desperate men are more inclined to make bad decisions.

The Investigation

The World Is Full of Charlies and Jacks

Walter Ward gave Sheriff Werner descriptions of Charlie Ross and Jack not long after offering his statement to DA Weeks. The Pinkerton detectives recorded his description of both men in their report:

> "Charlie Ross." Jewish. 30. Good Dress. 5′9″ or 10″. Weight 160 lbs. Smooth face (heavy beard). Wavy Hair. High Brow. Blue suit. Rain coat. Black and white check hat. Light collar. Cap.
>
> "Jack." Pasty face. Weight 150 lbs. 5′10″. Dope fiend. No nerve. Black straight hair. Black and white suit. Rain coat. Cap.[1]

These descriptions could have applied to any number of men found in Manhattan's cafés and cabarets. "Vague and meager" was how one detective described Ward's information about the men. It was surprising given the fact that Ward claimed these men had been hounding him for weeks and that he had met with them on several occasions.

In the evening after Ward handed over his statement about the scene of Peters's murder, Sheriff Werner and detectives from the New York City police department went searching for Charlie and Jack through the Tenderloin and the Lower East Side, visiting two well-known underworld hangouts for blackmailers and extortionists. The geography of the underworld was an intricate one. Knowing which kind of criminals could be found at which café or pool hall required skill and inside knowledge. Ward drove into the city with his lawyer Elwood Rabenold, following the detectives' car along the wet streets of a cool May evening.

On the corner of Forty-Ninth and Broadway, detectives went into the Ambassador poolroom, or as it was more properly known, the Ambassador Billiards Academy. Pool halls were a nineteenth-century invention, hangouts for racetrack gamblers. Owners put in billiards tables to give the men something to do while they waited for the racing results. During Prohibition, billiards academies were popping up all over Manhattan and Brooklyn, taking the place of the usual underworld bars and saloons, some of which put in their own billiards tables to make up for lost revenue. Alongside local hustlers and blackmailers, the poolroom hosted tournaments that brought in well-known players in the world of billiards. One estimate claimed that by 1921 there were 25,000 professional billiards tables in New York City alone.[2]

At the Ambassador Billiards Academy, detectives lingered for a while, asking questions of the patrons and the staff though coming up short on any information about Ross or Jack. They then drove down to the Lower East Side, to a small restaurant along Eighth Street. As he did at the Midtown pool hall, Ward stayed in his car with Rabenold, an odd behavior for a man who stated with firm conviction his desire to find those men who blackmailed him. "We tried to get Ward to amplify his descriptions of Ross and Jack," a frustrated New York detective told reporters who trailed along with the late-night investigators. "Every time we tried to ask Ward a question, his lawyer jumped right in," he added.

The entire outing must have felt like a waste of time for the detectives, moving along the city's seedier nightspots looking for two men with only vague details and common names. It was likely that few if any of the patrons would have been willing to talk to the strange new faces sitting at the bar or slumped at a corner table. The scent of the police would have been strong in a place filled with confidence men.

The evening dragged into the early-morning hours without any success or any new leads. Detectives wondered if the whole night wasn't just a show on Ward's part, a useless chase for men who might not even exist. "The name Charlie Ross," the New York City detective noted, "is a common name. It is the kind of name that would be assumed by an Italian named Russa or Russo, or a Hebrew named Rosenstein or Rosenberg or Rosenstamm. There are dozens of underworld characters who call themselves Charlie Ross."[3]

The search for the blackmailers would require more strategy than wandering around the seedier sides of Manhattan in the late-night hours with an unhelpful Walter Ward in tow. So it was not surprising when the name William Fallon appeared in the search for Charlie Ross and Jack.

Good-looking with fiery red hair, Fallon was one of the most successful criminal attorneys in New York in the early 1920s. Known for his fastidious appearance, in his college days Fallon devised a three-mirror system that allowed him to cut his own hair, a trick that gave him complete control over the way he looked from almost every conceivable angle.[4] This meticulousness was also evident in his legal skills and earned him the nickname the Great Mouthpiece of the underworld. His clients were notorious figures: bootleggers, thieves, gamblers, and more often, confidence men. He had a specialty in representing blackmailers and extortionists. He was also sometimes called Slippery Bill for the clever ways he got his clients acquitted through legal loopholes and courtroom antics. For Fallon, the courtroom was a stage for dramatic stunts that were meant to shock the jury and attract public attention.

In one case, while representing a man accused of raping a woman in his car, Fallon had the entire vehicle disassembled and rebuilt in the courtroom for the jury to see, including the bloodstained back seat. When the DA took the bait and asked the defendant to reenact the scene of the crime inside the car, Fallon encouraged the prosecutor to join in and act the role of his date, a gesture that prompted laughs from the all-male jury. The levity was a useful and strategic distraction that overshadowed the seriousness of the crime. How ridiculous it must have seemed to the jurors to watch this theater play out in front of them. Wasn't this all just a bit silly? And was this really a violent sexual assault or, as the defense argued, just rough play? As often was the case, Fallon's client was acquitted.

While the car stunt might have been extreme, Fallon learned early that distraction and exaggeration were useful tools in any courtroom performance. Perhaps it was his own love of Broadway theater and the actors who brought so much emotional power to their roles that inspired Fallon's approach. If we are to believe Fallon's biographer, the actors were as enamored of the attorney as he was of them. "It was not uncommon to find a Broadway performer" sitting in the public galleries when Fallon was defending a client," he writes, for "many theatrical folks believed that Fallon was more actor than lawyer."[5]

In June 1922, Fallon offered the only real hope Inez and Elbridge Peters had of solving their son's murder. Michael Sullivan, the lawyer from Salem, Massachusetts, representing the Peterses, retained Fallon to help them find Charlie Ross and Jack. Sullivan must have believed that if he could find those two men—notorious confidence men, as Weeks described them—then there was a chance to disprove Ward's story. And if anyone in the New York could find them, it was indeed the well-dressed, theatrical criminal lawyer with the perfectly coifed red hair.

"We are not trying to force our way into the inquiry," Fallon declared to journalists on the steps of the Westchester County Courthouse, standing next to Sullivan, "but we are anxious to get all the facts into the open." Fallon had a casual manner with the press, genial and humorous. "From what we know of the young Peters' life in Haverhill," Fallon continued, "we are prepared to say that he was not always a responsible youth, but he was never vicious. He was easily led, but we have found absolutely nothing either there or here which tends to implicate him in a blackmail scheme." He added that his firm had hired private detectives to begin his own investigation, and any information he found he would be happy to share with the district attorney's office. Fallon's intrusion into the DA's investigation was tinged with both generous assistance and subtle criticism.[6]

In Westchester, Weeks made public proclamations expressing his confidence in Fallon's ability to bring the two men to him even after the first few promised meetings were canceled. Wanting to avoid the throng of journalists at the courthouse and giving Fallon another opportunity to upstage the DA, Weeks instructed Fallon to bring the men to his home in White Plains. An avid gardener, Weeks spent the day tending to the spring planting, waiting for Fallon to arrive. But by day's end, he had heard nothing. "I have neither seen him nor heard from him since I talked to him last night," he told one reporter, his frustration and anger simmering in his words. "However," he said in a calmer tone, "I have every confidence in Mr. Fallon and his sincerity. He will bring Ross here if he finds him." He then added, "You know, Mr. Fallon was formerly associated with me as an Assistant District Attorney for two years, and I have great faith in him."[7]

Weeks gave Fallon his first job out of law school, hiring him as an assistant DA in Westchester County in 1914 and becoming a mentor to the young lawyer. During his time in the DA's office, Fallon would refine his very modern, media-savvy approach to the practice of law, much to the dismay of his colleagues. While Weeks must have seen in the well-dressed young lawyer with the sharp mind a rising legal star, if not a keen politician, he certainly could not have imagined what Fallon would become.

Few cases better defined Fallon's time in the DA's office than the 1915 indictment of Thomas Mott Osborne, the warden of Sing Sing prison. Harvard-educated and well-known in state politics, Osborne was a towering figure and one of the leading advocates for prison reform. Prisoners in the United States were often subjected to horrible conditions, including chained restraints, experimental medical treatments, poorly ventilated cells, and contaminated food.[8] Prison reform was a national concern in the early decades of the twentieth century, alongside Progressive Era efforts at better labor conditions, food-purity movements, and the devastatingly successful Prohibition movement. Osborne called the treatment of prisoners he witnessed "barbaric" and "medieval" and advocated for a wholly new approach to incarceration that focused on rehabilitation and not punishment.

As warden of Sing Sing, Osborne was able to implement his reforms, what some called the Osborne Method. Prisoners were given recreational time and better food and no longer had to wear the standard striped uniforms. Osborne also encouraged a democratizing of prison life, establishing an elected five-member panel of inmates to advise the warden and deal with prison conflicts. The Osborne Method garnered support by a growing group of charities and organizations advocating for prison reform.[9] Supporters organized a rally at Carnegie Hall in January 1916 that drew over 3,000 people. The event, open to the public, attracted a unique mixture of judges and politicians alongside former inmates, all applauding the many speakers who extolled the great work Osborne had accomplished as warden.[10]

Critics of Osborne charged that under his wardenship he allowed for lax conditions in the prison and abdicated his sworn responsibilities. More damning were allegations brought by more than twenty-two inmates that the warden had made sexual advances on some of the men and allowed sex among the inmates to flourish. Many of the men who made these claims disliked Osborne's reforms, as they limited their power among the inmates. The indictment against Osborne pointed to "various unlawful and unnatural acts"—a vague and indirect charge that gave prosecutors great leeway. The press described Osborne's indictment as a "malfeasance in office and for other crimes of such a nature as to be unprintable."[11]

Fallon and Weeks were under pressure from Republicans in the state capital in Albany to convict Osborne, hoping they could also silence the broader movement of prison reform that he represented. The prosecution became a political one. Weeks had the twenty-two inmates transported to White Plains and held in the county jail. It was a tactic that allowed the DA to more easily pressure the men into making shocking claims about their warden. The men were promised early releases if they could detail the "unnatural acts" they experienced and the abuses they suffered either directly by Osborne or by other inmates, abuses that Osborne allegedly allowed.

"We have affidavits," Fallon declared in court, "innumerable affidavits showing that this man is the worst kind of a degenerate, and for that reason should not be in the management of Sing Sing prison." One of the affidavits claimed that Osborne told an inmate, "You are a good looking boy; if I were a girl I would fall in love with you." Other affidavits were filled with scandalous and immoral details that never made it into the press, with articles simply noting that the subject of such testimony was "unprintable."[12]

Osborne's lawyers hired Val O'Farrell, a tall and gaunt private investigator who was building a reputation as America's Sherlock, a sought-after sleuth for high-profile crimes like kidnappings and jewel heists, often involving some of America's wealthiest families. O'Farrell came through the ranks of the New York City Police Department, from beat cop to lieutenant, overseeing the Tenderloin district on Manhattan's West Side—a post where he learned much about the criminal underworld.

O'Farrell conceived an elaborate and complicated scheme. He first rented an office space under the alias Colonel Trout in the building where the Westchester DA's office was housed while the old courthouse was being renovated. The men and women who staffed it were directed to do a simple task: eavesdrop on Weeks's office. In the dark of night, two of his men ran wires along the building's roof and rigged a Dictograph in the DA's office. An early form of intercom when it was invented in 1905, the Dictograph was originally designed as a way to communicate between offices within a large building, running wires along corridors and between floors. By the 1920s Dictographs were mostly used as sophisticated listening devices for amateur spies, private detectives, and police departments. The Dictograph allowed anyone to listen in on the private conversations of suspects, neighbors, or friends. The use of Dictograph transcripts in court varied from state to state, but rarely if ever was such evidence deemed unconstitutional. Conversations one might have in their office or behind the closed doors of their bedroom were not understood as private property—sound, the logic went, was not something one could own like one's letters or diaries. It was not until a series of court cases in the late 1920s that such invasive surveillance was deemed a constitutional issue, ruling one had the right to their private conversations.[13]

O'Farrell's staff compiled transcripts of the many meetings Weeks had with assistants, criminal attorneys, and politicians. He then created hybrid transcripts—part fact and part fiction—that amplified political corruption at the heart of Osborne's indictment. Once these new transcripts were made, they were neatly stowed away in the office file cabinets. O'Farrell then replaced his entire staff with new people who were completely unaware of the spying operation or what the file cabinets contained until the police, tipped off by O'Farrell himself, came storming into the office with warrants for all the files. Weeks flew into a rage at the evidence found, each meeting easily verified, though the doctored transcripts of those meetings pointed to a political scandal in the heart of the DA's office—a scandal that would make great copy for the morning papers.

After months of work, the case against Osborne fell apart. Prisoners recanted their accusations. Others took to the stand to claim that Fallon had promised early parole if they made damning statements about the warden. Eventually the court stripped away much of the indictment, as it lacked specific crimes, relying instead on general claims of "various unlawful and unnatural acts."[14] The failures of Weeks and Fallon sparked calls for an investigation into their handling of the prosecution. Weeks would leave the DA's office before those investigations began, and Fallon followed behind him.

Years later Fallon would remember the Osborne case as a pivotal one, where he learned the difference between a persecution and a prosecution. But it was this lesson, turned on its head, that made him such a great mouthpiece for the criminal underworld, making every prosecution an unfair persecution of his clients. It was also clear that both Fallon and Weeks were, at least in one instance, willing to let political pressure direct how they conducted their prosecutions. Seven years on, both Weeks and Fallon showed a mutual respect for each other—at least in public. Fallon once remarked about his former mentor, "Weeks is a fine fellow if you know him. But he is a hell of a man if he has it in for you."[15]

FALLON'S OFFICE WAS on the ninth floor of the Knickerbocker, a grand Beaux-Arts-style building on the corner of Forty-Second Street and Broadway in the heart of Times Square. Prohibition dealt a blow to the former Knickerbocker Hotel, particularly its bars and restaurants, forcing the owners to turn the once-lavish hotel into an office building. Fallon rented a series of thickly carpeted, wood-paneled, and high-ceilinged suites that must have appealed to his sense of grandeur and drama.

The day after Fallon addressed reporters on the steps of the Westchester County Courthouse, he announced that the elusive Charlie Ross and Jack would meet him at his Manhattan office and he would bring them to Weeks. The hallway and office reception room filled with reporters and private detectives eager to hear the men's story. Surprising to some, Fallon had hired the Val O'Farrell Detective Agency to help him track the men down, an unlikely pairing of two rivals.

But as the afternoon drew on, reporters learned that Fallon himself had fled out a back exit. "Disappeared" is how *The New York Times* described his escape. In his place, a detective from the Val O'Farrell agency told reporters that Charlie Ross and Jack had left the state, as they were fearful of being arrested. Agency operatives took the overnight train, what was called the Owl train, to Boston, where they were to meet with the two men early the next morning. This series of cat and mouse games with the press and investigators either showed an utter failure on Fallon's part or was in fact a calculated distraction to keep the mystery of the men alive.

Weeks, all but giving up on Fallon's promises, sent a Pinkerton detective to interview O'Farrell about the Boston meeting. O'Farrell's office was at the corner of Fifth Avenue and Forty-Second Street, not far from the Tenderloin where he used to patrol as a New York City policeman. It was at first a cordial meeting, O'Farrell's gray eyes and warm smile welcoming the detective into his posh office. There was nothing he would not do for DA Weeks, he said. He was confident he could find Charlie and Jack, though he added, "truthfully I do not think that either one of them know anything about the Ward case. We had them in tow for several days. The only reason they did not want to make an appearance was that they were in fear that Weeks would lock them up. But"—he spoke in a more promising tone—"if you or Weeks will guarantee me that you won't lock them up, I will see that you get them." It was a guarantee that the detective could not make and signaled, he thought, a growing evasiveness in O'Farrell's demeanor.

"Is it possible," the detective asked, hinting at the theory that Charlie and Jack may not even have been at the crime scene, "that before Peters was killed, he might have mentioned to Ward the names of Charlie Ross and Jack as being friends of his and Ward used these names in relating the alleged blackmail incidents?"

"In my estimation," O'Farrell jumped in before even pausing to consider the question, "there is absolutely no connection between Charlie Ross and Jack and Ward." Looking for Charlie Ross and Jack, he said, was like trying to "fish in a bathtub"—an absolute waste of time. He then suggested that the detectives were simply following false leads to generate more hours they could bill the Westchester DA's office, an insult that may have annoyed the detective, who must have felt some respect for O'Farrell and his growing reputation as the American Sherlock. Seeing O'Farrell was increasingly opaque in his responses, the detective decided to end the interview. In his report, he expressed real doubt that O'Farrell had any commitment to finding Charlie and Jack. If forced, the detective wrote, "it would be likely they would produce a couple of 'dummies' pretending that they were the persons who were known as Charlie Ross and Jack."[16]

At Young's Hotel in Boston, Harry Conners, an agent of O'Farrell's agency, met with two men he was sure were Ross and Jack. They went by the names Charlie Rowland and Jack Tuttle. The interview was short, as it became quickly apparent that these were not the men whom Ward described. At least that was what the agency told reporters. These men knew nothing about Ward, Conners said, adding, "The world is full of Charlies and Jacks."[17] After the Boston trip, O'Farrell dropped out of the hunt for the two blackmailers, and according to detective reports, he stopped working for Fallon altogether. Instead, rumors were that he had a new client, one that was more suited to his experiences with wealthy New Yorkers: the Ward family.

AS THE MYSTERY of Charlie and Jack deepened, the hope of actually finding the men diminished. Increasingly investigators believed the two men were in fact fictions of Ward's making. But Weeks and his private detectives were not ready to give up the pursuit. Without them, they had little hope of finding out what really happened the night Peters was killed.

Not long after the failed Boston meeting, a reporter with the New York *Daily News*, culling through old court documents, revealed that in fact Charlie Ross was the alias of a person who was living in the Bronx. His real name was Nathan Rosenzweig. In 1921 Rosenzweig, using the name Nat Ross, was indicted for the attempted extortion of a Wall Street banker. The shock of this news was only amplified by the revelation a few days later that Rosenzweig's lawyer was in fact the Great Mouthpiece: William Fallon.

Muzzle

When reporters from the *Daily News* tracked down Nathan Rosenzweig in his Bronx apartment, they found only his sister and brother at home. The tabloid described the woman as "hysterical with anger and grief," and when they inquired about her brother, she shrieked, "Nat is out of town," refusing to tell them anything more. Her anger only intensified when reporters asked her about Walter Ward, describing how she became "purple with rage" and shouted that the millionaire's son was "a scoundrel who lures innocent boys away from their innocence." There was no explanation about what she meant, but the implications were intriguing. Her answer did suggest that she knew of Ward and furthered the hope that Rosenzweig was indeed the elusive Charlie Ross.

But the sister's outrage was nothing compared to the brother's more violent response. He threated to kill the *Daily News* reporter if he came back around to snoop into Nat's life.[1] We could imagine why the Rosenzweigs might be so protective of their younger brother. Nat, it would be learned, had been involved in a queer sexual scandal a few years earlier involving a Wall Street banker named Orville Tobey.

Forty-four years old, Tobey was a junior partner at the commercial banking firm of Lawrence Turner and Company, where he had worked for nearly twenty years. Tobey was round faced with a thick mustache that he kept neatly trimmed. His World War I draft registration described him as stout, and at five eight and nearly two hundred pounds, that might have been a fair assessment.[2]

On a cool October evening in 1918, Tobey was taking a taxi to his West Fifty-Seventh Street apartment building where he lived with his invalid mother, aunt, and younger sister. He had moved to the apartment after his five-year marriage ended in divorce in 1912. His ex-wife, Grace Zimmerman, more commonly spelled Timmerman to soften the Teutonic sounds of the German name particularly during World War I, was the granddaughter of a wealthy immigrant family. The Zimmermans were bankers and lived in a Fifth Avenue mansion. Orville's path to working on Wall Street was likely helped by his in-laws.

As the taxi drove north, Tobey spotted a sailor walking along Lafayette Street. "Trudging" is how he described the sailor's movement. He motioned the driver to pull alongside the curb, and Tobey asked the sailor if he would like a ride. It was perhaps not an unusual thing to do then. World War I still had a month to go before a cease-fire, and New York was filled with recruits. During the war years Tobey was in the habit of inviting sailors and soldiers to his apartment for dinner with his family, to help them out as much as he could, often giving them money for theater. The sailor was appreciative of the offer of a ride. He shook Tobey's hand, politely and firmly, and told him his name was Nat Ross.[3]

Blond and of fair complexion, Ross was broad shouldered and stood about five feet ten inches tall. His face tended to redden in the cool air or when he was exerting himself, as he had been while walking up Lafayette that evening. The two spoke casually, small talk between strangers who had just met. Ross told Tobey about his experiences in the navy, life at the Brooklyn Navy Yard, his brief tour in the Caribbean, and short stay in Haiti. Each story spoken in a monotone pitch with few variations. He must have seemed a serious sort of guy. Tobey described his own travels for work, sugar plantations in Cuba and factories in South America. Perhaps both were surprised by the serendipitous pleasure of the moment, a casual encounter between two strangers finding similarities in their travels. Ross was heading to Midtown, so at East Forty-Sixth Street the taxi pulled to the curb. Ross "voluntarily wrote his name on a card," Tobey later related, "and asked me for my name and address" before he opened the taxi door and left.

It was two weeks later when Tobey saw Ross again. Most likely Tobey called Ross and invited him up to the apartment for coffee or dinner or some such pretext to see him again. Over the next few months, through the holiday season and into the new year, Ross would continue to visit Tobey, having dinners with the aunt and sister, spending an hour or more with the banker in his dark-paneled library, where Tobey often retreated in the evenings.

In January 1919 after the armistice was signed, Ross was discharged from the navy, leaving him in search of a job. Perhaps that's why his visits to Tobey stopped sometime in February. Or perhaps Tobey wanted some distance from the ex-seaman, concerned by how his constant visits and long evenings together alone in the library might appear to his sister.

In May, Ross returned to the West Fifty-Seventh Street apartment, only this time he brought a friend whom he introduced as Joe Brown, a slight man with thick black hair and pale skin, who, like Ross, was no more than twenty-five years old. The two young men had been friends since childhood. Or at least that is what Ross said.

Tobey must have enjoyed the men's company. Perhaps Brown talked about his delivery job at Barney Jacobs and Company, a Manhattan florist, where he said he had been working for the last few years. He liked the job, he said, as it was better than most work he had tried. Usually, his day was over by three in the afternoon. All this talk of work and jobs lead to Ross's request. "He was very hard up financially," Tobey remembered. "He had no money to get his food, and no place to go that night." Tobey gave him five dollars, but Ross asked for more. Tobey refused, which would have been difficult for the banker given his usual generosity. But it also might have been a feeling that Ross seemed different. After so many months of silence, to appear again and ask for money probably distressed Tobey, who might have thought of their friendship as more than simply financial. Aside from these concerns, as Ross and Brown left, Tobey didn't think there had been any bad feelings between them. He would, of course, ask around and see if he could find work for Ross.

It was a surprise then, the next day, when Brown called at Tobey's office and requested—*demanded* was the word Tobey used—that Tobey meet Brown and Ross on the corner of Wall and William streets in downtown Manhattan that afternoon. Tobey noticed that whatever good feeling existed the previous night had withered away in the tense tone of Brown's voice.

When they met on the street corner, Brown cut to the chase.

"We know what you are. You know what you are. You know what you have done to Ross," he said, his voice deep and low, his words moving with a quick, staccato rhythm.

"The little man,"—that's how Tobey described Brown, referring to his shortness—asked Tobey for $1,000. As the downtown lunch crowds moved past them, Brown went on.

"I know what took place up at the apartment. I know you are a degenerate." The word must have cut at Tobey, feeling like a betrayal of his trust in the sailor. Brown threatened to expose Tobey to his office, to go over to 64 Wall Street and tell his colleagues what kind of man he was. He threated to go up to his apartment on West Fifty-Seventh Street as well and tell his sister and mother and aunt what he'd done to Ross, right there in that apartment. Ross backed him up, claiming Tobey had "gone down on him" during his visits. The word *cocksucker* was used. It must have seared Tobey's skin as it came out of Ross's mouth.

How strange the scene must have looked on that May afternoon on Wall Street, the banker, the delivery man, and the former sailor walking and talking but bound by a tension simmering between them. The entire drama playing out in such a public place. Ross and Brown were leaving the city, planning to go to Texas. That might have given Tobey hope in that moment, that if he just paid these men off, they would leave town, disappear out west somewhere and never bother him again. He agreed to give them five hundred dollars that afternoon.

But of course that wasn't the end. The two men showed up at Tobey's office a few weeks later. There they were, right in the hallway.

Tobey recognized their voices. They came to ask for one hundred dollars more. Tobey escorted them outside, down the elevator and to the street. He walked with them away from the office building, tried to negotiate with them, but Brown again repeated his threats of exposing him at his office.

"I was incessantly annoyed with telephone messages," Tobey remembered. Brown, his distinctive staccato speech, demanded a meeting, demanded money. Mostly he called at 64 Wall Street. Sometimes at the apartment but not often. Brown was regularly seeing Tobey without Ross. Almost every two weeks they would meet on some street corner near his office, surrounded by the country's largest banks and financial companies, and the growing exuberance of stock market speculation. On one of those street corners, Tobey would pay one hundred dollars each time. It became a routine he must have despaired as he saw little hope of escaping.

At one meeting, Tobey brought an attorney friend, Charles Hann. It's unclear how Tobey knew Hann, except that they both worked in the same office building for different firms and had struck up conversations in the comings and goings of their days through the building's lobby. Tobey must have trusted Hann, given that he brought him into the mess of the situation, exposing him to the claims of his sexual perversions. Perhaps he found in Hann a sympathetic ally in what was becoming an unbearable secret.

Hann pretended to be a police detective and told Brown to "lay off this dirty blackmail game." Brown asked to see a badge, which only angered Hann more. Clearly Brown had little fear of the situation or little concern for his own arrest. It might have seemed to Hann and Tobey that this was not the first time he had played this dirty game.

"This man is a soiler of youth!" Brown shouted to Hann, breaking his usual low tone. It must have reverberated for a few feet and then some. When Hann suggested Tobey call over a street cop and have Brown arrested, Brown replied, "I'm not afraid of getting into trouble," adding, "This Mr. Tobey is a regular Harry Thaw."

"I've never seen such a brazen person before," Hann would later recall. Whatever hope Tobey had of bringing in Hann, to threaten and perhaps scare Brown away, dissipated within a few minutes of their meeting.

He eventually paid Brown and Ross thousands of dollars over eighteen months. Perhaps Tobey did wish to go to the police or reach out to Hann again or some other lawyer. Any of those options of course depended on the revelation of what Ross and Brown were claiming Tobey did to Ross. "A soiler of youth!" The phrase would have echoed in Tobey's mind, the words so brazenly spoken on the street corner in such a casual way. To defend against these accusations was clearly more difficult than paying what Brown was asking. Though as the months continued, and the demands increased, Tobey must have wondered how long he would have to live like this.

The dangers of this "dirty blackmail game" that Tobey found himself in were many. These games went by a number of names: *muzzle* or *mug* or more often *mouse*. In his 1937 book *The Professional Thief*, Edwin Sutherland relates one account of how the modern muzzle game was devised sometime around 1910 by a gang who frequented a poolroom in Manhattan's Tenderloin. Of course blackmailing men for queer sexual practices had a much longer history, but what Sutherland described was the more modern, organized scheme with a coded practice and language that emerged in the early decades of the twentieth century.

The muzzle started as a simple act of staking out subway bathrooms around Times Square. Upon spotting two men entering a stall together, the extortionists would barge in and, in their outrage, threaten to call the police until money or valuables were handed over.

The schemes became increasingly sophisticated. Why wait for the queer men to arrive at some bathroom stall? Why not bring them to you? The gangs started to use lures or steerers, young, handsome men who would, much like the badger scheme, draw a desirous victim into a hotel room, a comfort station, or a public bathroom stall and get the man into a compromising position before his muzzle partner barged in, appalled, outraged, and demanded money. Or flashed a badge and threatened arrest.

"Members of the mob . . . always appeared before any act took place," Sutherland explained, "or else the steerer stalled or postponed action if the other members failed to appear." It was perhaps necessary to make this distinction, to declare that the men working these muzzle schemes were not themselves interested in men. But we can imagine that the underworld, like the rest of society, had its fair share of queer men.

These muzzle schemes became so successful, gangs would organize traveling muzzle trips, with men working different cities for long periods of time. As the threat of public exposure and scandal was so great, and queer men were unlikely to go to the police for fear of being arrested, they were easy targets and vulnerable to repeated extortions. "The muzzle," Sutherland writes, "is one of the few rackets in which a go-back (second attempt) can be successfully staged. In some instances two or three go-backs on the same man are successful."[4]

Perhaps Tobey saw the coded stories in the press of other men in similar situations. The banker George Bancroft went to the police when he was lured to the University Apartment Hotel by a gang of men headed by infamous Dapper Don Collins, well-known for his cons and badger schemes and apparently not averse to muzzle schemes as well. Collins had inquired about investing in stocks but couldn't meet Bancroft in his Wall Street office. He suggested instead the hotel at Forty-Seventh Street and Sixth Avenue. Collins met him in the hotel lobby, and the men took the elevator to a private room. Inside, two men were waiting, flashing badges and making threats. "Collins threated to circulate improper stories about me," Bancroft stated, if he didn't pay him $5,000. Bancroft wrote the check and then went to the police.[5]

Seven men were arrested and charged with impersonating officers and carrying concealed weapons in July 1922 in Atlantic City, New Jersey. "Boardwalk Blackmailers," as one report named the gang, were preying on men who were vacationing in the well-known seaside resort. The phrasing may have had a bit of a double entendre for readers in the know, as Atlantic City had the reputation as a place of social and sexual adventure. Like many seaside resorts, Atlantic City was a leisure playground for visitors where the moral codes were often bent or broken. Queer men were known to walk along the boardwalk attired in outfits that would signal their queerness, such as tan shoes or red or lavender neckties.

In 1912 Woodrow Wilson bemoaned how the city attracted so many men who were far from the "home folks to watch them." "They are too apt to adjourn their morals and have a fling," Wilson complained. He was not speaking of queer men precisely, but the atmosphere invited all kinds and, of course, all kinds of blackmailers as well.

The seven men arrested had targeted Robert Haney, a Philadelphia businessman. Haney was alone with one of the men in the gang, possibly the lure, when others arrived, again flashing fake badges and threatening Haney. They forced him to write a check for one hundred dollars. Haney stopped payment the next day and went to the police. The men were from New York, Philadelphia, Baltimore, and Cleveland and had, according to reports, been connected to several blackmailing incidents from Boston to Philadelphia.[6]

BY THE FALL of 1920, after nearly two years of payments to Ross and Brown, Tobey had finally had enough and was willing to go to the assistant district attorney with his story. The ADA devised a sting operation involving Tobey paying the two men during a sidewalk meeting, with detectives nearby. When the payment was made the detectives arrested Brown and Ross.

On the car ride to the DA's office Brown affected a mild rage. That man, he said, referring to Tobey, "ruined this man"—pointing to Ross—"by committing degenerate acts upon him." Ross backed him up, both men now showing a certain anger. "It's true. He went down on me for four months," he said.

In the prosecutor's office both men used the only defense they had: that Toby was a degenerate, that he had defiled Ross, and that he was paying them to keep his secret. But they both were also brazenly honest and betrayed the fact that this was not the first mouse scheme for them.

"How are you living?" the ADA asked Ross.

"Off this man," Ross replied, referring to Tobey. He told the ADA that he and Brown had made somewhere around $7,000 off the banker and were willing to make a full confession, confident that Tobey would not press charges and go through with a jury trial.[7] Most likely the prosecutor knew this too, which is why he made a deal with Ross and Brown.

"If you get out of town and stay out I will not prosecute you on charges of attempted extortion," he told them. Ross and Brown took the offer. The ADA would later recall how both men "begged to be allowed to leave."

The police and prosecutor's sole response to months of payments and repeated threats was to force the men out of town, turn them on another city, where perhaps other queer men would become their targets, where more muzzle schemes could be devised. After all, the thinking would go, these queer victims were themselves criminals; their encounters with other men were serious felonies. Yes, Tobey was a respectable Wall Street banker, but there must have been the lingering distaste for the prosecutor and the detectives that he was, most likely, a degenerate. The offer to leave town could also have been what Tobey wanted. In this way, he could get on with his life, avoid the public scandal of a trial, and forget he ever saw Ross trudging along Lafayette Street on that brisk October evening two years earlier.

Eventually Ross and Brown returned to their game, again demanding money from Tobey. Neither had left the city as promised. At some point in the spring of 1921, Tobey agreed to press charges and move the case to court. Both men were formally arrested and charged with attempted extortion.

Once arrested, police and prosecutors learned the men were using aliases. Nat Ross's real name was Nathan Rosenschweig, sometimes spelled Rosenzweig. He told the DA he had changed his name to Ross. When he registered for the draft in 1917, he used Nathanial Ross. It was not uncommon for immigrants and children of immigrants to change their names and make them sound more English, particularly if one's name had the "cast of Jewishness," as one report referred to Ross.

Joe Brown too used an alias. His real name was Samuel Dreyfus.

His parents were Jewish immigrants from Russia who spoke little English and often struggled to find work. Dreyfus was living at home with his parents and two younger siblings in the Bronx, just a few blocks from Ross. The aliases would become a useful attack for the prosecution as they underscored the entire performance the two men enacted as part of their extortion of Tobey. It put into doubt the truthfulness of anything the men might have claimed in their defense.

The men were tried separately. Throughout his trial Dreyfus presented himself as a willing pawn to both Ross and Tobey. On the stand, he was often slow to grasp questions and at times appeared confused by the facts of the case. His voice was low, and the judge had to prod him to speak up so the all-male jury could hear him. This was particularly true when he was asked what Ross told him Tobey had done to him.

"Don't whisper it!" the judge exclaimed. His testimony was explicit in the facts of the sexual encounters, detailing how Tobey had "gone down on Ross," that he understood what sodomy meant, that no, that's not a word that Ross used to describe what they did, nor did he use the words *fluter* or *fairy* but rather *cocksucker* to describe his encounters with the banker.

Dreyfus claimed Tobey had paid him to take Ross away from New York, that he was more like an employee and certainly nothing close to an extortionist. He testified that at one point, just before the men planned to leave the city, a plan Tobey had allegedly hatched for them months after the payments began, Tobey said, "I know I am a coward. I don't know what to do, either jump into the river or commit suicide. It's driving me crazy." Dreyfus claimed Tobey turned to him for help and asked if he could keep Ross away from the city for a while. "There is one thing you can do to save me" is how Dreyfus described Tobey's pleas, making the younger man seem a savior for the distraught, suicidal banker.

Prosecutors drilled Dreyfus with questions about why he would hang around a man like Tobey. Why he would go meet Tobey even after Ross had told him what happened between them?

"You knew at the time he was degenerate?" the prosecutor asked.

"You didn't have any use for this kind of man? For outcasts, for people not fit to associate with ordinary people?"

"No sir," Dreyfus replied.

"Still you went down to see him in his office."

But it was Tobey's suspected criminal behavior that was also on trial. In his cross-examination, Dreyfus's lawyer amplified any suspicions the jury might have about Tobey' moral character.

"How many other boys were you sending money to during this time?" he asked.

"I don't believe I sent money to anybody during this time," Tobey said.

"You were entertaining other boys at your apartment, too?"

"We were during the War," Tobey replied, indicating the *we* as a family event.

"Not 'we.' Were you?"

"Yes, sir, I as a member of the family."

"Any other boys that you sent out of town?

"No."

"Any other boys you helped out with money?"

"No."

"Any other boys you got a job for?"

"Yes, sir, I have got jobs for two men."

"Sailor boys?"

"Soldiers."

"Sailor boys?"

"Soldiers."

In this breathless and repetitive exchange, the defense attorney pitched an image of Tobey as the predatory pervert targeting the hapless "boys" whom he entertained during the war years. We can imagine Tobey's shrinking resolve having to sit on the stand answering such questions that simmered with moral deviancy and criminality.

The defense attorney asked the district attorney if he made any "investigations whether or not the complaining witness was guilty of the acts charged him," inciting a heated exchange with the prosecutor.

"The issue here is not that this man is a degenerate or is not," the prosecutor declared. "The issue is what was in those men's minds when they asked him for this money." The objection was sustained, but the point made for the jury was clear: How can we trust a man like Orville Tobey?

It was, predictably, too much for Tobey to take.

Dreyfus was found guilty of attempted extortion and sentenced to three years in Sing Sing prison.

"You were a cruel, deliberate, and calculating criminal," the judge said at his sentencing. "You made the complaining witness live in fear of you for years."[8]

If there were any feeling of relief for Tobey, it would have been short-lived, as he knew he would have to go through the whole ordeal again with the trial of Rosenzweig. And that trial would, no doubt, make explicit the relationship between the two men with even more details of their alleged sexual encounters. It was likely that William Fallon, Rosenzweig's attorney, would make it a grand performance of perversity, turning Tobey into the villain of the entire show, doing what he did best, turning the prosecution into a persecution. One can imagine it was not something Tobey could endure. Tobey's lawyer offered a deal that gave Rosenzweig a suspended sentence. At first he refused it, hoping instead to go to trial, but Fallon convinced him to accept it, threatening to withdraw as his attorney if he didn't.

"If I hadn't listened to Fallon," Rosenzweig later told reporters, "I could have beat this case."

IT WAS WITHOUT doubt unnerving for Tobey to read the headlines in the *Daily News* in the summer of 1922 and see Rosenzweig named as a part of an "earlier extortion case involving a banker." Tobey was planning his wedding to Elizabeth Best that summer. The two would take a two-month-long honeymoon in Europe, traveling through France, Belgium, and Great Britain.[9] Tobey's lawyer thought it prudent to reach out to the *Daily News* and get control of the story, before reporters got too deep into that earlier trial, and rehash the details of the case. The newspaper agreed to keep Tobey's name out of the article in an exchange for an interview with the lawyer.

Rosenzweig, said the lawyer, "was an experienced blackmailer. My first impression of him was that he was an ignorant coward, but I soon unlearned that estimate." He added, "Ross had excellent knowledge of the law, and all the information we were able to pick up about him indicated that he had blackmailed hundreds of men before he blackmailed my client—and before he blackmailed Ward. I am convinced that he was a member or head of an enormous blackmail ring."

ROSENZWEIG DID FINALLY appear at the New York DA's office. He told detectives he had nothing to do with Peters's murder, that he had been making his weekly appointments with his probation officer and had been going to work each day. He was angry that his name had appeared in the Ward case, convinced that it was Fallon who put the idea into the reporters' ears.

Still not convinced of Rosenzweig's alibi, the DA called Walter Ward down to the criminal courts building. Detectives brought the two men together in an interrogation room. Ward took one look at the fair-haired Rosenzweig and declared without a doubt this was not the Charlie Ross who had been blackmailing him for weeks.

"I've never met this man before," he said. A few minutes later, he and his lawyer Elwood Rabenold walked out of the DA's office and left the building. It was a quick encounter, and one that must have left some uncertainty in the minds of the detectives about Ward's honesty.

William Fallon was not in the room when the two men met. Rosenzweig had a new lawyer. In fact, Fallon all but exited the case, failing to find Charlie Ross and offer some hope to the Peters family, not to mention Westchester officials, of solving a crucial mystery about the murder. Perhaps he too thought his former client was involved, and when it appeared he wasn't, Fallon quietly disappeared .

We can imagine investigators were left wondering who was lying. If they were to believe Nathan Rosenzweig's sister and her claims that

Ward lured "innocent boys away from their innocence," then Walter Ward did in fact know Rosenzweig, or at least had had some kind of encounter with him before. It's not clear why Rosenzweig's sister might have lied about her knowledge of Ward. What might she gain in making such a statement to the press?

On the other hand, there were reasons why Ward might have lied about knowing Rosenzweig. He might have wished to keep the pursuit of the blackmailing gang alive at a moment when many in the investigation were increasingly convinced that Charlie Ross and Jack were mere phantoms of Ward's story. As long as the blackmailers remained elusive, the only story of the murder was the one Ward and his attorneys devised. If Ward had known Rosenzweig, he might have wanted to keep a distance from the scandalous details of that earlier extortion case of Orville Tobey—details that were well-known to the detectives, DAs, and reporters. Rosenzweig's appearance in the investigation prompted new questions about Ward. Some were asking if Walter Ward had been entangled in an intricate muzzle scheme. Was he, like Tobey, a moral degenerate?

Peters and the Wolf

AMONG THE UNEMPLOYED EX-SAILORS AND EX-SOLDIERS WHO lingered in Bryant Park, James C. Clark was known as Skipper, a reference to his time in the navy and perhaps to his age. In his early forties, Clark was older than many of the men in the park, though he held his age well. He was handsome, square jawed, and leathery, with graying hair and rough stubble of beard. Like those younger men, Clark was drifting along, jobless, and trying to readjust to civilian life. When he saw the headlines about the murder of Clarence Peters, Clark was eager to tell his story, and the *New York American* was eager to listen.

According to Clark, the two met in the navy, during Peters's short time as a naval apprentice. After Clark was discharged in the summer of 1921, he reconnected with Peters, and they would "hang out" in Bryant Park on warm summer days. They also shared a room for a time at the Hotel Majestic, a fifty-cents-a-night boardinghouse on the Bowery, living on handouts. Peters told Clark he was getting money from the wealthy men he met in the park, but there was one man who interested him the most.

"I've got a lot of gentlemen friends," Peters told Clark, "but there's one guy I like best of all. He's on the police force at New Rochelle, and I'm going to shake all the others for him."

The shake was of course a reference to shakedown, or more precisely blackmail. If what Clark said was true, it would suggest that Peters was acting as some kind of lure, working blackmail schemes that Ward was orchestrating. "If he is such a great man," Clark asked, "why don't you shake him down?" Peters replied: "Not me. I'm getting enough as it is."[1]

Clark remembered sitting with Peters in the park in the summer of 1921 when a Peerless coupe drove up and parked along the curb on Forty-First Street. Peters walked over to the man, whom Clark described as "well dressed and prosperous looking." The three of them eventually went to a local restaurant on Sixth Avenue for lunch, with the well-dressed man paying the bill. Later that day, Peters handed Clark two dollars, saying it was from his "friend from New Rochelle," adding, "He wants to see you privately." Clark claimed he didn't follow up on the offer and didn't think anything more of the encounter until he saw Ward's picture in the newspaper. "That's the fellow," he said. "I'm willing to tell my story to the authorities at any time."

Reporters described Clark as mannered and intelligent, not the kind of man you might expect among those drifters in Bryant Park. A photograph of him, smiling and confident wearing a dark fedora, white collared shirt, and narrow tie, appeared on the *New York American*'s front page. It was proof that this man was real, even though James C. Clark was not his real name but rather an alias he used with reporters. At the Hotel Majestic, reporters did find that while Clark was well-known there, Peters had never registered under his own name. But just days after talking with reporters, and before his story was in print, Clark was no longer at the hotel, leaving behind an unpaid bill.[2]

DURING WORLD WAR I, Bryant Park, a manicured green space on the corner of Sixth Avenue and Forty-Second Street behind the stately New York Public Library, was taken over by a large tented YMCA canteen supporting servicemen coming through the city on their way to Europe. Perhaps this might explain why, in the years after the war when the country was caught in a deep recession, the park became a home for unemployed ex-servicemen, all wanderers in the shadows of the war's end. Bryant Park became notorious for such men who formed a community of drifters seeking ways to better their lives. For many the traumas of the war were still daily realities they had to endure as they tried to reenter civilian life.

In the fall of 1921, a rally meant to highlight the plight of these men was planned by the radical and charismatic activist Urbain Ledoux. Near the steps of the public library, surrounding the pair of marble lions named Patience and Fortitude that flanked the entrance, nearly 5,000 people gathered, eventually spilling onto Fifth Avenue, stopping traffic at the intersection with Forty-Second Street. Ledoux had planned a rather unfortunate event in which he wished to auction off jobless men to bidders who would pay them a decent wage. City leaders decried it as a "slave market" and called out a small army of policemen, arresting and attacking those who gathered, creating a near riot in the process.

"Freedom is dying in the United States," Ledoux bemoaned. "Until people rise and properly use the mediums they have in the pulpit, forum, and press they shall have no real freedoms."[3]

A few days later a local women's club took pity on the men and came to the park armed with cakes and donuts, a gesture that was greatly appreciated by the park habitués. Again, the police intervened, ordering the women to stop their charity work, while harassing the men and arresting those who fought back. "I've never witnessed such a thing in New York," one of the women told reporters. Another insisted she couldn't have imagined such a "thing could happen in an American community."[4] Editorials warned that such acts of charity for the drifters were only encouraging dangerous habits. "In Bryant Park," one newspaper decried, "the drifter has found undreamed possibilities of developing the fine art of living without effort," adding with a dire tone, "The drifter will prosper in this newly found stronghold and his numbers will grow."[5]

But another fact of Bryant Park in those years, a fact that didn't make headlines, was its queer life. Just a few blocks from Times Square, the park was well-known as a place to pick up men for sex or sociability. "Bryant Park has been a meeting place for years," one informant of a 1930s study of "sex variants" remembered about his experiences in the 1920s. "Every now and then the police would back the van up and clean it out," he said.[6] Along with Riverside Park, certain areas of Central Park, and Coney Island, Bryant Park was one point on a constellation of public places in the city where queer men went looking for fun and pleasure, while navigating threats of violence, robbery, and police harassment.

The park was also a place to recruit young working-class men for the many queer brothels in the city, secreted places set up in respectable-looking brownstones. One owner of such a place described having eight to ten men working for him. Most were around twenty years old, all were "tall, strong and heavily built," but few, he said, were homosexuals, as they engaged in "relations with men in order to earn money." He would find these men in his cruising along Riverside Drive, Forty-Second Street, Bryant Park, and the cafés in the Tenderloin and Times Square. He did admit that sometimes the men working for him blackmailed and threatened his clients to get more money, but added, "I try to get a more honorable class of boys."[7] Muzzle schemes held lucrative possibilities for drifters and jobless ex-servicemen. And, if Clark's story was to be believed, Clarence Peters was among them.

There were other men in the park who also remembered Peters. Ed Maloney, a former soldier and Bryant Park regular, claimed to have seen both Peters and Ward just a few months before Ward claimed the blackmail began. It's hard to tell what to make of these stories. It could be these men were simply making them up, motivated by the reward money.

But then far from Bryant Park, Harry Schneiderman, a marine recruit who arrived with Peters at Parris Island, also recalled Peters bragging about the wealthy men up north he could wire for money anytime he needed. It seemed to Schneiderman that Peters had been to New York City many times.[8] Peters was prone to making up fantastic stories of his past; investigators had already encountered several such stories from his transient farmwork in Massachusetts and New Hampshire. While his stories usually cast him in extraordinary situations well beyond his humble life in Haverhill, they were of course all lies. But to brag about wealthy men who could supply him money seemed a strange lie to tell. One might wonder why young Peters would make up such a morally dubious story for his fellow recruits.

WHATEVER TRUTH THERE was to Clark's story, it provoked a compelling picture about the seedier underworld of the city's queer life. The front-page article that included Clark's interview declared in large type, "Rich Men Met Poor Youths in Strange Group 'The Wolf' Led." The article detailed the "secret circle of poor youths and men of wealth" that was dominated by a "piercing eyed man known as 'The Wolf.'" This underworld circle of "extremes of social and economic life met" in parks, in Tenderloin resorts, and amid the "exotic atmosphere of magnificently furnished hidden apartments" around the city. It was, of course, not far from the truth in describing the queer landscape of New York in those years, but in the hands of the scandal-seeking newspaper editors, this landscape was as bleak and dire as any reader could imagine, mixing shock and intrigue at the same time.

Reporters interviewed Clark at a place in the "heart of the tenderloin"—the specific location was not revealed—which was the hangout of this "queer circle" where Peters and the Wolf were often seen. Readers were undoubtedly tantalized by the innuendo and unspeakable possibilities that lurked in the Tenderloin, suggesting that it held the secret to the Ward tragedy.

"Was Ward fearful of attack of one sort or another?" the newspaper asked, wondering if in fact the key to the blackmail mystery lay with finding the Wolf. The paper made clear that this Wolf was not the same as the notorious Wall Street speculator David Lamar, whom the press had dubbed the the Wolf of Wall Street during his indictment and trial for fraud in 1914. A number of wolves lurked in New York in those years.[9]

Clark's interview was reprinted in newspapers across the United States, including the *Haverhill Evening Gazette.* "It is absolutely not so," insisted Fred Magison, the Haverhill attorney who, after Michael Sullivan's departure from the case once Fallon's efforts failed, was now working for the Peters family. Magison was friends with the Peterses; he and Elbridge's late half brother were law partners. Inez and Elbridge were adamant that Clark's claims about their son were complete fabrications, contending yet again that Clarence was never away from

Haverhill for more than a few days.[10] But then, Clarence might not have told his family everything he was up to. When he left to join the marines, Inez and Elbridge were made aware of his plan only once he had arrived at Parris Island and sent a letter about his intentions. It seems likely that, if true, Clarence would have kept his trips to New York, and the many wealthy gentlemen he met there, a secret from his family.

THERE WERE OTHER stories as well, brief reports in the press that hinted at Ward's secret life. It was said that Ward frequented men-only parties at the Lenox Hotel and Hotel Brunswick in Boston where servicemen mingled with civilians and where, perhaps, he had first met Peters. Witnesses told investigators they saw Ward and Peters at such a party at the Lenox Hotel and that Ward left with Peters and other men and drove around the city with them. At one of these parties, a photograph was taken of Ward, the subject of which might have been the leverage for blackmail.[11]

In Boston, Pinkerton detectives working for Weeks pursued these rumors. At the Hotel Brunswick they checked the guest registry for the past year. They found an R. H. Ward who was a guest in November 1919, but that was the nearest to a Ward they could find. Clerks couldn't remember this Ward nor what he was doing in Boston. At the Lenox Hotel they had the same experience, a registry absent any Walter Ward, or even Ralph Ward, his brother, or George Ward, his father. Though it didn't seem to occur to these detectives that most men who wished to rendezvous with another man in a hotel room or to slide into the underworld of queer parties for a weekend rarely used their actual names when signing in to a hotel.[12]

With little success at the front desks, detectives made an appointment to speak with Lemuel Prior, owner of both hotels. Prior it turns out was well acquainted with George Ward and Ralph Ward, as they visited Boston regularly and stayed at the Lenox Hotel, though apparently didn't sign the register. Prior would often have dinners with the Wards and the manager of the local Ward factory. But, he told detectives, he knew nothing about Walter Ward and, in fact, never knew that George had another son until he saw the newspaper accounts of the case. He was completely perplexed by the news of the family scandal and the sudden appearance of a new Ward family member.[13]

A few weeks later, detectives from the Browne-Rykert detective agency, also working for Weeks, interviewed a Mr. Dougherty, the city editor of the *Boston Advertiser* newspaper, searching for information about the men-only parties in Boston hotels. Dougherty, detectives believed, might have knowledge of such events from his contacts in the city's business community. Dougherty claimed that Walter Ward was indeed an intimate friend of Lemuel Prior and would visit the city often. Prior would host what the editor called "wild parties" filled with liquor and young men between the ages of seventeen and twenty-two. Rumors were, Dougherty said, that Prior was a "degenerate."

This information was echoed by detectives in New York who were investigating people who knew Prior. Prior traveled to New York often. One informant told detectives "there was no doubt about Prior being a degenerate." Another informant, described as a "prominent hotel man" confirmed "there is no question as to his being a degenerate."[14] There was of course every reason to believe that Prior, standing in front of the Pinkerton detectives, would twist the truth about his encounters with the Wards. After all, it could be quite a scandal if word got out that he was the host of such wild parties of young men. Prior, the owner of two well-respected hotels in Boston, would certainly not want to be associated with such scandalous behaviors. It was better, he might have thought, to pretend that he didn't even know Walter Ward existed.

THEORIES ABOUT THE queer relationship between Ward and Peters were not only hinted at in the press. Some arrived in more explicit terms in the mail addressed to District Attorney Weeks. H. F. Newfield, owner of Photo-Root, Inc., a printing and photography shop, detailed his own assessment of the case in a long letter. He advised a careful medical exam of Ward to determine if he was a degenerate, as he was convinced that the entire case was based on Ward's attraction to

Peters. His theory came from his own experience observing a local restaurant, "where men of this type hung out, sometimes as many as 20 or more at a time." He noted that these men had a "peculiar glitter about the eyes, movement of hand and legs slightly different to the everyday person," and declared that, in general, such men were "cunning, deliberate liars, and speak glibly in a friendly sort of way." He added that his interest in the case was one that every citizen should take—that justice was done.

After extolling Weeks's virtues as a DA, he ended with a simple request: "I have a large collection of photos of celebrated persons, if you have one handy of your good self, autograph it and send it to me. My thanks in advance."[15] It is not known if Weeks responded to Newfield's request.

In light of the *New York American* articles, Weeks directed detectives to make inquiries about Ward in the nightclubs and cabarets around the Tenderloin and Times Square. There were rumors that Ward was known to associate with "uncouth" characters in the city and to frequent places popular with underworld gangs; most of the places were exclusively for "young toughs," as one report described them.[16] Detectives began with the more popular places in the Tenderloin: Palais Royal, Broadway Gardens, Little Club, Pre-Catalan Café, and Piccadilly Rendezvous—names that conjured the exotic and the decadent.

Waiters at the Little Club on West Forty-Fourth Street did confirm that Walter Ward had visited the year prior but had little memory of whom he was with or how often he came. The manager at the well-known Broadway Gardens, an upscale club for underworld figures at Seventh Avenue and West Forty-Sixth Street, said they had never seen Walter Ward there. One informant, close to the club's owner, Billy Gallagher, told detectives if Ward was a heavy spender, he would have been known to everyone. They did say that George Ward, Walter's father, was a frequent patron and "lavishly entertained women" at the club. They also claimed George was rumored to be a mouse, that underworld vernacular for degenerate.

George's exploits were also remembered by waiters at the

Pre-Catalan Café, who described him as a "high flier" and a "daddy" to many of the girls on Broadway. But then the manager did concede that some of what he had heard about George was just rumor and not something he witnessed himself.[17]

In their inquires around the pool halls, namely the Ambassador Billiards Academy, detectives learned more about Walter. Harry Bosky, a well-known confidence man, told detectives that Walter Ward was without a doubt a degenerate and had been "shaken down" on two occasions that he knew about.[18] Detectives returned some weeks later and met with three "notorious blackmailers" known as McCarthy, Lloyd, and a man called Speed. They were part of the gang of men arrested in Atlantic City for the extortion of Robert Haney just a few weeks earlier and, detectives noted, "make a specialty of 'shaking down' men of wealth after succeeding to get them in questionable positions." Detectives brought up Walter Ward to elicit some information the men might have but without any success. All three men had jumped bail in New Jersey and were wanted by the police, so they may not have been that eager to answer questions about the sensational Ward case from private detectives.[19]

WELL BEYOND THE Tenderloin, detectives were also asking about Ward's sexual tendencies in New Rochelle. Was he a degenerate? Might he have inclinations to such behavior? Was he in fact a "cocksucker"? That's the word they used in their interview with Frank Cody of the New Rochelle Police Department. Cody had defended Ward's actions in the days after he offered his statement. As chief of police, Cody might have had some insight into Ward, or at the very least known if there were rumors about the handsome and enigmatic police commissioner. One might think that Cody would have dismissed the questions outright. But surprisingly, he was more tentative about the possibility. He said that if Ward was in fact a "cocksucker," he showed no signs of it. For Cody, such men lacked courage and were, as a "general thing," cowards. Ward was, without a doubt, no coward. As evidence of Ward's courage, Cody reminded detectives that during the workers' strike at the Ward Bakery a few years earlier, Ward "donned overalls" and risked his life to deliver bread throughout the city and thwart the efforts of striking workers. The Pinkerton detectives, well-known for their strike-breaking successes, might have agreed with Cody's theories of courage.[20]

In Sutton Manor, the same detectives interviewed the neighbors of the Wards. Or at least tried to. As the investigation continued and new, ever more scandalous stories appeared in the press each day, most of the good residents of the Manor locked their doors to the strangers who were snooping around the neighborhood. They kept their shades down and told their gardeners and maids and chauffeurs to avoid any questions that might come their way from the press. Word was spreading that even those strangers who presented themselves as detectives could not be trusted. It was increasingly common for reporters to pretend to be detectives to get the locals to answer questions, to get a neighbor or friend of the Wards to betray a trust or confidence that might then be in the morning edition. Beware, was the whispered plea among the Manor residents that spring and summer.

Ernest and Jane Stolz were less fearful than some of their neighbors. They lived in a large Dutch Colonial at 122 Echo Avenue, about two blocks from the Wards. Ernest owned a company that manufactured what were then called earphones, or rather hearing aids. "It multiplies sound waves far and near," the ads proclaimed.

The Stolzes had known the Wards ever since the young couple moved to Sutton Manor. Ernest told detectives Ward was a "high class fellow, a shrewd and keen, nervy fellow with a strong will power." Ward was a kind of "whole show" guy, he said, meaning he often needed to run things on his own terms, which resulted in a domineering personality, particularly concerning his employees. But, Ernest insisted, he was "the last man in the world [he] would size up as a degenerate." Jane Stolz agreed and said Ward's character and habits were "exemplary" and dismissed any suggestion that he was a degenerate or had any associations with cabarets and resorts of the underworld.

They both expressed what a splendid woman Beryl was and that everyone in the Manor could hardly understand how she had endured the daily strain of all this trouble. But they both made clear that their impression of the entire affair was just that, an impression, as they had not ventured to ask the Wards directly about the murder. However, there was much discussion among the neighbors, Ernest said, and "the whole thing is a mystery which no one seems to understand."[21]

The Stolzes had their own theory about the blackmail that concerned racetrack losses Walter refused to pay. When threated with exposure and hounded for the money, he killed Peters in the "spur of the moment" as Walter, Ernest repeated, "is a quick tempered, nervy fellow, who, when driven to the wall would fight." But then of course, both Ernest and Jane were not so certain this theory made sense, as welching on a bet was hardly worth all the secrecy and public scandal, and certainly not a good reason to put his lovely wife through such torture. It did appear that while residents of the Manor were tentative in talking about the case to the press and detectives, they were quite eager to play amateur sleuths among themselves in trying to solve the mysteries of the crime.

At the Sutton Manor boathouse, detectives spoke with William Sweeney, the seventeen-year-old son of Thomas and Ida Sweeney, who lived in a small Colonial on Sutton Manor Road. Among the Manor residents, the Sweeneys were clearly of more modest means. Thomas was a traveling salesman in the cotton industry, and the Sweeneys' home was filled with six adult children and a son-in-law. Unlike many of their neighbors, the Sweeneys lacked any live-in help.

At first William was reluctant to talk to the detectives, as he was told to "keep his mouth shut," though who told him that was unclear. One might imagine that among those in the Sweeney household, as among other Manor residences, talk of the Ward scandal was not uncommon, and William, the youngest of the family, might have been directed to avoid any questions about the Wards from strangers. He also might have felt compelled to resist such directives, to reveal what he knew and what was whispered. He had heard that Ward was a "rounder"—a drunk who spent a lot of time out at bars—and a reckless driver, particularly through the streets of Sutton Manor; that he also heard a rumor Ward killed a man in Manhattan by running him down with his car; that two of Sweeney's male friends who had gone out with Ward several times and knew for a fact that man was a "fairy." The term needed some explanation, as the detective noted in his report that *fairy* was "a common expression or term applied to degenerates." Though when pushed for the names of these friends, Sweeney resisted.

"I refuse under any circumstance," he said.

For the detective this adamant refusal cast doubts about Sweeney's claim. "I don't think much of it," he concluded in his report.[22]

One has to wonder why William Sweeney would even risk revealing such information in the first place. What did he have to gain from calling Ward a fairy to the stern-eyed, dark-suited Pinkerton detective after he was warned not to talk to such men? While the detective might have dismissed his claim as mere rumor, the more he asked questions, the more a contradictory image of Walter Ward emerged, neither confirming nor denying the possibility that a queer blackmail scheme was behind Peters's murder.

Ideal Sherlock Mystery

THE FAMED BRITISH MYSTERY WRITER ARTHUR CONAN DOYLE had some advice for Frederick Weeks. In June Conan Doyle stood along the Hudson River talking with the press before he was to board the RMS *Adriatic* and return to England. Reporters were eager to see what the creator of Sherlock Holmes would think about the most compelling real-life murder mystery of the moment.

While Conan Doyle admitted to not having a deep knowledge of the case, from what he had read he thought it would make an "ideal Sherlock mystery," adding that Sherlock would most likely "confine his attention to the Ward family alone, leaving the actual murder to unravel itself after the blackmail mystery was solved." When asked if he thought blackmail was indeed the cause of the murder, the writer channeled his fictional detective.

"Sherlock Holmes always took facts given him," Conan Doyle told reporters, "and proved them falsely before dropping them."

But it was Conan Doyle's more untraditional approach to the crime that struck some of the journalists gathered. "I am positively certain," Conan Doyle declared, "that in many mysteries of this kind a psychic, working from a spiritualistic trance, has reconstructed the picture of the tragedy and has been able to put the police in the way of solving it."

While a psychic may not uncover the motive for the murder, Conan Doyle conceded, he or she could, in communicating with Peters's spirit, learn in "exactly what conditions Peters met his death." He illustrated how a medium could hold a piece of clothing Peters wore at the time of his murder, which would help the medium communicate with him. But it would have to be someone friendly to Peters as, he suggested, "I don't believe Peters has been dead long enough or was of great enough intelligence to communicate with a stranger." He also stressed that the medium would have to be empathetic, as "heaven does not like a board of inquiry" when calling forth a spirit.[1]

It was perhaps not what reporters expected of the great mystery writer, but Conan Doyle's response should not have been too surprising. For the previous two months the renowned writer had been touring the United States, lecturing on what he described as the "new revelation" of spiritualism. In the later years of his life, his singular obsession was promoting spiritualism, a belief that the dead can communicate with the living and that séances and mediums could lead anyone to connect with those on the "other side."

Advertisements for Conan Doyle's lectures showed a keen showman. He hired a well-known management and promotion company to handle the tour. In a series of lectures at Carnegie Hall that kicked off the tour, tickets ranged from fifty cents for high-tiered seats to $2.50 for the front row. Every seat in the venerable hall was filled for his three nights of lectures, though one might imagine many in the crowd came to see the famous writer rather than to listen to his theories about the spirit world.

At the podium, Conan Doyle spoke with a commanding voice, deep and declarative. The focus was a series of "psychic photographs," each projected on a large screen onstage and displaying a variety of apparitions. Conan Doyle described the story behind each image, letting the audience ponder the particulars of the hazy black-and-white scenes in the darkened hall. The photographs showed men and women and children. Some were Conan Doyle's relatives; others were strangers, old women or soldiers killed in World War I, some with bullet holes still visible in their temples. "He vouched for the authenticity of them all," noted a *New York Times* reporter who witnessed the event.

Conan Doyle was also keen to dispel any doubts, denouncing critics in the press who questioned the truth of the photographs as of little intelligence.

At one point, he showed a ghostly photograph of his own son, who'd died from injuries during the Battle of the Somme in 1916 and had appeared to him in a séance in England where the photograph was taken. "It is not a good likeness," he declared, "and shows him at about the age of sixteen or seventeen, although he died at twenty-two." He did not to linger on the personal loss, though one can imagine how Conan Doyle's own grief was a compelling motivation for his interest in speaking to the dead. Spiritualism would have this power, this possibility for so many who came to listen to his lectures in the years after the tragedies of war and the influenza pandemic of 1918 and 1919 when so many died. Conan Doyle moved from the personal particulars of the loss of his son to the general evidence the photograph offered. Those in the audience at times gasped; at other times murmurs of disbelief hummed through the hall. But on the whole, the audience appeared taken by what they witnessed in those mysterious and captivating images of the ghostly dead.[2]

"These pictures show that there are certain laws on the other side which have to be observed," he told the audience. One curious claim he made was that there were, to his knowledge, no flappers in the spirit world. Those bobbed-hair, short-skirted women of the younger generation had, in his estimation, reverted to more traditional Victorian fashion once on the other side.

Conan Doyle's ideas about communicating with the dead may not have been that strange in the spring of 1922. The country was enthralled with the mysteries of radio, which seemed as perplexing as any séance. Music and news reports were floating along radio waves like never before. In public parks and ocean liners people enjoyed orchestra music performed miles away. At the Hotel Pennsylvania in New York guests danced into the early-morning hours to music that "seemed to come from nowhere," as one report described it, but was in fact performed by an orchestra in Newark, New Jersey. Summer resorts were planning on transmitting radio broadcasts to their guests. "When lounging in a swimming pool or under the shade of some willows," one report noted, "you will hear news of world events and charming music." There were experiments in music broadcasts on public buses and in local shops. "One of the latest fads now is to be entertained with radio music while having a shave," noted a report from California. But listening was not always a simple task of plugging in a radio. Picking up clear radio waves was complicated work that required skill. Newspapers began publishing radio sections in which, according to one writer of the era, "thousands of hitherto utterly unmechanical people puzzled over articles about regenerative circuits, sodion tubes, Grimes reflex circuits, crystal detectors, and neutrodynes." Sounds were emanating from everywhere, if one only had the proper tools for listening.[3]

Out in the Hudson River that June, Guglielmo Marconi, inventor of the radio, was aboard his yacht, named the *Elettra*, which also served as his floating laboratory, listening to radio waves from Mars, which was the closest it had been to the Earth in nearly a decade. "Several times I heard mysterious sounds I could not understand or explain," Marconi told reporters. "I do not think they were from Mars. In fact, I am not certain if Martians are trying to communicate. But," he added, sounding every bit like a spirit medium, "I was there to do everything possible to record messages if any were sent."[4]

CONAN DOYLE'S LECTURE tour created a national debate about spiritualism. Firsthand accounts of his events detailed his ideas of psychic phenomena in newspapers across the country, prompting both an excitement about the famous author's untraditional claims and a deep skepticism from ministers who found in Conan Doyle's new religion a threat to traditional Christianity. Some called him mad, others an advocate for free love and the ruination of the family, while one pastor declared that a writer who had spent so much of his life studying crime had himself become as abnormal in his thinking as the criminals he created.[5]

But the harshest criticism for Conan Doyle's beliefs came from an unexpected group: the Society of American Magicians. In early

June 1922 magicians and illusionists gathered at New York's Hotel McAlpin's grand ballroom for the annual dinner of the society and to listen to Conan Doyle give a keynote lecture. Famed illusionist and society president Harry Houdini had invited Conan Doyle. The pair first met in London in 1920. They shared a compelling interest in spiritualism, though with starkly contrasting motives. For many in the room, and most acutely for his host Houdini, to see a writer who created the master sleuth of rationality and logic become obsessed with mediums and the spirit world was both intriguing and complete lunacy.

Magicians had the most pointed critiques about spiritualism for they could see the pretense behind the séances and the psychics. Houdini had been investigating the phenomena for decades. While publicly he appeared curious about the practices of mediums, privately he referred to it as the "spook industry."[6]

Joseph Rinn, a friend of Houdini's and a member of the Society of American Magicians, was blunter in his skepticism. Rinn wrote a syndicated critique of this "spook industry" for *The New York Herald.* "For the small sum of six dollars," Rinn declared, "any one may entertain any of Sir Arthur's spirits and put them through amazing tricks." Rinn offered a $5,000 reward to anyone who could in fact produce a spirit manifestation that was not, after his investigation, found out to be a simple act of illusion. "If Sir Arthur Conan Doyle and the spirit photographers will only include on their investigating committees a few experts in 'magic tricks,' like myself and Mr. Houdini or any other members of the Society of American Magicians," Rinn challenged, "we will, I am quite sure, be able to explain every one of the 'supernormal phenomena' which have deluded the author of Sherlock Holmes, and we will endeavor to produce all of the tricks in the bright sunlight of Broadway where everyone can see how we make the ghosts come and go at will."[7]

At the McAlpin, Conan Doyle had his own sort of trick for the room: a short silent film depicting prehistoric animals. "These pictures are not occult," he declared to his attentive audience, "but this is psychic because everything that emanates from the human spirit or human brain is psychic. It is not supernatural. Nothing is. It is not preternatural in the sense that it isn't known to our ordinary senses." He went on to describe that what the magicians were about to witness was the "joining on the one hand of imagination and on the other hand of some power of materialization. The imagination, I may say, comes to me. The materializing power comes from elsewhere." It must have sounded all quite abstract and esoteric and a mystification that the magicians would have been keen to recognize.

Before starting his film, Conan Doyle declared he would not answer any questions about it "either from the press or others present." With that, he let a dramatic pause linger in the room, creating a palpable anticipation.

Then the lights in the room were lowered, and the black-and-white film projected on the wall. In it were a series of vignettes of dinosaurs in action: brooding mastodons, flying pterodactyls, and heavy-hoofed eohippus, huge prehistoric horses. There were fights among the animals in some scenes, playing among them in others. One can imagine the wonder and awe in the room watching such creatures come to life, or at least as much as film in those early years seemed lifelike. Beside those daunting and dusty displays of bones at the American Museum of Natural History, seeing such creatures animated in this way must have been a captivating experience.

The film prompted a range of emotions among the magicians, with confusion being a common one. Without context or explanation, what was anyone meant to make of these scenes of long-extinct animals? As one reporter described the sentiment in the room, "No one knew whether the motion picture of prehistoric animal life was 'psychic,' 'imaginative' or just 'fake.'"[8] Keeping to his word, after the film ended, Conan Doyle left the hotel without answering questions, leaving everyone to wonder what they had just witnessed.

The next day Conan Doyle wrote Houdini to explain his little trick. The film was a Hollywood creation, part of a movie that was based on Conan Doyle's earlier book *The Lost World*, which the filmmaker allowed him to use. "The purpose was simply to provide a little mystification to those who have so often and so successfully mystified others," he wrote. It was, in effect, a trick on the masters of tricks.

But it also raised the question of what is true and what is fake. The film, in all its crude special effects, gave the impression of being actual footage of prehistoric animals. Not unlike a good murder mystery, the entire presentation played with the spectators' sense of evidence, skirting a line between rationality and belief. The film made possible something that seemed so utterly impossible and for a brief moment captivated the audience of spiritualism skeptics.

Houdini contained his annoyance with his guest's stunt. In his reply to Conan Doyle he made a joke of the evening, noting that the one positive thing to come out of his film presentation was how it "created a great deal more newspaper talk than anything on the program."[9]

The two men simmered a rivalry, each eager—desperate, one might even say--to convince the other of their understanding of spiritualism. If Conan Doyle could get Houdini to profess the merits of this new religion, that would be a huge victory for his own efforts. Houdini's desire to persuade the creator of Sherlock Holmes about the realities of the many tricksters and frauds of the "spook industry" would further validate so much of what the master magician had found over his years of research. In *A Magician Among the Spirits*, published in 1924, Houdini recounted his decades-long study and investigation into spiritualism and concluded,

> I say unflinchingly I do not believe, and more, I will not believe. I have said many times that I am willing to believe, want to believe, will believe, if the Spiritualists can show any substantiated proof, but until they do I shall have to live on, believing from all the evidence shown me and from what I have experienced that Spiritualism has not been proven satisfactorily to the world at large and that none of the evidence offered has been able to stand up under the fierce rays of investigation.[10]

A few weeks after the society dinner in New York, Conan Doyle invited Houdini and his wife, Bess, to the Ambassador Hotel in Atlantic City, one of the newly built grand hotels meant to turn the seaside town into the Monte Carlo of North America. Conan Doyle's wife Jean had recently begun to conduct her own medium sessions using automatic writing, a process by which the spirit communicates through the medium in the form of writing. The couples spent afternoons on the beach and evenings in the hotel gardens. At some point, Jean offered to hold a séance to try to communicate with the spirit of Houdini's mother. Houdini agreed. In their hotel suit, Conan Doyle pulled the curtain closed to block out the late afternoon light and views of the ocean. Houdini remained open-minded, curious to the experience, hoping, he later recalled in *A Magician Among the Spirts*, "that I might feel once more the presence of my beloved Mother."

As the séance began, Lady Conan Doyle went into a trancelike state and her writing hand began immediately to transcribe the spirit's words. Houdini remembered how quickly his anticipation turned to regret as he didn't even feel a "semblance" of his mother's spirit. But Lady Conan Doyle continued on, transcribing a long letter that ended with a declaration about the importance of her husband's work. "God bless you . . . for what you are doing for us—for us, over here," Jean wrote. It was all a bit too much for Houdini, for he could easily see the pretense of the whole affair. But it was something more apparent that troubled him with the performance of automatic writing. His immigrant mother, while having lived in the United States for nearly fifty years, could neither speak nor write in English. When Houdini related this fact after the séance and the curtains were opened, Conan Doyle didn't hesitate in his response. The spirits, he said, become "more educated" the longer they are on the other side, and clearly Houdini's mother had mastered English after death.[11]

The entire experience would be the final and fatal rift between the two men. In the coming months Houdini would become more vocal in the press about his criticism of Conan Doyle and his skepticism of spiritualism. In dismissing ghostly presence, what spiritualists called manifestations and what the press called spooks, Houdini declared: "As to 'manifestations,' I have been present at thousands of seances, and my eyes—the eyes of a trained and practical magician—saw the workings of many mediums, and I knew that the 'manifestations' absolutely were caused by natural means. The average observer would not see these things. He would believe the faulty evidence of his senses."[12]

THERE IS NO indication that investigators took Conan Doyle's advice and sought assistance from a medium to solve the lingering questions around Peters's murder. But, as luck would have it, Frederick Weeks and Sheriff Werner found themselves at the Hotel McAlpin just a day before the banquet of the Society of American Magicians. The two men came to interrogate a mysterious figure who emerged from the city's underworld claiming to know what had really happened on the night of Peters's murder.

The Rat

It was nearly seven in the evening as Frederick Weeks and Sheriff Werner walked north toward Herald Square on their way to the Hotel McAlpin. The noise of the elevated trains rattled above them and crowds navigated the streets around the square, the frenetic energy of cars, delivery trucks, and the occasional trolley chirping down Broadway.

At twenty-six stories tall with 1,500 guest rooms, the McAlpin was the largest hotel in the world and one of the most luxurious in the city. Standing on the corner of Broadway and West Thirty-Fourth Street, it dwarfed the surrounding buildings, casting a heavy shadow over the Sixth Avenue El as trains sped north and south. Guests could choose between the ornate Louis XIV dining room or the more intimate terra-cotta Spanish-style grill. There was a whole floor for night workers that was kept quiet during the daytime, three distinct men's baths—Turkish, Russian, and hydrotherapeutic—a large pool and gymnasium, a fifteen-chair barbershop, and a wing of shops specializing in women's clothing on the women-only floor, which catered to a guest who would prefer "all her neighbors were women and that her every wish will be the duty and pleasure of other women." There were two circulating libraries, one for new fiction and one for business, and a complete hospital and surgical ward. The hotel also had its very own orchestra, often performing at the grand ballroom on the top floor of the hotel with dramatic views of the city.[1]

As the men entered the hotel lobby, bright and marbled and bustling, Weeks told the Pinkerton detective who had accompanied them to stay near the entrance and keep watch for people coming and going. They then took the elevator to the twelfth floor and walked down the narrow hallway to room 1292. There they met with two reporters from the *New York American*, the hotel detective A. C. Dennison, his assistant William Dorsey, and a lanky man with curly dark hair, brilliant blue eyes, and a thick mustache named James Cunningham, though many knew him by his nickname: Jimmy the Rat.[2]

TWO DAYS EARLIER, the *New York American* published a shocking article in which Cunningham claimed Peters was not in fact murdered on King Street, but rather was shot at the Ward's home in Sutton Manor and later dropped along the road by Ward. Using the pseudonym Martin O'Hare, Cunningham wrote a letter to the newspaper detailing the crime and claimed that James Cunningham was in fact the key to solving Peters's murder. It was a strange, imaginative, and boastful performance, motivated, it seems, by the reward money the newspaper dangled in front of readers for information about Peters.

"I notice to-day that you have offered a reward in the connection with the 'Ward Case,'" the letter began, and then detailed how the crime involved racetrack betting and a certain gang of confidence men who preyed on wealthy men. Walter Ward, Cunningham claimed, was involved with this gang but, he clarified, not as a target. "Ward's connection with that gang mystified him," he wrote, referring to himself in the third person, as Ward "was well to do and yet seemed to be in the confidence of the crooks and didn't seem to be used for a sucker."

According to Cunningham, Ward was concocting a scheme of his own, in which he was working with the blackmailers to secure thousands of dollars from his father, which he would split with the gang. The blackmail was not in fact directed at Walter but rather at George Ward. It was George's money the blackmailers were going after. This would explain Walter's cablegrams to his father as George was sailing back on the RMS *Majestic* and his father's stern rejection of any payments to blackmailers. Cunningham, working with three other blackmailers, set a trap for Walter at his Sutton Manor home on the night of May 15—a trap that would implicate young Ward and give George evidence of his son's scheme.

Peters, along with another man Cunningham named as Charles Rodgers, met with Ward to discuss his plan just before midnight and well past the card game that Beryl had hosted that evening among neighbors. Another accomplice named Joe Jackson was to enter the house through the basement with a lawyer who worked for George Ward. The men were to quietly climb the steps to the first floor and linger near the library door, eavesdropping on the conversation and revealing Walter Ward's scheme.

What Jackson didn't expect was to encounter Fifi Ziegler, the Wards' temporary maid, who happened upon Jackson in the dark hallway, startling her into a frenzied panic. She burst into the library shouting, "Burglars! Burglars!" Seeing the men outside the library door, Ward jumped to his feet, pulled out his pistol, and fired several shots. One shot hit Peters in the chest, and two shots wounded Joe Jackson in the shoulder and the forehead, though both he and Rodgers managed to flee to their car and drive away. Cunningham claimed the men came to his apartment in the Bronx and told him the story before driving the wounded Jackson to Stamford, Connecticut, to a doctor Cunningham knew who could treat him. Cunningham also claimed that two New Rochelle policemen, who were on patrol that evening, arrived at the Wards' house not long after the shooting. Ward dismissed them both, claiming the "police commissioner will handle the situation."[3]

Cunningham's story prompted scandalous headlines and caused "a sensation in Westchester," as some reports described it. Weeks maintained his calm demeanor when he addressed reporters the morning the story broke: "I don't know what to make of this, but the whole thing will be run right down."[4] Werner sent police and detectives to the Wards' house along with Assistant District Attorney Frank Ferris just hours after the morning edition of the *New York American* arrived on the newsstands. Frank Cody, the police chief of New Rochelle, also sent his men to Sutton Manor, creating what must have felt to the neighbors like an all-out police raid that morning, with several police cars descending on Decatur Road, and a stream of officers, detectives, and lawyers pushing through the crowd of reporters and climbing the stone steps to the front door.

Walter left earlier that morning for his office at the Bronx factory, so Beryl greeted the men with her usual smile. She had no objections to the men searching her home, though she did call Allan Campbell, Ward's attorney, who arrived about twenty minutes later, red-faced and angry. By then the house was overrun with men searching every room, armed with "electric flashlights" and magnifying glasses to explore the "darker places of the home," as one report noted. A breathless Campbell complained to Ferris that the search was without a warrant and demanded it all to cease at once. Ferris ignored his objections and reminded Campbell that the men were invited into the house by Beryl and there was nothing he could do to stop it.

"Search warrant or not, I'm here under orders from District Attorney Weeks and I'm going to search the house," he told Campbell. In frustration, Campbell tore a small piece of paper from his notebook and wrote his protest on it, calling the act "unwarranted and illegal," and signed his name. It was a weak gesture with little legal weight. As the police continued their search, Campbell went to the terrace on the side of the house, its stone arches framing a view of Echo Bay, and spent the next few hours pacing back and forth and, as reporters observed, "puffing furiously on his pipe."[5]

It had been two weeks since Peters's murder, and this was the first time authorities had examined the Ward's home for clues about that night. "Tardy" was how some reporters described the feverish searches then underway. From the street, reporters watched as men moved through upper-floor rooms, shadowy figures behind the windows, occasionally emerging on vine-clad balconies. The search was said to be thorough; every "nook and cranny" from the cobwebs in the basement to the third-floor closets filled with "winter underwear and what not" were examined.

Much of their attention was focused on the library, pulling out the books from the recessed shelves; "encyclopedias were heaped and unheaped," reports noted. They examined the moldings and wood paneling with magnifying glasses, looking for any trace of scratches or nicks or signs of repair. They pulled back rugs in the library, in the circular foyer, and on the grand staircase that branched in two directions, one side going east, one going west. They found no bloodstains on the carpets or the floorboards. No signs of stains at all. "There were no chips of splintered wood or pools of deep red on the Ward library carpet," one report declared. Though of course the rugs could have been replaced. Damaged wooden paneling could have been repaired with a precision that made it look as good as new.

At one point, Ferris and a detective appeared on the front porch of the house and descended the stairs. Reporters clustered along the curbside, thinking they were going to take questions. Instead, the two ignored reporters and walked across the road to 78 Decatur Road, an Italianate-style house with a red-tiled roof and white stucco walls, where Waldo and Ruby Shuman lived. The Shumans were good friends of the Wards'. Beryl Ward had called them the night Walter was writhing in pain on the library floor from his overdose of iodine, and Ruby came right over even before the doctor arrived. Waldo had made complaints to the police about the annoying reporters asking questions, knocking on doors, trampling through the gardens looking for servants to get information on the Wards. Their ten-year-old daughter, Laura, had in fact taken the bait of a reporter who offered her a bit of money in exchange for a few photographs of the Wards. Ruby intervened just in time. The whole incident prompted the Shumans to demand the police clear the entire Manor of the press with little success.[6]

That morning, with police cars and detectives descending upon the Wards' house, it would have been yet another frustrating day of traffic and meddlesome reporters milling around Decatur Road. Waldo Shuman, a stockbroker on Wall Street, had left early that morning. When Ferris knocked on the Shumans' door, Ruby answered and invited the men in, closing the blinds to keep out the reporters' cameras. She told the men she hadn't heard any shots from the Wards' house that night. She had been there most of the evening, playing cards with the neighbors, she said. Given her long friendship with the Wards, one can imagine she gave the detective and the assistant district attorney a direct and curt complaint about pursuing such crazy leads that appeared in the morning news, listening to such men who were nicknamed Jimmy the Rat, and further upsetting dear Beryl over such wild accusations. How could the police even imagine a murder occurring right there on Decatur Road in Sutton Manor? After about five minutes, Ferris and the detective left the Shumans' home and walked back across the road, each somber faced while dodging the many reporter questions thrown at them.

By lunchtime, Ferris called the search off. The policemen and detectives left with nothing to confirm Cunningham's story nor any new clue in their investigation. "Not a bit of evidence in the house. We looked the place over from top to bottom," one New Rochelle policeman told reporters, and then offered a slightly odd compliment about Beryl Ward's housekeeping: "Everything was as clean as a shoe."

Sheriff Werner was more tentative with his comments to reporters. "We found nothing that would substantiate the story published in the New York newspaper," he said. "Our report will be made to the District Attorney and we have orders to say nothing." When asked if he had concluded Peters was not in fact killed at the Wards' home, the sheriff turned blunt: "I did not say that. I said that we found nothing to substantiate the story."

This sentiment was echoed by Frank Cody, who also told reporters, "I do not believe there is any substance to the story," as if reading from a script. Cody wondered about the *New York American*'s eagerness to publish a story that, in his mind, was dubious at best. When asked if he believed the story was "authentic," he declined to say but did declare with a tone of hyperbole: "I will stake my place that neither Peters nor anybody else was killed or shot in the Ward home on the night of May 15–16." Cody obtained signed statements from every policeman on patrol near Sutton Manor the night Peters was killed, and each confirmed they had heard nothing unusual from the Wards' house. "I am standing implicitly on their combined statements," he said. "I know my men." We can imagine, however, that few were surprised by the police chief's statement, or the fact that "his men" would deny that a murder happened in the house of the New Rochelle police commissioner.[7]

In White Plains, Weeks reminded reporters he was actively pursuing the investigation and reassured the public about his office's efforts. "All along I have had a lot of leads that I couldn't tell the public about," he said. "Everything we get we investigate even though some of it is a waste of time."[8] He didn't indicate that the search of the Wards' home or Cunningham's story were a waste of time, but the implication was there. While Weeks might have made this claim publicly, privately, he and Werner made plans to meet Cunningham in New York the next day.

That afternoon, Beryl Ward was cutting flowers from her garden with her Boston terrier, Bebe, at her feet. Reporters tried to engage her about the search of the home and Cunningham's story about the murder. "I really have nothing to say now," she said, holding large pruning shears in her hand. "Probably," she added, "I shall never have anything to say about the matter. So far as I am concerned it is done with." Reporters noted that she was affable, and she appeared "entirely untroubled."[9]

THE TALL WINDOWS of room 1292 at the McAlpin looked out onto the darkening city sky over Herald Square. One window was propped open to let in some air. Cunningham sat in a high-back desk chair, his narrow shoulders stooped forward, his small red bow tie slightly askew. As the men questioned him, street noise seeped into the room, car horns, the rattle of subway trains, and the muffled sounds of passing conversations that floated from the sidewalks. Cunningham was combative at times and other times despondent. At one point he jumped up from his chair and bolted to the window, ripping up a few papers he held in his hand and throwing the pieces out into the night air. Those on the street had no idea that the confetti falling from the sky might have been connected to the famous murder case they read about in the morning headlines.[10]

Cunningham repeated to Weeks much of what he'd written in his letter to the *New York American.* How he was for years a private detective hired to investigate blackmail schemes at the racetracks. "The kingpin of the blackmailers has a motto," he said. "'You can always get a man through a woman!'" adding that the blackmailers used "women of country-wide repute—many of them well-known stars of the stage and screen." Sensing a certain doubt among the men in the room, Cunningham continued: "They may call me a liar. But I tell you that this blackmail ring comprised wise turf operators, beautiful women, and men of such prominence that they shrank from the slightest breath of scandal."

He said he had worked for a Canadian racehorse owner, a Commander Ross, who employed Cunningham as his personal assistant and investigator. He also claimed to have worked for the famous Jockey Club in Manhattan, instructed to "clean up scandals that happened in connection with actual running of races." His job was to "clean up the Turf," he said. He eventually ran afoul of Arnold Rothstein, the notorious gambler and bootlegger, however, and was fired from the Jockey Club.

Cunningham spoke with a certain authority, a certain believability that no doubt made him a good undercover investigator, a man able to navigate the underworld with the skills of an actor. In fact, his résumé included work in the theater—a "specialist in theatrical lines" is how he defined it—and as a press agent for an upstate New York theater. He also worked as a private investigator for the Thiel Detective Service Company in 1918, and for a brief time he worked for Val O'Farrell, though publicly O'Farrell denied he'd ever employed him. His story is "undiluted goulash," snapped O'Farrell when reporters inquired about Cunningham's claims.

It was during his work at ferreting out extortion schemes among racetrack habitués that Cunningham met Walter Ward, whom he described as a "gay young fellow like many of his wealth and position." Ward was well-known for his "wise money." As he said this, Cunningham paused for a moment before adding, "Know what I mean?" his right eyebrow raised slightly. The term was a reference to those who made large bets that always win. This piqued Cunningham's interests, for a man who consistently wins could either be incredibly lucky or incredibly shady. It was known that Ward employed a clocker, a man well-versed in racehorses who traveled across the East Coast and South documenting race times on particular horses and reporting back to Ward. There was a good deal of money spent on securing a sure bet.[11]

Cunningham claimed Ward was part of a racetrack gang, and he and his father, George, helped such gangs "to get other men," luring them with champagne and beautiful women. The more Cunningham investigated Walter Ward, he said, the more "powerful obstacles" were thrown in his way.

"I had accomplished results—wonderful results," he said, "but I was getting dangerous. I was actually threatening the stability of racing by threatening the graft of the men who fixed races and used their beautiful decoy women at night to trap men." Eventually he was barred from the racetracks, and his private detective license was revoked.

"To shorten a long yarn," Cunningham sighed, "my license as a private detective was taken away. I was notified that I had better make myself scarce about the race tracks." This blacklisting made it impossible for him to work. Then he heard of Charles Rodgers's scheme to blackmail George Ward.

AFTER ABOUT TWO hours of listening to Cunningham's many stories about his experiences of underworld criminals and racetrack crimes, detailing with confidence a number of meandering tales involving the well known and the lesser known of the crime world, Weeks had heard enough. He directed his detectives to detain Cunningham as a material witness and bring him to White Plains where he was held on a $5,000 bond in the county jail.

"Cunningham has some information," he told reporters. "Whether he gained it at first hand or has overheard underworld gossip which he has elaborated and sought to capitalize for his own benefit is not yet clear. He will be held at least until it is clear."[12]

It was an unexpected move given the fact that Cunningham's story seemed to have produced little evidence of its veracity. Weeks's statement to the press suggested that even if some of Cunningham's statements proved false, there might be a kernel of truth in the underworld gossip. Reporters, however, would have noticed that there was nothing in Cunningham's story that indicated how young Peters was involved in the alleged scheme. How was it he had found himself sitting there in Ward's library, just hours after arriving from South Carolina? And how, after nearly three weeks since leaving Boston for the marine training base and only having a few cents in his pocket, was he the number two man in what appeared to be a complicated blackmailing plot?

It was likely Weeks felt obligated to arrest Cunningham as some public display of action, a show that the investigation was proceeding at a good pace, even if nothing new had yet emerged to disprove Ward's statement. Editorials continued to criticize Weeks's investigation and question the competence of those involved. The *New-York Tribune* noted that while no evidence was found in the search of the Wards' home, authorities had "contented themselves with looking for proof of the newspaper yarn," and reminded readers that "no members of Ward's family and none of his servants were questioned. Nor have they been questioned since he told his remarkable story of the killing." The editors concluded with a stinging jab at Weeks and Werner, one of many lodged against the men by the press. "Seldom in the history of criminal practice in this country have officials been so inert," adding, "the citizens of Westchester county are more and more asking why."[13]

AT THE COUNTY jail, Cunningham sulked on his "steel bunk in an atmosphere heavy with disinfectants and fried food," as one reporter described the scene. He hadn't expected to be arrested. In fact he told the editors of the *New York American* before his meeting with Weeks, "I know everything, but I'll know nothing when authorities put me behind bars." He made good on this threat, as he refused to cooperate with detectives in verifying details of his story. "They locked me up," he complained. "Now let them run around and find out what they can get without my help, because apparently it isn't appreciated." While he may have been lacking credibility for his story of the crime, he did not lack self-importance. "You can't get anywhere without me," he boasted. "As long as you keep me locked up in here, you'll run around in circles. Let me out and I'll prove everything I've said."[14]

His mother came to White Plains along with a lawyer she'd hired to seek his release. Ruth Cunningham took a room at the small hotel across from the courthouse. She told authorities that her son had nothing to do with Peters's murder and certainly would not have been involved with such a gang. He was "romancing," she told reporters in describing the nature of her son's fantastical claims about the crime. Her lawyer, Maurice McCarthy, was more direct, calling the story "ridiculous," and expressed a desire to seek Cunningham's release as soon as Weeks was through questioning him.

For Cunningham, being detained in jail felt like a betrayal by the editors of the *New York American*. He said he was "bitter" toward the paper and claimed he wrote the letter as "bait" to get the editor's attention. When he met with them, he thought it best to give only a few details, imagining they would pay him some of the reward money for more specific information. In the letter he signed as Martin O'Hare, there was a postscript describing how many of the details in the letter were simply "hearsay"—that's the word he used with detectives—and were meant to prompt reporters to investigate before they published the letter. He complained that the press was the cause of his predicament, that they were "hungry for a story" and rushed the letter to print, pushing Cunningham into the spotlight and eventually into a jail cell in White Plains.

We might understand his defense as that of a man who was used to seeing others as the cause of his plight. Or rather, a man who found ways of distorting reality in his favor, to play along the imaginative lines between facts and fictions, allowing him to create a version of himself that was flexible and changing.[15]

Imaginative was often how people described Cunningham. One informant said he had a very "imaginative brain," while Val O'Farrell, outraged by Cunningham's story, described him as "a paranoiac with creative criminal imagination," and then flatly claimed he was an "unmitigated liar."[16] A doctor hired by the *New York American* called him the "most remarkable psychological character that has ever bubbled to the surface in a great criminal mystery" and added that he was a shrewd, cunning, and crafty trickster of the underworld.[17]

In White Plains, while detectives found Cunningham uncooperative, they also described him as engaging and talkative about his life in the underworld. One detective noted that he would make a good "scenario writer" for the theater and felt Cunningham concocted the whole story about the shooting at the Wards' home from details found in newspaper articles. But, he added in his report, his statement would be "thoroughly investigated."[18]

IN THE DAYS that followed, Sheriff Werner took officers to Stamford, Connecticut, to investigate claims that a Joe Jackson had been wounded in the Ward house and driven to a doctor there for care. He rounded up taxi drivers who might have assisted in this effort. None could recall any injured man on the morning of May 16. Cunningham named Daniel Hanrahan as the Stamford doctor who treated Jackson. There was in fact a Dr. Hanrahan in Stamford, but he was surprised to see his name in the news.

"I am much at sea as to why my name was mentioned," the doctor told reporters. He said he had never met Cunningham nor treated a man named Jackson, nor did he know Walter Ward. "I have not treated a man for wounds or any other injuries in May or any other month," he said, standing on his porch speaking with a certain controlled anger. "That story is utterly false and I am willing to have the house searched to prove the truth of what I say."[19] Like their search of the Wards' home, the Stamford inquiries were a wild chase that amounted to nothing.

Pinkerton operatives investigated Cunningham's background, uncovering what one might have expected: a mysterious and shadowy past. Detective Dorsey at the McAlpin described him as a "hotel beat," as Cunningham had a pile of unpaid hotel bills that stretched across several cities. Onondaga Hotel in Syracuse, Emerson Hotel in Baltimore, United States Hotel in Saratoga, and in New York City, the Hotels

Breslin, Pennsylvania, and Commodore each declared Cunningham owed them money, leaving some to wonder if the man ever paid for a hotel room or simply slipped out the side door in the early-morning hours.

In his year with the Thiel Detective Service Company, Cunningham worked as a shadower, casing clients for background information for the detectives. Near the end of 1919 he was fired from the agency for what the director phrased as a "general indifference to work." A former colleague at the agency remembered Cunningham as having an "imaginative mind" but also as a man as "slippery and clever as they make them," who "operated without honor or regard to how, when, or where the axe would fall." If Cunningham lacked a story about a particular client he was working on, he would "make one up." He described how Cunningham was capable of anything and "was always out for a dollar wherever he could get it." Though strangely he did confess that if Jimmy the Rat was involved in the Ward case, he was probably the "mastermind" behind the entire crime. What emerged was a contradictory picture of a man who was both brilliant and cunning but seemingly lacking in ambition. It was becoming clearer to investigators that whatever information Jimmy the Rat had about the murder of Clarence Peters, it was most likely wrapped in a layer of lies.

WALTER WARD ARRIVED at the White Plains jail with his lawyer Allan Campbell to identify Cunningham. The two men met in the jail reception room.

"Hello, Ward! How are you?" Cunningham shouted as he saw Ward coming through the door. Campbell followed his client into the room and stood with Sheriff Werner. The room had a yellowish late-afternoon light, casting long shadows on the walls.

"What do you mean? I never met you before in my life," Ward snapped, visibly annoyed with the casualness of Cunningham's greeting.

Cunningham lit a cigarette, his long, thin body relaxed as he stayed seated. "Oh, yes, you did too, and you know it," he replied. "You just don't know me with this mustache." Cunningham winked his left eye and brushed his mustache with his hand as he smirked to Ward.

"I don't know this man," Ward retorted as he turned on his heel to face Campbell. "Come on, let's get out of here." The two men left through the jail entrance and out to a waiting car.

Rumors around the courthouse had circulated, and a crowd of people had gathered near Ward's car, smiling and waving as he exited the jail. Among the crowd was a group of excited boys and girls who pressed close to the car's running board at it slowly moved along, some of the kids shouting with apparent affection for the confessed murderer, "Oh you Wardie!" as he drove away.[20]

Cunningham's lawyer, Maurice McCarthy, had not been notified about the meeting between his client and Walter Ward. In talking with reporters, he made his anger over being kept in the dark about the entire encounter clear.

"Ward," he said, "confessed to a crime and was originally held on $10,000 bail. My client confesses to nothing at all, is charged with nothing at all, and is held on $5,000, proportionately to his financial standing a much greater security."[21] It was an irony that was hard to miss. The confessed killer freely walked in and out of the county jail, but an alleged material witness to the crime remained behind bars.

McCarthy filed a writ of habeas corpus to get Cunningham released. "My client was willing to co-operate to clear up this alleged blackmail plot," he told Judge Seeger, the same judge that issued Ward's bail. McCarthy argued that Cunningham was simply a witness to the blackmail plot and was not involved in the shooting of Peters. "There is not a scintilla of evidence upon which to hold my client," McCarthy continued, "only an affidavit that states Cunningham is essential to a solution of the case."

Weeks argued that Cunningham wished to stay in jail, that he even "preferred jail" to being out, a phrasing that suggested Cunningham was under some threat by men on the outside. Judge Seeger eventually sided with McCarthy. Weeks agreed on a lesser bail of $2,500, which Cunningham paid on bond.[22]

Despite the many questions surrounding Cunningham's character, the mounting claims that he could not be trusted, and the growing sense that his story of Peters's killing was pure fiction, Weeks devised a plan to keep him under surveillance, hoping perhaps that he would still be useful. Cunningham was a "great value to the prosecution," Weeks argued in court. It was a claim the DA was standing by both publicly and privately, despite the skepticism of the Pinkerton detectives. Weeks's continued focus on Cunningham suggested he had few other leads in the case.[23]

THE HOTEL BELMORE was a small and shabby establishment on the corner of East Twenty-Fifth Street and Lexington Avenue, with rooms starting at eight dollars a night. "Phone and electric fan in every room," their small ads in *The New York Times* announced. Detectives with the Browne-Rykert Detective Services rented room 405 for Cunningham and 406 for themselves. Cunningham convinced authorities that once word of his release made news, Jackson, whom he was friendly with, would seek him out at that particular hotel, where he knew Cunningham would often stay, registering with the alias Collins.

Unbeknownst to Cunningham, detectives had rigged a Dictograph in room 405 so they could listen in on any conversations Cunningham might have. A detective sat with Cunningham in his room, a second detective sat in the adjoining room, listening and taking notes, while a third detective watched the comings and goings at the Hotel Belmore entrance from a room in the Hotel Amsterdam across the street. It had all the resources and manpower of a serious surveillance, as if the authorities, and the agency operatives, were convinced that Jimmy the Rat was going to produce a break in the case.

But reading the detective notes it was clear that Cunningham was stringing the men along. One afternoon, Cunningham asked the detective to go out and "purchase some refreshments." Upon the detective's return, Cunningham appeared excited and said that a representative of Jackson's had called while the detective was out, though he had little information to offer. It was quite possible, Cunningham told the detective, that Jackson and Rodgers had him under their own surveillance to determine if he was trying to "double-cross" them—that's the term he used. What Cunningham didn't know is that the detective in the adjoining room listening on the Dictograph knew there was in fact no phone call at all.

It continued in this way for weeks. At one point, detectives described how Cunningham's "sweetheart," named only as Miss Morris, arrived at the hotel. Cunningham asked detectives to go out and get some refreshments for them, and then asked them both to leave the hotel for the evening as he wished to spend the night with the woman. The detectives refused.

In another incident, Cunningham disappeared, and when detectives called to Miss Morris's apartment, she told them he'd left early in the morning but should be back soon, and that they should call back around one o'clock. When they called again in the afternoon, she explained that Cunningham had received an early-morning phone call requesting that he meet agents of Jackson's at the Hotel Adelphia in Philadelphia. Infuriated, detectives demanded Cunningham call them to set up a meeting with Weeks and Werner upon his return.

In Rye, New York, at Werner's house, Cunningham was interrogated by Weeks and the sheriff. He related details about this trip to Philadelphia, how he waited in the lobby of the Hotel Adelphia but no one arrived to meet him. He suggested the entire trip was an effort to "look him over" and, yet again, to make sure Jimmy the Rat was not double-crossing them. When Weeks asked how he had paid for the train tickets, Cunningham explained that his brother had given him the money "last night." Weeks pressed on, wondering how his brother would have given him money for a ticket to Philadelphia the night before he received the phone call requesting him to travel to Philadelphia. Cunningham, pausing to consider the conundrum and finish his cigarette, revised his story and claimed it was in fact a housemate by the name of McNally who had actually loaned him the money that morning.

"I'm disgusted with you!" Weeks exclaimed in a rare moment of rage. He admonished him and told him he was now skeptical that any part of his story was in fact true, and that if he didn't "get down to business," he would put him in jail again. Cunningham appeared unmoved by the DA's irritation. He sat in the middle of the sofa and lit another cigarette.

In contrast to Weeks's clear exasperation, Sheriff Werner still had faith in Cunningham, still felt he could provide useful information. But the sheriff wasn't always the best judge of witnesses.

AMONG THE DETECTIVES, Cunningham's story was understood as more distraction than solution. The *New-York Tribune* reported that skepticism of Cunningham's claims led detectives to believe he was a "plant." One underworld informant told detectives that there was so much "double crossing with rats like Cunningham" he wouldn't be surprised if it wasn't O'Farrell who concocted the entire story of the shooting at the Wards' home, and the fictious characters of Rodgers and Jackson, just "to throw the authorities off the track." It was a shocking charge, suggesting that the famous private detective was attempting to distract investigators from the real motive for Peters's murder. It also added more speculation that O'Farrell was now working for the Wards, helping direct the inquiry into seemingly useless directions. It's difficult to say what hand if any O'Farrell had in Cunningham's appearance in the case. As the 1914 indictment of Thomas Osborne showed, O'Farrell was not against deliberate distractions for his clients. And Jimmy the Rat's story did keep rumors of Ward's racetrack gambling in the headlines for weeks.

"We do not expect to find the solution of the case at the racetracks," one investigator told reporters.[24] That did not dissuade continued inquiries into Ward's gambling debts as a source of blackmail and Peters's murder. Ward's attorneys had suggested that from the start.

Weeks was increasingly left with fewer and fewer leads as he continued to subpoena witnesses for the grand jury. He often compared the investigation to a knotted fishing line: the difficultly of untangling each knot inevitably led to more knots. As the summer solstice neared, a different metaphor would become a better description for his investigation: a fishing expedition.

The Devil's Dance

A HEAT WAVE TOOK HOLD OF THE NEW YORK AREA IN EARLY June. Temperatures neared ninety degrees, and hospitals filled with people suffering from heat exhaustion. On Saturday, June 10, Governor Nathan Miller, on a tour of the state with an eye to his reelection in November, nearly fainted at an event on Long Island. Presiding over the unveiling of a monument for local Civil War heroes, Miller was about ten minutes into his speech when, standing at the podium in the late-morning sun, he turned pale and a feeling of nausea took hold. After a brief rest and a glass of water, he returned to the podium hoping to finish his speech but only a few minutes later had to end abruptly and leave the event.[1]

While still recovering from the incident, the Republican governor made a detour on his way back to the state capital to White Plains for a meeting with William Ward, the long-serving and powerful Westchester County Republican Party "boss," as the press called him. Nothing in the Westchester County Republican Party happened unless William Ward approved it. Ward was of no relation to Walter Ward, but it was well-known that he had a hand in Walter Ward's appointment as a police commissioner in New Rochelle, perhaps even seeing a bigger political career for the handsome and ambitious commissioner.

Miller won by a narrow margin in 1920 against the populist Democrat Al Smith, who easily carried the five boroughs of the city while

Miller was more popular upstate. A staunch conservative, Miller spent years as a corporate lawyer, helping Andrew Carnegie create his large corporate empire through mergers and trusts. As governor, Miller was a strident supporter of Prohibition. In his first months in office, he signed the Mullan-Gage Act, which put in place some of the most restrictive Prohibition laws in the country. The act gave police unrestricted power to search for alcohol wherever they suspected it, including random searches of citizens on the streets. It also allowed for private citizens to bring charges against their neighbors for the possession of alcohol. Within weeks, the police arrested tens of thousands of New Yorkers, creating chaos in the courts and siphoning the police from other efforts. Whatever popularity he'd had back in 1920 was gone by the summer of 1922. In the upcoming election, he would once again face Al Smith, but this time he wouldn't have the momentum of Warren G. Harding and the national Republican ticket behind him. And, more troubling, he wouldn't be free of the increasing scandal over how Republicans were handling the investigation.[2]

So Miller's detour on that hot and humid Saturday made sense. The meeting between the governor and the party boss included a "White Plains official," though who exactly was veiled in secrecy. It was well-known that William Ward was "violently opposed to any move to bring about any interference from Albany into the Westchester conduct of the Ward case," according to the New York *Daily News.* The concern was not so much of the governor meddling into local affairs, but rather how it might play into ongoing criticism. "The vigorous Democratic minority," the *Daily News* continued, "has already been handed too many rounds of political ammunition for the next local campaigns by the press criticism of Weeks, Werner, and the lethargic prosecution of Ward in White Plains." Of course, for his part, Governor Miller may have seen an opportunity to save his drowning support by demonstrating his concern for justice in the state. He was keeping an open mind about intervening, telling reporters, "I may investigate the whole business."[3]

Many were urging Miller to do just that. Maurice McCarthy, James

Cunningham's lawyer, sent a telegram to the governor encouraging him to consider taking over the investigation. "Any information in my possession relative to the Ward Case is at your disposal," McCarthy wrote, adding, "Will give you fullest cooperation in solving this alleged blackmail plot."[4]

McCarthy wasn't the only one asking for the governor to step in. A damning editorial in *The Evening World* condemned "the whole conduct of the case" as "inexplicable" and "absolutely incomprehensible." It pointed directly at Weeks, criticizing his actions as "far less than his duty," and warning that such "non-feasance weakens trust in the administration of the law." It concluded by appealing to Governor Miller, who the editors believed was "duty bound to look into the matter and supersede the lackadaisical officials with prosecutors who will get action."[5]

Privately, the *Daily News* city editor Phil Payne wrote a sharp letter to Miller nearly demanding he intervene in the investigation. "There seems to be little doubt that a policy of obstruction has been followed by the authorities at White Plains," Payne wrote, detailing failures in the investigation. "There is an honest belief that justice is being perverted in this case," he concluded. Miller replied a few days later. "The Governor cannot personally look after the various criminal investigations in the different counties of the state," he wrote, and argued that any intervention by the governor could only happen on "clear grounds plainly established," which Miller claimed had not "been presented to me in the Ward case." While Miller may have been leaving open the possibility for intervening publicly, privately he had little interest in getting entangled in the case.[6]

Members of the Westchester County Republican Committee, which included Weeks and Werner, discussed the continuing uncertainties of the case. The committee was soon to devise their ballot of candidates for the November elections and didn't want this case to linger in the press for much longer. Many on the committee wished for a quick indictment and trial, all wrapped up by the end of summer, clearing up the entire case by September and taking it out of the headlines. The plan depended on Weeks, and it seemed that the DA, who was a loyal Republican Party member, was increasingly upsetting the party bosses.

FORECASTERS HAD PREDICTED the heat wave would finally break on Sunday. As thousands of people gathered along the Hudson River and Long Island Sound to find some relief from the heat and humidity, the western skies turned from gray to nearly black. Witnesses described the storm as a "big black cloud that swirled and dipped toward the earth." Others said the approaching storm clouds resembled the "funnel shape of the western wind clouds."[7] Across the region, the storm came on suddenly and moved with quick and furious speed. It cut a path of destruction across Westchester County and parts of New York City.

At Clason Point Park, a working-class amusement resort near the East River in the Bronx, the storm brought down a large Ferris wheel, killing seven and injuring thirty. Along the coast of City Island, a fat finger of land that stretches into Long Island Sound south of New Rochelle, small rented boats and canoes were caught up in the gale, many capsizing, others taken far from shore. The island looked like a "war-wrecked city" *The New York Times* observed. Frantic parents were "besieging the police station with requests for information concerning their missing children." Many were asking why there weren't more rescue boats on scene as soon as the storm passed.

The storm's fury was over in a matter of fifteen minutes. "The city and its residents were entirely unprepared for what is believed to be the worst storm that the city has ever experienced," one newspaper declared. In the following days, reports put the death toll somewhere between fifty and seventy-five, with hundreds more injured or missing and believed drowned. Authorities initially characterized the storm as a severe summer squall with winds in excess of eighty-five miles an hour. They later described it as a series of small tornadoes that created a path of destruction about three hundred miles wide. "The devil's dance of little tornadoes" is how one newspaper described it.[8]

While the courthouse in White Plains suffered little damage from the storms, the term *devil's dance* could have easily described the activities going on inside the building. Weeks was reportedly feeling confident that an indictment would be handed down within a few days.

Since early June, nearly twenty individuals had testified, from neighbors and colleagues of the Wards' to authorities involved in the investigation. It was the testimonies of those closest to Ward that would be important and the most difficut to secure. The Wards' Finnish cook, Amy Mild, was asked about the Wards' reactions to press accounts about the killing. Lulu Barrows, the Wards' nanny, was also questioned, though she was not in the home the night of the murder. She had been on vacation at the end of May. Or at least that was how her absence was explained by the Wards.

It was instead Fifi Ziegler who was in the house that night. Reporters referred to her as either French, Swiss, or Alsatian. Her identity was hazy, as was her employment with the Wards. Ziegler was hard to find. Detectives tracked her down working for a family on Long Island. According to reports, she was let go just a few days after Ward's confession was made public. Some questioned the timing of her leaving. Ziegler told the New York *Daily News* before her testimony that "maybe I heard something about the affair at breakfast the morning after it occurred," adding, "but I don't remember anything definite." On the stand, she did remember at least one thing. She claimed that after the morning of the murder she overheard Walter Ward say, "I couldn't do anything else." It was a mysterious sentence dangling there in the grand jury room without much context. She claimed she heard nothing else between the Wards and could not confirm what time Walter came home that morning.[9]

Palmer Tubbs, Walter Ward's assistant at the Bronx factory and fellow police commissioner, corroborated Ward's story about the two blackmailers, Charlie Ross and Jack. He told jurors that two men with those names had called and visited Ward at his office the previous March, just about the time Ward claimed the blackmail scheme began. Ross and Jack had two meetings with Ward at his office. Tubbs described the physical traits of the men and at one point was questioned about the nationality of Ross.

"I never heard him speak except once," he replied. "He spoke good English. I wouldn't say he was a foreigner."

Tubbs did say that when the men met with Walter they were "all smiles." He recalled how Walter gave him a ride home to New Rochelle on the evening of May 15 and that when he left Walter at 6:00 p.m. near his home he seemed fine. His testimony would produce a huge gap between the time Ward dropped Tubbs off that evening and the time he returned to Sutton Manor in the early-morning hours the following day.[10]

For members of the Ward family, it wasn't their testimony that made headlines so much as the many ways they avoided any questions from the district attorney. Beryl Ward drove herself to the Westchester County Courthouse just a few days before the heat wave took hold. As a light rain fell, she ascended the courthouse steps wearing a gray cape edged in chinchilla and a gray sport hat with pheasant plumes.

Once inside, she dodged reporters and climbed two flights of stairs rather than wait at the bank of elevators where she would be an easy target for photographers. She sat most of the morning in the witness lounge, reading magazines. On the stand, she confirmed her identity and the date of her marriage to Walter. When asked about the night of Peters's murder, she refused to answer on "advice of counsel." As a spousal witness, Beryl had the law on her side. When asked what Walter had told her about that night, she again refused to answer. When asked what time Walter arrived home on the morning of May 16, once again she refused to answer. Weeks requested that Justice Joseph Morschauser direct Beryl to answer that last question since it was not confidential information but rather known to other members in the Ward household. Fifty-nine-year-old Morschauser had been on the bench for nearly two decades and was well-known for deciding cases based on his sense of justice rather than adhering to the finer points of the law—a quality that earned him the nickname Uncle Joe. He was also well-known for his dislike of divorce trials, given his beliefs in the sanctity of marriage.[11] Responding to the judge's directive, Beryl did confirm that her husband returned home at 4:30 a.m. on the morning of May 16. Weeks asked if Ward had telephoned that evening to say he wouldn't be home until late.

"Yes, the maid took the message," Beryl replied.

"Was Mr. Ward in the habit of coming in late in the morning?" the grand jury foreman, Auckland Cordner, asked.

"Not as late as that," Beryl replied.

"That was an usual occurrence?" he followed up.

"Yes, sir," she replied.

Weeks did ask about a published report in which Beryl said she could "clear this thing up if given a chance."

"The only remark I made," she responded, "was there was no women in the case and I suppose I must have said I would like to talk, but had been advised by Mr. Ward's attorneys not to." And with that, she left the grand jury room.

A swarm of reporters surrounded Beryl and Allan Campbell as they made their way to the courthouse lobby.

"You fellows have been talking a lot about secret stairways and the mysterious spiriting in of witnesses," Campbell announced, referring to the intricacies of the remodeled courthouse, "so we are going to show you, Mrs. Ward is going to leave by the front door of the Court House."

It was unclear whose idea it was to leave in such a public manner, but it did appear that Beryl Ward was increasingly enjoying her newfound notoriety. As she walked down the front steps, she posed for the cameramen, smiling to her left and right. When one photographer caught her face in an awkward pose, she turned to him and said, "Be a good sport," and then looked directly at his camera smiling as he snapped another, more complimentary photograph. "You boys have had enough now," she said and walked back to her car.[12]

WHEN SERVERS APPEARED with two subpoenas at George Ward's home in the Bronx, one for George and one for his son Ralph, who also lived at the home, they found the men had left the state to attend a bakers' conference in Pennsylvania. Both had been utterly silent since Walter Ward's confession of killing Clarence Peters. Ralph had appeared at the courthouse back in May to provide bail money for his younger brother but avoided reporters' questions.

George Ward was practically a ghost, avoiding all requests for comments and spending much of the time since his return from Europe well outside the reach of the Westchester authorities. "Fled over border" is how one newspaper described George Ward's movements that June, conjuring the image of someone in exile. Or on the run.[13]

After the bakers' conference, George traveled to Williamsport, Pennsylvania, to testify in a case of patent infringement involving the Ward Bakery Company. A published photograph of him leaving the courthouse surrounded by lawyers and private detectives declared the "millionaire baker was well guarded and numerously counseled in Pennsylvania." After the trial, he traveled to Pittsburgh, where he stayed with friends in the wealthy suburb of Sewickley Heights and enjoyed a number of rounds of golf. "He refuses to discuss the case of his son," reporters noted. He was later spotted in Cleveland, Ohio, allegedly there to discuss plans for a new bread factory in the city. When reporters confronted him outside his hotel, he refused to make a statement or to say whether he would return to New York to face the grand jury.

"I'm beginning to think," Sheriff Werner told reporters with unusual understatement, "that he doesn't want to come to White Plains to testify."[14]

George Ward was not the only missing Ward family member that the grand jury wished to question. Beryl's mother, Mrs. Laura Curtis, had also been subpoenaed but was nowhere to be found. Detectives questioned her neighbors, who lived in the respectable Victorians along Arlington Avenue in Brooklyn and those near her Belle Harbor summer home, but found few leads.

Mrs. Schafer, a former friend in Belle Harbor, described how she had rarely seen Curtis in the past several months. "Mrs. Curtis has made different friends in the last year," she said. "She has been going out to wild parties. I don't like that kind of life and have not gone out with her." One of those wild parties was the Saturday before Walter made his confession public to officials in Westchester. Curtis had attended a dinner party at the home of the Mr. and Mrs. Waldner, where cocktails were abundant and Curtis drank and played cards until 2:30 in the morning. One of those who attended the dinner party, a Dr. Pflug, described Curtis as a "damn good fellow," who "can drink like the rest of us." Dr. Pflug, detectives noted, had apparently "imbibed freely" before their interview and was quite open with detectives.

"We raised hell while we were there," he said, describing the Saturday-night festivities. But, he added, he didn't think Curtis knew anything about the murder, as she had a carefree attitude all night. If she were concerned about her daughter and son-in-law, he said, she was "a damn good actress."[15]

The Sunday morning after that dinner party, Curtis called her daughter. Mrs. Waldner told detectives that Beryl asked her mother to come to Sutton Manor immediately, and the Waldners drove her back to her house and helped her pack before driving her to New Rochelle.

"There was considerable excitement around the house," Waldner remembered about the Sutton Manor residence when they arrived, adding that Mrs. Curtis was planning on leaving town. But Waldner was keen to note that neither she nor her husband had been told about the murder on that Sunday morning and that neither had seen or talked with Curtis since they had left her in New Rochelle. Detectives were dubious of her claims. In fact, everyone detectives talked with who knew Laura Curtis claimed they hadn't seen her since before her son-in-law had admitted to killing Clarence Peters. Whether Curtis had in fact ghosted her friends, or whether her friends were protecting her, was not clear. What was clear was that Laura Curtis was very skilled in the art of dodging a grand jury subpoena.[16]

RALPH WARD DID eventually face the grand jury, though he had very little to say. He detailed his father's travels, explained they were planned weeks earlier and were in no way an effort to avoid testifying.

He provided a neatly typed itinerary of his father's business travels over the coming months. Chicago, Cleveland, Youngstown, South Bend, and Mount Clemens, Michigan, in late July. Each stop took George farther and farther away from White Plains.[17]

Weeks was also interested in what Ralph knew about the blackmail and murder. He asked him whether Walter had told him about the blackmailing scheme, and whether Walter had asked to borrow large sums of money. To each question Ralph replied simply, "He did not." He did note that in the two months before the murder he was critical of his brother's behavior in the office.

"Coming late in the morning and going away early in the afternoon, dividing his responsibility with persons under him, rather than assuming the responsibility he was supposed to maintain," he said. He added he didn't think his brother was acting "normal," that he suffered from constant headaches, but Ralph couldn't say whether he was in fact sick. Weeks then asked Ralph when he had first heard about the murder.

"The first I heard anything about it was on the night of May 17th," Ralph replied.

"From whom did you hear it?"

"My father," Ralph said.

Weeks pushed further: "What did he say to you?"

"I don't believe I have to answer that question, do I?" Ralph asked.

Weeks, startled by the response, retorted, "It isn't privileged."

"I will decline to answer you," Ralph replied.

"On what ground?"

"That anything I might say that father told me would be only hearsay as far as evidence of the case is concerned," Ralph explained. Weeks reminded Ralph that he was not the judge of hearsay in the grand jury room and that he could refuse only if his testimony would incriminate him.

Weeks tried again: "The question is what did your father say to you?"

"I decline to answer that until I have some further advice on it," Ralph replied, adding, "I am giving you my understanding of what my attorney told me about the things I was supposed to answer and not to answer as far as my rights are concerned."

"What do you think your rights are?" Weeks asked.

"I believe they told me I could only answer questions about things I heard from Walter or saw Walter do." Weeks retorted that his attorneys' advice was wrong, explaining that the grand jury investigation was not a trial and that they were "entitled to information from any source in order to thrash out and get at the truth." He reiterated that Ralph needed to answer the question.

"I think I will have to be guided by my own attorneys," Ralph replied, calmly and directly. Weeks threatened Ralph with contempt of court. Ralph continued to refuse to answer.

"Don't you think it would clear your brother if you did tell it?" Weeks asked.

"I don't think there is any question about that."

"Don't you think it would be preferable to establish the actual killing in self-defense rather than have this jury feel they should bring an indictment for murder?"

"Well, that's for the jury to decide," Ralph said.

"But if you are able to clear your brother by a statement of what you know don't you think it is pertinent and essential you should do it?"

"Well, there are ways of doing that. I don't care to undertake it and I decline to answer the question," Ralph said.

"You understand," Weeks, clearly frustrated with Ralph's reserved reticence, asked, "an inference might be drawn that will not be to the benefit of your brother's case?"

"I appreciate that."

"Still appreciating it you take that stand?"

"Yes, sir."

"In your mind," Weeks continued, "you are satisfied that your brother killed this man and that he did it in self-defense?"

"Absolutely!" Ralph's voice raised to show his unwavering belief in the story that his father had told him and the statement that Ward had offered. To the jurors, Ralph's resistance to answer Weeks's questions must have looked more like dodging the truth than upholding the rules of the grand jury proceedings. Why, they might have wondered, would Ralph not want to clear up this entire matter?

The next day, Ralph arrived at the courthouse early in the morning and "disappeared in a labyrinth of winding corridors," as the press reported. At some point he was handed a subpoena to appear before Justice Morschauser to answer the questions he'd refused during the grand jury inquiry. Again Ralph was silent on what his father had told him about the murder of Peters.

"You have to answer this now," Morschauser said. "This is a different case." What the judge meant was that Weeks was building a case of conspiracy against George Ward for his continued refusal to return to New York and face the grand jury. Ralph was now being asked to testify about his father's whereabouts but also what his father knew about the murder.

"Then you order me to answer your question?" Ralph asked the judge.

"Yes, I order you." To which Ralph related what his father told him.[18]

There is nothing in the remaining court records about what Ralph told the judge in his chambers on that morning of June 15. But in the coming days, a curious story circulated in the press about the reason for the alleged blackmail, often attributed to Ralph Ward. The story claimed that Walter had started to frequent the Empire City racetrack in Yonkers, New York, during the summer of 1921. There Ward became acquainted with "track louts"—men who provided tips on the races. These men were also part of a gang of blackmailers who were led by Charlie Ross. At first, the tips made Ward a lot of money and only drew him deeper into the scheme. Ross would meet Ward at his office or call him on the phone to provide tips for the next weekend's races. Detectives learned from an Empire City bookmaker by the name of Johnny Walters that in the summer and fall months of 1921, Ward made a number of bets, earning him over $10,000 in winnings. "Ninety percent of the time he knew what he was betting on before he did the bet," Walters told detectives, adding, "And you can take it from me he was no sucker." Walters felt sure Ward's success was not just luck.[19] His winning continued. Until it didn't. Eventually the tips turned sour, and Ward started to lose a lot of money. But even on losing bets, the tipsters demanded their fee. As one report observed, "If the horse won, Ross won; if it lost, Ward lost both ways."[20]

The cycle of gambling racked up a substantial amount, and Ward decided he was through with the tips and the bets. But the gang wasn't interested in letting Ward go, so they threatened to expose him for his gambling debt. How would it look, they suggested, the upstanding businessman, police commissioner, father of two in respectable Sutton Manor drowning in the mire of bad racing bets and associating with such race louts? Ward apparently was unconcerned by the threats, until they told him about an incident from Walter's past when he was first married. Ward was shocked by the details they had of the incident. Then, according to reports, he began paying these men "hush money" to protect his reputation and his family.

But by the early spring of 1922, after months of payments, he told the blackmailers he was done. It was then that the gang threatened Ward again, only this time it was an incident in George Ward's past they said would be revealed if he didn't keep paying them. It seemed that Walter had fallen into a never-ending scheme of threats and payments and needed a way out. Confronting the gang on King Street was Walter's attempt to end the blackmailing once and for all, and to protect not only his family, but his father as well. As one report described it, his confession to the killing of Clarence Peters was "colored as the condonable act of an honorable fighting man."[21]

Whatever truth there might have been to this new story of the blackmail, it furthered the image of a vulnerable Walter Ward who acted in self-defense in his murder of Peters. And while the story might have explained part of the crime, it still did not explain how Peters was involved in the blackmailing. Nor did it explain the secret that was so scandalous it led Ward to kill a man.

A week after Ralph Ward spoke to Justice Morschauser in his

chambers and the new story of his racetrack betting made headlines, another, more scandalous story about Walter Ward from the summer of 1921 emerged. The center of that story was not one of New York's racetracks, but rather a modern apartment building on the edge of Harlem called the Poinciana.

Poinciana

Laura Wright worked as a housekeeper at the Poinciana, a large apartment building on the corner of West 120th Street and Amsterdam Avenue. "New Ten Story Fireproof Apartments," the ads for the building announced in 1913 when it first opened. The apartments offered "massive rooms, with plenty of sunshine; handsomely appointed; embodying the newest improvements." By the early 1920s, the residents of the Poinciana were mostly white professional women, either single or engaged.

In the summer of 1921, Wright had worked at the building for nearly two years, having been hired when she was only seventeen years old. Each morning she walked to the building from her apartment in Harlem. She enjoyed her work, as she found the Poinciana quiet and most of the residents kept to themselves, rarely speaking to or even noticing her. The superintendent of the building, Fred Olsson, and his wife were kind, though Mr. Olsson often forgot her last name, and would usualy refer to her as "the laundress." Wright and her husband, William, both with little more than a fifth-grade education, left their native South Carolina sometime after World War I when they were still adolescents, joining the Great Migration in those years when African Americans escaped the abuses of Jim Crow for opportunities in the North.[1]

Sometime around late July, the Olssons asked Wright to take care of the cleaning and laundry of a new tenant, a handsome bachelor who was subletting apartment 9-L between July and September. Wright must have heard the rumors about this tenant, the late-night parties he hosted, the women who came and left throughout the evening, the drunk guests who stumbled through the lobby in the early-morning hours. When Olsson let Wright into 9-L every few days, she didn't know what she would find. While the tenant was usually careful with his suits and shirts and straw hats, keeping them tidy in the armoire, she often found gin and whiskey bottles strewn about the floor and dirty clothes left on furniture or hanging on the back of the bathroom door, where a large silk robe often hung. Expensive-looking jewelry—diamond tiepins, rings, pocket watches—were also casually left around, on the bedroom nightstands, the chair cushions, or the counter of the small kitchenette.

On one occasion she found a pair of men's silk pajamas in the trash can, torn and cut as with a knife. She didn't know what to do with them. Fred Olsson told her that if they were in the trash, then mostly likely the tenant didn't want them anymore. It must have seemed a shock to Wright to see such expensive things treated with such carelessness. While she had occasionally encountered the handsome bachelor of 9-L in the hallways and the lobby, she never spoke to him beyond a *hello* or *good afternoon*. She did eventually learn from the other Poinciana staff that he worked in the automobile industry and that his name was Walter Ward.

BACK IN JUNE, Miss MacGregor, who rented apartment 9-L and worked as a secretary to the president of U.S. Steel, placed a classified ad to sublet her apartment between July and September. When Ward came to see the two-room furnished apartment with views of Amsterdam Avenue, neither MacGregor nor Fred Olsson knew anything about the prospective tenant. But he must have made a good impression. They had no reason to doubt Ward when he told them that he was a bachelor and he wished for a place in the city while his family was on vacation in Canada.

It was not the only lie Ward told. On his sublease application, he listed his address as "63 Sutton Manor" rather than 63 Decatur Road in Sutton Manor, a slight variation of the truth. A more deliberate lie was his description of his occupation. He claimed to work in the automobile industry, specifically as a purchasing agent at the Bronx Equipment Company, which was a subsidiary of the Ward Bakery Company. The Bronx Equipment Company mostly made machine parts for the bread factories and the company's delivery trucks. The application was a mixture of facts and fictions, allowing Ward to hide in the shadowy space between the two.

As the Poinciana rented only to a certain class of people, Olsson was diligent in vetting applicants for leases. It was a shock then when Olsson talked with one of Ward's references, a manager at the Kelly-Springfield Tire Company, and was told that the applicant was actually a member of the wealthy Ward baking family—and he lived with his wife and two children in New Rochelle.

Olsson called Ward immediately.

"What are you trying to put over on me?" he demanded.

Ward cut the conversation short, left his office, and drove over to the Poinciana to have a conversation with Olsson far from the ears of his colleagues and any curious switchboard operators. According to Olsson, Ward explained how "people who he did not want to see were after him. And for that reason, chose an apartment where he would not be known, instead of a hotel." He told Olsson, "You know how rich people are bothered or annoyed by persons they don't want to see."

It's unlikely that Olsson could sympathize with Ward's plight. While he was dubious that the Poinciana could provide the anonymity Ward desired, he was willing to play along and, in his words, "help him out." He suggested his wife or Laura Wright could look after Ward's apartment, cleaning and doing his laundry privately. This way Ward would not have to send his laundry out and risk the staff seeing the name tags on his clothes when they were returned. Both the Olssons agreed to keep his identity a secret among the building staff. For this service, Ward paid an additional twenty-five dollars a month on top of the one-hundred-dollar monthly rent. He always paid in cash, Olsson remembered, describing how Ward usually carried around thick rolls of hundred-dollar bills. While he approved the sublease, Olsson would eventually come to regret his decision.[2]

WARD MOVED INTO apartment 9-L on July 1, 1921, at about the same time he allegedly got involved with the racetrack tipsters—the gang of track louts, as they were called—who began feeding Ward winning tips on horses. He must have felt incredibly lucky in those summer months as he enjoyed a string of big wins at the races and reveled in his life as a bachelor at the Poinciana, what some newspapers were calling his "clandestine retreat" or, more suggestively, his "love nest." Soon Ward was hosting nightly parties at the apartment, though usually they were not too loud and did not disturb the neighbors. He had a regular supply of alcohol brought to the apartment by a young, sheepish man who carried the bottles in a large suitcase through the lobby. Ward had given the man a key and directed the building staff to always allow him access.

It was not only the mysterious deliveries that Ward received that surprised the building staff, but also the steady stream of women. The doorman, Dan Washington, described how most nights Ward brought two and three women to his apartment, though he couldn't remember details of any of them.

Edgar Huggins, the elevator operator, also remembered what he called the "regular parade of women" Ward brought to 9-L. "I never saw a man have so many different women," he told detectives. "He brought as many as half a dozen there in a day." Huggins, an immigrant from the British West Indies, had a front-row seat to Ward's entertaining, riding up and down the elevator with each of Ward's new guests.

The visits had their own routine to them, as Huggins explained:

> He would bring one woman there say about 7 or 7:30 and would then come down with her, take her away in his coupe. An hour, maybe two or three hours later, he would come back with another woman, take her to his apartment, stay for an hour or two, bring her down, take her away and come back with another woman, as late as midnight and

> after and keep her there for a couple of hours, then take her away in his coupe.

This parade became gossip among the Poinciana staff, prompting all kinds of speculation. "It didn't seem as though he could just sit there and talk with them," Huggins offered, "and he could hardly be having intercourse with all of them. I don't see how he could. I couldn't do it to as many as he had in one day in a week. We used to think he was, you know, sucking them."[3]

One night, Huggins remembered, a policeman came into the lobby well past midnight asking about the owner of the coupe parked along Amsterdam Avenue. Huggins directed him to apartment 9-L. When the policeman returned, he told Huggins, "The fellow is alright. He's chairman of the New Rochelle Police Commissioners." One can imagine how Ward flashed his heavy badge, making a big show of it, and probably giving the man a shot of gin or whiskey while persuading, or perhaps threatening, the officer to just ignore his car. Huggins remembered that Ward continued to park his car in front of the building each evening, legal or not, for the rest of the summer.

Olsson recalled another time when Ward flashed his badge. At about the time Wright took over housekeeping duties in July, Ward complained to Olsson that some of his jewelry was stolen, nearly $1,000 worth, he claimed. Olsson told Ward he was not very smart leaving such valuables around like that, but Ward ignored his comment. Ward said he knew who took the jewelry and pointed the finger at Wright. He gave Olsson his badge and told him to find her at her apartment in Harlem and to threaten her with arrest if she didn't return them.

"Of course I had no intention of carrying out his wishes," Olsson told detectives. "I know better than to go up around the colored section on such an errand, and besides that I knew the laundress did not steal his jewelry."

When Mrs. Olsson returned from her vacation, she was furious at Ward's directive. She "laid the law down" with Ward, as Fred Olsson described it. She was direct, telling Ward that Laura Wright did not steal and that it was probably one of the women in his "gang." That's the term she used to describe the parade of women coming through his apartment. She suggested he call the police and have detectives investigate the theft, but Ward was quick to dismiss that idea. The subject was never brought up again. What became clear was how easily Ward used his police commissioner badge as a cover for any number of privileges and abuses.[4]

Olsson also recalled noticing two guns Ward kept in the apartment, one in the bedside table and one in the closet. He would later testify that both guns looked very similar to the .32 Smith & Wesson pistol and the .38 Colt automatic Ward offered up to Sheriff Werner as the weapons used the night of Peters's murder. Olsson was shown the .32 Smith & Wesson and asked if it looked like the one Ward kept in the Poinciana apartment.

"It looked exactly like that," he said. He also recognized the .38 Colt, as Ward had handed it to Olsson to hold on one visit to his apartment. Whether the pistol was the same or whether it just looked the same was unclear. But the fact that Ward had a pistol in the summer of 1921 that looked exactly like the pistol he claimed Peters used to threaten him nine months later must have seemed a strange coincidence to investigators—and one that could not be ignored.[5]

WHY WARD FELT the compulsion to rent an apartment on the Upper West Side of Manhattan that summer is unclear. Rumors were circulating that Walter and Beryl had been having problems for some time. One person, who had "close contact with the domestic situation" at the Wards' home, told reporters that the Wards were "estranged," though to "outward appearances amicable."[6] Pinkerton detectives learned that when Beryl Ward spent the previous winter in Palm Beach, Florida, she had been "morally indiscrete," though the report did not detail the nature of this indiscretion. When Walter found out about Beryl's behavior, it caused, in the detectives' words, "domestic trouble" and may have led to Ward poisoning himself with iodine in April 1922.[7] As the investigation drew on, reporters and detectives were getting a better picture of the Wards' marriage and how Walter's private life might lead them to the motive for the blackmail.

One incident that they were investigating happened a few months before Walter proposed to Beryl in the spring of 1915. Ward often traveled to Pittsburgh as secretary of the Ward-owned Brooklyn Tip-Tops baseball team. Walter, who was twenty-three at the time, met Marguerite Smith, the daughter of Albert Smith, who played for the league's Pittsburgh Rebels. Soon the two were the subject of Pittsburgh gossip for their parties and extravagances. Ward was known as a generous spender and "the life of the party." He lavished Smith with money and expensive clothes.

Not long after they met, Smith moved into Ward's hotel suite, where their parties became the "talk of Pittsburgh night life." Reporters with *The Philadelphia Inquirer* tracked Smith down in June 1922. "We were very good friends," she claimed, and admitted she had traveled to New York with Ward, visiting him at his home in New Rochelle and at least one time on his yacht. Walter and Beryl moved to New Rochelle around 1917, suggesting the affair between Smith and Ward continued well after Ward was married.

But it seems that Smith was not the only woman Ward was involved with back then. He was also having an affair with Martha Kendall, a vaudeville performer and waitress at the bar of a hotel where Ward often stayed.

"I knew her very well," Smith remembered, describing how Kendall and a friend of hers would always attend the Federal League games and were "on intimate terms with members of the Pittsburgh and Brooklyn teams." But, Smith added, "when Ward was in town they used to drop their other admirers and cling to him for he was the gayest spender of them all and was clever and attractive besides."[8]

In 1922, Martha Kendall was living in Los Angeles, operating a "modiste," or designer dress shop, on Hollywood Boulevard. She was blunt when a reporter from the *Los Angeles Times* came to interview her.

"Find the woman in the case," she said, "and the Ward blackmail mystery will be solved." Kendall was "scathing in her denunciation of Ward," the reporter noted. She described him as having a near obsession with entertaining women. "Some were married, some unmarried and some had children," she claimed, adding that he was known for squandering large sums of money and boasting about his conquests. "He was a man absolutely without honor when it comes to women," she declared, her simmering anger evident in each comment.[9]

"Yes, he made love to me—the kind of love he made to many, many other women," Kendall claimed. "But I was different. I was not dazzled by his money nor his good looks." It was then that Kendall related Ward's violent tendencies. "When he realized I had not fallen into his web, he attempted to abduct me." She described how Ward, with the help of his chauffer, broke down her apartment door and tried to kidnap her.

Kendall brought criminal charges against Ward, but the case was settled out of court. R. H. Jackson, who was counsel for the Pittsburgh Rebels and a former DA in Pittsburgh, represented Ward. Though it would be one of his last cases, as just a few months later he was disbarred after his conviction for stealing money from a client.

Kendall received somewhere between $1,000 and $10,000—the exact amount varied in press reports. The other uncertainty about this settlement was who exactly paid it. Some reports claimed Ward's friends, while others said it was George Ward who paid Kendall off to protect the reputation of his son—and presumably the company as well. Whoever put up the money, the incident never made it to the press at the time. And, as luck would have it, the entire incident also disappeared from the courts. When reporters went looking for the court documents in 1922, they were told all the files were missing.[10]

After the settlement, George Ward demanded his son's return to New York. In May 1915, Walter proposed marriage to Beryl. The same month announcements of Beryl's engagement were published in Brooklyn society columns, a small profile of Walter as the treasurer of Federal League appeared in a number of newspapers, describing the twenty-three-year-old as a "clean cut" and "business-like chap" who "looks on life seriously."[11] Both the marriage proposal and profile seemed an effort to transform Walter from party boy to respectable businessman. But by the summer of 1915 Walter had returned to Pittsburgh, resuming those "gay parties" that had become so notorious. It seems unlikely that Beryl was unaware of Ward's escapades, Kendall's lawsuit, or the many rumors that were circling around her fiancé. But whatever concerns she might have had did not dissuade her from marrying Walter that September.

Without the court files, it is impossible to tell what exactly happened between Ward and Kendall. When the incident made headlines in the investigation into Peters's murder, it was often described as a blackmail scheme devised by Kendall demanding money from Ward. Smith hinted at this scheme in her interview with *The Philadelphia Inquirer,* which described how blackmailers "lured Ward into their hands" and suggested that the earlier incident might be behind Clarence Peters's murder. But blackmailers tended not to bring lawsuits against their targets, as it would risk exposing the secrets at the heart of the extortion. This story of blackmail may have been cooked up by Ward's supporters to deflect from the facts of the incident.

Kendall, of course, dismissed claims that she was blackmailing Ward. He "always cried blackmail when he was in trouble," she told the *Los Angeles Times.* Smith appeared to have nothing but disdain for Kendall, suggesting a rivalry that had lingered for nearly a decade.

"In my opinion," Smith told reporters with a pointed criticism, "all she is seeking in her purported exposure and her offer to testify regarding Ward's past is notoriety and possibly a generous travel account." These contradicting claims only muddied the truth about what actually happened in Pittsburgh so many years earlier.[12]

Then some clarity emerged in an unlikely place. Weeks after Kendall and Smith cast doubts on each other's stories, a small article bubbled up in the New York gossip rag *Broadway Brevities*:

> Referring to the Ward case, did you know that the little lady said to have been the principal in the Pittsburgh incident ran a millinery shop downstairs on 45th Street near the Princeton up to a few months ago? Under the name of "Marguerite" and was a familiar figure in the all night places with the little girl known as her sister. And told the whole story to certain friends here but the amount named by her was $25,000 not $1,000. And that there is a little

> son, according to the same lady's account, as the result of the midnight invasion figuring in the Pittsburgh scandal?

Despite the newspaper's dubious reputation as a tabloid scandal sheet, detectives immediately tracked down the editor, who directed them to the informant of the story, a chiropractor by the name of Dr. Souchelle. He claimed that while traveling in Pittsburgh in 1914 he met a woman named Rose Mary Kendall, whom he described as five feet six inches tall with red hair and working as a singer in a cabaret at the Hotel Lincoln. Kendall, the doctor remembered, told him how she brought a lawsuit against Walter Ward after he forced his way into her apartment and raped her. "Criminal assault" was the term the doctor used. Kendall became pregnant with Ward's child, giving birth to a boy. Ward eventually settled out of court for an astounding amount of $25,000. Souchelle claimed that he had spoken to Kendall in New York many times since their first meeting.

Souchelle's story lent more credence to Kendall's public claims about her relationship with Ward. One can imagine that when the *Los Angeles Times* reporter came to her shop on Hollywood Boulevard asking about Ward, she would have explained it as an attempted kidnapping rather than a sexual assault. Such crimes were little talked of in the press, and when they were, they often cast shame on the victims. "I'll tell all I know, if they ask me, not till then," she told reporters with a tone that was both direct and discreet.[13]

For investigators, the stories of Ward's three months in the Poinciana, and the many women he entertained there, fit a pattern about his private life. Perhaps the blackmail did stem from one of these women? The challenge was to find them. But few on staff could remember details about any of the women parading through the lobby.

"I could not begin to describe any of them," Huggins told detectives. Lilian Kist, who worked the switchboard in the lobby of the building, rarely got a good look at Ward's guests. Except one time, she recalled, when she noticed a woman with reddish hair, wearing a black dress and a large black hat. Kist noticed her from the side as she and Ward waited for the elevator but couldn't describe the woman with any detail.

Ward would often direct the switchboard operators to tell anyone who called that he was not home. There was one woman, Kist remembered, who called often. When Kist told her that Ward was not home, she would say, "Tell him Schuyler called." While Kist thought Schuyler referred to the phone exchange, it was actually the name of one of Ward's women: Peggy Schuyler. Petite and red haired, Schuyler was a frequent visitor to apartment 9-L and most likely the woman Kist saw standing at the elevators. Mrs. Olsson had unexpectedly stumbled upon Ward and Schuyler in his apartment one morning, when she thought Ward had already left. The two were talking, and Schuyler was wearing that silk robe that Wright had seen hanging in the bathroom. Slightly embarrassed and made uncomfortable by the encounter, Olsson apologized and left abruptly.[14]

According to some news reports, in the years before World War I, Schuyler was a singer at a roadhouse in Westchester, those notoriously seedy taverns that catered to underworld figures, hiding in the shadows of Westchester's image as a respectable suburb. One roadhouse was known for its plentiful whiskey and raunchy cabaret shows that left "nothing to the imagination," as one detective noted. Sometimes patrons were treated to a live sex show. An "exhibition of copulation by a nude couple" was how a detective described it.[15] Schuyler's personal relationships varied from underworld figures, criminal lawyers, and wealthy businessmen. One informant told detectives that Schuyler also went by the name of Peggy Neal and among her friends was known as Toodles. It was as Peggy Neal that she brought a lawsuit against a hotel owner in New Rochelle for breach of promise—a common tactic some female blackmailers used to entice wealthy men to pay them and avoid a scandal.[16]

In the early-morning hours of Labor Day, a woman believed to be Schuyler got into a raucous argument with another woman at Ward's apartment. Huggins described it as a complete "hair pulling and scratching encounter." The shouting spilled into the hallway, waking up the neighbors who complained to the staff. At some point, Ward left the apartment, and the shouting match between the two women only intensified. Schuyler apparently had had enough of Ward after that. Speculation in the press suggested it was Schuyler who drew Ward to the racetrack blackmailers, his gambling debts, and eventually the fateful night on King Street.

The next day, Olsson complained to Ward that this kind of behavior could not continue in such a respectable building. He meant the late-night parties and inebriated guests, but he also meant the parade of women that was clearly becoming a problem for the building's residents. He threated to evict Ward that day, but Ward quickly turned apologetic and promised to tame his behavior.

By the end of September, Ward's lease expired, and MacGregor was due to return. Ward packed up his trunks, and two Ward Bakery workers took them back to New Rochelle on a bread delivery truck.[17] The building's management company was so dismayed by Ward's conduct that they resolved never to allow him to have an apartment at the Poinciana again.[18]

Through June and July, detectives continued to search for the women who frequented Ward's apartment, interviewing cabaret and theater owners, talking with chorus girls about what they may have known about Walter Ward in the summer of 1921. The press was, unsurprisingly, dubious about the character of the women who frequented apartment 9-L.

None of the women, *The Evening World* reported, "so far as known, were persons who were on friendly terms with Ward's wife and relatives, or who would have been admitted to the social circles in which he moved in New Rochelle and Brooklyn." It added, "Their visits and the evidences of their conduct in the apartment were of a nature to be used as a basis of blackmail threats."[19]

While inquiries by detectives and reporters proved little use, it seems, for a while at least, investigators were taking Martha Kendall's advice: "Find the woman in the case, and the Ward blackmail mystery will be solved."

A Perfectly Normal Prisoner

Rumors began circulating that the grand jurors were "thoroughly dissatisfied" by the progress of the investigation and frustrated by Weeks's failures to produce key witnesses. Ralph Ward's resistance to jury questions epitomized how the entire investigation was uncovering little beyond what was already known, and certainly not much beyond Walter Ward's initial statement. Some of the jurors wanted Judge Morschauser to appoint a legal advisor to replace Weeks.

Whatever truth there was to those published rumors, and however thin the testimonies had been, on the afternoon of June 15, Auckland Cordner, the grand jury foreman and a New Rochelle real estate developer, handed down an indictment of first-degree murder. Short on facts, the indictment was clear on the intentions behind the killing of Clarence Peters. It read in part: Walter S. Ward "with force and arms, in and upon one Clarence E. Peters, in the peace of the said People then and there being, feloniously, willfully, unlawfully and of his malice aforethought, did make an assault." Just one day shy of a month since Peters was found murdered along King Street, Walter Ward would finally face a jury. The charge of first-degree murder was a capital offense in New York State. If convicted, the handsome baker would face the electric chair.[1]

Armed with the arrest warrant, Sheriff Werner sent his deputies out to find Ward. Some men went to Sutton Manor, some to Ward's office at the Bronx factory, and others to the offices of Rabenold &

Scribner at 61 Broadway in Manhattan. It was there that deputy sheriff Frank Cherico found Ward.

"You're under arrest," he shouted down the hallway toward a seemingly surprised Ward. "You've been indicted for murder in the first degree."

Cherico and Ward, along with two Westchester police officers, took the subway to Grand Central station. From there the plan was a circuitous and accommodating path from the city, taking the men first to the Bronx factory where they picked up Ward's chauffer, who then drove the men to Sutton Manor where Ward was allowed to gather clothes for his expected jail stay. After packing a small bag, Walter was escorted by Cherico back to his chauffeured car for the drive to White Plains.

Beryl reportedly sobbed when Walter told her the news of his indictment. "As he walked down the steps to his automobile," Cherico told *The New York Times*, "she buried her face in her hands and leaned against the door."[2]

The extraordinary accommodation given to Ward had eaten up much of the afternoon. By the time the men arrived at the courthouse it was already a little after six o'clock. Ward looked nervous as he entered Joseph Morschauser's courtroom. Gone was his usual energy and smile. As Weeks announced the indictment for first-degree murder, Ward gripped the table in front him, struggling, it seemed, with maintaining his composure. Allan Campbell, Ward's attorney, requested a postponement until the next day, which Morschauser allowed.

"I commit the defendant to jail," he said. "There is no bail in this case. You know that?" he asked, turning toward Ward as he stood near his lawyers.

Warden John Hill assured reporters that Ward would be treated like any other prisoner. "There will be no luxe imprisonment this time," he told them in a gesture of toughness meant to stifle criticisms of how the warden had handled Ward's earlier stay at the jail.

The next morning reporters observed that Ward looked pale and haggard; his body gestures lacked the confidence of the last time he had appeared in court. "His eyes were puffed and his smile was infrequent and seemingly forced," one reporter noted. Weeks began the hearing charging Ward with first-degree murder and reading out the indictment. Ward pleaded not guilty. Campbell reserved the right to change his client's plea if the evidence warranted. And then he raised the issue of the trial.

"There is a matter that I would like to present now, because it seems to me to be paramount," Campbell said, his tone calm and respectful, "and that is the fixing of a date for a speedy trial. The case has a number of special circumstances which we perhaps do not need to go into at length because your honor is somewhat familiar with the proceedings that have gone on up to this time." Morschauser reminded him that it was not up to the judge nor the defense lawyers to determine when to bring the case to trial. That was in the hands of District Attorney Weeks.

Campbell persisted. "It seems to me," he continued, "that the logical process to go through is to have the case tried as soon as possible because if he is innocent, he should not suffer that period in jail, his health not being of the best, and if he is guilty, there is certainly no harm or wrong or injustice done, in having the case tried at once." Campbell's request was with an eye to the approaching summer months, when the courts were usually in recess through August. Ward might have to spend the entire summer lingering in a county jail cell.

"There are a number of men out here in jail that are waiting to be tried," Morschauser retorted, his patience fraying.

"I do not want to antagonize Your Honor," Campbell replied.

"You do not antagonize me," Morschauser said, and then suggested the defense could help in getting a speedier trial. "If you could produce these two other men," he said, referring to Charlie Ross and Jack, "probably you would have no trouble in having him tried right away."

But there were other reasons why a speedy trial was impossible. "The District Attorney has the right to conduct his office in the manner in which he thinks it should be conducted," the judge said. "There are many reasons why he cannot go on with the case now, I can see. Relatives that he needs as witnesses in this case are not in this state. He has a right, in my judgment, to wait until he gets them here." Weeks

Crime scene photograph along King Street (*Westchester County Archives. May 16, 1922. Walter Ward Papers*)

Map of Kensico (Daily News, *April 28, 1923*)

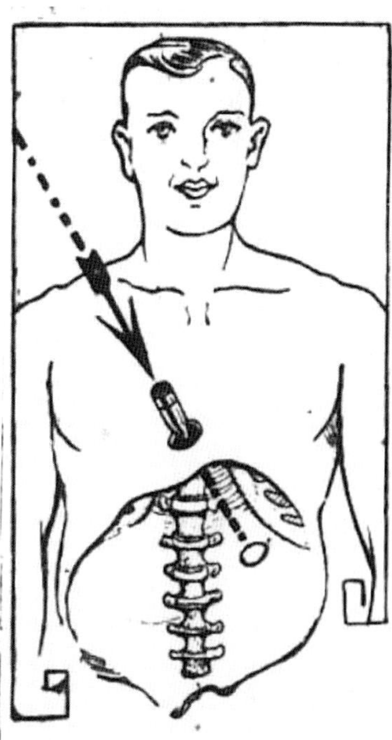

The bullet that killed Peters struck him in the middle of the breast bone. It ranged downward, making an exit wound four inches to the left of the spine and six inches below the point of entrance.

New York American illustration of bullet wound (New York American, *May 25, 1922*)

THE LARGEST MORNING CIRCULATION IN AMERICA

DAILY NEWS

NEW YORK'S PICTURE NEWSPAPER

FINAL EDITION

Vol. 3. No. 284. 24 Pages. ** New York, Tuesday, May 23, 1922. 2 Cents

BLACKMAIL DEATH MYSTERY

Page 2

The slain man, Clarence Peters (above), former marine, was killed by millionaire, latter, says, when Peters and companions demanded $75,000 under threat of death.

This photo-diagram shows how Clarence Peters was slain, according to Walter S. Ward's account of his battle with blackmailing gang near Kensico Reservoir.

Walter S. Ward, son of the head of well-known baking firm, who tells how he was forced to shoot.

Mrs. Walter S. Ward.

BULLETS, NOT MONEY.—Walter S. Ward surrendered yesterday as slayer of Clarence Peters, whom he shot, he says, in battle with blackmailers. He was released on bail.

Gladys E. Zielian, new Mrs. Carroll.

Bradish Johnson Carroll Jr., who must choose between bride and his father's fortune.

SURPRISE WEDDING.—Divorced quietly a month ago, Bradish Johnson Carroll Jr., heir to millions, wed chorus girl and faces disinheritance.

OFFSTAGE DRAMA.—Jeanne Robertson (above with lawyer), actress, told in court yesterday of a battle in her apartment with a suitor and her rescue by army captain.

Front page of the New York *Daily News* after Ward's confession, with photo diagram of shooting (Daily News, *May 23, 1922*)

Inez and Elbridge Peters (*May 25, 1922. Justin Peavey Private Collection*)

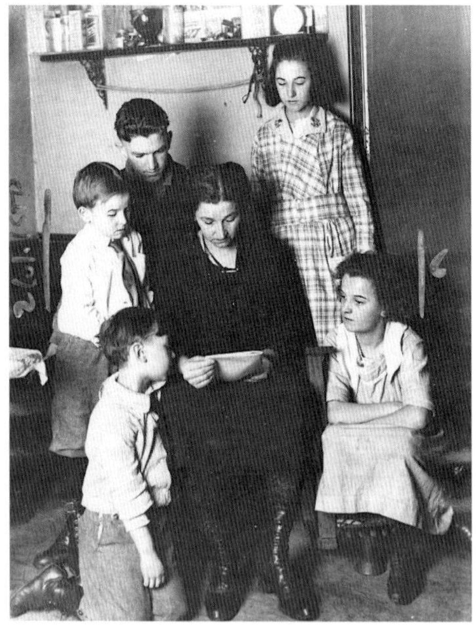

Inez Peters with her children (*January 6, 1922. Justin Peavey Private Collection*)

Walter Ward (*n.d. Justin Peavey Private Collection*)

Early Hardy, uncle of Clarence Peters (*September 20, 1923. Justin Peavey Private Collection*)

Image of Beryl Ward with children used in court (*n.d. Justin Peavey Private Collection*)

Clarence Peters (*May 27, 1922. Justin Peavey Private Collection*)

Ralph Ward and Walter Ward (*July 27, 1923. Justin Peavey Private Collection*)

Walter and Beryl Ward before the verdict (*September 21, 1923. Justin Peavey Private Collection*)

Justice Robert Wagner (*Harris & Ewing Collection. n.d. Library of Congress Prints & Photographs Division*)

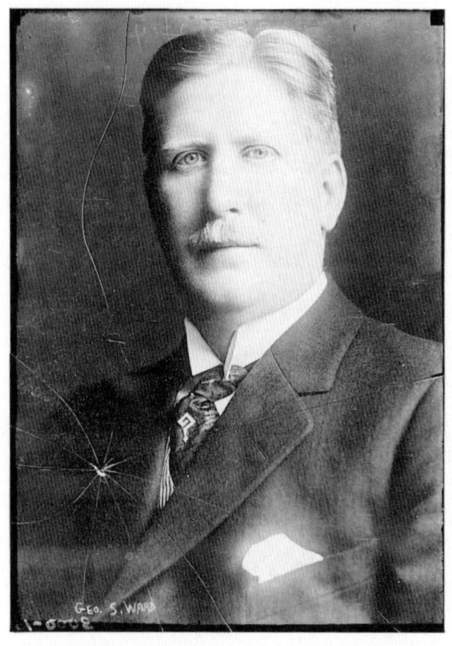

George Ward (*George Grantham Bain Collection. March 2, 1914. Library of Congress Prints and Photographs Division*)

Sheriff George Werner
(*n.d. Justin Peavey Private Collection*)

Coroner Edward Fitzgerald (*May 26, 1922. Justin Peavey Private Collection*)

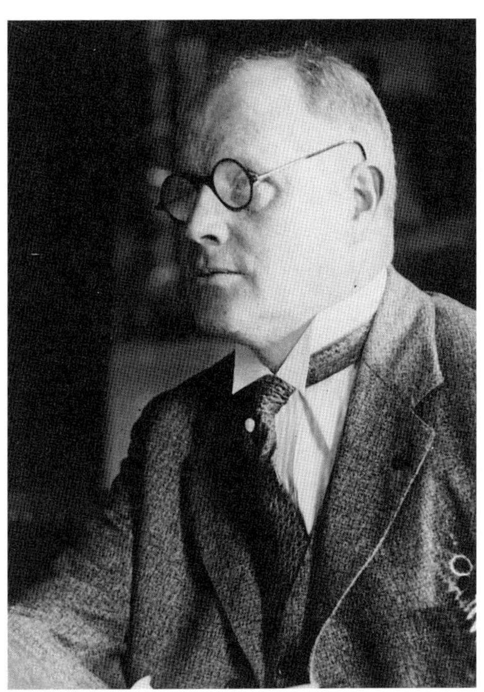

District Attorney Frederick Weeks
(*May 25, 1922. Justin Peavey Private Collection*)

Attorney General Carl Sherman (*September 14, 1923. Justin Peavey Private Collection*)

Morris McCarthy and James Cunningham (*June 3, 1922. Justin Peavey Private Collection*)

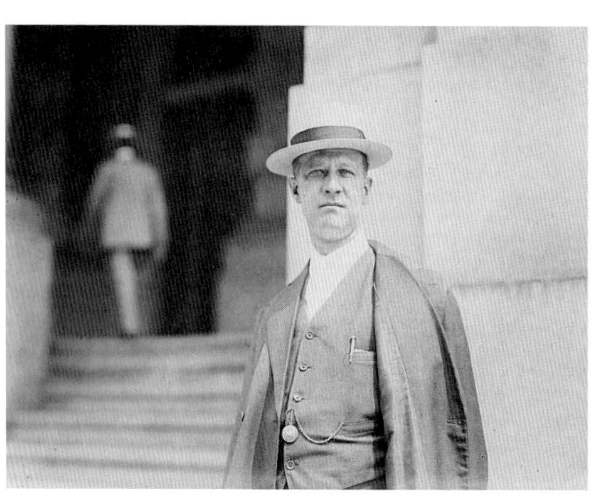

Governor Alfred Smith (*George Grantham Bain Collection. May 18, 1920. Library of Congress Prints and Photographs Division*)

Queenie Jones in England (*May 2, 1923. Justin Peavey Private Collection*)

Joseph Medill Patterson
(*George Grantham Bain Collection. n.d. Library of Congress Prints and Photographs Division*)

Crowds gather outside the courtroom (*September 20, 1923. Justin Peavey Private Collection*)

Old Westchester County Courthouse (*"Westchester County Courthouse, White Plains, N.Y." c.1917. Library of Congress Prints and Photographs Division*)

Ward Bakery
Bronx Factory
(*n.d. Justin Peavey Private Collection*)

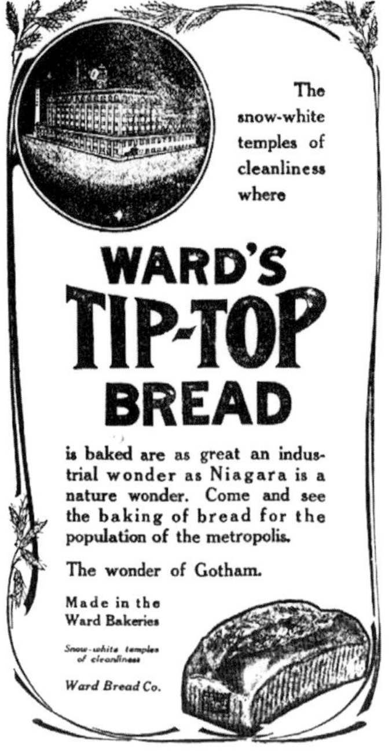

Ward Bakery Advertisement
(Brooklyn Daily Eagle, *November 8, 1911*)

WARD THREATENED WITH NEW BLACKMAIL AS "ROSS" FLEES

Daily News illustration of the investigation as a silent movie
(Daily News, *May 29, 1922*)

was decidedly silent through much of these exchanges between the two men.

Morschauser and Campbell went back and forth about the appearances of witnesses who would, as the judge indicated, clear up vital facts of the case. Campbell protested that it was not the defendant's "responsibility for their appearance," a claim that contradicted Ward's initial statement when he and his lawyers were actively pursuing the whereabouts of Charlie Ross and Jack. Campbell then pivoted back to his initial request.

"I simply want to go on, further distinguishing this case from the cases of other people awaiting trial," he argued.

"Why should it be distinguished?" Morschauser snapped back. He reminded Campbell that there were in fact other defendants in the county awaiting trial. "A colored man, who has been in jail here for several months," he said. "They stand equal before the law. He has to be tried first. I do not know why you should urge this anyway."

It was true. Everod Blankes, an African American, had been sitting in the county jail since February after he was arrested for the murder of Frank Harris. Blankes was convinced by a dream that Harris was having an affair with his wife. The press described Blankes's violent attack on Harris as one "frenzied with jealousy."[3]

"I know pretty well about some of those other men from general experience," Campbell said, offering his own assessment of men like Everod Blankes and how they differed from men like Walter Ward. "A good many of them do not want to be tried, are in no great hurry. That is the difference." Perhaps sensing the judge's impatience, Campbell didn't linger too long on such speculations about the nature of criminals who, for some reason, wished to stay in jail. The uniqueness of his client and what distinguished this case from others was, it seemed, Ward's background and social status. Moving along, Campbell turned to the problem of the indictment itself.

"What I want to say," Campbell clarified, "is that there is no evidence against this man. That is our contention, from the very beginning, that there is no evidence—"

"There is evidence that he shot him, isn't there?" Morschauser interrupted. "He shot him?" The judge had clearly reached his boiling point with Campbell's request. "This case will go on in the ordinary way," he concluded. And with that Walter Ward was escorted back to his jail cell.

Ward had chicken for dinner that night, and then read and smoked in his cell and showed little sign of nervousness about the situation he was facing. He was "a perfectly normal prisoner," Sheriff Werner told reporters, continuing to sound like Walter Ward's publicist.[4]

IN THE FOLLOWING days, Campbell took his arguments for the need of a quick trial to the press. Standing on the steps of the courthouse he pointed to the facade of the building. "Have any of you fellows ever noticed the inscription across the front here?" he asked, gesturing to the engraved frieze. There was a pause in the moment. Reporters' heads turned upward, some shielding their eyes from the sun's glare to read the words: TO NONE WILL WE SELL TO NONE WILL WE DELAY TO NONE WILL WE DENY RIGHT OR JUSTICE. After a few seconds, Campbell continued, "We want an immediate trial. Our client is facing a summer in jail and he has the right to have a jury pass on his case." In response to a question about the absence of George Ward, Campbell remained elusive, stating that George would be called as a witness at the trial, but added he didn't "know whether he will remain outside the jurisdiction until the trial or not. He is out there on business." Then, in a rebuke to Morschauser's claims in court, he directed reporters to "find out how many cases there are awaiting trial. The only one we have been able to discover is that of a negro mentioned by Justice Morschauser the other day."[5]

As the days stretched into weeks, the prospect of a quick trial seemed increasingly unlikely. In response to Campbell's claims that his client is being denied a speedy trial, Weeks used his usual bluntness with reporters.

"The answer to Ward's lawyers is that when the case is ready for trial, we'll go to trial," and, he added with a measured tone, "Not one minute before." A few days later he made this point even stronger:

"I would resign before I would go to trial before I have my evidence ready. They cannot stampede me."[6]

Isaac Mills fielded questions about the nature of the blackmail, and in particular the secrets that emerged in the story that Ralph Ward allegedly disclosed in Morschauser's chambers. "Everything relating to the defense will be brought out at the trial," he told reporters outside his home, adding after a brief pause, "if it seems necessary." He continued: "You can't blame him for not wishing to bring humiliation upon his family until it is absolutely necessary." It was a striking admission really, further fueling speculation about the skeletons in Ward's closet that could clear up the mystery of the entire case. Mills's use of the word *humiliation* only made the secret that much more tantalizing, conjuring all kinds of speculation about what shame the Ward family was hiding. "You can't expect the defense to put forth the defense until the prosecution has made a case," he added. "You can't expect us to say more than that."[7]

Reports of Ward's time in jail described a man despondent and withdrawn. He spent most of his days sitting in his cell, smoking, reading, or staring out at the exercise court. He rarely spoke with other inmates, though he did speak with Joseph McMuller, the prison cook, offering advice about the prison bread. "You've got a little too much yeast in this bread," he suggested to McMuller, who, it was reported, was happy to have the master baker's advice. Usually, Ward declined the prison dinners and instead had his meals sent in from a local restaurant.

Like all the prisoners, Ward was allowed visitors on Wednesdays and Saturdays, though in those weeks after his indictment there were only meetings with his attorneys and occasional visits by his brother Ralph. Beryl Ward stayed isolated in Sutton Manor, avoiding the press. While reports suggested Walter didn't wish for her to see him in jail, her exile might have been an orchestrated plan to keep Beryl away from the cameras and reporters' questions that she was often eager to engage.[8]

As the weeks dragged on, Ward's attorneys continued to push for their client's release. They successfully petitioned for access to the grand jury minutes, convinced that the indictment had little evidence behind it. Campbell claimed in court that the foreman of the grand jury, Auckland Cordner, "had a bias against the defendant," showing from the very beginning of the investigation a "hostility" against the defendant and to his wife and brother. According to Campbell, Cordner had been up for the position of police commissioner in New Rochelle but lost out to Ward and, the defense complained, was using the grand jury to attack the reputation of the entire Ward family. Campbell also argued that the daily headlines of false leads and exaggerated claims "created an atmosphere in the grand jury room that was hostile to their client." The newspapers conducted a "front page campaign," he said, that was meant to pry open the motive behind the blackmail to fill their news columns. The arguments were clear: Ward was the victim of a corrupted investigation and a biased press.

But the criticism of the press coverage didn't stop Ward's attorneys from also using the press. When they finally did get the grand jury minutes, they promptly leaked portions of them to support their consistent claims that Ward was being blackmailed by a gang of men over racetrack losses. They circulated Tubbs's testimony claiming two men, one named Ross, had met Ward a few times at the Bronx factory office, pushing back on the growing speculation that Charlie Ross and Jack were mere inventions of Ward's imagination. Excerpts from Beryl Ward's testimony confirmed that Ward did not come home until the early morning hours on May 16 and that Peters had never been to the Sutton Manor home, and when asked if Ward was in the habit of carrying a gun with him, Beryl replied, "No, sir; not that I ever saw."[9]

Armed with the grand jury transcripts that showed the prosecutor had no real evidence to dispute Ward's initial statement, Ward's attorneys petitioned to dismiss the indictment. In Justice Seeger's courtroom where Ward had been initially arraigned back in May, Isaac Mills argued for the release of his client with an impressive performance of hyperbolic outrage.

"Never since the days of the Spanish Inquisition," the seasoned jurist declared, his voice deep but shaky, "has a greater outrage been perpetrated than was perpetrated in the grand jury room." Journalists and friends of the Wards' filled the courtroom, marveling, no doubt, at the stamina and animated presence of the seventy-one-year-old attorney, as well as his skills at dramatic rhetoric. For nearly two hours he painted a picture of a man so grievously wronged it would be a miscarriage of justice to keep him jailed one minute longer.

"I want you to look at him," Mills declared as he gestured with his hand toward his client. Ward looked tired and thin, the press noted. His pale face was wrinkled, and his characteristic smile seemed forced.

"Does he look like a cold-blooded murderer?" Mills asked. Next, he pointed toward Beryl, sitting right behind Ward in the gallery.

"I wanted his wife here. There she sits," he said, while turning his back to the judge to look directly at Beryl and forcing all eyes of the courtroom on her. "Does she look like a wanton, as the black-haired foreman of the Grand Jury tried to impress on the world?" Mills intoned, referring to Cordner's direct questions of Beryl during her testimony. "I wanted their two children here," and, forgetting that Beryl had refused to bring them to the hearing, Mills gestured back toward the gallery. "I want the court to look up on the innocent who will be the sufferers in their generations to come."[10]

Mills paced in front of Seeger's bench, gesturing with his hands, respectful but also pointedly critical. He claimed Weeks had suppressed the fact that Peters was a "desperado and a thug," a claim that Ward's attorneys loved to repeat. Weeks had only "suspicions" about Ward's initial statement, Mills declared, based on two facts: that Ward had an interest in betting on the horses and his decided delay in reporting the murder to authorities. In dismissing the first doubt, Mills described how men in Westchester have a tradition with horse racing. "Where Ward came from, every man loved horses."

As for the delay in confessing the crime, Mills was adamant Ward did the responsible thing. Rather than confessing to the New Rochelle chief of police Frank Cody, his "subordinate," Mills said, he instead told his father, George, and then consulted with his "trusted attorneys," coming forth to surrender himself, in Mills's words, "on the third day." The echoes of biblical redemption would not have been missed by the judge and those in the courtroom.

Mills also evoked the Bible when he addressed the scandal of the Poinciana: "Your honor knows the frailties of men. I simply say that 'let him who is without sin among you cast the first stone.'" As Mills took his seat next to Ward, the echoes of his voice felt more like that of a sermon, casting Ward as a family man and an unfortunate sinner but certainly not a killer.[11]

Weeks rose, his voice softer and his argument more pragmatic. He lacked the dramatic rhetoric, the punctuated pauses, the gestures to those in the courtroom. Instead, he noted the deep concerns about the Poinciana story that had only recently come to light, and the potential new evidence that incident might produce. He explained the timeline of the investigation and cast doubts about the key facts of Ward's statement, the time of the shooting, the absence of the two witnesses Charlie Ross and Jack, and the mystery of the bullet hole that pierced Peters's shirt but not his vest. The bullet hole, he argued, indicated deliberation on Ward's part and justified the first-degree murder charge. While Seeger sat quietly through Mills's nearly two-hour oration, as Weeks moved through his short outline of the prosecution, he was often interrupted by questions from the judge. It was clear to everyone in the courtroom that Seeger was not convinced by the state's argument.

After a two-hour adjournment, Seeger returned to the courtroom. "Gentlemen," he said, "I think instead of writing a decision, as you are all anxious to have one immediately, I will make it now verbally." He continued: "This case is an unusual one. Its unusual character lies in the fact that there is no evidence of commission of a crime except such is contained in the defendant's own statement. If what he states is true in its entirety, no crime has been committed, because he says clearly that he acted in self-defense." Ward must have felt buoyed by these opening remarks.

"It does appear clearly, however," Seeger continued, "that the defendant took a human life. That fact alone is sufficient to raise a question of fact. This court cannot determine the truth or falsity of the defendant's statement." Seeger went on to describe the prosecution's case as "barren" of any evidence for the motive of the killing and also "barren" of any evidence to show Ward's killing of Peters as deliberate or premediated. But, he added, the district attorney could not take as true Ward's statement.

"I think there are facts which must be submitted to a jury," Seeger declared and then opened the door for Ward's freedom.

"But in view of the fact that the defendant has voluntarily surrender himself," Seeger concluded,

> that he has at all times given evidence that he is not attempting to flee, and because of the absence of any evidence in this record tending to show that there was any deliberation or premeditation on his part in the killing, because of the doubt that I feel that the facts warrant an indictment for the crime of murder in the first degree, and because the courts have held that a voluntarily surrender favors admission to bail, I think, under all the circumstances, that it would be unjust to keep a man who had surrendered himself in this manner to the courts in confinement awaiting trial. I have concluded to admit him to bail.[12]

For the second time in as many months, Justice Seeger released Walter Ward from jail. As the judge's gavel strike echoed in the courtroom, Ward smiled broadly and turned and kissed Beryl as his friends and neighbors gathered around him.

"I have nothing but thanks and kindness for the uniform courtesy with which I was treated at White Plains," Ward told reporters later. "Everybody was kind to me. I occupied a regular cell and sought no special favors of any kind." He added, "I'm mighty glad to get back to work and believe there's plenty of it waiting for me."

At the Bronx factory the next day, employees gathered to greet Ward as he arrived. They gave him a "hearty welcome," as one report described it. "I was touched by the reception," Ward said. "You never can tell how many real friends you have until you get into trouble. It seems great to be back on the job, but it also seems queer not to be able to tell how much sugar and flour we have on hand."[13]

After Seeger's decision, Weeks refused journalists' questions. Anonymous sources informed reporters that he considered the judge's refusal to dismiss the indictment a "big victory" and that he was focused on his investigation, pursuing all leads that came into his office. He still believed that he would be ready to go to trial in the fall.

Weeks continued to pursue the conspiracy case against George Ward, subpoenaing Ward family members and their Sutton Manor neighbors in an effort to force the elder Ward back to the state to testify. Laura Curtis, Beryl's mother, suddenly materialized. She was served a subpoena at the Ward's Sutton Manor home, where, she claimed, she had been living for several weeks. She appeared in White Plains wearing a large white feathered hat, a velvet dress with a string of pearls cascading to her waist, and a fox stole wrapped around her arm. But it was less about what she wore that intrigued the press than whom she came with: her attorney, the former Westchester district attorney Lee Parsons Davis. Weeks's appointment as DA came after Davis stepped down to return to private practice. Now the two men, former colleagues, would face off in court.

"The report that Mrs. Curtis has avoided service of a subpoena is absurd," Davis argued. He added, "Mrs. Curtis had been living with her daughter at her home in New Rochelle for the last month and could have been reached there readily." Davis was pointedly critical of Weeks's conspiracy investigation, calling the proceedings "illegal." He declared, "I intend to test the validity of the proceedings by advising Mrs. Curtis to refuse to answer, although she has nothing to conceal."

"They wanted me to put Mrs. Curtis in jail," Weeks later told reporters, "but I saw through it."

The district attorney conceded Davis's argument and agreed to question Curtis outside of court and, more troubling, not under oath. Sitting in Weeks's office Curtis claimed that she was at the Wards' home on the night of May 15 attending her daughter's card party, but she did not see Walter come home. She also claimed that Ward did not tell her anything about the blackmail plot nor Peters's killing, nor did she know anything about a conspiracy by George Ward to hinder the investigation. The entire meeting took only fifteen minutes.[14]

Judge Morschauser described Davis's action as just another one of his "bluffs." But it was a bluff that worked. Weeks now faced the possibility that every witness he summoned to testify in the conspiracy investigation—Ward family members and their neighbors—would also declare the proceedings illegal. Weeks's only recourse would be to jail them all, and that was certainly not what he wanted to read in the morning news. By late July, he announced the conspiracy hearings would be postponed indefinitely.

After the announcement, Allan Campbell told reporters that the district attorney was simply "attempting to gratify the daily press and discredit Ward."[15] But as Campbell criticized the attacks on his client, he and his colleagues were secretly pursuing new claims about the character of Clarence Peters.

Queenie of Haverhill

In early July, while he was lingering in his White Plains jail cell, Walter Ward received a letter from a Mrs. J. Jones, 15 Bartlett Street, Haverhill, Massachusetts.

> Dear Sir,
>
> I have wrote [*sic*] these few lines to you because I have no idea who your attorneys are. At the same time I may be of assistance to you. Ask your attorneys if they have a detective name A.B. Monroe. He belongs to Pinkerton Detective Agency and led me to believe he was working for your case for your benefit. I have good reason now to believe otherwise after bringing another man here yesterday in an automobile.
>
> If such is the case let someone see me quickly for my daughter and myself have already given him important information intended for yourself. He told me our information had been sent to your attorneys. Somehow I doubt it. We were asked to keep everything secret and have done so up to now but I saw something in the paper here last night which has made me write this letter, for I may keep quiet too long and make it too late to help you.

He told us it would save your life after we told him our story.

Please act quickly.

Yours respectfully,
Mrs. J. Jones

On the top of the letter, Mrs. Jones wrote and underlined, "Please keep my name and address from paper men at present." And along the corner, she added, "Keep your courage and I can help you, I'm sure."[1] She also included A. B. Monroe's business card with his address and phone number in Boston. Monroe was in fact a Pinkerton detective working for the district attorney's office and assigned to Haverhill to investigate Clarence Peters. Whatever prompted Mrs. Jones's suspicions about Monroe, they were correct.

It is hard to tell if Ward was encouraged or concerned by Mrs. Jones's offer of assistance. We do know that he handed the letter over to Allan Campbell, who soon sent his law partner, Samuel Miller, and one of their own detectives to Haverhill to investigate.

MRS. JONES WAS known in Haverhill as Goldie Jones. At the house on Bartlett Street she lived with her husband, Joseph, her twenty-one-year-old daughter, Queenie, and her five-year-old son, Roland. At least that was how she described her family to the neighbors.

The Joneses had lived in Haverhill for less than a year. Sometime in 1919 they left their native Birkenhead, England, an industrial town outside of Liverpool, and immigrated to the United States. Since then, they'd had a habit of moving around. A few months in New York, a few more in Boston, then a move to a small apartment in Roxbury, a neighborhood in south Boston, followed by nearly a year in Revere, Massachusetts, before they ended up on Bartlett Street in Haverhill.

Joseph Jones was a slender man in his midfifties and sported a thick black mustache that made him look older than his age. His experience was in the meat trade. As they moved from place to place, he supported the family by finding work at the local butcher, though such jobs usually paid a meager salary. While in Haverhill, Joseph worked at the United Butcher Shop in the center of the city, and money continued to be a problem.[2] Goldie's daughter, Queenie, was, by all accounts, a modern woman. Her hair cut short in a bob, she was often seen around Haverhill in drop-waist cotton dresses that hung off her slight frame. Detectives described her appearance as the "type known as a flapper."[3]

Sometime in late June 1922, Goldie Jones started telling Pinkerton detectives what she knew about Clarence Peters. It seemed everywhere you looked in Slipper City that summer someone was asking questions about young Clarence. The city was "flooded with Pinkerton men," the *Haverhill Evening Gazette* declared, "and they were investigating every movement the boy ever made."[4] Some detectives were working for Ward's attorneys; others were paid by the Westchester DA's office. It was often confusing to know who was who. Though sorting out who was asking the questions was easier than sorting out the stories themselves. From operators at the telephone exchange, workers at the Carlton Fruit Company, sales ladies at a small shop that sold wooden heels, trolley conductors and ushers at the Academy of Music to William Smith, who owned the popular Smith Lunch Café and William Mobley, the proprietor of the busy Professor Bill Artist Bootblack near the train station, comments about the oldest son of Elbridge and Inez Peters were in great supply.

Mobley, an African American who had arrived in Haverhill in the 1890s from Kentucky, had built a local empire expanding from a small shoeshine stand to a prosperous business of hat blocking, cleaning, and dyeing company. By the 1920s, he owned several properties in town, including the Orpheum theater, and was well-known among lawyers and businessmen.[5] Mobley claimed he'd seen Peters with a well-dressed man outside his shop back in April and "wondered what Peters and a man of this type were doing together."

William Smith had employed Clarence for a short while for manual labor around the café but thought Peters was not very smart. He described him as "big and good looking. The women were very fond of him." Smith also recalled Peters came into his café with a well-dressed, wealthy-looking man who purchased his most expensive cigars. The man "looked kind of bashful, also manicured fingers and swell clothes," Smith remembered. Peters told Smith the two of them were "going where we can make some big money." It was the last time he saw Peters.

It was hard to tell which stories to believe. One informant told detectives that both Smith and Mobley were being paid to "invent" stories about Peters and his mysterious, wealthy friend. By whom was unclear. Sifting through the truths and lies was part of the work, for despite the fact that Clarence Peters had so few friends, almost everyone in Slipper City had a story to tell about him.[6]

But the Jones family apparently had a particularly convincing one. Tall and confident, Goldie Jones used peroxide to bleach her hair a bright blond, which made her very "noticeable" on the streets, according to one local informant. With her direct way of addressing people, buttressed by an English accent, Goldie could easily command a room. "Imposing" is how one detective described her. She claimed that in England before the war, she had been a singer and a stage actress. We can imagine that few who encountered her would have doubted such claims.[7]

At the house on Bartlett Street, Goldie told a Pinkerton agent working for Weeks that Clarence had visited them many times during that spring, as he and Queenie had become good friends. Before he left Haverhill in April, Peters was at their home nearly every day. She remembered how Peters had a certain talent for storytelling, engaging her and Queenie with his adventures overseas in the navy and even his trips to New York City. "I always looked on his stories of wild life and gay times as a bluff," Goldie told detectives. But when he told the Joneses that he was leaving for White Plains and New Rochelle where he "had a very wealthy friend," they apparently believed him.

At some point in their many conversations, Goldie told Peters she wished to return to Liverpool, but the trip would cost two hundred dollars. Peters offered to help and promised he could get the money from his friend in New Rochelle and send it to her. He also promised to send a diamond ring for Queenie. Rumors were that Queenie and Clarence were dating, though detectives heard similar stories about other young women around town. The *Haverhill Evening Gazette* reported that Clarence had asked many of these young women to marry him, but all had refused his proposals. Perhaps Queenie was his last chance, if in fact we can believe the Joneses' story.

But Goldie began to get suspicious of some of the detectives, and particularly A. B. Monroe, whom Goldie initially believed was working for Walter Ward's attorney. That's when she wrote the letter to Ward, prompting Samuel Miller's visit to discuss what the Jones family knew about Clarence Peters. Whatever she told them, Miller found the information compelling, as he set up surveillance at 15 Bartlett Street.

When Detective Monroe returned to talk with Goldie, she told him Peters wrote out his White Plains address on a small scrap of paper and gave it to Queenie, asking her to write to him. Monroe asked to see the address, but Goldie couldn't find that scrap of paper. She did say she would be happy to go to New York with the agent and "turn over" the address to Walter Ward's attorneys.

It was at that moment that the detective realized Goldie had been talking to others. "I'm not with Ward's attorneys," the detective clarified, at which point Goldie jumped up from her chair and started to shout at him. "She became excited," he wrote in his report. Goldie accused the detective of deceiving her, of pretending to be working for Ward but in fact working for the DA's office. She raised her voice and kept shouting harsh accusations at the detective, poking the air with her finger with each claim. "You told me that all the information I gave you was going to Ward's attorney," she shouted.

It was possible that the detective had deceived Goldie, had told her what she wanted to hear to get information on Peters. But then why drop the act on that afternoon in early July? It was more likely that Goldie, the former Liverpool stage actress, delivered a convincing performance. As her anger raged on, Samuel Miller and a detective by the name of Matthews climbed up the basement steps and entered the kitchen. Still in a fit, Goldie left the room and walked out to the back porch.

Miller was the younger of the two, dark haired, stout, and shorter than Matthews, whose bushy hair was nearly all gray.

"Are you working for Ward?" Miller asked. Monroe denied he was, leaving the men to assume he was working for the prosecutor's office. The conversation quickly became adversarial, with Miller firing a series of questions at the agent: Was he a "Pinkerton man"? Had he turned over any evidence from Haverhill to Weeks or to any other attorney in the case? What information had he found out about Peters's last weeks in Haverhill?

Refusing their questions, Monroe made his way to leave but not before the two explained that they had installed a Dictograph in the cellar and that they would be listening in on any conversations Goldie Jones would have in the coming days. We can imagine the scene verging on the comic and absurd, as detectives were spying on detectives, and no one knew for sure who was working for whom. For the next few days, Miller and Matthews shadowed Monroe as he moved around Haverhill making clear they were watching what the DA's office was learning about Clarence Peters.[8]

THE EDITOR OF the *Haverhill Evening Gazette*, George Houston, had little sympathy for Walter Ward or his agents skulking around town asking questions, digging up dirt on the Peterses' son. He knew the family and had no doubt that whatever delinquencies Clarence had committed in the past, he was not a violent criminal. "He was a poor boob," he told detectives, "sub-normal, but surely not guilty of any serious crime."

In May as Peters's murder made national headlines, Houston went to New York to interview the investigators and attorneys. He had a tense meeting with Allan Campbell in his firm's Broadway office. Houston had been dubious of Ward's statement from the start and found little insight from Campbell, who evaded most of his questions. The editor left the meeting even more convinced that something just wasn't right with the entire story.

So when Miller and Matthews came by the newspaper's offices

in July, just days after the incident in Goldie Jones's kitchen, Miller reminded Houston of that earlier interview in New York and hoped the editor could help them out with their investigations around town. They said they could prove "two very serious crimes against Peters," a claim that enraged the editor. According to detectives, Houston's response to the men was so volcanic and obscene that he refrained from including it in his report as the words "would not look well."[9]

At some point, the district attorney's investigators decided to out Goldie Jones's story, exposing how Ward's attorneys were trying to hide a witness. Houston published a front-page article on July 26: "Peters Planned to Obtain Cash from Rich Man." The facts of the article were taken almost verbatim from the detective reports, detailing the story Goldie had told in her kitchen, the confrontation between Ward's agents and A. B. Monroe, as well as their Dictograph operation in the Joneses' basement.

When *Gazette* journalists went to Bartlett Street to interview Goldie for the article, she said Campbell had told her to "keep her mouth shut"—a task that proved particularly difficult for the former actress. As Slipper City readers learned that the Joneses were involved in the case, many were probably not so surprised. But when they read that Ward's agents had set up a Dictograph in the basement of the Joneses' home, it must have seemed to some like the entire town was filled with spies.

The *Gazette* article was picked up by *The Boston Globe* and *The New York Herald*, circulating Jones's story well beyond Haverhill and making Goldie and Queenie the newest central characters in the ongoing investigation.[10] Weeks was surprised by the entire story. "There may be Ward detectives working on the case," he told reporters, "but as yet I have had no report from my man in Haverhill," adding that the Joneses' story was in fact "news to him."

Weeks's statement was a complete lie of course. Ten days earlier, Harry Scott, superintendent of the New York Pinkerton office, had sent a letter to the DA expressing his concerns with the Jones family and had included the detective report detailing the encounter his agent had had at Goldie's house:

> We are attaching report of our Opt. A.B.M. dated Boston, July 12. No doubt you will find same quite interesting. Boston office has been instructed to make every effort to learn the real identity of the men Miller and Matthews. The writer does not know either of these names as being connected with the Ward defense. However, they are probably detectives, and if so, we have instructed Boston to work along the lines that Queenie Jones is possibly a coached and paid witness, and this is something, of course, which will be of the utmost value to you in case investigation develops a situation of this kind. We have felt all along that Queenie Jones was coached by someone, and if it is possible for us to get her to admit that she is a framed witness, it will no doubt aid your case materially.[11]

We don't know what Weeks said in his reply to Scott, but his public claims of ignorance about the Joneses' story point to an orchestrated deception. By planting the article, the prosecution turned the tables from doubts about Clarence Peters's character to questions about why Allan Campbell might be silencing witnesses. Perhaps Weeks and his agents did not wish to repeat the James Cunningham debacle, getting caught up in the fantastical stories of a material witness who, in all likelihood, was planted by the defense. And Goldie Jones was no James Cunningham. As one agent reported, "when dressed for the street," Goldie was an "imposing woman" and, if properly coached, would make a "dangerous witness."[12] If the Jones family really did have compelling information about Peters—information that would seemingly confirm Ward's story—why, readers might have wondered, were Ward and his attorneys so eager to keep them quiet?

INEZ PETERS CALLED the article a "pack of damn lies" and told detectives that Clarence barely knew Goldie and Queenie. She acknowledged the Joneses came to Clarence's funeral to express their condolences. But in the weeks after, both mother and daughter were spreading stories about Inez and Elbridge and the dire homelife their children endured. It got so bad, apparently, that Inez had to take the matter up with an attorney, which put an end to the Joneses' town chatter. Inez repeated to detectives that Clarence had never had a gun, as he was too "soft hearted to hurt anyone." He never even went hunting, she said, which was a near rite of passage for young men in Haverhill.

At the United Butcher Shop on Merrimack Street, detectives found Goldie, Joseph, and Queenie and asked them about the *Gazette* article. Joseph said the headline was a lie but refused to explain why. Goldie was equally tight-lipped, though when asked if the newspaper stories were true, she said "there was a lot of truth in them" and left it at that. As was her nature, she found it hard to keep quiet for very long. She admitted she felt sorry for Clarence, suffering as he did at the Peterses' home, taking another jab at Inez and Elbridge. There was, she said, "a great deal of good in the lad that could be brought out by kindness and a full stomach."

She then lowered her tone and looked directly into the detective's face. "Clarence Peters is no blackmailer," she said. "I'll say that to you or anyone or before sixteen judges." She repeated this point a few times in the conversation. Queenie stood next to her mother, serious faced and nodding in agreement. Detectives expressed surprise to see Queenie out of the house on Bartlett Street, which they had under surveillance for weeks. Goldie was quick to reply, "There is good reason for remaining in seclusion."[13]

Detectives soon started asking more questions about the Jones family. Joseph's coworkers were surprised to see his name in the papers. One colleague said for "three to four weeks" Joseph knew nothing about the Peters's case, and then "he knew all about it."

Their former landlady in Boston, a Mrs. Walker, said she took them in even though they were strangers because of the "strength of them being English." She soon regretted her decision, as she found the family "strange." Goldie and Joseph were often fighting at night. Walker could hear their loud arguments through the walls. It was Goldie she heard most often shouting at her husband and using "rotten language at times." She wondered if the two were actually married. When the family left, they took furniture that Walker had loaned them and refused to give the items back when she asked about them.

In Revere, the stories were similar, with neighbors expressing complaints about the Joneses' behavior and their loud fights in the evening hours. Queenie was known to "entertain young men" at the house when her parents left her alone. One informant claimed the family owed back rent, and "numerous bill collectors were looking for them."[14] There were few around Revere who had anything nice to say about the Joneses, remembering instead the many unfavorable rumors about them that still lingered many months since the family had left.

At Brown's Market in Revere where Joseph had worked, detectives spoke with his supervisor, a man named Eugene McGillicuddy. He remembered that Joseph was all right as a worker, but "Mrs. Jones seemed to be a trouble maker." But it was McGillicuddy's story about Queenie, what many in town were often gossiping about, that interested the detectives the most.

Queenie's brother Roland was actually her son, fathered by an American sailor by the name of Arthur Elliot. Detectives tracked down Elliot, who told them he had met Queenie during the war while stationed in Liverpool, though in England Queenie went by the name of Jessie Smith. He was twenty-one, and she was seventeen when the two first met. Elliot explained that Joseph had entered into a bad business deal with a meat supplier and had left town for a while, only to return to exchange one exceptionally common English name for another—the Smith family became the Joneses.

Elliot recalled how he and Jessie had had sex the first night they met and continued to see each other for the next two months. He remembered when he went to visit her, he often had to "race four or five other sailors to get there first," as she was having sex with all of them. The Smiths did treat him in "fine style," Elliot conceded, and for a sailor far from home, their hospitality was much appreciated.

When Elliot returned to Boston at the war's end, he knew nothing of Queenie's pregnancy until the Joneses arrived in the United States. As Queenie held the young Roland in her arms, Goldie demanded Elliot marry her daughter. He never mentioned to detectives if he questioned Roland's paternity. It seemed he simply believed the family's claims, perhaps out of guilt or a sense of honor or succumbing to Goldie's particular skills at intimidation. Whatever the case, Elliot agreed to marry Queenie to make, in his words, the "child legitimate."

The two married on May 15, 1919, in Boston. On the marriage certificate Queenie is identified as Jessie Collette and her father as Robert Collette, indicating that Joseph was perhaps her stepfather. Goldie went by the name of Jessie Johnson, suggesting that Goldie and Joseph may not have been married. Changing their name from Smith to Jones back in England was not the first time the family had assumed new identities. It all must have been a confusing situation for young Elliot, marrying into a family who were experts at deception, feeling perhaps that he had been drawn into some kind of con by the very people who treated him so well during the war. But the deceptions would only grow deeper. Soon after the wedding, Elliot learned that Roland had already been adopted by Goldie, putting into doubt his own rights to his son—if Roland was in fact his son.

Elliot's relatives told detectives that Queenie was not right for him. "She was slack and not a good helpmate, nor a good housekeeper," one family member recalled. The marriage deteriorated quickly and Elliot devised an escape plan not long after the ink on the marriage license dried.

Stationed at the Deer Island naval base in Boston Harbor, Elliot kept his distance for the next two years, rarely seeing his wife or the family. His absence prompted Queenie to have him arrested for nonsupport. In court, Goldie testified that her daughter was at "death's door on account of Elliot's actions." Then in February 1922, a formal divorce was granted on the grounds of cruel and abusive treatment, a claim Queenie argued before the judge, and Elliot did not contest, hoping, one can imagine, to be done with the entire affair. While the judge granted the divorce, he denied Queenie the right to resume her maiden name. Though we can imagine that such a condition would have mattered little to the Jones family.[15] It was a few weeks after the divorce became final that Clarence Peters began to visit the Jones home and allegedly promised Queenie a diamond ring.

IN EARLY AUGUST, just three weeks after the article was published in the *Haverhill Evening Gazette*, 15 Bartlett Street had been emptied out. Joseph could not find anyone to buy the household furnishings, so workers from a secondhand shop hauled the few pieces of furniture, along with the dishes and pots and glasses to their shop on Pecker Street.

Gossip among neighbors and Joseph's coworkers at the United Butcher Shop suggested the family was going back to England. But others suspected they were instead on their way to New York. Elliot's grandmother told detectives that Goldie telephoned to say the family was moving to New York for a while. But, she said, when they returned to Haverhill "they would have a lot of money, enough to buy Arthur an automobile." Elliot, understandably, wanted nothing to do them.

The truth of their move was found at the Haverhill Post Office, where Goldie Jones left a forwarding address effective July 31, 1922: "General Delivery, New York City, N.Y."[16]

Housecleaning

When J. Henry Esser took the podium at the Westchester Biltmore Country Club in early September, he was buoyed by increasing support for his district attorney nomination. The forty-three-year-old Esser was a stout man, balding and round faced with light-blue eyes. He was a good Republican Party member and deeply concerned by the handling of the Ward case. His speech would be one of the first political events at the newly completely country club, built on a former estate and anchoring an entire village of large mansions that surrounded a rambling golf course. The club's main building, with its stucco-and-brick facade, sat on a grassy hill and resembled a Florentine prince's country villa. In the dining room, with its wood-beamed ceiling and white plaster walls, Esser addressed nearly 150 Republican women, who all came to hear the candidate's ideas on changing the Republican Party.

"This scandalous failure of justice is laid squarely at the door of the Republican Party," he declared, speaking with a fiery excitement and pointed criticism of his party and, in particular, Weeks's handling of the Ward indictment. He accused the party of concealment and fraud and claimed the Ward case has become a weapon in the hands of the Democrats.

"Republican voters can and should do their own housecleaning in this county," he told the women in the room, apparently appealing to their sense of domestic duty. If nominated, Esser declared, he would call upon Weeks to refrain from bringing the case to trial, as he feared Weeks lacked a solid case to convict.

"If Walter Ward is a guilty man," he said, "he should never be tried and acquitted on a half-baked case, and therefore given immunity from all further prosecution." More pointedly, Esser accused the DA of yielding to wealth and power rather than to the rule of law, something that Democrats had been complaining about since Ward's confession.

"We are face to face," he said, "with the problem of whether a rich man is entitled to any different treatment before the bar of justice than a poor man."

Esser's appeal for justice was a sharp sword pointed not only at Weeks but also at William Ward, the sixty-seven-year-old Republican Party boss in the county. His power was so well-known, the press often referred to the local Republican Party as the Ward Organization. According to Esser, that grip on power had led only to corruption, most clearly evident in the district attorney's office.

"I stand here in the political arena," Esser vowed in a gesture of political idealism, "to hold aloft the torch which has fallen from the hands of the District Attorney. I will dare, so long as the strength is given me, to fight for the dignified, efficient, and impartial enforcement of our laws, regardless of whom I have to oppose."[1] There was generous support among the Republican women, their applause spilling out the open windows onto the nearby golfing greens.

Esser was part of a group of Republicans who saw the 1922 election as a ripe opportunity to seize power away from William Ward, prompting a primary fight that the *New-York Tribune* described as a "war on Ward."[2] Days after Walter Ward's release on bail in July, the group announced their plans to challenge the party boss. The press labeled the group "insurgents" or, more objectively, "independents." In their vehement opposition to William Ward, they were more often referred to as the anti-Ward candidates.

Esser emerged as the most vocal critic among the group. The failures of the Peters investigation became a powerful wedge in their efforts to diminish William Ward's influence over every political post in the county and state, from congressional representatives to police commissioners, from sheriffs and county clerks to state supreme court nominees. Anyone who wished to be on the ballot for the Republican Party had to find favor with William Ward.[3]

Just days before the September primary, Esser, suffering from a broken rib due to a fishing accident, traveled to New Rochelle to give a speech not far from Walter Ward's Sutton Manor neighborhood. The event prompted menacing letters to the candidate. "If you dare come to New Rochelle and start any of your talk about the Ward case, you will get something worse than broken ribs," one letter threatened, adding mysteriously, "Weeks knew what was good for him." Esser publicly denounced such threats to a crowd of nearly five hundred people.

"These scandalous, threatening letters," he told his listeners,

> have not been sent to me because of anything I have said or will say about the trial of Walter Ward. It was about my demand for the indictment of the two alleged blackmailers who Ward says were with Peters when he shot him to death that has roused the underworld of New Rochelle and possibly elsewhere to make these threats of violence against me.

Esser then pointed to the corruption in the DA's office and the soiled reputation of the fine people of New Rochelle.

"I stand on my promise," he declared, "if elected, to remove this blot from the City of New Rochelle." In a gesture of populist sentiment, he empathized with the city's residents, who, he declared, "want to know the truth about this affair, and they want justice done. They do not want it said hereafter that murder or blackmail may be committed in New Rochelle and go unpunished."

Esser's message was consistent throughout his campaign, harnessing public outrage over the handling of the Ward case while decrying the corruption the case epitomized. Esser was a committed Republican, and while his campaign criticized William Ward's hold on the party, it was also an effort to save Republicans from a November defeat.

"This mess lies squarely at the door of the Republican Party," he told the crowd, relying on his reliable trope of cleanliness: "We cannot evade it or escape it. We must clean it up. If we do not the people may hand the job over to the Democrats to do."[4]

WHILE THE INSURGENTS used Weeks's handling of the Ward-Peters case as a bulwark against the Republican Party leadership, William Ward had been supportive of Weeks's nomination throughout the summer—at least publicly. When the Westchester County Republican Committee met in July, they nominated Weeks with enthusiasm. It might have been a surprising move to some, as the DA had not expressed much interest in running for office. William Ward was direct and confrontational in his support of Weeks.

"The Republican organization does not go before the voters in any spirit of apology," he declared. "The Republican office holders have conducted their offices with ability and dignity."

A fellow party member echoed this sentiment when he nominated the DA, stating, "We want a man of moral courage, who will not be stampeded by public clamor." Perhaps such declarations were a bargain Weeks made with the committee, an endorsement of his character that was also a measure of the Republican Party's courage to stand by morals rather than public opinion.[5]

However strong those public endorsements had been, in the waning days of August, Weeks suddenly and, for some, unexpectedly withdrew his nomination. His statement to the press was a simple one: "I cannot practice law and be District Attorney, and I must give more time to my practice." In public, his reasoning to step down was for his son, who was studying law and for whom he wished to leave his law practice. But to many, his decision had been predicted for some time. His investigation into Peters's murder continued to stumble and had become a threat to Republican reelection, as the insurgent candidates made clear in their many campaign speeches. The rumors that his support among his Republican colleagues was increasingly thin only intensified the public rifts between him and his party.

"By retiring voluntarily from the field," Esser complained, Weeks "has made it easy for those who will do so to claim that he would not risk a campaign with the Ward murder case as an issue; and," he continued, "that he would not venture an encounter with those political influences behind the Ward defense."[6]

It was true. Weeks owed much of his political career to the very men who wanted this case to just disappear, not the least of whom was Ward's lawyer Isaac Mills. The respected judge had been a staunch political ally and friend of Weeks's since before he was first elected DA in 1914. But in the summer of 1922, that friendship had reached a breaking point.

"I'll run my own office," Weeks told Mills in a private conversation in July, just before Ward's release on bail. According to some reports, it was a rebuke that would break the two men's decades-long friendship and create a rupture in the Republican Party as well. Just how much Weeks was willing to confront those "political influences" behind the Ward–Peters case was uncertain. Perhaps his withdrawal from the nomination was forced by those in the party. Perhaps he was simply exhausted by the political pressure and public scrutiny the investigation had exacted. The Ward case became such an albatross. Whatever the reason, the hope of removing Weeks from the ballot, by force or choice, did not in fact remove the scandal of the murder investigation on the upcoming election.

In August, a few days after he announced he would not be on the ballot, Weeks showed his increasing desire to be done with the entire case.

"The trial will be brought on when I am ready," he told reporters who were hounding him for a trial date. "I have the whip hand and no one can force me to go to trial until I decide to do so."

Ever the purveyor of striking metaphors to describe his work, Weeks seemed more eager to threaten with the whip than to actually use it. He had at that point already ended the contract with the Pinkertons. The superintendent of the New York office, Harry Scott, sent Weeks a sixteen-page invoice itemizing the lunches, suppers, telephone calls, train tickets, taxi fares, and the mysteriously phrased "Necessary Expenses Seeking Information," as well as the daily wage for each agent who worked on the case over the last four months—twelve dollars a day was the going rate. The bill totaled $2,780.15—or about the amount of a down payment for a modest-sized home in Sutton Manor.

When asked if any new developments had emerged in the case over the summer, Weeks was terse: "No, I am not giving more information to the press. I'm not talking about the Ward case anymore."[7]

DESPITE THEIR STRONG presence in campaigning that September, the group of insurgents failed miserably at the polls, taking only 5 percent of the ballot victories. Esser lost to Arthur Rowland, the assistant DA under Weeks who replaced his supervisor on the ballot. The vote count was not even close, with Esser losing by nearly 7,000 votes out of 18,774 votes cast. Rowland would go on to win the DA post in the November general elections.[8] The Ward Organization emerged undamaged.

While Rowland's victory secured William Ward's control over the district attorney's office in White Plains, in the state capital that November, Republicans had less to celebrate. They lost their huge majorities in the state house and senate, and Democrats flipped fifteen of New York's congressional seats. The biggest victory went to Al Smith, the forty-nine-year-old populist Democrat who had been defeated by Nathan Miller two years earlier. He made a huge political comeback in beating the Republican by more than 375,000 votes, the largest win in the state's history. The victories in New York were felt across the country as Democrats won on state and national ballots.

"I expected a big Democratic sweep," Smith told reporters on election night. "This is greater and bigger than I expected and imposes a greater obligation on me, a great responsibility I hope I can meet."

The sharpest differences between the two candidates for governor were their stances on Prohibition. Miller was a firm believer in the

Eighteenth Amendment and used his office to promote the dry movement in any way he could. His widely unpopular Mullan-Gage Act was even more draconian than the federal Volstead Act, outlawing the production and possession of alcohol across the state and giving police wide powers to search anyone they suspected of carrying alcohol.

"When you get rid of the lovely picture painted by the press," Smith said about Miller, "of the welfare and economy Governor, the friend of the common people, of labor and of women and children, what is left is a real reactionary Governor of the old-fashioned Republican school." Smith campaigned as a so-called wet candidate, and his anti-Prohibition stance appealed to urban voters and immigrants, particularly in his hometown of New York City. Residents of the nation's largest city were increasingly tired of the dictates of the moral reformers that Nathan Miller and his Republicans represented. Which is why few were surprised when Smith won every precinct in the city.[9]

THREE DAYS AFTER the November elections, Isaac Mills was once again standing in front of Judge Morschauser and once again requesting a trial date.

"The District Attorney has had the matter in his hands for six months and three days, and he ought to be able to present his case if he has one," Mills argued. He complained that it was unfair to his client to hold up the trial. Weeks, he said, should be "man enough" to say that he has not enough evidence, rather than to let the indictment linger on for so many months. "If I cannot get a trial for Mr. Ward," he concluded, "to which he is entitled after this long delay then it is my duty to bring about, if possible, a dismissal of the charges."

John Mack, assistant district attorney, argued for the prosecution, as Weeks was increasingly absent in the case and clearly had little energy left to wield that whip hand he'd declared weeks earlier. Mack contended that the investigation was ongoing and that the state had a right to take its time.

"There is no denying that all that is left of Peters is a little mound of earth," Mack argued. "This man should be held until every bit of evidence has been run down. We have spent money and we are going to spend lots more to help solve this mystery."

Mills retorted that the only real mystery was the nature of the blackmail itself. "For obvious family reasons," he said, "he does not wish to give that information, and he should not be compelled to give it unless the people first make out a case against him. The revelation of these stories," he said with a certain disdain, "can serve only to satisfy the prurient public curiosity."[10]

Morschauser wasted little time siding with the prosecution. "At this time motion denied without prejudice," he declared.

WITH AN EYE to Weeks's exit from the district attorney's office on January 1, Mills filed yet another motion on New Year's Eve to dismiss the indictment against Ward. Three days later, Ward and his attorneys were back in court arguing their motion. Only this time, they stood before the often accommodating supreme court justice Seeger, the man who had twice admitted Ward on bail.

Mills detailed the facts of the case and plotted the timeline of the DA investigation and argued nothing had been uncovered to dispute Ward's original statement. Mills wondered why the district attorney's office had been so curious about how Peters, "plying his nefarious trade, was shot and killed by his intended and outraged victim."

As Beryl Ward sat behind her husband, calm as usual, Mills declared that blackmail was worse than killing, as it threated Ward's children and had slandered his wife. He concluded with an image of Ward as father and husband who had endured enough at the hands of the prosecutor's office.

"He has in no manner sought to evade prosecution," Mills declared, "and there is not the least danger of his running away. If further evidence should be discovered by the prosecution, and another indictment found, he will be here ready to meet the accusation." He concluded, "Justice must have a heart."

Newly elected District Attorney Rowland, only three days on the job, offered less of an argument and more of an accommodation for the defense.

"There is no doubt that this case is still fraught with a great deal of mystery," he told the court. "I doubt very much that we as yet have the full God's honest truth." He claimed that thousands of dollars had already been spent on the investigation following every lead imaginable, "but we have been able to get nowhere. We are in the same position as we were in several months ago."

Rowland's statement sounded as if he either knew very little of the investigation or, taking a lesson from his predecessor, decided that this six-month-long case was not going to mire his first term as DA.

"The case has become old. It is stale," Judge Seeger declared from the bench, suggesting the murder indictment was akin to an old loaf of Tip-Top Bread. He continued,

> Under the constitution, Ward was entitled to a trial. But there has been no evidence brought out to overcome the truth of the statement Ward made through his attorney when he walked in this courthouse and declared he had killed a man. Killing a man in self-defense is no crime. The State has shown nothing to prove Peters was not killed in self-defense. It is therefore better for the State that this motion is granted.

Seeger's decision ended the six-month-long investigation, and the charges against Walter Ward were dropped. Ward, looking vindicated and relieved, walked with Beryl arm in arm out of the courthouse. The normally reticent Ward stopped at one moment before getting into a waiting car and told the press, "I am so happy."

Later that afternoon, journalists went to Weeks's home for a comment on Seeger's decision. They found only his maid, who pointedly told reporters the former DA had "gone out of town," and she didn't know when he would return.[11]

News of Justice Seeger's ruling made front-page headlines across the country. "Walter Ward, Rich Baker's Son, Freed of Murder," the *Dayton Daily News* declared in Dayton, Ohio. The *Anaheim Bulletin* in California announced, "Walter Ward Freed on Charge of Slaying." The *Detroit Free Press* included a photograph of a smiling Ward captioned, "Rich Baker's Son Who Is Freed of Murder Charges," as did the *Bangor Daily News* in Bangor, Maine, with its large-font headline: "Ward Freed on Charge of Murder." In Juneau, Alaska, editors of *The Alaska Daily Empire* betrayed a sense of relief with their headline: "Mysterious Shooting Case in New York Finally Dismissed."[12]

The New York press also seemed exhausted by the six-month investigation with its many twists and turns that all led back to Ward's original statement. "An Expensive Mistake" is how the *New-York Tribune* described the case, pointing to the costs of the DA's investigation. "There has never been any real evidence against him beyond his own story of the shooting," the editors complained, pointing fault at both Ward's privilege and the incompetence of the investigation. Ward's path to justice and the district attorney's reputation would have been better served, the editors contended, if they would have approached the case as they would with any "ordinary citizen."[13]

It was a common criticism in those cold days of January, a lingering sense that there were in fact two systems of justice: one for the rich and one for those "ordinary" citizens.

But, the editors appeared to concede, what really could be done about it?

An Uncertain Justice

Grief-Stricken Mothers

INEZ PETERS STOOD ON THE PLATFORM AT THE HAVERHILL train station on a cold and gray January morning. She wore her heavy, dark wool coat and simple black boots, as the forecast called for snow later in the day. Black was also the color of her dress—a symbol of mourning she'd often worn since Clarence's funeral six months earlier. She might have been nervous, standing there with her attorney, Fred Magison, as the two discussed the trip that would take them to Albany, New York, and a meeting with newly elected governor Al Smith. Magison had connections to Democratic assemblymen in Albany who had helped set up the meeting. Haverhill neighbors pooled what little money they could to help Peters purchase her ticket. She was not the kind of woman who ever imagined meeting a governor. She still struggled with the publicity that this entire tragedy had thrust upon her. As she stood in the gray morning light, we can imagine her repeating a stanza from a poem by Haverhill native John Greenleaf Whittier that Clarence often recited to her:

> Through this dark and stormy night
> Faith beholds a feeble light
> Up the blackness streaking;
> Knowing God's own time is best,
> In a patient hope I rest
> For the full day-breaking!

Whatever fears she might have had in meeting with the New York governor were tempered by the frustrations of finding some peace about her son's murder. For months, Clarence often appeared in her dreams. *Nightmares* were perhaps a better name for them. She described how "Clarence's spirit" would stand off in the distance and try to speak to her. But she could never make out his words. "I could see his lips move. I see the tears on his cheeks, but he can't speak to me," she said. She took to shouting Clarence's name in her sleep, waking up Elbridge and her children in the dark hours of the morning. Elbridge must have wished for some way to help his wife, though such behaviors were rarely talked about. And besides, how could Inez find any help for her nightmares when she couldn't even pay for her own train ticket? She was certain that she would continue to be haunted by her son's spirit until Walter Ward was brought to justice.

After six months and a barrage of theories about her son's death, Inez Peters remained convinced that Clarence never knew Walter Ward until the night he was killed. His life, she said, "was such that he couldn't have known him." She believed Clarence was hitchhiking his way home from New York when the two men met. "I don't know why Ward killed him," she said. As she boarded the train, we can imagine how determined Inez must have been to rid herself of that mystery and those terrifying dreams of her muted son.[1]

IT MADE SENSE that Peters would appeal directly to Governor Smith. The populist Democrat had just won a landslide victory in New York and was a national political figure. Many considered him to be the next Democratic Party nominee for president. It was an unlikely rise for a man who grew up Catholic on the Lower East Side with little education beyond public school. The child of Irish and German immigrants, Smith spent much of his early life in overcrowded tenements. His first job at the Fulton Fish Market eventually led to a government position that drew him into the city's powerful Tammany Hall political machine, where he rose through the ranks to eventually be elected to the state assembly in 1904. He was an anomaly among his many Ivy League colleagues in the assembly, never having gone to college himself. The journalist H. L. Mencken described Smith as "amiable, hearty, and decent"—all qualities that endeared him to his constituents and to working-class voters across the state. Smith spoke in the vernacular of the working-class and cared about their concerns. He also spoke with the tenor of a stage actor, a skill he learned at a young age acting in local theater productions, shaping what would become a dramatic public presence. One contemporary described Smith's voice as a "nasal twang." When he took to the floor of the assembly, one reporter noted, "nobody had to put their hands to their ears to hear what he was saying. His powerful voice is at times almost sinister."[2]

Smith believed government had a role in regulating businesses and protecting and improving the labor conditions of the working class. In 1911, then assemblyman Smith and state senator Robert Wagner created the Factory Investigating Commission, more commonly known as the Triangle Commission, as it was formed after the infamous 1911 Triangle Shirtwaist Factory fire that killed 148 women workers in Greenwich Village. For four years, the commission investigated labor conditions across the state, held public hearings, and interviewed workers and owners. Frances Perkins of the Consumers' League, who had been investigating storefront bakeries, was on the commission and recalled how Smith would inspect firsthand worker safety on the factory floor and often climbed through windows or pushed through jammed doors to test the safety of fire escapes. Smith and Wagner went beyond just factories and inspected upstate vegetable farms and canneries. They toured overcrowded tenements where women and children did piecework such as sewing, making paper flowers, or rolling cigars for low pay. Throughout the state, commissioners found appalling conditions, prompting a raft of new laws regulating child labor and workplace safety. The most important legislation was the introduction of a minimum wage for women workers—a radical proposition in an era when both of the leading political parties were dubious about government's involvement in the free market. Perkins recalled how

Smith's experience on the commission was one he "never recovered" from, shaping a new political vision for the assemblyman.

Like many working-class voters, Inez Peters might have seen in Smith a politician who understood the struggles of people like herself, who knew what it was like to be poor and to stand on the outside of power and privilege. "I came here today," Peters told reporters outside Smith's office in Albany, "to plead with Governor Smith for justice, because I have read of his great devotion to his aged mother, and I felt that he would see that justice was done."

The meeting lasted nearly thirty minutes. "I am asking for justice at your hands," Peters told Smith. She impressed upon him the hardships she had endured. "I don't remember ever having any good luck," she said. "I have had ten children. Only five of them are alive. Three were taken from me within the past five years." She stressed that she did not wish to punish Walter Ward if he was in fact innocent of the crime. But, she said, her son deserved to have a jury hear the case. "If some poor boy had killed my son," she implored Smith, "I honestly believe he would have been tried and either convicted or acquitted a long time ago." Magison detailed for the governor a timeline of the case and how Ward's statement did not match the evidence. "The facts disprove every statement made on behalf of Ward," he said, adding, "What we do know is that Walter Ward killed Clarence Peters and he is a free man today." His summation for the governor was simple: "All we ask is that you have the state make a thorough investigation into the killing of Peters." Inez sat quietly through much of the meeting, holding back tears and dabbing her eyes with a black-bordered handkerchief as she listened to her attorney recount the facts of her son's death.

The governor expressed deep sympathy for Peters. "I don't care how much wealth the Ward family has," he told her. "If I find there is sufficient evidence to force Walter Ward to trial, he will explain to a jury the killing of your boy." He added, "I know it is hard for a parent to lose a child. And it is doubly hard to lose a son in such a way as your boy met his death."[3]

Whether moved by Peters's pleas of "the grief stricken mother," as the press described her, or prompted by Magison's arguments,

Smith emerged from the meeting resolved to reconsider the investigation, directing his staff attorneys, Owen Potter and James Parsons, to look into the case. It was one of the first tasks for the newly elected governor. He could have moved quickly with an order to have the attorney general set up an extraordinary grand jury to reinvestigate the entire case, with the power to call witnesses and subpoena evidence. But Smith took a more cautionary approach, still perhaps uncertain whether he should even get involved in a local murder investigation.

He must have heard the rumblings in the state assembly to open a legislative inquiry into the case. One Democrat assemblymen described the investigation done by Weeks and Werner as a "gross dereliction of duty" and complained that the district attorney's office in Westchester needed a "good cleaning out, and had needed it for years." Another Democrat, representing Manhattan, asked, "Do you mean to tell me that Walter Ward with all the wealth at his command hasn't made some financial settlement upon the poverty pinched Peters family?" He added, "I want the Governor to rip that case wide open. Let's prove to the people of this State that there is equal justice for the rich and the poor."[4] Some in the assembly argued that Justice Seeger should be impeached. While Democrats introduced resolutions to begin hearings into the case, they remained in the minority in both houses. Efforts for a legislative inquiry would be difficult as Republican assemblymen were sure to block such moves. If Inez Peters had any hope of finding justice, it would have to come from Governor Smith.

Days after Peters's meeting with Smith, a small editorial appeared in local newspapers across the country titled "The Still Small Voice." The title recalled a line from the Old Testament about the power of following one's conscience, that inner voice that drives us toward moral action. The syndicated, unsigned editorial appeared in nearly the same format in small-town newspapers from Roanoke, Alabama, and Stonewall, Oklahoma, to Mound Valley, Kansas, and Wood, South Dakota. While explaining the Ward–Peters case, the article pointed to the injustices of the crime in rousing rhetoric. "Ordinarily, such a menace to society would be locked up, tried for murder, sent to the electric chair, to prison for life, or acquitted according to the facts developed," the editorial proclaimed, referring to Walter Ward. "But this was not an ordinary murder," the editorial complained, arguing that the Ward family has spent millions to keep Walter out of prison, including buying more ads in influential newspapers in exchange for favorable reporting. In pointed language, the editorial demanded justice for Inez Peters and called upon other mothers to have their voices heard. "Every mother in America should write a letter to the governor of the great state of New York demanding that the investigation be searching, at least that it be more thoroughly undertaken than the travesty of justice that set free the gilded assassin."[5]

By late January, letters began arriving at the governor's office almost daily. Many were written in pencil on thin ruled stationary; their loopy, cursive handwriting often betrayed grammar and spelling errors. The sentiments in each letter were the same: mothers from across the country pleading to the governor to reopen the investigation. "If Christ in his Glory does hear a poor sinner's plea," wrote Mrs. H. N. Sherva from Iowa in reference to Inez Peters, "should not we, who profess to walk in his footsteps, also hear her pleas, judge righteously? Give her justice."

While appeals to Christian values were common in the letters, more often they were overshadowed by outrage about class privilege and injustices in the legal system. "As one of the many mothers of our U.S.A., I insist on a most thorough investigation of the dismissal of the murder indictment against Walter Ward," wrote Mrs. A. R. Hall from the farming town of Colville, Washington. "This dismissal of a self-confessed murderer is an insult to American justice. Justice deals with criminal fact, not financial." Mrs. Frank Salvage, the wife of a farmer who lived not far from Colville, wrote, "I would like for you to thoroughly investigate this affair for it's getting to be a common thing that the judge and jury are bought off as they were in this case. And if there is not a stop put to it it's going to be not many years until the poor class will be shot down like dogs and nothing said." The president of the National Association of Army Nurses of the Civil War wrote out of a duty she owed "to all mothers to speak for the poor mother whose heart is being wrung with an agony." She called the investigation a "burlesque" and declared the case "should stir every citizen of the land who believes that justice is not a commodity to be given to the rich and denied to the poor."[6]

For some mothers, the case recalled a familiar reality. Mrs. S. Vornes of Michigan described a similar incident in her town, when a young man was murdered by the son of a millionaire. "The circuit judge was taken to the home of the father 3 weeks before the trial and royally entertained. Now was there any justice in that?" she demanded, adding, "The accused got on the stand and even told that this was the third man that he had killed and still they let him go free." She ended with a familiar refrain: "I make this plea as a mother that is bereaved of a son. I am a mother of two boys. If one was cruelly shot, I certainly would thank anyone for trying to help bring them justice." Mrs. Williard Imes of Indiana saw in the case a longer history of abuse. "During slavery," she observed, "white people of the south were allowed to murder any black that happened to cross his path. This was carried out even after the war. This murder by a millionaire's son on the poor Boy compares with those of the south during slavery." She concluded with a dire warning about the times: "If money is allowed to protect murderers the end can only be Ku Klux—Bolsheviks and anarchists. This is only one case, and there are many. If it is allowed to go ahead, can you blame people for turning against the government?"

While as much as the letters were filled with anger, they also held a poignancy about the grief and struggles of the poor. "We lost our son last spring by accident," one woman wrote, "and I surely sympathize with the poor mother." Another declared, "Us poor mothers are struggling through life trying to produce citizens to be proud of. But if a rich man can shoot them down, and use a little of their surplus gold and hold their head up and March on, what can we do?" Mrs. Mary Newman, a sixty-four-year-old widow from Indiana, wrote,

> I offered three sons on the altar in the "World War" to make the world safe for all good people, and I can not sit in silence while the "Criminal Rich" make a mockery of

> law. It seems this crime is being committed for a "Criminal Rich Man's Son" who occupied a feather cushion like most of his kind during the last war. You know how it was.

She concluded with a tone of despair: "I am only speaking for one poor old mother for there are millions who have lost all hope in justice for poor people through dangerous judges." The letters were a powerful testament to the frustration so many felt about the abuses of the justice system—abuses that the grieving Inez Peters clearly symbolized for many across the country.

These letters remained private. There is no evidence that their pleas were ever reported on in the press at the time, nor did Smith mention them to journalists. The governor's staff kept them in a file folder labeled WALTER WARD CASE, where they still sit in the Alfred E. Smith papers at the New York State Archives. As the letters continued to arrive through February and March, the governor's staff must have wondered who was behind that editorial that had ignited mothers across the nation to demand justice.

Voice of the People

WALTER WARD SAT AT HIS LARGE MAHOGANY DESK IN HIS Bronx factory office. He smiled across piles of paperwork at a woman reporter from the New York *Daily News*. It was unheard of for newspapers to hire female journalists for crime beats, but the three-year-old New York tabloid was eager to break norms. Julia Harpman was well-known for her crime reporting at the tabloid. Respected for her dogged reporting, she had her own bylines on stories of murder, theft, and blackmail. But there were other women reporters at the paper who pursued the scandals and murders that the *Daily News* relied on for its compelling headlines. Of course, while Ward had little interest in talking with the press, he most likely had no idea that the young woman was in fact a crime reporter.

As she entered Ward's office, his face "broke into a polite but not exactly happy smile," she noted, describing how his "well-tailored shoulders of great breadth" rose above his cluttered desk. She described Ward as looking haggard and pale; his face showed deep lines around his mouth. While he might have enjoyed the pleasure of the company, once Ward realized his guest worked for the *Daily News* he showed little patience for her questions.

"If you were a male reporter," he told her, "I'd take you by the neck and show you the elevator." His restraint turned into frustration, complaining about the press and particularly the young tabloid. "They feed the public with sensational attacks on men of wealth," he intoned, and then quickly shifted to his more familiar silence as the "muffled roar" of the bread machines hummed in the background of their meeting. The reporter persisted, going down a list of questions she had prepared. To each Ward shook his head, refusing to answer.

Then, pausing for a moment and smiling at Ward, she asked with directness, "Do you think you would be at liberty if you were a . . . poor man?"

Ward groaned, "Oh, God!" At that point, he rose from his chair, walked to his office door, and seized it open. "You can tell your paper that I refuse to talk," he declared. The hum of the bread machines grew louder in the office, surrounding the reporter as she left. Despite his refusal to answer questions, the entire scene made for great copy in the next day's paper.[1]

THE FORTY-FOUR-YEAR-OLD FOUNDER and editor of the *Daily News*, Joe Patterson, was eager to get Walter Ward back in court. The day after Justice Seeger's dismissal of the indictment, the tabloid published a scalding editorial, decrying Seeger's decision. "There still is a bit of difference between a million dollars and poverty when both stand before the bar of justice," the editorial asserted. "A million dollars may hurdle the bar; poverty can't." It was a claim the paper had made since the early days of the investigation, but now, the ambitious upstart among the New York press, the *Daily News* declared that the case was no longer about a singular incident but about a larger question of class privilege and the American justice system. "Ward's lawyer," the editorial concluded, "in pleading that his client be dismissed, declared that 'Justice must have a heart.' And Justice, deaf, dumb, blind, and hog-tied, proceeded to 'have a heart.'"[2] It was the kind of fiery rhetoric that Patterson deployed even as most of the other city newspapers had left the case behind.

WHILE WARD REFUSED answering the reporter's questions in his Bronx office, another *Daily News* reporter tracked down former DA

Weeks in his newly opened law offices in White Plains just across the street from the courthouse. Armed with a list of questions, some of them, according to the newspaper, "asked by citizens in letters to the *Daily News*," the reporter found Weeks reticent and combative. "I have retired from public office," Weeks replied, and then barked, "I have nothing to say about the Ward case." When the reporter persisted, Weeks pushed back: "I won't read your questions. I don't want to see them. I absolutely refuse to discuss the case." In the courthouse that same reporter tried to interview DA Rowland. "Oh, I haven't any time to be bothered with questions about the Ward case," Rowland sighed before disappearing down a side corridor and a back door into his office. "The public be damned" is how the newspaper characterized both men's responses to their reporter's questions, positioning the tabloid as a public advocate.[3] For Patterson, pursuing the Ward-Peters case furthered his political tendencies while also building his fledgling paper's influence.

NAMED AFTER HIS maternal grandfather, Joseph Medill, the longtime owner and editor of the *Chicago Tribune* and former mayor of the city, Joseph Medill Patterson grew up in luxury. Both Ward and Patterson were inheritors of family fortunes and expected to fulfill their roles in the family businesses. They could have easily been friends having lunch at the University Club in downtown Chicago or drinks at the Westchester Biltmore Country Club. And while both men owed their success in life to family fortunes, each made use of that privilege in very different ways.

Patterson's mother hired him a valet when he turned fourteen, a service he quickly despised. Instead, he chose to distance himself from his family's wealth through a kind of sartorial rebellion he would embrace through his entire life: tattered tweed jackets, frayed pants, and scuffed shoes. While Patterson attended the proper East Coast schools—Groton boarding school followed by Yale—he had for much of his young adult life disliked the mores and values of the privileged class he found himself in. After Yale, Patterson worked as a journalist reporting on the Boxer Rebellion in China—though he arrived too late—and disputes along the U.S.-Mexico border. He cast himself as a working-class journalist on those adventures, wishing to uncover the injustices endured by those caught within the larger political conflicts. He earned only fifteen dollars a week as a reporter, though his family fortune paid him an additional two hundred dollars a week.[4]

In Chicago, he tried his hand at city government. Unlike his grandfather, who had been the Republican mayor of the city, Patterson campaigned for a reform-minded Democratic candidate—whom the *Tribune* strongly condemned. When the Democrat won, Patterson was made commissioner of public works. But he soon became disillusioned with city politics, frustrated by how the mayor's office sank into the same sorts of corruption he'd campaigned against. "Money is power and dominion," he told a reporter after he resigned his post as commissioner. "No one possesses it, but it possesses everybody." In his late twenties, he came out as a socialist. "It isn't fair that because my grandfather worked hard and left money," he told a reporter in New York in 1905 while attending a socialist conference, "I should have everything and many people should have nothing. All sources of production should be vested in the people." He added, "In other words, as I understand it, I am a socialist." It was the kind of declaration that could have easily been dismissed as youthful idealism among Patterson's family and his friends from Yale, though years later Patterson recalled how his embrace of socialism was, for his family, akin to being an abolitionist in the antebellum South.

When his father died suddenly in 1910, Patterson, along with his cousin Robert McCormick, took over as coeditors of the *Tribune*. The pairing was more rivalry than partnership, as the two men had very different views of the *Tribune*'s direction, and Patterson found himself once again drawn into the conservative tentacles of the family business. But it seems he moved into his new role with a certain spirit of innovation. In 1917, he launched the Tribune Syndicate, one of the earliest wire services in the country, which circulated *Tribune* articles and editorials to newspapers across the country. It became a powerful tool to influence readers well beyond the shores of Lake Michigan.

In the winter of 1923, Patterson used the syndicate to publish the editorial "The Still Small Voice" in small-town newspapers, prompting mothers to write those letters to Governor Smith at the same moment the *Daily News* began its campaign to bring Ward back to court. Patterson's keen concern for social injustice was coupled with his expert skills at generating populist sentiment.

Patterson conjured the idea for a daily *Picture Post*–style tabloid while serving in the 149th Field Artillery in France during World War I. He was inspired by a meeting he had in London with Alfred Harmsworth, the Edwardian aristocrat and newspaper publisher who founded the lucrative tabloid *Daily Mail*, which had a circulation of 800,000 readers who were attracted to the tabloid's sensational headlines and photograph-rich layout. It was often called the "busy man's newspaper" for its appeal to the working class. Harmsworth told Patterson that New York City was a perfect market for a similar tabloid. Besides, if Patterson didn't start one, Harmsworth warned, he might himself.

On June 26, 1919, with funding from the *Tribune* board, Patterson's idea for a tabloid in the country's largest city became a reality when the first issue, initially called the *Illustrated Daily News*, hit newsstands. "Its interests will be your interests," Patterson informed his readers in that first edition. "We shall give you every day the best and newest pictures of the interesting things that are happening in the world." And, he promised, "It will be aggressively for America and for the people of New York, and will have no entangling alliance with any class whatever."[5] Patterson chose his words carefully, knowing perhaps that a publication aimed at working-class New Yorkers would have a scent of bolshevism in those reactionary years after World War I when labor strikes were common and government surveillance campaigns against anarchists and communists swept the nation, led in part by the ambitious twenty-five-year-old J. Edgar Hoover.

Managing his small editorial team in New York from his offices in Chicago, Patterson sent telegrams and letters directing them how the tabloid should look. "Guard against the tendency of too many too long stories," he wrote to his managing editor Phil Payne, suggesting he use "bigger pictures" and larger headlines.[6] "Try to get in a couple of crime pictures every day," he wrote to another editor. "That is, you can get direct action pictures showing how the crime was committed, or at least get in pictures of people connected with the crime either as victim or criminal." He added, "It is essential to get more news pictures. That is our life blood and if we do not excel in that we are done for."[7]

Payne, a good-humored but quick-tempered editor who mostly had experience in small-town newspapers, eagerly stretched the possibilities of Patterson's tabloid. Two of the paper's more innovative features were the Voice of the People, which published letters from readers, and the the Inquiring Photographer column, which assigned a photographer to canvass the streets of the city asking one particular question for the day and publishing the responses with a photograph of the person interviewed. These direct appeals to the man-on-the-street approach to journalism, along with games and contests, drew in readers and fueled circulation.[8]

When Governor Smith requested his attorneys look into the Ward case, the Inquiring Photographer column asked New Yorkers their opinions about Smith's decision, and the answers were overwhelmingly positive. Brooklyn musical director Warrant Purisch praised the governor's actions, though doubted it would come to anything. "Money in this country is all powerful," he said. Helen Ballon, a secretary in Queens, said it "was a good decision for Governor Smith to make. Rich and poor should be treated alike by the law." Insurance broker R. M. Battersby said he admired the governor's "fairness of mind" and thought the case should be reopened.[9]

These columns had the veneer of popular sentiment while also prompting debate—something Patterson knew was good for circulation. He encouraged what he called "knocks" in the Voice of the People section, which were letters highly critical of government or business. "For goodness' sake," he complained to his editors, "remember to publish knocks, and vicious ones, every day." Sometimes, editors themselves would write such "knocks," trying to stir up debate that would then play out on the editorial pages. Such orchestrated populist approaches to the news made Patterson's tabloid a thoroughly modern newspaper.

Though controversy was not dishonesty. "I don't care to be a tool for common or garden blackmailers whose favorite stunt is to threaten publicity," Patterson wrote to Payne in 1923. Even on the editorial pages, Patterson was keen on getting the facts right, directing Payne to avoid "inflammatory editorials not based on truth." "Where there is a wrong or oppression," he advised Payne, "we strive to correct it but we never should do so by the use of false premises."[10]

By early 1923, the *Daily News* had a circulation of half a million, an astounding feat for a newspaper competing against the likes of the *New-York Tribune* and *The New York Times*—both of which saw their circulation sag in those postwar years.[11] It would soon have competitors and a growing chorus of critics. One contemporary complained that as the city's tabloids grew in popularity "radicalism fell," arguing that they presented "American life not as a political and economic struggle, but as a three ring circus of sport, crime and sex."[12] Certainly Patterson was attuned to that circus and used each ring to drive circulation. But he also knew that the circus was often where political struggle played out.

IN LATE FEBRUARY the Democratic assemblymen Louis Cuvillier introduced a resolution for an inquiry into Clarence Peters's murder. The Republican-controlled assembly sent the resolution to the Ways and Means Committee to assess whether it was prudent to spend money on such an investigation. The move was meant to kill the resolution before it could even be discussed on the floor. Cuvillier accused his Republican colleagues of "gross carelessness and inefficiency" in the handling of his resolution. "I am prepared to ask for an appropriation of $1,000,000, if that amount should be necessary to produce justice in this case," declared Cuvillier.

In committee, he laid out the miscarriage of justice and raised questions about Judge Seeger's motives in dismissing the indictment.

His rhetoric was pointedly inflammatory. Ward left Peters's body "to lie there like a carcass of a dog," Cuvillier declared, inciting his Republican colleagues. They in turn defended the investigation. Westchester Republican senator Walter Westall retorted, "There is no doubt that justice has been administered in this case, Mr. Cuvillier, in the minds of anybody except your own, and that dirty, lying little sheet, the *Daily News*." As expected, Cuvillier's resolution died in committee along with any hope of a legislative inquiry. There would be no justice for Clarence Peters's murder, Cuvillier told reporters, because Walter Ward "is wealthy and thinks he is above the law."[13]

The *Daily News* made much of the attacks on its campaign to bring Ward back to court. "Facts are a stubborn thing," the paper declared, "whether presented in the *Daily News*, in the Assembly, or not presented at all." Just days after the Ways and Means Committee voted down Cuvillier's resolution, the paper's editorial page turned its attention to Governor Smith. "The *Daily News* has asked for justice," the editorial declared, "nothing more and nothing less." As for Senator Westall's "snarling accusation," the tabloid retorted, the senator represented "voices of those who dodge facts and fear justice." It concluded with its familiar and pointed campaign: "Walter Ward should face a jury. The Governor of this State has the facts of the case before him. He has the power to act. Gov. Smith, it's your move!"[14]

Not unsurprisingly, readers' letters in the Voice of the People supported the tabloid's editorial stance. "If Ward is guilty, then he alone must suffer the remorse," declared one reader, adding, "Let us pin our faith in Gov. Smith. If he is great enough to be Governor then he is great enough to do what is right in the Ward case." Similarly, a reader from Brooklyn wrote, "I truly share your opinion that the law should take its regular course in this case as in all others, thereby deciding in a definite way whether this ordinary individual is justified in the eyes of the law in the killing of the penniless youth, Peters."

More often, the letters thanked the *Daily News* for its relentless campaign, suggesting how popular opinion was on the side of the newspaper. A reader from Manhattan offered a familiar refrain:

"Congratulations to THE NEWS and its harp, the harp on which THE NEWS has so often played the most welcome strain," adding,

> Let us hope that the outcome of the case will prove once and for all time there is no double standard of justice, that the laws governing the middle classes also obtain when violations have been committed by those of the wealthier classes. It is the spirit of fair play on the part of THE NEWS which endears your paper to its thousands of readers.[15]

To many, it appeared public sentiment strongly supported a new investigation.

Fred Magison, Inez Peters's attorney, wrote to Governor Smith in March, asking if he had made any decision about reopening the case. Reminding the governor of their January meeting, Magison wrote, "I was encouraged by your manner and apparent interest in the cause I presented, and believed that you would act speedily and effectively in the matter." He detailed how he provided a transcript of the grand jury testimony and "pointed out wherein the law had been violated by Ward," concluding, "Two and one-half months have now elapsed and I have not heard from you."

Smith turned the letter over to his counsel James Parsons, who wrote a terse response, criticizing Magison's understanding of the case. "I disagree with the statement in your communication," Parsons wrote, "that there is any proof that Ward shot Peters, or that Ward, or even his attorneys in his behalf in his presence, confessed that he shot Peters." Parsons's continued by explaining the scene of the murder based on Ward's statement: "In fact, the so called confession is to the effect that when Peters ordered Ward to leave the car that this order resulted in a grab for the revolver in Peters' hand, thereby deflecting the shot from Peters gun, and that immediately there was a fusillade of bullets, and not proof nor any statement the bullets from Ward's gun shot Peters." Parsons also disagreed with Magison's assertion that "there was any misconduct or illegal acts" by either Sheriff Werner or DA Weeks.

Parson's unfiltered defense of Ward and the Westchester authorities must have confused Magison, though his reply suggested he was more infuriated than perplexed. "My letter was addressed to the Governor, asking advice as to when he was going to reach a decision in the Ward case," he wrote. "I didn't ask for your criticism of my findings, or for an expression of your views in the case. Certainly, I didn't ask for a defense of Ward, and that seems to be about all your letter contains. I am quite familiar with the Ward case. Everyone, except you, agrees that Ward killed Peters. I am not going to try to convince you." Magison concluded with resolve: "I shall not bother you further with this matter. I have no reason to hope that the Governor will act favorably on my petition if he pays any attention at all to the advice he gets from you."

It's unknown if Magison showed Parsons's letter to Inez Peters, as it would have further dampened her hope that the governor might intervene. The correspondence came just weeks after Republicans defeated Cuvillier's resolution in the legislature, leaving few options open. So it must have been a surprise to Magison and many in Albany when Governor Smith announced in late March that he would in fact reopen the case. "The Attorney General's office," Smith stated, "is making, by my direction, a thorough investigation into the Ward-Peters murder. That is all I can say now, except that from a personal consideration of the facts and inquiries made by my direction, I have reached the conclusion that this thing ought to be cleaned up once and for all."

It was a brief statement, without any explanation for his rationale or details of what led him to his decision. The press called the announcement "unexpected." We might speculate on the "inquiries" that Smith made about the case. Clearly Parsons did not encourage this decision. Perhaps Cuvillier, angered by his Republican colleagues, persuaded Smith to seize the case for political reasons. It may have been that stack of poignant and pleading letters from mothers across the country asking for justice for Inez Peters. Or perhaps the thirty-two-year-old Carl Sherman, the newly elected attorney general and former federal prosecutor from Buffalo, convinced Smith that the case needed to be "cleaned up once and for all."

Of course it might also have been the many weeks of the *Daily News* campaign. Joe Patterson and Phil Payne thought so when their tabloid reported on Smith's announcement.

> The action of Gov. Smith marks another step in the three months fight of the *Daily News* to accomplish just one thing, to discover why a millionaire's son should not be required at least to justify in court and on trial his admitted act in slaying a penniless waif, a youth of nineteen, who had crossed his path in the course of some of his eccentric activities.[16]

As he had with Smith's predecessor, Nathan Miller, Payne had been lobbying the governor privately for some time, writing letters and having at least one personal meeting. "Needless to say," Payne wrote to Smith the day after the announcement, "I am very much gratified at the stand you have taken in the Ward case. I feel sure that a thorough investigation by the Attorney General's office will eventually result in Ward being brought to trial and will restore the confidence of the people of New York State in our judicial system."[17]

There was a heavy burden of expectation placed on Attorney General Sherman to solve the many uncertainties of Peters's murder. It was a challenge the new attorney general seemed eager to take on. "The investigation will be as complete and thorough as I can make it," he told reporters. "Nothing that will aid us in dispelling the fog of mystery that had enveloped this case will be left undone. I am determined to sift the case to the bottom." We can only wonder if he was prepared for how dense the fog would become in the following weeks.[18]

False from Start to Finish

Carl Sherman made a pledge. "I am prompted to make this investigation in the open," he told reporters. "There is something in this keen public interest that is tantamount to a demand from the people that this case be laid open." His promise of transparency was a sharp rebuke to the capricious way the crime had been handled the previous summer. "Personally," Sherman declared, "I feel that the public is entitled to know, particularly in view of the fact that there is a general impression that much has been shielded from view in the past." He continued, "Not only will the newspaper men be permitted to attend the examination of witnesses, but the records will be made available to them in order that they may inform the public. There should be nothing to hide, and I can see nothing to be gained by resorting to star chamber proceedings."[1] Whatever Sherman felt about the case, his criticism about how the initial investigation had been handled was pointedly clear.

Tall and thin with deep-set eyes, Sherman was known for his quick temper and impatience, as well as his keen prosecutorial skills. But as he swore his oath of office in January 1923, there was one history-making fact about Carl Sherman: he would be the first Jew to hold the attorney general post in New York State. Born in Olmütz, a city in the northern region of the Austro-Hungarian Empire, Sherman immigrated to the United States with his parents when he was only four. The family settled in Buffalo. There his father built a tobacco business. Sherman attended law school at the University of Buffalo. He ran an unsuccessful campaign for state senate before serving as assistant district attorney for the Western District of New York, a position that honed his skills at navigating prosecutorial responsibilities amid outside political pressures.[2]

His move to the attorney general post felt as much a personal victory as a community one. From a young age, Sherman had been active in Jewish organizations in Buffalo, including the Jewish Young Men's Association and the Jewish War Relief Drives during World War I. He served as president of the Manhattan Social Society, the largest Jewish group in the city. The *Buffalo Jewish Review* celebrated his election victory. "Mr. Sherman's honor is shared by the Jews of Buffalo," the paper announced on its front page, "as they have always considered him one of their most active young men in civic and Jewish communal affairs."[3] In an era of strong nativist and anti-immigrant sentiment, a Jewish immigrant from eastern Europe taking control of the attorney general's office would have unsettled many in the state. Sherman's tenure would last only one two-year term, defeated by a Republican challenger in 1924. He never held public office again. But in the state capital that spring of 1923, whatever thoughts he might have had about his political future were overshadowed by the pressing need to get to the truth about the murder of Clarence Peters.

SHERMAN'S CONDUCTED HIS inquiry under the Peace and Safety Act, a World War I-era state statute meant to root out spies and subversives to ensure "public peace, public safety, and public justice." It was a stretch to use that law for an inquiry into a local murder investigation, but Sherman seemed to have few reservations. His first task was to subpoena nearly fifty witnesses, many of whom had already testified to the grand jury in the summer of 1922. He summoned the witnesses to Albany to testify, a transcript of each day's proceedings given to the press for the morning editions. The list included those who arrived on the crime scene the morning of May 16, including Frank Taxter with the Westchester County Light Company, state trooper Harry Green, and coroner

Edward Fitzgerald. They summoned Sheriff Werner, fingerprint expert Ray Hill, New Rochelle mayor Harry Scott, and police chief Frank Cody. They also summoned Fred Olsson, superintendent at the Poinciana, as well as the elevator operators and Laura Wright, the cleaning woman who worked for Olsson. Others included Palmer Tubbs, fellow police commissioner and former personal assistant to Walter Ward, two of the Ward Bakery switchboard operators, and a mechanic in the company's garage, among other employees. Even Ward's attorneys were called to testify. Reading through the transcripts and reports of these inquiries, the contradictions and doubts about Ward's statement of what happened on King Street grew with each new witness.

Sherman enlisted Assistant Attorney General Wilber Chambers to help with the investigation. A decade older than Sherman, balding, and sporting a trim mustache, Chambers had been with the attorney general's office since 1910 and distinguished himself in prosecuting complex cases often related to corporate fraud and labor regulations. Chambers had lived in New Rochelle for over twenty years and was active in the local Republican Party.[4] Perhaps Sherman saw in Chambers someone who could filter the scent of political prejudice that the investigation provoked in the minds of some.

When Ward's attorney Allan Campbell took the stand, he remained evasive and at times uncooperative. "I respectfully decline to answer" was Campbell's usual refrain, citing attorney-client privilege. He did recall that the meeting in DA Weeks's office on the morning of May 22 had been a cordial one between Ward and the authorities. At one point, Campbell noted, Weeks stood up and, in a gesture of praise, said to Ward, "They would have got me, all right, if I had been there." Ward apparently said nothing in response. Campbell related how he and the other attorneys sat with Ward, Coroner Fitzgerald, and Sheriff Werner in the DA's office for nearly two hours as staff prepared paperwork for the arraignment. Apparently, to the astonishment of Sherman, the men discussed little about the actual shooting. No one was "interested in asking any details of the shooting at all, of any of you?" an exasperated Sherman inquired.[5]

"Well, I think they were interested, I do not recall," Campbell replied. The evasiveness continued. Chambers asked why Campbell waited so many days to bring Ward in to authorities. "I can not answer that question without going into confidential matters," Campbell replied. He refused to even confirm when he became Ward's attorney in the case.

On questions about the statement itself, Campbell remained stubbornly reserved. While he described how he and Rabenold had drafted the statement at Rabenold's house the weekend before Ward appeared before authorities, Campbell refused to confirm if Ward himself had actually authorized the statement or offered any information for the drafting of it. He even refused to confirm whether Ward had even seen it or read it before it was turned over to authorities.

"Do you mean to tell us," Sherman pressed, "that you presented this statement with the name of Walter S. Ward on it regarding his action, without consulting about it? Without receiving his authority to make it public?" Campbell refused to answer.

Taking another approach, Sherman asked, "Did you make that statement on behalf of Walter S. Ward?"

"Yes," Campbell replied.

But when Sherman went further and asked if he had Ward's authority to present the statement on Ward's behalf, Campbell "respectfully declined to answer."[6]

Elwood Rabenold took the stand next. He sat in front of Sherman as a newly elected Democratic state senator from Manhattan and proved even more opaque than Campbell. Despite earlier testimony by Coroner Fitzgerald and Sheriff Werner, Rabenold claimed he wasn't even in the DA's office on the morning of May 22. "The Sheriff is mistaken," he said, claiming he had been in federal court in Manhattan that morning. When questions turned to the drafting of the statement, Rabenold refused to offer any clarity.[7]

"Where did you get the facts for the statement, whether they are facts or not?" Chambers asked. Rabenold declined to answer, citing privilege. Sherman retorted, arguing the statement was a public document, and as such his office has a right to know where the information for Ward's statement came from.

"I think we have the right to know about anything you did make public," Sherman said. "What you want to keep to yourself, you have a right to keep to yourself, but what you have given to officials we claim the right to interrogate."

Rabenold held his ground calmly: "How it came into being is entirely apart from the thing itself. You have the thing itself."

A clearly frustrated Sherman declared, "The assertion of privilege may be carried too far," and then demanded that the state senator explain his rationale for refusing to answer questions related to the drafting of the statement.

"There was a time in this case," Rabenold replied,

> when my instructions to my entire office were that we should extend to the authorities every possible facility for getting at the facts, in which we were as anxious as they, in order that those facts be known. That attitude towards the officials was abused. After it had been abused, not once, but at least three times, seriously abused, we changed the attitude and the change of attitude continues till now.

What were these three abuses, we might wonder. Rabenold enumerated each. First, the unannounced arrest of Ward in June and the increase in his bail from $10,000 to $50,000 after reporters and detectives found crime scene evidence that contradicted his statement. Second, the search of the Ward home based on claims by James Cunningham, claims that Rabenold described as a "wild indefensible dream of a crazy criminal." And finally, the grand jury indictment on first-degree murder, which, he claimed, lacked "a vestige of legal evidence to support it." For these reasons, Rabenold asserted, he and his firm ended their cooperation with the DA's office and were certainly not inclined to assist in Sherman's inquiry. It was a bold statement that questioned the district attorney's investigation, the entire grand jury's proceedings, and the attorney general's own authority to conduct his inquiry.

Failing to find any new facts about Ward's story, Sherman and Chambers turned to the crime scene investigation. Deputy sheriff Frank Cherico testified that he believed Peters had been brought to the roadside. "The way the body was found. I don't think he dropped there when he was shot." Chambers asked if he thought it would be possible for one man to have placed Peters along the side of the road. "It would have been quite a load for one man," Cherico noted, "unless he was a strong man."

Like Cherico, state trooper Harry Green also stood by his initial theory that Peters was shot elsewhere and brought to the side of King Street. Green testified that the heels of Peters's shoes were not dug into the ground, but rather lay on top of the soil, and recalled how oddly composed the body had been. "I don't see how he could have fallen in such a perfect order," he told Sherman.

As he had a year earlier, Green's former supervisor, Eugene Roberts, disputed such claims. "It looked to me as though he had just fallen back after receiving this blow almost in the solar plexus," he stated. When Sherman pressed him that Peters could have been laid down in that position, Roberts repeated his theory.

"I always maintained that Peters was shot where he fell, from the dirt on his shoes, that corresponded with the same ground as where his body rested," he replied. He explained how he and his men searched the entire area around the body and found no evidence of a struggle, nor of gunshots except for the shell casing of the .38 caliber bullet. The lingering question of where the bullet landed when it exited Peters's lower back remained a mystery.[8]

The guns came into doubt when police chief Frank Cody testified that the .32 Smith & Wesson pistol that Ward claimed Peters had used might have been the same one that Cody gave Ward back in 1920. "It was a small sized revolver," Cody said, "something like the one there," pointing to the .32 pistol that lay on the table with the other evidence. But, Cody contended, it was hard to remember exactly which kind of pistol he had given Ward, and besides they all looked similar. The New

Rochelle Police Department kept no records of the guns they acquired through arrests and searches, making it impossible to know if the serial number on that Smith & Wesson was the same as the one Cody had handed Ward. Pistols, it seemed, slipped through police headquarters will little accountability. This was also true of the .38 automatic Colt that Ward obtained from Cody in December 1921. "It was lying on the desk, with some other revolvers, and he saw it," Cody recalled. Ward picked it up and said, "That looks like a good revolver, have you any use for it?" Cody then let Ward take it home. The police chief never asked Ward why he might have the need for two handguns.

Sherman also pressed the police chief on a crucial perplexity about Ward's story: his fear that his life was in danger by the blackmailers. As police commissioner he had a large force of nearly seventy men he could have enlisted to pursue a gang of blackmailers. If Ward "had wanted detectives in plain clothes or officers detailed to protect him in any way or to protect his house," Sherman asked, "he could very readily have secured such assistance?"

"He surely could, yes, sir," Cody replied with little hesitation. "He was the boss, we were there to do what he told us." So why, we might wonder, did Ward not use his authority and privilege as police commissioner to catch the gang of blackmailers? He certainly was not shy about using his badge for advantage, as his actions at the Poinciana in the summer of 1921 illustrated. Even Lieutenant John McGowan with the New Rochelle police, who had helped with the search of the Wards' home in early June, testified about his confusion on this point. "Why didn't Ward come to Headquarters and tell Chief Cody or me about it," he wondered on the stand. "We'd have covered him up by getting after the blackmailers. There would have been no notoriety and the murder might have been avoided."[9]

As contradictions about the crime scene continued to accumulate, Chambers questioned the exact nature of how the shooting happened. He summoned Dr. John Black, who conducted the autopsy with his assistant Dr. Henry Vier. Neither doctor was called in front of the grand jury in 1922, so their testimony for the attorney general was the first time they'd made public their concerns about the case. "The shot was well designed to accomplish death," Black testified. When asked if Peters might have been able to walk after being shot, both doctors confirmed that he might have been able to stagger or stumble but definitely not walk. "The man died a quick and violent death," Vier confirmed.

Both doctors were perplexed by Ward's description of the shooting. The autopsy showed that the gun had to have been directed downward at Peters's chest, as the bullet had entered the right side of his chest, cut though his torso, exiting the lower back toward the right side of his body. This trajectory would have caused massive internal bleeding, making Peters's death quite quick. If Peters's killer had been standing next to him, the other man would have had to be "considerably taller," Black noted. If he had been standing on the car's running board and Peters stood on the road, the height differences were still questionable given what autopsy results showed. Vier said he found powder residue on Peters's clothing: the doctors determined, with fair certainty, that the .38 Colt had been fired at close range.

Chambers had the doctors reenact the scene, with Black playing Ward and Vier Peters. As the two entangled their arms, acting out the encounter described in Ward's statement, it became clear how improbable his description had been. "The bullet," Black declared, "would go in a direct, straight course, or else it would take the opposite course from what it did." In other words, as Ward was left-handed, and Peters had the pistol in his right hand, when Ward grabbed Peters's right wrist and pushed it upward to deflect the shot, the bullet from his own gun would have cut into Peters's chest and made a direct line through his torso. Or if Peters had been standing below Ward, Ward's bullet, fired from his .38 revolver held in his left hand, would have made a downward arc through the left side of Peters's torso. But that contradicted what the autopsy showed. There was also another curious fact. As Ward was holding Peters's right wrist, his arm would have been stretched across Peters's chest, blocking Ward's gun and making it difficult to fire at Peters in the few seconds of the struggle. Either way you consider the encounter, the facts of the autopsy cast doubt on most of Ward's claims.

Not satisfied with the doctors' reenactment, Chambers and his legal assistant stood up and tried their own test of the encounter, this time using the actual guns. Chambers climbed on the seat of a wooden banker chair, while his assistant stood in front of him, planting one foot on a thick legal volume and the other on the chair seat to balance himself. The two men entangled themselves, Chambers holding the .38 pointed downward and his assistant with the .32 stretching against his boss's resistance. A *Daily News* photographer captured this odd tableau for the paper's front page. The angle of such an encounter and the struggle between the two men made it highly improbable that Peters would have fallen back in such a composed fashion. Black contended that the only way the bullet would have cut through Peters's body in the way that it did, with Ward shooting with his left hand, was if Peters had been in some "twisted or unnatural position."[10]

GIVEN THE UNCERTAINTIES the autopsy presented and the doubts about whether Peters was actually murdered along King Street, Chambers made plans to reenact the shooting at the crime scene to determine if nearby witnesses could in fact hear a barrage of gunfire, as Ward had claimed. Chambers took two state troopers, a few reports, and three new witnesses: Brooklyn contractor Leslie Irvine, his son, Frances, and friend Albert Stewart. These three men were returning from a furniture delivery in Connecticut in the late-night hours of May 15 when they encountered a problem with their truck, forcing them to spend the entire night parked along King Street just a mile south from the discovery of Peters's body. It was a clear and quiet night, they remembered, and they told State Trooper Green back in May 1922 that they had heard no gunshots that night. Each of the men expressed little interest in getting involved in the case, and detectives from the DA's office never interviewed them, nor were they summoned to testify before the grand jury. It was only when reporters from the New York *Daily News* tracked them down that their story become public.[11]

Chambers wished to test the witnesses' theory. On a clear May evening, he and the three witnesses stood where their truck had broken down, along with a small crowd of onlookers and journalists. A mile north, two state troopers stood where Peters's body had been found. After three tests that evening, when the troopers fired twenty-one pistol shots into the air, only two or three were heard where Chambers stood. Farmer Clarence Eckhardt, who lived up the hill from the crime scene and had been one of the first to find Peters's body, told investigators he had heard nothing on the morning of May 16. But when the troopers fired those test rounds into the air, Eckhardt heard all twenty-one gunshots while sitting in his home, making it nearly impossible to have slept through the shoot-out Ward alleged between him and the blackmailers.

"The whole affair has been very unsatisfactory," Chambers told reporters after the test. "There was entirely too much noise," he added, noting that traffic along King Street made it difficult to hear gunshots a mile away. He suggested perhaps an early-morning test would better recreate the conditions when Peters was killed. While he said the "test was not conclusive either way," he did arrive at one crucial insight about the crime: Peters, he believed, could not have been murdered on King Street. "As a result of the test and from other information," Chambers told reporters, "I am thoroughly convinced that the story of the shooting as related by Ward's attorneys is false from start to finish." He added, "Ward killed Peters under different circumstances and in another locality. Peters' body was carried to that lonely spot."[12] If Chambers and Sherman were now convinced that Ward's statement was indeed untrue, then the question of motive became even more mysterious. And the only ones who would know about motive were the Wards themselves.[13]

RALPH WARD TOOK the stand with a certain casual defiance. "A thin curl of cigarette smoke issued from his tight lips," one report noted.[14] As he had in front of the grand jury, Ralph confirmed that he'd heard about the shooting from his father, George Ward.

"What did your father tell you?" Sherman asked.

"I decline to answer," Ralph replied.[15]

When pushed, Ralph stood by what his lawyers had told him a year earlier, that conversations he'd had with his father would be deemed hearsay. Sherman reminded him that the attorney general's office was trying to ascertain the facts of the case, and what Ralph had learned from his father would be crucial for their inquiry.

"Whatever your father told you we want to know," Sherman demanded.

"I am sorry, I cannot tell you."

George Ward was, not surprisingly, on vacation at a spa in White Sulphur Springs, West Virginia, and beyond the reach of the attorney general. When asked if his father was willing to come forward and testify in the inquiry, Ralph was decidedly unhelpful.

"I have not the least idea," he said, taking another long drag on his cigarette. Sherman seemed baffled that Ralph had no idea when his father would be returning to work. He pressed Ralph further. "Well, he may come back tomorrow, or not for a month. I don't know," Ralph replied.

Something that Ralph did know had to do with a $20,000 loan his brother had taken out in the winter of 1922 from the Corn Exchange Bank in New York. Walter had used some of his company stock as collateral for the loan. "He told me that he had to get some money," Ralph testified. The bank gave Walter a short-term ninety-day loan that would come due in early April. Ralph too helped his brother with the collateral by offering nearly one hundred shares of his own stock holdings. Ralph had no idea why his brother needed the money, and when he asked, he said Walter would not tell him.

Ralph recounted how his brother had become deeply involved in racetrack betting in the fall and winter of 1921. Walter had promised to quit betting—a promise that Ralph said he did not keep. The manager of the Corn Exchange Bank testified that Walter ordered the sale of most of the collateral stock in early April, as he hadn't the money to repay the loan. The sale included some of Ralph's stock as well. Later testimony confirmed the stock sale. George Zacharias, assistant treasurer of the Ward Bakery Company, showed Sherman the company ledger indicating a sale on April 5 of 102 shares, totaling $20,400. As Zacharias testified, that was the only stock sale that Walter Ward had made since he first became a shareholder in 1915.[16]

By the beginning of April 1922, Walter "seemed to be constantly worried," Ralph said. "He had headaches almost every day and was not acting like himself at all." It was about this time that Ward disappeared, leaving no word with Beryl or his brother about where he had gone. Palmer Tubbs had suspicions on where to find his boss: at the racetrack in Bowie, Maryland, a small town about twenty miles east of Washington, D.C. Tubbs contacted Lieutenant John McGowan with the New Rochelle Police Department and asked if he would go and find his boss.

"We had only been there a half hour when I spotted Ward" going into a betting booth, McGowan told Sherman. "He must have been making a heavy bet because it was the highest priced booth at the track," McGowan remembered. "They wouldn't take bets less than $50.00 at the booth."

Tubbs instructed McGowan to shadow him. Ward was alone making those big bets on thoroughbred racing, though with little success. Had Ward taken the loan money and traveled to Bowie, a place where he could be anonymous among the crowd of high-stakes betting? Was he desperate to double or triple his money and return to New York ready to pay off whatever debt he owed?

Eventually Ward boarded a train to Washington, D.C., and McGowan telephoned Tubbs with the information. Tubbs dispatched Ralph Ward to the nation's capital to bring his brother back home. McGowan never spoke to Ward, nor did he try to question him. "He was the commissioner," he told Sherman, "and I was afraid he might get sore."[17] Returning to New York having squandered a small fortune, Walter sent a cablegram to his father requesting nearly $40,000. Walter would not tell his brother why he needed the money, but Ralph suspected gambling debts. When asked if he thought his brother was being blackmailed, Ralph's reply was curt: "I never thought of that."

The timeline that Ralph set out about his brother's financial troubles must have been illuminating for Sherman and Chambers. It presented a picture of a man in need of cash while also struggling with a gambling habit that seemed quite out of his control. Such details that Ralph willingly offered supported his brother's initial statement about the blackmailing gang. From the earliest days of the investigation, racetrack gambling debts had been floated as the reason behind the blackmail plot. It was the story the dubious Jimmy the Rat told DA Weeks a year earlier. But were these financial difficulties related to blackmail? Ralph's testimony left the possibility open, which perhaps was precisely the point. If not outright refusal or silence in response to questions about the crime, ambiguity would be useful as well. One thing did become clear: Ward was desperate in the spring of 1922 for a large sum of money. What exactly he needed the money for was still a question that Sherman and Chambers could not answer.

WHILE SHERMAN HAD accumulated substantial doubts about the facts of Ward's statement, he had little direct evidence to dispute the claims of what happened on King Street. Neither Sherman nor Chambers believed Ward's story of how the murder happened, but they had no other plausible alternative theory of the crime—at least no theory that they made public. One detail they were convinced of was that Peters had to have been murdered elsewhere and brought to that quiet place along King Street and laid out in such a composed manner. But where he had been murdered, and why, remained a mystery. Their entire inquiry, presented in the open, was getting murkier with each new doubt.

As the men continued their inquiries, a new revelation came not from witness testimony but rather a letter from England. "I have information," Sherman announced to reporters at the end of April, "that attorneys acting for Ward together with several of their agents, had the Jones family under their wing for a period of time at various apartments and hotels in New York City."[18] Goldie, Joseph, Queenie, and little Roland, who mysteriously disappeared from Haverhill in July 1922 after claiming they had information about Peters, were ready to tell their story.

Dirty Trick

In early January 1923, just days after the indictment against Ward was dropped, Bertha Robinson, an agent with Rabenold & Scribner, stood at the Cunard ticket office and purchased four tickets on the SS *Albania*, scheduled to set sail for Liverpool on January 13. The ship was modest in size and amenities, offering only four public rooms and two small decks. Robinson paid $420, along with an additional twenty dollars war tax for two first-class cabins for the Jones family, who apparently had little choice in the matter of returning to England.

Her colleague Samuel Miller, an attorney with the firm who investigated the Joneses in Haverhill in the summer of 1922, collected the tickets the day before the ship was set to sail. Both Robinson and Miller accompanied the family to the ship, meeting them on the West Side pier on a cloudy January morning. They wanted to make sure the family got settled in their cabins, though such concern had little to do with any affection for them. Rather Robinson and Miller feared the family would try to elude departure and remain in the city.

It must have appeared odd to some of the passengers to witness the family board, escorted almost like prisoners. The crew of the ship, according to one report, noted how the Joneses stood out among the first-class passengers, as their "style of dress did not gibe with that usually adopted by first-class travelers."[1]

The voyage across the North Atlantic was rough, making their arrival to Liverpool at the end of the week a relief. The lawyers had promised the family they would cover the cost of their resettlement in England. Ask the purser for the money once you dock, they told Goldie. But as the SS *Albania* maneuvered into port, the purser was baffled by Goldie's question. "No one gave me any money for you," he told her. We can imagine the shock and anger she must have felt at that moment, recognizing the lawyers had betrayed their trust after all they'd agreed to. The anger would have simmered as the family disembarked, standing on the pier, facing the ornate grandeur of the Port of Liverpool building, its colonnade dome dominating the skyline. "A dirty trick" was how Goldie later described their arrival in a letter to a friend.[2]

FOR NEARLY SIX months, the Joneses lived in relative secrecy at 508 West 149th Street in Manhattan. Miller, who had orchestrated their move to New York in July 1922, testified he'd supported the family, paying one hundred dollars in rent for the apartment and a stipend of about forty dollars a week, though he couldn't remember the exact amount when questioned under oath. After Joseph found work at a butcher shop on Amsterdam Avenue near the apartment, Miller reduced the stipend to about thirty dollars a week. On the stand, Miller deflected any connection between Ward and these payments.

"I did it within my own discretion, personally," he testified, an answer that cleverly twisted the facts. He claimed Walter Ward was not his client, nor was he acting on Ward's direction. But, when challenged by such hairsplitting, conceded he had been supporting the Joneses as a "member of the firm of Rabenold & Scribner." When asked if he had requested the Joneses to move to New York, Miller again deflected.

"I didn't bring them. They came with me," he said.[3]

However Miller wished to describe the Joneses' move, the reality remained: Ward's attorneys brought the family to New York at the end of July 1922 and supported them in secret for nearly six months. Whatever importance the family held for Ward's defense, the attorneys clearly didn't feel the need to keep them in New York once the indictment was dropped. By the time the family was escorted onto the SS *Albania*, Rabenold & Scribner had spent nearly $2,000 on their Haverhill witnesses. Or, to describe it another way, if Joseph had continued his work at the butcher shop, he would have had to work about a year and half to earn that much money.

Goldie remembered their move to New York in a letter to a friend, written a few days after she arrived in Liverpool. She had nothing but anger for the way the attorneys had treated them. The lawyers had her "make an oath" that she would not talk about the case to anyone. Once back in England, she no longer felt any allegiance to that oath.

> Now I know what they are and that they got rid of us by sending us to England, and if the state knew all, they would have let the case go to trial long ago. Not only that. They only put down what would help Ward. They told us not to tell the rest. If they only knew what we could say for the state's benefit the state would have kept us in New York. Now I understand why we got away so quickly. They were afraid of the case being reopened. They were always afraid we would tell and that is why we were hidden away. Of Joe they were scared because he was really a state's witness, I mean, would have been a good witness for the state.
>
> They even made us give away our home in Haverhill and we could claim for what we have lost, and Joe having to give up his position for their benefit. Why, they even said we must not write to our friends, nor must we let them know where we were, nor must we have visitors. Why, Mr. Miller told Queenie to say things that weren't true.[4]

The letter was drenched in recriminations and revenge but also took a different tone about what she knew of the crime. In New York, she had told the landlord's wife that the crime was "plain murder" but she and Queenie were "saving that man from the electric chair."[5] Six months later she claimed she could help the state in its case against Ward. It was hard to tell what exactly the Joneses knew.

Even more mystery and uncertainty can be found in a letter Joseph Jones wrote in March to a friend in New York, where he described how the lawyers demanded both urgency and secrecy in their move from Haverhill. His home was "practically given away," he wrote, because of these demands. Then he detailed the family's relationship with Peters.

> We were on intimate terms with Clarence Peters. He used to visit our home. I was the last to speak to him, as far as I know. He borrowed from me the money to pay his fare to Boston the day he left. There are other things I explained which I do not intend to disclose in this letter. And I could enlighten you more but I don't wish to put it on paper at present for various reasons.

Joseph's reticence to put into writing certain details made his letter cloudy with innuendo. Earlier in the letter, he declared, "I shall give you the main details of what I know, but you must understand there are things which I can only give verbally."[6] What might those things have been, we can only speculate, as there is no record of Joseph giving testimony. Whatever Joseph knew, it was too damning or too shocking to be written in a private letter.

JULIA HARPMAN, THE *Daily News*'s crime reporter, broke the story of the Joneses in late April 1923 using private correspondence, affidavits, and other documents the family supplied the tabloid. Harpman detailed how Goldie and Queenie had several meetings with attorneys through the late summer and fall of 1922, including Miller, Rabenold, and Campbell. Each meeting followed a similar plan: coaching both women to repeat false claims about Peters. They asked Goldie if she thought Peters was a "degenerate." When she said no, the attorneys corrected, "Yes, he was—and a blackmailer too." Goldie continued,

"They told me to say that I knew that Peters had received letters addressed to him in care of the White Plains post office, telling about a certain millionaire who would pay to keep something quiet."

After several such meetings, the two women started to believe the lies. "Miller kept telling me to repeat over and over that Peters was a blackmailer," Goldie told Harpman, "until I believed it." Eventually Goldie and Queenie surrendered to the forceful tactics and signed statements they said they didn't believe. "It was not true," Goldie said. "I knew it wasn't at the time. I am sure Peters was not a blackmailer. I don't believe he ever knew Ward."[7]

The revelations of Peters's story threw more confusion into Sherman's investigation. If Goldie had vital information about Peters, prompting her to write to Ward in July 1922, then why would Ward's attorneys need to coach her and Queenie to lie? What did the Joneses know about Walter Ward that his attorney's wished to keep secret? What was clear is that Goldie and Queenie went along with the lies in the hope of continued financial support. She did tell a relative of Arthur Elliot's, the hapless ex-husband of Queenie, that the family would return to Haverhill with plenty of money, offering to buy Elliot a new car. Perhaps attorneys instead offered a trip back to England and money to resettle. But when they arrived in England without any of the promised money, Goldie and Joseph reversed their earlier claims and found friends in New York and reporters at the *Daily News* who were willing to listen to their story.

But then, we might wonder, which story were they to believe?

The day after the *Daily News* published Harpman's article, reporters asked Sherman if he wanted to bring the family back to New York to testify. "Yes, I'd like to have them here," he responded with a noted lack of enthusiasm. But, he added, "I haven't the money to meet the expense."[8]

In a brazen move, Rabenold & Scribner sent a letter to the attorney general the next day, citing his comment in the *Daily News* and offering to help with expenses. "We would like very much to have the Jones family come to New York," the letter read in part, the disingenuous tone seeping through the sentences, "so that they could be examined and cross-examined on oath. For the purpose we offer to contribute one-half of their expenses."[9] It seemed the law firm had not spent enough on the Jones family. We don't know if Sherman responded, though there is no evidence that the Joneses were asked to testify.

Sherman knew that while the family's story made for compelling tabloid copy, in court their testimony would float in the air, shifting with each question thrown at them from either the defense or prosecutor. They'd lied before, signing an affidavit they now claimed was false. Who's to say they wouldn't be lying on the stand as well? Whatever the Jones family knew about Peters would linger in speculation and deceit. The Joneses would drop out of the Ward–Peters case by May. Queenie eventually took Roland and moved to Canada where she tried to forget everything she knew about Walter Ward or Clarence Peters.[10]

Five to One

DAILY NEWS MANAGING EDITOR PHIL PAYNE FELT GOOD ABOUT his efforts over the many weeks of Sherman's investigation. Early on as testimony made headlines, he wrote to Patterson in Chicago with a tone of vindication. "I felt very gratified with the developments," Payne wrote. "Examination of a few of the witnesses proved the statement we have made about the case. Every newspaper in the city carried Ward on the first page."

The Ward-Peters case was not only front-page news, if we are to believe a letter to the *Daily News* by C. T. Corcoran published in the Voice of the People column. "In street car, subway, elevated, shops and on the street we seem to hear of nothing but the Ward case," Corcoran wrote. "Everywhere the opinion is the same—'Ward should be brought to trial.'" The writer added, echoing the editorial stance of the tabloid, "It is pleasing to note the absence of bitterness in these demands. It has been my experience that all of them have been based on only a desire for justice."[1]

In May 1923, the *Daily News* began asking readers on its editorial pages a simple question: "Can a Rich Man Kill a Poor Man in New York and Not Be Tried for It?" Each new story of Sherman's inquiry was another occasion to demand a new grand jury. "The investigation," an editorial in early May declared, "has been led on and on until it has assumed the appearance of a chase after some will-o'-the-wisp." In another, the tabloid pushed back against Sherman's complaint that the

Daily News was being "unreasonable" in its relentless criticism of the slow progress of his inquiry. "Would this paper be considered reasonable if it had had as little to say about this case as the rest of the daily papers?" the editors asked, adding, "Certainly if we had maintained a policy of silence, Mr. Sherman would have no Ward case to bother him now." It was, the editorial concluded, those who had "whitewashed" Ward and those who "stood by and let them get away with it" who were being unreasonable.[2]

After the Jones story was published, the tabloid gave Smith a simple ultimatum. "What more do you want, Governor?" the paper demanded. "Daily consideration, and reconsideration of the Ward-Peters case is a thing that alternately bores one to tears and moves one to rage," the editorial complained. Reminding readers of the many facts that emerged from Sherman's inquiries, dismissing others such as the "putrid details" of the "mythical blackmailers," which the editors were clearly convinced never existed, the paper then asked, with an exasperated tone, "When will an Extraordinary Grand Jury be called to reindict Walter Ward?"[3]

It was a Friday morning when the tabloid's demand hit newsstands. By early afternoon Carl Sherman announced his recommendation. "Without in any way indicating my belief in the guilt or innocence of Walter S. Ward," he said, "I believe that sufficient grounds exist for the submission of all available facts to a Grand Jury with a view toward procuring an indictment charging Walter S. Ward with such an offense as the facts would warrant." Sherman pointed to the "conflicting testimony" of his investigation that required detailed examination and presentation before a grand jury. "A conclusion of justifiable homicide," Sherman added, "is here entirely lacking."

Governor Smith wasted no time in accepting the recommendation. "I will name the Attorney General as the prosecuting official to take the place of the local District Attorney," Smith announced in the early evening hours on that Friday. In establishing an extraordinary grand jury, the governor not only had the power to appoint the prosecutor but also the judge, drawn from the state's supreme court, though Smith declined to name the judge in his announcement. "I will probably act officially on Monday," he said.[4]

IN HAVERHILL, AS one might expect, news of Smith's decision made the front page of the *Haverhill Evening Gazette.* While the article pointed to Sherman's diligent investigation over the recent weeks, it was the work of a relentless press, in particular the *Daily News* campaign, that Slipper City readers were told made the difference in the case.

"Those 'in the know' do not give credit to Mr. Sherman nor to Governor Smith," the paper informed, "for it is openly declared both in the capitol . . . and throughout New York City's environs that if it were not for the bold, persistent publicity given the case and the demands made upon the state officials by the NEWS and, occasionally by other newspapers, that the Ward case would have been dropped forever and even forgotten." The *Daily News*, the article celebrated, pursued "the most audacious series of stories and editorials ever printed."[5]

Fred Magison, Inez Peters's attorney, praised the tabloid for its efforts. "It is the most remarkable and commendable demonstration of journalistic enterprise in the annals of criminal jurisprudence in the United States," he wrote with clear exuberance. He lauded the tabloid's "tireless and unceasing demand that Ward be brought to justice" and added that Patterson's picture post "aroused a public sentiment so overwhelming that even the tremendous opposition that the Ward millions command was inundated and swept away by a mighty tide of public opinion."[6]

In the days after Smith's announcement, bookies across the city began taking bets on Walter Ward. The odds were five to one he would not be indicted again. Ward of course loved a good bet, and those odds would have surely made him happy.[7]

Let Us Have the Fish

The Wards liked to speed. While cars in the early 1920s would reach a top speed of only about forty-five miles an hour, Walter and Beryl tried to get as close to that limit as possible. Beryl was caught going thirty-five miles an hour through Westchester in the summer of 1922—her third time being stopped. She had her daughter, Betty, and son, Willard, in the car, along with their nanny, Lulu Barrow. In court, she admitted she was in the wrong but claimed that the street had few side streets, making it safe to "step on it," as she said. Besides, she told the judge, everyone else was doing it. With her past warnings, she had no option but to pay the twenty-five-dollar fine.

Walter, well-known for his speeding through Sutton Manor, found himself in front of the justice of the peace in early June 1923 for speeding through the small village of Mamaroneck. He was not a stranger to such tickets. Sometimes, as police commissioner, he would call upon police chief Frank Cody in New Rochelle to help him out with a fine. But on this occasion, just a week after a new grand jury was announced, Ward appeared in court, pled guilty to the crime, and paid his twenty-dollar fine.[1]

Catching the Wards had become its own news story as the spring stretched into summer in 1923. In March, when Carl Sherman's inquiry seemed likely to begin, Beryl left for Bermuda. "I have nothing at all to say," she told reporters, who, much to her surprise, tracked her down along the pier before she boarded her ship. "I am going away to rest," she declared, adding with a tone of disdain, "You reporters are all pests. I don't want to say anything. I'd like to be left alone for a while."

Months later, as Sherman was eager to talk with Beryl about the night of May 15, she and her mother, Laura Curtis, were nowhere to be found. "Exiled" was how the press described their absence. It would later be learned they had taken the kids and the servants and traveled to Atlantic City for the summer. When an officer found the Wards in the lobby of the Chelsea Hotel and Garden in the resort town, he attempted to serve them with a subpoena to testify, but they "refused service." They knew they were within their rights and far from the reach of any New York State subpoena. The officer recalled how the women, after refusing the subpoena, walked past him, through the lobby, and into the elevator.[2]

But it was George Ward's ongoing exile from New York that continued to frustrate the attorney general. Ralph offered little information about his father's return when questioned in April. "He may come back tomorrow, or not for a month," he said. When an officer arrived with a subpoena at George Ward's home in early July, the butler informed him that Ward had not been home in nearly a year. At the Bronx factory, the receptionist told the officer the same story.[3]

JULIA HARPMAN INTERVIEWED Inez Peters for the *Daily News*, drawing a sharp contrast between the Wards' exile to hotels and spas and Peters's return to the factory floor. "Imagination can conceive no greater contrast," Harpman wrote, "than exists between the maker of bread and the wiry, nervous, dark-eyed and poverty stricken woman who has found it necessary to 'go into the shop' so that her five children may eat." Peters told Harpman that she had to find work at the shoe factory as Elbridge's illness had worsened. "I've taken my little fourteen-year-old daughter out of school now and she is taking care of the little ones while I go to the shop," she said. The struggle with grief and the unresolved case was a constant haunting for Peters. "I try to stop thinking about it," she said, "but, even at my work, when I am trimming the leather, no matter how busy my hands are, my brain won't stop. Sometimes I think I shall go crazy, worrying about it all the time."[4]

At the Westchester County Courthouse, Sherman and Campbell sifted through one hundred prospective jurors for the extraordinary grand jury. It was an arduous task of finding residents who had no bias against the case, no opinion about Ward or his victim. By late June, twenty-three citizens had been selected, which included a painter from Yonkers, a secretary from New Rochelle, a grocer from Ossining, and a farmer from Mount Kisco. There were three real estate agents, one banker, two construction contractors, a bookkeeper, and a florist among the men. There were, of course, no bakers on the jury.[5]

Governor Smith appointed his long-time friend and political ally supreme court justice Robert Wagner to preside over the grand jury proceedings. Wagner had been the cochair of the Triangle Commission with Smith back in 1911. The two men had similar political backgrounds, coming through the Tammany Hall political machine of New York City to rise to statewide office. Wagner had immigrated with his family from Germany when he was eight years old. His father found work as a janitor for a building in Yorkville, a German enclave on Manhattan's Upper East Side. After success at City College, a beacon for immigrant children in the city, Wagner attended law school and soon entered politics. In 1918, he was elected to the state supreme court. A *New Yorker* profile of Wagner described him as the "janitor's boy" and presented the judge as the embodiment of the rags-to-riches story of immigrant success.[6]

In New York State the supreme court had original jurisdiction over both civil and criminal cases. The appeals court, on the other hand, served as the court of last resort. The First Judicial District of the New York Supreme Court, on which Wagner served alongside thirty-five other justices, had jurisdiction over Manhattan and the Bronx. Known as the busiest jurisdiction in the state, the court received nearly 15,000 new cases annually by the early 1920s. The courts were able to hear only about 9,000 cases a year. This workload, Wagner noted, required a "mental and physical endurance" that had become unbearable. The situation became so bad that in 1923, with a backlog of nearly 22,000 cases, Wagner chaired a commission aimed at reforming the administrative proceedings of the court. So when Al Smith called on him to preside over the extraordinary grand jury, Wagner clearly had his hands full.

Wagner had almost no experience with criminal cases. His expertise on the bench rested in civil law, often involving labor relations and business regulations—concerns that had distinguished his political career. It was in civil cases that Wagner was better equipped to demonstrate his undeniably modern judicial philosophy, which saw the law as dynamic and responsive to the needs of a changing society. Wagner was public and direct in his criticism of conservative judicial doctrines of constitutional originalism. "We worship too much the importance of precedent and antiquity," he would declare. In one ruling in 1923, Wagner wrote, "Words must be interpreted and understood in their most natural and obvious meanings," adding, "We as courts are not bound to close our eyes to what as men we know."[7] We can imagine that Wagner's acceptance of Smith's request had as much to do with his sense of responsibility to his old friend as with his concern for the injustice the Ward-Peters case had come to symbolize.

The first issue Wagner ruled on was the question of the cablegrams between George Ward and his sons. Sherman had been eager to read them for over two months. In the face of Ralph Ward's silence and George Ward's exile, those transatlantic communications could provide the key to the motives behind the killing and reveal the reasons for the alleged blackmail. When Sherman had subpoenaed the cablegrams back in April at the start of his inquiry, it prompted a separate legal fight. The Wards filed an injunction against the Western Union Telegraph Company and the Postal Telegraph and Cable Company to prevent Sherman from getting their cablegrams. Sherman argued they were crucial to his inquiry to ascertain whether Ward's claim of being blackmailed was true.

Allan Campbell argued that the communications were private property and contained sensitive business information including earning figures, conditions of certain factories, and plans for future plants—all information that, if it became public, would "tend to damage" the Ward business. Campbell also argued that as the attorney general had conducted an open and transparent inquiry, there was every reason to believe that the content of the cablegrams would find its way to the front pages of the morning editions.

In April, supreme court justice Ellis Staley agreed with the attorney general. "The law does not recognize cables or telegrams as privileged communication, to the extent that their use may not be required in aid of justice," Staley reasoned. He added, "If we adopt this construction of the law, the telegraph may be used with the most absolute security for purposes destructive to the well-being of society. The correspondence of the traitor, the murderer, the robber and the swindler would become things so sacred that they never could be accessible to the public justice."[8]

Two days later, the appeals court disagreed but not on the question of property rights. Rather it found that Sherman's larger inquiry, conducted under the 1918 Peace and Safety Act, did not grant the attorney general authority to subpoena witnesses or private communications related to a local murder investigation. Such actions, the court argued, could be done only through a grand jury, what the court described as the "great bulwark of the innocent." Lacking the legal procedures and secrecy of the grand jury, the court noted that Sherman "failed to protect Ward from notoriety but made public announcements that his investigation would be conducted in the open," which, it argued, stripped Ward of "all the privileges and safeguards which otherwise would be accorded him." Sherman's inquiry, the appellate court declared, was well beyond the bounds of the law.[9]

But that was in April. By early June, Sherman had the authority of a grand jury and once again subpoenaed the telegraph companies. Ward's attorneys once again tried to stop it.

"I challenge my adversaries," Isaac Mills argued in front of Wagner, "to produce a single fact which would tend to prove these messages are of value to the case." He again claimed that the communications were private property and declared the attorney general was simply on a fishing expedition.

"Are you intimating that I am guilty of contempt of court in subpoenaing these cables?" Sherman retorted. "If there has been blackmail," he continued, "there are conspirators. Who they are or to what extent they conspired I don't know. But there was a conspiracy and these cables were used in some way in the circle of circumstances which went to make up the scheme." Twisting Mills's metaphor, Sherman declared the grand jury certainly did have the power to "fish" for evidence if necessary.

Wagner took two days before siding with the attorney general.

"Telegrams are privileged only where oral communication would be," Wagner reasoned. "Hence my conclusion is that the documents in question are not privileged communication."[10] It was a surprisingly brief ruling that ended weeks of legal battles and would finally reveal the contents of those infamous cables.

Once unsealed, Sherman found that all ten of the cablegrams were partially composed in code. Even the signatures were coded, Ralph signing his Hap and George using the company's signature bread, Tip-Top. Since the nineteenth century, telegrams were often written in code, partly to keep the messages secret from the preying eyes of telegraph workers but also to lower the cost, as telegrams were usually charged by the word. With the help of specialized code handbooks such as the *ABC Code* or the *Acme Code*, a sender could keep their messages private, allowing one to condense whole phrases or sentences into five seemingly random capitalized letters. This was particularly useful for sensitive legal or business communications, and so the fact that the Wards had been communicating in code was not surprising.[11]

Deciphering the code was another matter.

When Ralph Ward appeared in front of the grand jury, Wilbur Chambers questioned the coded parts of the cablegrams. When shown a message from April 1922 and asked to decode it, Ralph was his usual evasive self.

"Of course I cannot well identify it with these code words in it, which I don't recall," he replied. "You see, it is a year and a half since I used code, and I only used the code on messages I sent now and then. And I really cannot recall these words."[12]

Even the direct phrases in the communications were a mystery. One message Ralph sent to his father included the phrase "Walter believes difficulty closed without settlement." When asked to clarify, Ralph had little knowledge of what that referred to, as Walter had told him nothing about what he needed money for in the spring of 1922.

In the end, the long-sought-after cablegrams became their own subterfuge. While some of the coded parts could be deciphered, much remained hidden. Sherman's hope that the cablegrams would answer the questions behind Ward's motives was extinguished. As one report noted, the messages, once read to the jurors, "proved less startling than was expected."[13]

RALPH WARD WAS more forthcoming in other parts of his testimony. He did reveal that he asked his father for $90,000 for Walter, a figure much larger than earlier reports. While George Ward initially agreed to the amount, once he learned from Walter it was for blackmail, he directed Ralph not to give his brother a penny. George did tell Ralph the entire story of the blackmail, the same day George returned on the *Majestic*. But Ralph still held to the argument that what his father had told him was hearsay and refused to relate the story. At that point the jurors became frustrated with Ralph's continued defiance.

"That is what we are seeking," one juror confronted him. "A justification for that act, but we cannot get it, as you people have closed right up and don't say a word."

Another juror, relying on the often-employed fishing metaphor, asked Ralph to come clean about what he knew.

"Pull in the bait," the juror implored. "Give us what is on the end of the fishing expedition line. That is what we are here for now. The bait is out. Now give us the information. Let us have the fish."

Ralph calmly and politely refused and characterized the entire investigation as a "persecution," echoing Elwood Rabenold's constant refrain about the case. He claimed his family was, at the beginning, diligent in helping authorities "solve the thing," but it quickly became apparent that, in his words, "we were greatly discouraged, and we saw politics playing an important part, and other influences, which had nothing whatever to do with the case."[14] Ralph left the grand jury room offering yet again few insights about the reasons behind the murder.

The fish remained in the water.

Unprintable Practices

THE ATTORNEY GENERAL SUBPOENAED SEVENTY-THREE WITnesses, requesting their presence in front of the extraordinary grand jury. Many had already testified before the 1922 grand jury or had traveled to the state capital just a few months earlier to answer questions as part of the attorney general's inquiry. Throughout the humid weeks of July, the grand jurors heard the contradictory theories about the crime scene investigation, details of Peters's autopsy report, testimonies from Ward's neighbors and colleagues, his gambling habits and financial troubles, the scandal of Ward's bachelor apartment in the Poinciana, the character of Clarence Peters, and the timeline of his travels in April 1922 from Parris Island, South Carolina, to New York. Much of the testimony rehearsed what was already known about the case—facts and observations that cast doubts on Ward's initial statement but offered little beyond speculation.

William Fallon, who had recently been indicted for bribing a juror, reemerged as a witness about his unsuccessful search for Charlie Ross and Jack.[1] In an unusual move for the well-known criminal attorney, Fallon slipped past reporters outside the courthouse and quickly made his way to the grand jury waiting room. Reporters noted how quickly he reemerged from a side door, suggesting his testimony had been brief.

Frederick Weeks told the grand jurors he accepted Ward's statement at first. "It looked very, very plausible," he said, "and after I mulled it over a couple of days, why I didn't believe it at all." He testified he thought Peters was killed somewhere else and brought to King Street. But it was the nature of the alleged threat that he said was the most difficult part of his entire investigation. Weeks recalled a confrontation with Ward's attorneys in his office. "For god's sake," he'd told the attorneys, "if this blackmailing occurred you talk about it, as you suggest, race track stuff, lay your cards on the table. Out with the stuff." Campbell paced "up and down with his hands in his pockets, very much excited." He told Weeks, "We will not be forced either by the public or popular clamor to say what the blackmail is." It was this encounter, according to Weeks, that put him "on the outs" with Ward's attorneys. "They abused me plentifully," he told the jury.[2]

Palmer Tubbs, who was a police commissioner in New Rochelle and for two years Walter Ward's assistant, offered a mixed portrait of his former boss. Not long after Tubbs testified in the first grand jury, detailing how two men, one named Ross, came to visit Ward at his office, Tubbs was fired from the company. Ward explained to his assistant that the company was reorganizing their workforce, and Tubbs, according to Ward, was "the weakest link." Ward was a "hard man to work for," Tubbs testified, and described his former boss as "very cold blooded, close mouthed, but," he added, "the most wonderfully alert mind in the purchasing game." It was not the most flattering of descriptions for a man suspected of murder.

Elbridge and Inez Peters took the train to White Plains to testify on the character of their son. The couple stood on the steps of the courthouse. Inez, dressed in mourning black, leaned on her husband's arm as they faced reporters. "Our boy met a violent death," Elbridge told reporters, "and then, to make it worse, the man who killed him branded him as a despicable blackmailer. His mother and I know that Clarence was not that type." As the two made their way to the train station, Elbridge turned to the reporters and declared, "I want justice."[3]

Earl Hardy, Clarence Peters's uncle who identified the body, also traveled to White Plains. He testified that while Peters had been in a few "scrapes" in the past, he couldn't imagine his nephew entangled in such complex con games. "I don't think he had a mind capable of doing the things they reported in the papers," he said.[4]

WHILE THE GRAND jury witness list would have been familiar to anyone following the case over the past year, one name was new: William Mundia. Twenty-five-year-old Mundia worked as a chauffeur and lived in a small apartment with his Italian immigrant mother, Angela, and older brother, John, on West 106th Street in Manhattan. Mundia's World War I registration card described him as medium build and medium height with dark eyes and dark hair. But he never did serve in the war. The card was stamped INSANE and listed his place of employment as the "Matteawan State Hospital, Beacon, N.Y."

Built in 1892, Matteawan State Hospital for the Criminally Insane sat among forests and pastures in the hills near the Hudson River, about seventy miles north of New York City. Consistently underfunded and overcrowded, the facility treated some of the most violent criminals in the state. One of its more notorious patients was Harry Thaw, architect Stanford White's killer. Why Mundia was incarcerated in Matteawan is unclear. One article reported that he had been convicted of "malicious mischief," carrying a concealed weapon, and assault. Records from the hospital, even a hundred years later, remain private under state law, so it is impossible to determine what treatment he may have received or when his treatment ended. What we do know is that at some point Mundia had been released on parole and by 1920 was back living with Angela and John working as a chauffeur. We also know that the only way one left Matteawan was with a certificate signed by one of the hospital's doctors confirming the patient's recovery.[5]

Mundia found himself back behind bars in June 1923, having violated his parole. On his second day in the West Side Jail in Manhattan, he told the guards he'd swallowed a handful of pins in an effort to kill himself. It turned out he swallowed only one pin. But as they rushed him across town to Bellevue Hospital, Mundia claimed he had been a friend of Clarence Peters's and knew Walter Ward. It must have seemed an odd comment to the staff, but one that prompted them to contact the police. His confession led him to Sherman and eventually to the witness stand in the White Plains grand jury room.[6]

Mundia testified that he met Walter Ward at Cushman's cabaret in Greenwich Village, a place known for its illegal alcohol, uptown slummers, and petting parties. In January 1923, eleven young women were arrested at Cushman's in a sweeping police raid, which included sixteen other cabarets in the Village. Proprietor Robert Cushman was charged with "impairing the morals of minors." In a newspaper column, F. Scott Fitzgerald decried the raids and arrests. He blamed Prohibition, which made such places an "adventure" for the young. "Those girls at Cushman's," Fitzgerald wrote, "weren't vicious any more than the flappers in my novels are vicious."[7]

Allegedly Mundia and Ward not only enjoyed Cushman's nightlife, but also went to cabarets in Harlem and attended private parties in the city. While Mundia described Ward as a "degenerate," exact details of their parties and Ward's behavior were too scandalous for the press. "Unprintable practices" was how *The New York Times* described Mundia's testimony. At the private parties, Mundia claimed Ward paid him twelve to fifteen dollars for what one newspaper called "depraved practices," though what that meant was left to the readers' imaginations.

A more explicit moment came when Mundia told the grand jurors he had been "going with" Ward for a few months before the murder and that they both knew all the "faggots." It must have been a shocking claim for the grand jurors, and one that few newspapers even printed. When *The New York Times* published the story of his testimony on its front page, the editors had to clarify for its readers that the term *faggot* was slang for "sexual perverts." It was the first time the newspaper had used this term to describe homosexuals, educating, no doubt, some of its morning readers on queer vernacular.

While the relationship between Mundia and Ward might have sparked surprise, his account of Peters's murder held its own spectacular details. According to Mundia, he met Ward on a road near the crime scene in the early-morning hours of May 16, 1922. The two men stopped their cars, and Ward came up to Mundia, telling him he'd shot Peters. "He told me," Mundia testified, "he had just knocked him off." Mundia claimed he'd first met Peters along the Hudson River docks in April 1922 and had seen Peters with Ward at Cushman's a few times in May. Ward told Mundia two men named Jack Rogers and Charlie Ross were supposed to murder Peters, but they refused, so Ward had to do it himself. Both Ross and Rogers had been paid off for their silence.

"I will give it to you as I have to the other skunk," Ward allegedly said to Mundia along the dark roadside in the early-morning hours, holding his .38 Colt in his hand. But his threats were short-lived. Ward lowered his gun and offered Mundia a check to keep him quiet about the crime and supposedly all he knew about Ward. When Sherman asked Mundia what was the size of the check, the chauffeur misunderstood the attorney general's question.

"It was this big," he replied, gesturing with his hands to indicate the check's physical size. Later he clarified it was for $5,000, though Mundia refused the offer, as he did not have a bank account. This odd exchange, along with a series of contradictory facts, must have cast doubts in the jurors' minds about why Mundia had been called to testify in the first place. His descriptions of both Ward and Peters were inaccurate. His claim of meetings with Peters in April and May contradicted the established timeline for Peters's movements from Haverhill to Parris Island. The meeting and conversation along the Westchester roadside on the night of the murder seemed too coincidental, too fantastical to be believed.

"Do you realize the enormity of your crime if you don't tell the truth?" a clearly frustrated jury foreman asked Mundia.

"Yes, sir," Mundia replied.

The foreman then warned him, "You are saying a great many things that these intelligent men could not possibly believe."

When confronted by the fact that Peters could not have been in New York in late April and early May, as Mundia had described, he replied, "Say what you please," and then fell silent.[8]

Sifting through the facts and fictions of Mundia's testimony was a particularly acute task for the grand jury. Why Sherman brought

Mundia in to testify is unclear. Though perhaps it was all those "unprintable practices" that intrigued Sherman, for it was not the first time that homosexuality was at the heart of the investigation. Initial inquiries into the murder focused on the sexual possibilities behind the murder. Sherman was certainly aware of James Clark's story in the *New York American* a year earlier, which alleged Ward's interest in working-class men and Peters's relationship with wealthy men in the city. He would have read the detective reports from Boston and Sutton Manor, where informants described Ward as a "fairy" and a "degenerate" and where detectives asked if Ward could be a "cocksucker."

And then there was a letter Sherman had received in April from C. V. Knightley. For several years Knightley had worked as a secretary at the Boston YMCA, where he claimed he had met Peters on several visits. Ward too was known to visit the Y, according to Knightley. The YMCA, with its private room rentals and social activities, was often a hub where queer men could find social and sexual encounters. When a national scandal erupted in Newport, Rhode Island, in 1919 involving sex between U.S. Navy recruits and local men, it was the Providence YMCA that became the center of the investigation. "The Army and Navy Y.M.C.A was the headquarters of all cocksuckers," one investigator noted. In cities along the East Coast, the queer activities at the Y were well-known.[9]

"I know about Peters' relations to Ward," Knightley wrote. "They were of the 'Solly' type." *Solly* was a kind of crude term for *homosexual* in the 1920s. How Knightley knew the nature of their relationship he did not explain. Did Peters and Ward meet each other at the Boston YMCA? Knightley suggested that George Ward knew of his son's sexual desires and "cautioned silence" when Knightley raised the matter with him.

On the afternoon of May 15, 1922, Knightley recalled meeting Clarence Peters in Pennsylvania Station in New York City. Peters asked to borrow five dollars, as he was trying to get to New Rochelle, showing a postmarked letter "addressed in a female hand," Knightley noted. Knightley then detailed how the murder really happened. "Peters was shot at Mrs. Ward's bedroom door," he claimed; the blood-splattered mat was burned. Walter Ward took Peters's dead body to King Street and dumped it there. "No other men were present," he said. We don't know how Knightley came upon this information. His description was so matter-of-fact in his letter, it was as if he had been told it by Ward himself. Despite the tone of confidence, Knightley did make clear that he wished to "avoid publicity" and had no interest in making a public statement.

There is no record that Sherman called Knightley to testify to the grand jury. The letter might have seemed too cryptic and unsubstantiated. The theory that Peters had been murdered at the Wards' home on Decatur Road had already been thoroughly dismissed. But the claims about the homosexual encounter—those unprintable practices the press alluded to—between Ward and Peters continued to linger in the case, if only in shadowy speculation. Despite the seemingly unreliable details Mundia offered, the fact that he took the stand in the grand jury room made clear that the attorney general was not discounting the queer possibilities behind the crime.[10]

AFTER A MONTH of testimony, the grand jury was ready to deliver its verdict. On Friday, July 27, Walter Ward, along with his lawyers and brother Ralph, arrived at the Westchester County Courthouse. According to one report, Ward was "immaculate as well as indifferent," smiling for the photographers who surrounded him in the courtroom. He wore a well-pressed brown suit with white striping. In one hand he grasped a rolled-up magazine; a large diamond ring on his finger flashed as he twisted the magazine in a small gesture of nervousness that betrayed his seemingly calm demeanor.

"Walter S. Ward," the court clerk intoned, "you have been indicted for the crime of murder in the first degree."

When Wagner asked for Ward's plea, Isaac Mills shouted, "Not guilty!"

"I think the defendant should speak for himself," Sherman retorted, and Wagner agreed.

Mills then nudged Ward: "I plead not guilty." The court was filled with journalist and spectators, including DA Rowland. Those in the back rows cupped their ears to hear Ward's plea, his tone muffled in the cavernous courtroom. As they did in the summer of 1922, Ward's attorneys requested an immediate trial. Wagner suggested a trial date in two or three weeks.

"A week," Mills complained, "may mean a lot to a man seeking a little more sunshine."

Sherman of course knew he would need time to prepare the case and gather certain witnesses. "I'd like to set a definite date," he told the court, "but there are many witnesses to be called and some of them are out of jurisdiction." It was a direct criticism of George Ward's ongoing exile from the state.

"Why should that cause a delay?" Mills asked. "Why can't we go on immediately? How many witnesses does the Attorney General want? I don't think there is any new evidence in the case." He then criticized Sherman as an outsider, meddling in the affairs of the local district attorney.

"The Attorney General," Mills continued, "has come into this county declaring that he is dissatisfied with the manner of which this case was handled by our officials."

"I resent that remark!" Sherman shot back, his quick temper on full display. "I have never made such charge." Wagner defended Sherman and quickly ended the debate. Pragmatic in administrative processes, Wager finally set the trial date for September 4.

PRAISE FOR THE indictment filled the Voice of the People column in the *Daily News*. "One of the greatest moral victories in history," wrote Thomas Keating. Not surprisingly, many of the letters were strategically selected for their praise of the tabloid. "To the NEWS and the NEWS alone belongs the credit for the reindictment," wrote Sumner Forsythe. "What a valiant fight for justice it has been on the part of your newspaper and what a signal victory it has led to."[11]

An editorial in *The New York Times*, titled "A Mystery Under a Mystery," observed the layered uncertainties of the case and questioned the public's appetite for the crime. "There has been a feeling, that back of the murder or homicide was something else, darkly mysterious," the paper noted, "and that it was against the disclosure of this something else that the desperate fight of Ward's counsel really was made. The result has been the arousing of intense curiosity and some rather queer resentment that what the public wanted to know should be kept from them."[12]

As Ward's attorneys left the courthouse, they were in an upbeat mood, which was odd given that their client had just been indicted for the second time on the charge of first-degree murder. They gave reporters the impression that finally the mysteries and secrets behind the murder would emerge into the full light of day.

"Well, I'm glad it's over," Senator Rabenold told reporters. "There are two sides to this case, and now we'll be able to tell our side of it."[13] Many might have wondered if Rabenold really meant what he said.

Mousetrap

In early August, headlines about Walter Ward's indictment were eclipsed by the sudden death of President Warren G. Harding, which threw the country into national mourning. Harding was on a trip to Alaska when he suffered a bout of food poisoning coupled with pneumonia. His doctors advised the president to recover in San Francisco rather than risk the long train trip back to Washington. Heeding his doctor's advice, Harding took a suite at the Palace Hotel in the city. News reports claimed that the president was doing much better and a full recovery was imminent—a prognosis that ended with a sudden deadly stroke on August 2.

"News of the death of President Harding not only greatly shocked officials in Washington," *The New York Times* reported, "but took the capital completely by surprise." Telephone lines were jammed in the nation's capital, and at big hotels, "dancing was immediately stopped and a hush and gloom settled over the crowds." In New York, Governor Smith expressed his condolences, stating the president's death was "a terrible loss and a terrible shock to the nation and practically to the entire world."

The mysteries of Harding's death provoked wild claims that the president had been poisoned by his doctor or his wife, Florence, who, some believed, was insanely jealous about his ongoing affairs, which were well-known around the nation's capital. Florence refused to have an autopsy to determine the exact cause of death. Instead she had Harding embalmed within an hour after he died. More likely, his deadly stroke was caused by his poor health, an enlarged heart, and a misdiagnosis by his doctor. The mystery about his death would, however, linger for years, with books and articles speculating about who might have killed the president. Such theories were made more acute when scandalous revelations of graft in the Harding administration emerged in the months after his death, fueling congressional hearings and court cases for nearly a decade. But the public knew little of these scandals in those early weeks of August 1923. Instead, as Harding's casket traveled by train across the country, large crowds gathered in towns and cities along the route to mourn his loss. "It is believed," *The New York Times* reported, "to be the most remarkable demonstration in American history of affection, respect and reverence for the dead."[1]

AS THE NATION mourned, Allan Campbell and Isaac Mills filed a thirty-two-page petition requesting access to the extraordinary grand jury testimony and a motion to dismiss the indictment. They made a number of legal challenges to how Justice Wagner and the attorney general had "misadvised" the grand jury in their deliberations. They charged directly that as the first indictment had been dismissed, this new inquiry produced "no evidence that the homicide committed by Ward was a crime." They listed all seventy-two witnesses who testified, noting how many had testified in 1922 and offered nothing new to the case a year later. About the new witnesses, they cast doubts as to their relevance to the case. Chief among them was William Mundia, who, they noted, "was brought from some jail or insane institution in New York" and "who declared he knew something about the Ward case, and who acted in such a way that he was examined by the authorities to determine his sanity."[2]

The attorneys went to great lengths to point to bias in the entire grand jury process. Campbell noted how when he testified, he remembered some jurors had the *Daily News*, and, in fact, he witnessed "one grand juror reading the 'Daily News' while the testimony was going on." He suggested that the entire inquiry had been tainted by the campaign of the New York tabloid. "The 'Daily News' has carried as a prominent place daily in its editorial column in large type the following statement: 'Can a rich man kill a poor man in New York and not be tried for it?'" Campbell noted, "and has during the course of the grand jury proceedings as well as prior thereto conducted a campaign in its editorials and news columns in favor of the indictment." The petition included five pages of excerpts from the tabloid, illustrating the bias of the paper and suggesting the influence it had on the grand jury's investigation.

Ward's attorneys successfully got their motion heard in front of Justice Seeger, who had been quite favorable to Ward in the past. It was Seeger who had allowed Ward's freedom in 1922 on bail, and it was Seeger who had dismissed the first indictment in January 1923. In an open letter to the Justice, the *Daily News* all but declared his participation in this new stage of the case an obstruction of justice: "We believe that you, Justice Seeger, are sadly mistaken in permitting yourself again to be drawn into this case. If the second indictment against Ward is dismissed, it will be the greatest travesty of justice in the annals of any State."[3]

Soon after the indictment was handed down, Sherman hired Manhattan attorney Thomas O'Neill as a special deputy attorney general for the case. O'Neill had a reputation as a strong litigator in criminal cases and an expert in negligence law.[4] In Seeger's court, O'Neill argued that Ward's attorneys couldn't be trusted with the grand jury testimony.

"The disclosure of the Grand Jury minutes would tend to defeat the ends of justice," he argued. He pointed to the many witnesses whom they never were able to subpoena, such as George Ward and Beryl's mother, Laura Curtis. He pointed to the failed attempts by agents in Atlantic City to bring Mrs. Curtis and the Wards' maid, Lulu Barrows, back to White Plains to testify. He pointed at the ways the Ward attorneys secreted away the Jones family, hid them in the city, and then forced them out of the country after Seeger dismissed the first indictment. These willful efforts to thwart the investigation,

O'Neil declared, "indicate what might happen to some of our important witnesses if they get the Grand Jury minutes."

"They have the names of these witnesses from the indictment," Seeger retorted.

"Well, they may have the names of them, but that alone isn't enough," O'Neill replied. "They haven't got the addresses either, of all of them, so far as we know." At one point, O'Neill read into testimony letters from Goldie Jones detailing how Ward's attorneys had treated them. Mills interrupted, declaring, "I can't see the slightest relevancy to all this."

"I can't either," Seeger replied and, without hearing any other arguments, granted the defense's motion for access to the minutes.[5]

Of course once Ward's attorneys got their hands on the 1,024 pages of grand jury testimony, they did what the attorney general had feared, and what they had done back in the summer of 1922: they gave them to the press. Staff at the Rabenold & Scribner offices on Broadway sent the testimony to a printer and produced hundreds of copies to be given to journalists.[6] We can imagine the weight and size of each copy, hauled in boxes into the lobby of the law firm, ready for any reporter who requested a copy. If it had been bound and circulated to the local bookstores of New York, it just might have been a bestseller that August. Throughout the following weeks, excerpts from the testimony were republished in article after article in the New York press. It was a clear strategy to cast doubt over the entire indictment.

Back in court pursuing a motion to dismiss the case in front of Justice Wagner, Elwood Rabenold criticized the attorney general and the entire investigation. He pointed directly at the testimony of William Mundia. "The Mundia fiasco was evidence of the attitude of mind on the part of the Attorney General," Rabenold declared, "satisfied only with gore, salaciousness and sensation." He argued that Ward was being persecuted, not prosecuted, and demanded that the entire indictment be dismissed.

"They want a trial," O'Neill retorted. "Then why all these elaborate motions whose only object is to stop the trial?" He continued,

"This prosecution is not based on Ward's wealth. He is entitled to every right that a poor man is entitled to but they don't understand that he is not entitled to any more. They got a *de luxe* reception when they came to give him up." O'Neill called Ward's statement a "silly tale" and denied that Ward was being treated unjustly. "Ward is not being persecuted," he said, "but is being prosecuted because he concededly killed Clarence M. Peters and did not tell about it until after his identity had been established, and then presented a statement nearly every part of which is shown by the minutes to be false and to a great extent impossible."[7]

Justice Wagner ruled against the defense. He reasoned that given the evidence presented, "all the issues including that of self-defense are questions of fact to be determined by a trial jury upon the weight, character, and credibility of the evidence." He also denied Ward his request for bail: "It is only where there are exceptional circumstances that a defendant charged with homicide is released on bail pending the trial. No such unusual circumstances appear to me to be present."[8]

Friends sent letters and notes of sympathy to Ward to his jail cell after Wagner's ruling. "I am ready to go to trial any day and prove my innocence," he told Warden Hill. Ward asked Hill to put him to work in the jail. While Hill did not assign Ward to scrub the kitchen or bathroom floors, the *Daily News* reported that he had apparently been tasked with making two wooden mousetraps to catch mice that had been nibbling their way into the flour bags in the jail kitchen.

"If Ward made good mousetraps," a *Daily News* editorial observed, "doubtless by this time the two mice have paid the penalty for their minor crimes. But if his mousetraps were of no better construction than mousetraps for Justice which his lawyers and unseen political friends have been making for months past, the two mice probably still are enjoying their freedom."[9]

Privately, *Daily News* managing editor Phil Payne wrote to Joe Patterson about the outrage and frustration by the defense attorneys at having to try their case in front of Justice Wagner rather than a more accommodating judge. "I am reliably informed," Payne wrote, "that Justice Seeger was told by the political boss who secured his appointment to lay off the case at once." Seeger, it seemed, was tending to his own private scandal and did not want to get involved any further with the Peters case. Another favorable supreme court justice was also eliminated, as his court appointment had been orchestrated by Isaac Mills, and Sherman was keen on exposing this conflict should he need to.

But the political intrigue was not as compelling for Payne as his delight with the publicity the *Daily News* was getting through the many legal maneuvers of the defense attorneys. He pointed to how their courtroom arguments and motions to dismiss were heavily "devoted to attacks upon THE NEWS" and how a "great many New York papers have used the name of the DAILY NEWS throughout their publication of the Grand Jury minutes." Payne concluded, "I am convinced that our determined fight for justice in the Ward case has enhanced our prestige wonderfully and has had a great deal to do with our circulation gains within the past few weeks."[10]

Fly into the Air Like Smoke

Carl Sherman stood in front of the jury box in the dark-paneled Westchester County courtroom on the morning of September 17. Tall and lanky, he was dressed in a blue suit and white shirt and looking confident for his opening argument. Behind him, the gallery was standing room only. Spectators tried to push their way through the heavy double doors into the hot and stuffy courtroom, as officers struggled to keep the crowd orderly. "Not since the trial of Harry K. Thaw when he sought his release from Matteawan asylum," one article noted, "has there been so much excitement around the White Plains court house."[1]

Sherman began by thanking the jurors for their patience.

"It is quite likely that the trial will drag on some time," he told the twelve men, "and I am quite sure that you all will continue to exercise patience, because it is a solemn duty which we have to perform."[2]

As expected, it had taken several weeks to seat a jury, which prolonged the start of the trial. Both sides went through nearly two hundred potential jurors, each one quizzed on their knowledge of the case and their potential bias. Ward sat in the courtroom through the entire process, gesturing his approvals or disapprovals to his lawyers. In the end, the twelve men, including a farmer, a machinist, a real estate broker, a grocer, a butcher, and a men's clothier, among others, took their seats in the jury box on that Monday morning in September prepared to determine Walter Ward's fate.

The *Daily News* described Sherman as having a "flint in his voice, and fire in his eye."[3] Whatever fiery presence Sherman may have had, it simmered underneath an earnestness in his words.

"The State must prove, and expects to prove," Sherman began, "that Walter Ward shot Peters dead with intent and design in him to do it. In other words, cold-blooded, deliberate murder."

Sherman recounted Ward's story of what had happened on King Street. As he read Ward's original typewritten statement to the jury, certain details were spoken with an incredulous tone. He called the statement a "master piece," the phrase dripping with ridicule. He then cast doubts about each claim, from the mysterious two men Charlie Ross and Jack who had never been found, to the lack of any sign of a struggle along the roadside, to that curious position of Peters's body laid out perfectly composed, and most acutely, to the claims that Peters had been involved in a blackmailing gang for weeks before the murder.

"He could not any more have been in a blackmail plot," Sherman told the jury, "than I could have been at that time."

He then turned to Walter Ward, sitting next to his lawyers, his legs crossed, looking relaxed and calm and wearing a new gray suit. Beryl and Ralph sat right behind him in the gallery. Sherman, animated and raising his voice, waved the statement in the air and shouted, "Peters had no more chance of getting $75,000 out of Walter Ward than I had!" The dramatic gesture captured the full attention of the entire room.

As he detailed the sequence of events around the murder, Sherman described how the bullet had entered Peters's body, using his own torso as a diagram, pointing to the entry point near the center of his chest, and moving his finger across the side of his body and turning to the jury to illustrate the exit point. Connecting himself with young Clarence Peters was clearly a strategy for Sherman, an effort to create an image of the ex-sailor beyond his arrests and incarcerations in reformatories. Sherman knew well that Ward's lawyers were keen on making the case about the character of Peters rather than the dubious claims of Ward. He often referred to Peters as the "sailor boy" or simply "boy," conjuring an innocence in the jurors' minds.

"When we finish, we will have disproved every essential part of the Ward statement. It will fly into the air like smoke!" he exclaimed. As he neared the end of his opening argument, his earnestness turned into anger. Clenching his right hand, Sherman pounded the heavy oak table in front of him, the thud echoing through the courtroom, and declared, "There will be nothing left except the fact that Walter Ward, with malice and design, pulled the .38 revolver on Clarence Peters, who was unarmed, and shot him through the heart, deliberately and with premeditation."[4]

It was a powerful and determined opening for the attorney general, a "flogging," as the *Daily News* described it. Sherman's main strategy was to cast deep doubts about Ward's original statement, to show the jury that Peters's murder could not have happened the way Ward had described it and that his claims of self-defense were all a lie. But doubts alone would not be enough to convict Ward of first-degree murder. And many in that courtroom must have known all the bluster and drama would get the prosecution only so far.

Before Sherman even sat down, Isaac Mills, who led Ward's defense in the trial, rose and motioned for a dismissal of the entire case. Compared to Sherman, who just turned thirty-two years old, the gray-haired and bespectacled Mills appeared the wise and experienced jurist who could still command a courtroom with ease despite his age and noticeably diminished hearing.

"I move that the indictment be dismissed on the Attorney General's opening," Mills motioned, declaring that these were the same facts and no more than in the previous indictment. As we might expect, Wagner denied his motion.

For Ward's defense attorneys the strategy might have seemed simple, and one that Mills and Campbell had been pursing for over a year. Raise doubts over the testimony of the seventy-one witnesses set to testify for the state and make the jury believe that Ward's story of the murder was the only plausable truth about what happened on that lonely road.

Duncan Rose, the White Plains pharmacist, described how he'd found Peters's body along the side of the road in the morning on May 16. "The dead boy was lying flat on his back, his feet together and his toes pointed up," Rose testified, noting that his feet were about two inches apart and that on his vest "every button was buttoned." Assistant Attorney General Chambers offered the jury photographs taken that morning of the body along King Street. "Did you see any injuries about Peters?" Chambers asked.

"No," Rose replied.

"Did you see any blood?"

"None.

"With his vest buttoned, as you looked at him, did you see any sign of a bullet hole?"

"No, sir."

"Did you see any gun around there, broken glass, any signs of a struggle?"

"Nothing. I only saw the body."[5]

Allan Campbell questioned Rose about his encounter with men who appeared to be "foreigners and laborers," in Duncan's words, and their two trucks on King Street, just a mile or so from where Peters's body lay. Might those men have moved the body? Campbell asked. Might they have positioned him along the road in the manner that Rose had found him? Rose could not deny that possibility.

Frank Taxter, the lineman for the Westchester County Light Company, claimed he'd found the body much as Rose had described it. But he remembered how Peters's right hand had been resting on his thigh, and there was sand on his palm, in contradiction to most of the other witnesses from that morning.

State trooper Harry Green, one of the first officials to the scene, recounted what he remembered about the crime scene and the state of Peters's body. While questioning Green, Sherman introduced Peters's clothing as evidence. His suit and white shirt, a dark circle seared around the bullet hole, were passed around to the twelve jurors to inspect. Sherman held the bloodstained vest in his hand as he asked Green how he'd found the body and what he'd noticed around the crime scene. Green, wearing a tight tweed suit and a small dark bow-tie, recounted how he removed Peters's coat and vest and then saw the bullet hole. He also testified how he'd found the bullet casing.

"I got down on my hands and knees and searched all around. Trooper Ralph Colins was with me and we looked for bullet marks on the rocks, the trees, and the underbrush. We found nothing."[6]

But Green, who prided himself on his keen memory, quickly proved an unhelpful witness. He often struggled with many of the details. "Indistinct recollections" is how one newspaper describe them.[7] He claimed the bullet casing was from a .32 pistol, until Campbell reminded him it was from a .38 automatic. Campbell also pointed out that in Green's grand jury testimony, he'd claimed Peters's feet were six or seven inches apart, but at trial he now agreed with Rose that the feet were much closer together, no more than two inches apart. With a tone of frustration, Campbell asked if Green had been coached to get his testimony more consistent with others who had been to the crime scene that morning, prompting indignant objections from Sherman.

Changing one's earlier testimony became a theme as the trial went on. Dr. Henry Vier, who assisted in the autopsy, testified that he found no powder marks on Peters's clothing.

"Did you see anything to indicate powder marks on Peters shirt?" O'Neill asked.

"No sir," Vier replied.

"In regard to the burn, you have been in doubt as to whether it was a powder burn?"

"I have."

"Didn't you testify in April, 1923 that it was powder marks?" Campbell asked.

"I did."

"Now you have changed your mind?"

"Yes."[8]

One key leg of the prosecution's case rested on doubts about the two guns Ward claimed were used on the night of Peters's murder—the .32 Smith & Wesson and the .38 Colt automatic. The prosecution was convinced that the Smith & Wesson had not been Peters's gun, but rather one that Ward had received from New Rochelle police chief Frank Cody back in 1920. O'Neill questioned Cody on the stand.

"I show you this Smith and Wesson," O'Neill started, "and ask whether it looks exactly like the one you gave the defendant."

Mills jumped up to object, which Wagner overruled.

Cody examined the gun, turning it over in his hands, and said, "As I remember, it looks exactly like it." Campbell then offered Cody the .38 Colt automatic and asked him if it looked exactly like the gun he'd given Ward.

"Yes, it looks exactly like it," Cody replied. Cody also testified he had seen Ward use the .38 Colt at target practice with the police department just a few weeks before Peters's murder. Ward, Cody recalled, always hit the target and often hit the bull's-eye.

Under cross-examination Cody conceded that he had not seen Ward with the Smith & Wesson since he'd given it to him and that there was no way to identify whether that particular gun was the one he'd handed Ward.

Before Campbell returned to his chair, O'Neill rose and called his next witness: Allan Campbell.

"I order you to the stand. Do so now," O'Neill intoned, while the defense attorneys tried unsuccessful objections. It was a dramatic move calling Ward's lead attorney to testify in such a sudden way. A reluctant Campbell took the stand. After a series of questions about Campbell's initial involvement in the case, O'Neill asked if the two guns were in fact those that Walter Ward had given him and that he'd then given to Sheriff Werner on May 24, 1922. Campbell confirmed they were and with that left the stand.

While Sherman and O'Neill may have been convinced that the Smith & Wesson was in fact not the one Peters had used, it seemed unlikely that anyone in the courtroom, or among the jurors, would have been swayed. While the .32 pistol may have looked "exactly" like the one Cody had given Ward in 1920, the prosecution couldn't establish for certain that it was, without a doubt, that same gun. "The failure of Chief Cody to make the identification," the *Brooklyn Daily Eagle* reported, "plainly was a sad blow to the State's Attorney."[9]

It was crucial for the state to lay out the timeline of Peters's movements from Parris Island to New York, confirming train tickets and departure and arrival schedules. Corporal Winfield Buzard with the U.S. Marine Corps at Parris Island, South Carolina, testified to Peters's departure on May 14, 1922.

Buzard confirmed that Peters had no weapons of any kind when he arrived, nor when he left. On his departure, Peters had asked Buzard if he had any better clothing to give him than the clothes he'd worn when he arrived. The corporal had offered him a brown suit that had been unclaimed by one of the recruits who had been admitted to the service. Peters then spotted a low-cut pair of patent leather shoes.

"He told me he was a dancing instructor," Buzard testified, "and he would like to have those shoes." Curiously, while Buzard did confirm Peters's suit as the one he gave him, Peters, it seems, was not wearing those low-cut patent leather shoes when he was murdered. What happened to those more stylish shoes?

On cross-examination, Campbell asked if Peters had told him why he was being discharged from the marines.

"He said on account of a wife and child," Buzard recalled. Buzard's testimony increasingly portrayed Peters as a man filled with lies.

Campbell went through all the items that Buzard remembered Peters had taken with him when he left Parris Island. Buzard could not recall seeing the cheap cigarette case and what the press often described as the "dainty" handkerchief, the one with the lavender border and lavender pansies stitched in the corner.

"Did you see this lady's handkerchief in his possession?" Campbell asked, holding the handkerchief in his hand.

"I did not," Buzard replied.

"I move to strike the answer," Chambers objected, "on the ground that there is no evidence yet that it is a lady's handkerchief." It was true. Since the first time the press had described the handkerchief, it was always assumed to be feminine given its lavender stitching and flower pattern. Justice Wagner ordered the answer struck from the record.

"When he told you about going away," Campbell continued, "did he tell you something about his plans?"

"No."

"Did he tell you something about his inclinations?" Campbell asked, clearly pushing a line of inquiry about Peters's personal life. O'Neill's objection was sustained.

Buzard did testify that on one hot afternoon before Peters was rejected for service, he'd told him a story. "If I was on the outside, I would not be working. I would be driving out to the park some place," he told Buzard. Though he was not exactly sure, Buzard believed Peters talked of driving around in a Stutz car, "the windshield laid back and taking a nice, cool breeze." It was this reference to the Stutz that the defense wished to highlight, connecting, perhaps, to the Stutz car that Ward claimed met him and Peters on the night of the murder. It was certainly a small detail being stretched to support Ward's statement. But then so much of the testimony in the first week rested on small details, on how many inches were between Peters's feet, how many buttons were undone on his vest, the origins of that "dainty" handkerchief or the cheap cigarette case. The small details either cast doubts about the facts of the crime or confirmed other facts of Ward's story. Both sides depended on such small details.[10]

For the many spectators who crowded into the stuffy courtroom, the end of the first week of the trial revealed only the familiar circumstantial evidence and puzzling contradictions that had followed this case for months. "The humdrum witnesses," one report called it, "with their unimportant stories."[11]

So it was a shock when, in questioning Sheriff Werner near the end of that first week, Campbell was forced to reveal a sworn affidavit that offered a different theory of the blackmail. In it, George Ward was the real target, with the gang threatening to expose Walter's "immoral acts" if George Ward did not pay them cash or hand over property. But perhaps it was not only the new theory that was shocking. It was also the source of theory: the dubious and fanciful informant James Cunningham.

On the stand, O'Neill asked Sheriff Werner why Ward had not filed a complaint against the blackmailers so as to issue a warrant for their arrests.

"Mr. Rabenold came in," Werner explained, referring to Ward's attorney, "and told me that he would not allow Ward to do it and had advised him not to." The exact reason was not made clear.

On cross-examination, Campbell, defending Rabenold's decision, produced James Cunningham's affidavit dated August 1922. In the sworn document, Cunningham named the two blackmailers as Stanley Lewis and Jack Rogers, whom he described as an Italian with a "sallow complexion, smooth face and dark hair." Cunningham claimed George Ward had been threatened through letters and phone calls that he would be disgraced after exposing Walter's "immorality and immoral acts" if they were not paid. Walter himself had been drawn into the scheme, asking his father for the money, to protect his reputation.

Was this new statement evidence for why George Ward had avoided returning to New York State for so many months and refused to cooperate with any of the investigations? What exactly were those immoral acts that Cunningham alluded to in this affidavit? And was Walter himself part of this scheme in order to extort money from his father?

For Campbell, the Cunningham affidavit showed why Ward did not file a police report since a warrant had already been issued for the arrests of the two men. While the defense had little interest in showing Cunningham's statement, O'Neill had forced their hand, knowing full well the content of the affidavit. So it was no surprise when Campbell wished to "wait until our case if necessary" before reading the affidavit to the court. O'Neill jumped to his feet and volunteered to read it. Taking the affidavit, he stood in front of the jury box and recited all four paragraphs.[12]

We can imagine that for many in the courtroom, a statement by

Cunningham, even a sworn statement, would have been looked at with skepticism. Cunningham was a "puzzling figure" as *The Boston Globe* described him.[13]

For investigators, Cunningham's claims were mere fabrications offering little to solving the crime. For the prosecution, making Cunningham's statement public was a particular tactic that had less to do with the dubious nature of the witness behind the affidavit and more with compelling the evasive and reticent Ward to testify. "The Cunningham affidavit," as one legal observer told reporters, "is another wedge that will force Walter Ward to the witness box. Then you will see the real pyro techniques."[14]

His Story Is Still Unexplained

As the trial entered its second week, the crowds outside the courthouse grew larger. Journalists took note of a curious fact that of the three hundred or so spectators who lined up each morning eager for a seat in the gallery, many were women.

The *New York American* dismissively referred to them as "bevies of gum chewing flappers."[1] One reporter noted the competition among the women: "A hundred women—gray haired grandmothers, and bobbed misses of high school age—push and pummeled one another in the halls of the court house." State police had a difficult time controlling the crowds. Women pressed their faces against the small square windows in the courtroom doors each morning, scanning for the best seats. Older women brought their knitting to occupy their hands during the day's testimony. Others brought lunch boxes so as not to lose their seats during the noon recess.

One morning a few of the women protested for better courtroom seats. They shouted, "We want equal rights!" and others joined in. As their chants echoed through the marble halls of the courthouse, guards were forced into giving the women preference in the gallery.[2]

The press began referring to the women as "murder fans," and the objects of their affection were the Wards themselves. Walter and Beryl had become celebrities; their youthful good looks were as familiar in the newspapers as the newest silent-film star's or stage actor's. Each morning as Walter Ward was escorted out of jail, women in a local insurance-company office stood at the windows and waved at him as he made his way to court. He often returned their salutes. But it was Beryl Ward who had become the center of the "murder fan" interest, according to one report. She told reporters that she'd received more than 2,000 letters from women across the country. While she admitted some of the letters condemned her husband, most expressed sympathy and a "belief in Walter's innocence." She said she was "going to answer every one of them" as soon as she felt strong enough."[3]

So when Carl Sherman announced, "I call Mrs. Beryl Curtis Ward to the stand," on that Monday afternoon of September 24, a hushed silence took hold of the courtroom crowd. Walter flushed red at the sound of his wife's name, gripping the arms of his chair and making a slight gesture to stand up before his lawyers pulled him back down by the elbows. It was the one moment in the trial when Walter appeared genuinely upset. Beryl stiffened when she heard her named called. Reports described how she stood up looking frail and weak and made her way to the witness stand. "Like a little mouse," the *New York American* noted. "She crept into the chair, the same girl who sixteen months ago was so gaily young, so pretty and so unafraid with her bright, direct eyes and her disarming smile."[4]

On the stand, wearing a navy blue dress and matching cloche pulled down tight over her forehead, her hands visibly shaking, Beryl looked out into the crowd of faces, still and quiet, all waiting in anticipation of her testimony.

"Mrs. Ward, what time did your husband Walter Ward come home in the morning of May 16th?" Sherman asked.

"Between 4 and 5 a.m.," Beryl replied. Her voice was barely audible beyond the first row of spectators. Many times, she was asked to repeat her answers.

Sherman then asked about Lulu Barrows and the Wards' cook, Amy Mild. Beryl detailed how she had not heard from Mild since last November, when she'd left the Wards' employment. Barrow, the children's nanny, was still in Atlantic City.

"She is out of the state," Beryl told Sherman. Beyond these questions of the household staff, Sherman asked nothing else. A wife, of course, had immunity from testifying against her husband, and so Sherman's questions were meant, it seems, to confirm a timeline of May 16 and establish the whereabouts of the other two witnesses who were in the home that morning. Sherman's questions made clear that the Wards were keeping both Barrows and Mild away from the trial, casting suspicions about why they would be silencing the two women.

Campbell, on his cross-examination, questioned why Beryl and her children were in Atlantic City.

"I had been ill last winter," she replied, "and went to Bermuda to stay for some time, and I became very lonesome without my children." She explained she had moved to Atlantic City in April. It was at this point that Campbell offered a photograph into evidence. It was an image of mother and children, caught on the terrace of the Sutton Manor home on a sunny afternoon. Newspapers reproduced the photograph next to reports of her testimony, conjuring, no doubt, sympathy for the young mother.

"When Mr. Ward came home, the night you have spoken about," Campbell asked, "did he give you an explanation of why he was out late?"

"He did," she replied, tears welling up in her eyes.

"Was that explanation satisfactory?" Campbell persisted, prompting Sherman's objection, which was sustained by Wagner. But Campbell continued to dig, asking what explanation Walter gave his wife.

"We object as improper cross-examination," O'Neill shouted, calling the line of inquiry "a self-serving declaration."

"It is not self-serving," Mills interrupted.

"Certainly what he stated to her is surely self-serving," O'Neill retorted.

Wagner sustained the objections.

Beryl's time on the witness stand took less than fifteen minutes and, to what must have felt a disappointment to many in the room, revealed nothing about the blackmail story. Beryl had declared early in the case that she knew everything about the blackmail. Now, sitting on the stand under oath, a room full of "murder fans" hoping she would reveal the mystery behind her husband's actions, she held firm to the Wards' impenetrable silence.[5]

By coincidence or deliberate planning, Inez Peters testified that same Monday afternoon. As the attorney general called Peters to take the stand, two large oak doors on the side of the courtroom swung open, and she walked out, draped in a simple black dress and wearing a large black turban, to which a heavy mourning veil was attached with a "dagger like" hatpin, as one report described it. Once on the stand, she pulled the veil back from her face and, as the *Haverhill Evening Gazette* detailed the moment, raised her "wide, work-worn hand, with a black stone ring" as the oath was administered.[6]

The press made much of the differences between Beryl and Inez. "Youth and fashion contrasted with age and mourning," *The New York Times* wrote. "Sisters in tragedy," *The Boston Globe* announced, drawing a sharp distinction between the two. "One, old and tired," the newspaper observed, "the other also drooping and weary, but charmingly dressed and still youthful." It was a strange contrast between two women who differed in age by only twelve years and who both were taking care of young children. The distinctions were, of course, less about age or fashion and more directly about the class difference. But as contrasting as the two women may have appeared, "both were fighting," *The Boston Globe* noted, "for what each believed to be justice for a man."[7]

On the stand, Peters faced Walter Ward for the first time, though she often kept her eyes cast downward; her voice, like Beryl's, was soft and at times shaky.

"I want only justice, not vengeance," she stated. She testified that Clarence was a "good boy," though occasionally he got himself into "scrapes" and sometimes arrested. When O'Neill referenced a few of Clarence's arrests, Peters was quick to dismiss them. About his car theft, she explained he took it "only for a ride down the alley." She did concede that her son could be "unsteady" and often changed jobs, but she added, when he was released from reform school it was always "for his good behavior."

"What was the largest week's pay your son ever earned?" O'Neill asked.

"Twenty dollars," she replied.

"And he gave it all to you?"

"Yes," she replied.

O'Neill then held up two letters that Clarence had written from Parris Island.

"He wrote these letters to me," Peters testified, "and they prove he was not the kind of boy who would blackmail anyone." O'Neill tried to introduce both as evidence, but Ward's attorneys objected, arguing they had no bearing on the crime itself. Wagner sided with the defense.

O'Neill returned to the witness. "After receiving those letters from your boy," he began, pausing for a moment as Peters dried her eyes with a black-bordered handkerchief, "the next time you heard was that he had been shot out on this road?"

"Yes," she said, her response muffled by the handkerchief.

As O'Neill sat down, Mills stood and addressed the judge. "No cross-examination for Mrs. Peters," he said.

She then stepped down and exited the same side door she'd come in.

"Justice is all that we want to see," she told reporters outside the courthouse, standing next to Elbridge.

"We have no personal feeling of vengeance against Walter S. Ward," she said. The Peterses were unable to sit through the many days of the trial and had come down only that morning to testify. Inez told reporters she did not want to sit there and look at Walter Ward. But their absence from the courtroom was also a matter of money.

"My husband and I have lost a lot of time by this case," she said. "In order to come down here today I had to hire a girl to take my place in the stitching room," she explained, referring to her job at the shoe factory, which earned her three dollars a day. "You know that they would not keep my job for me if I did not," she told reporters. "That cost money. My husband is a carpenter. He gets five dollars a day. Every day we lose means eight dollars to us. And that counts when you have five children."[8]

PERHAPS THE BIGGEST shock in the trial came on the morning of Tuesday, September 25, just seven days into the trial, when Carl Sherman announced three simple words: "The state rests." We can imagine a collective gasp among the spectators. It was a sudden and unexpected move. Sherman had called only thirty-two of his seventy-one witnesses. He didn't call Ralph Ward for example, or William Mundia, though the latter may have been a risky witness.

The move seemed confounding even to the defense lawyers, who asked for a short recess. As the session resumed, Mills made a series of motions to strike out certain testimony related to the identification of the two guns and the James Cunningham affidavit. Wagner denied each motion. Mills's final motion was a third attempt to have the entire indictment dismissed.

"There is nothing new," Mills declared in court. "It is the old, old case which Mr. Justice Seeger said was 'stale.'"

Wagner had little patience for the constant motions to dismiss. "As the evidence now stands," he declared from the bench, "the matter is one for the jury to decide. The motion is denied."[9]

THE NEXT DAY, more women than ever lined up at the courthouse entrance, hoping to finally witness what many believed would be the dramatic testimony of Walter Ward. "Women were far in the preponderance in the crowd which assembled long before court convened," one report noted. Would this be the moment the ever-reticent Walter Ward would finally tell his side of the story? Would he detail what really happened on King Street and clear up the many contradictions and confusions about Peters's murder? Would he make public the scandalous secret at the heart of the blackmail that allegedly drove him to kill? These questions simmered in the air that morning, as the guards again tried to control the crowds, people jostling for the few empty spots at the back of the courtroom to stand.

But after Wagner took his seat and the twelve men were called into the jury box, Isaac Mills rose and addressed the court with a simple statement.

"The defense rests, your honor."

It was a confusing and disappointing surprise to everyone in the courtroom. Ward's defense would offer not one witness, not a single piece of testimony, nor any evidence to support their claims about how Peters was murdered. Walter Ward would remain silent, as he had been for sixteen months. Some in the courtroom might also have remembered when Ward's attorney Elwood Rabenold claimed in late July that they were eager to "tell our side" of the story. Clearly they had changed their minds. Walter Ward would stand by the original statement his lawyers had offered back in May 1922, confident that nothing of Sherman's case disproved their claims.[10]

IT WAS AN overcast afternoon. Gray light streamed through the courtroom window as Mills stood before the jury box, note cards in his hand, ready for his summation. Mills began with a pointed criticism of the prosecution.

"Do you jurors want any man persecuted? Do you want any man unfairly treated?" he asked. He then declared that his client had been "most unfairly prosecuted by the State." He dismissed Sherman's entire case. Reminding the jury that his client need not prove his innocence but that the State had to prove his guilt, Mills described the prosecution as failing to bring "the slightest shadow of proof" against Ward.[11]

He attacked Sherman's tactics, declaring he'd coached witnesses so the testimonies about the crime scene would appear consistent. Crucial to their defense was to cast doubt over the entire crime scene and the way Peters's body was found. Mills pointed to the differences in testimony about how the body was positioned, how his hands were lying, where the body was in relation to the road. He suggested that those "foreign men" that Duncan Rose had seen in their truck on his commute to work might have moved the body.

"They had come up the road," Mills said. "They had seen the body. They had gotten out and maybe they carried it back a little from the edge of the road." With all the discrepancies about the crime scene, Mills argued, there was "no accurate observation."

Mills also cast doubts about the vest, which witnesses recalled as being buttoned all the way up when they'd found Peters, making it difficult to understand how the bullet had pierced only his shirt and not the vest. Mills held up the vest to the jurors, and then pointed to the absence of a button at the top of the vest.

"There never was any button for the upper buttonhole," he declared. Mills reasoned that as Peters's body was lying lifeless, this detail was overlooked by the witnesses. But certainly, he argued, that absent button would explain how the bullet had pierced only the shirt and not the garment.

Perhaps one of the more dramatic claims of Mills's summation was that of Peters's role in the entire blackmail plot. He described Peters as a "blackmailer by hire," arguing that Peters, who had only just arrived in New York a few hours before his death, had "hired himself out undoubtedly that evening for a few paltry dollars to serve as the gunman." Mills added, "Can you imagine anything worse?" This new theory that Peters was a gunman for hire was meant to account for the many incongruities between Ward's statement and the timeline of Peters's arrival in New York on May 15. Maybe Ward didn't know Peters at all. Maybe Peters was just in the wrong place at the wrong time. How odd, some in the courtroom might have thought, that Ward now seemed confused about how Peters was even involved in the alleged blackmail scheme.

Mills went on a familiar tirade about blackmail as the "vilest and most detestable of crimes." As he had in the past, he called it worse than murder, for it was an attack on a man's character.

It was at this point that Beryl Ward began to cry and, to many in the courtroom, appeared to have slumped in her chair. Smelling salts were administered to revive her, and she recovered quickly.

The "gunman for hire" theory furthered Mills's other vital contention: the questionable character of Peters. He connected the victim's many arrests for theft with the plot against Ward.

"I tell you, my friends," Mills said in a more conversational tone, "in these days, almost every crime of violence is connected with the stealing of an automobile." More directly, he highlighted Peters's history of crime.

"You know what he was," Mills suggested. "It gives me no pleasure to speak badly of the dead. But, you know his record." He continued, "Let me say, however, that these repeated acts of thievery show a confirmed disposition. There is no crime more dangerous than that of thievery," adding, "Blackmail is but a species of it." In this claim, Mills dismissed the prosecution's contention that the .32 Smith & Wesson was not his gun. "There is no evidence of that," he declared, only speculation.

In contrast to Peters's dangerous past, Mills ended his four-hour-long summation, which was filled with biblical references and legal doctrines to highlight the virtues of his client, by asking Ward to stand up, and he again presented the photograph of Beryl Ward with her two children, passed it around to the jurors, and took a pause in his summation so that each juror had a chance to look closely at the photograph.

"Do you think these are the children of a murderer?" Mills asked. He then declared that Ward was of "good character, peaceable, orderly, law-abiding" and asked the jurors to put themselves in his place.

"Suppose you had gone astray," he speculated, referring to claims of Ward's betting habits. "Suppose you had fallen into the hands of evil men and they discovered something of the past which affects your character and standing." He asked, "What would you do?" It was a compelling moment appealing to the jurors' own secret indiscretions as a plea for empathy for Walter Ward.

"Do you think that they ought to be called upon to throw wide the door of their closet," Mills continued, "and disclose to the public the skeleton hanging there? Of course not." Everyone has a secret, Mills suggested, but Ward should not have been punished for it. Nor should the family have to endure such public scrutiny.

"I commit to your keeping, to your consciences, to your judgment," Mills concluded, "as men of sense and honor and decency, this man, this woman, these little children, for deliverance from this horrid persecution, unjust, and unprecedented, which has tormented them for sixteen months."

FOR CARL SHERMAN, his closing argument must have felt like a boulder being pushed up a hill. It was true that he had not presented any direct evidence that disputed Ward's claims, no witnesses on the morning of May 16, and no one aware of the blackmail scheme. He had instead only circumstantial evidence and testimony that pointed to the improbability of Ward's story. Sherman was prone to courtroom drama, and his summation would depend on it.

"When a lawyer has no defense," Sherman began, "he must seek propaganda, a smoke screen, or camouflage. But," he continued in a challenge to Mills, "I am here to talk to you about facts—evidence, cold, hard facts."[12]

Sherman dismissed criticism of his prosecution, that he browbeat the grand jurors into an indictment and that he coached witnesses at trial. He reminded the jurors that a year earlier another grand jury had also come to the same conclusion: that Walter Ward should be brought to trial. And, he declared, turning and pointing his forefinger at Ward, that is because "this man is guilty of murder in the first degree. His story is still unexplained."

As he did in his opening argument, Sherman moved through the courtroom with energy, often bending over the jury box, staring directly into the faces of each juror. The young attorney general's performance, his voice booming all the way to the back of the gallery, his speech direct and succinct and uncluttered by legal theories or religious references, stood in contrast to the bespectacled and erudite Mills, who anchored himself in front of the jury box as he delivered his closing.

"What is the issue before you?" Sherman asked. "It is: Did Walter S. Ward, with this gun, fire a shot through the heart of Peters striking him dead? It is conceded that he did." After a long pause in which Sherman looked across the courtroom, the spectators frozen in attention, he raised his voice.

"It is conceded that he did!"

And with that he grabbed the .38 Colt automatic and waved it in the air. "Sometimes a jury, on circumstantial evidence, hesitates to convict," he said. "Is there anything circumstantial about this gun?"

Sherman raised doubt about the origins of the Smith & Wesson. Putting down the Colt, he then grabbed the .32 pistol and turned to the jury. He reminded them that the story of how Ward obtained the gun had changed during the trial, as defense attorneys argued that Ward returned to the scene and took the gun.

"Why would a man come back to the scene of a crime at the dead of night—to pick up a pistol?" Sherman asked, his tone of disbelief echoing around the courtroom. Sherman also asked, if this was not the .32 pistol Cody had given Ward, then why didn't Ward simply prove it?

"You could say," Sherman declared as he pivoted toward Ward, "I still have the gun that Cody gave me. Here it is." He then turned back to the jury, still holding the Smith & Wesson: "I charge that Ward killed an unarmed man, and lied about it."

He then moved to the motive of the crime, the alleged blackmail plot.

"You don't want to know the details of that secret, and neither do I," he said, "but don't you want some proof of how these alleged blackmailers operated? Don't you want to see some of these terrible letters he says they wrote him? He simply says, 'I've been blackmailed; you've to take that as a fact.'" It was the key mystery of the case that justified the self-defense argument and a mystery that only the defense could solve. "Isn't there some evidence of the blackmail you'd like to see?" Sherman implored the jurors.

But the most dramatic moment came when Sherman and O'Neill enacted the shooting as Ward's statement described it. O'Neill held the Smith & Wesson and placed a foot on a rung of his chair to mimic Peters, who allegedly stood on the car's running board. Sherman held the Colt in his left hand and reached across O'Neill torso to grab his wrist, whipping his arm upward as O'Neill pulled the trigger. The small clap of the pistol's hammer echoed through the courtroom. Sherman aimed his Colt at O'Neill's chest but did not pull the trigger. In a rapt courtroom, "prosecutor and assistant stood motionless," the *Daily News* reported. "Then Sherman slowly turned his head to the jury in a silence of deep significance." Sherman's right arm, still holding on to O'Neill's wrist, would have been in the way of a shot to his chest.

"You have seen with your own eyes," Sherman said, "the impossibility of his story. His right arm holding the hand of Peters would always have been in front of his gun."

Sherman next pointed to James Cunningham's affidavit, which Mills dismissed in his closing as preposterous. For Sherman it pointed to a motive and the reason Ward did not go to the police to file a formal complaint. He didn't do that, Sherman declared, "because those blackmailers were Ward's friends—he was their pal."

In responding to Mills's claim that the prosecution has offered no alternative theory about the murder, Sherman played off of the gunman-for-hire theory. He proposed to the jury that the two blackmailers might have met Peters while he was hitchhiking from Philadelphia back to Haverhill and offered Peters a job in the blackmail scheme against George Ward. Sherman then suggested the blackmailers turned against Walter.

"Did they pose Peters as a man who knew all about the plot to extort money from the father? Did Ward, in a blind range and a desire to conceal his act, shoot Peters down?" As a theory, like so many alternative theories of Peters's murder, this one required a heavy dose of speculation and imagination. There was, as Mills noted in his summation, no other "truth" to the story in Ward's statement—a statement that had become, over the past sixteen months, its own declaration of fact even if it left so many questions unanswered.

"The statute," Sherman concluded with a call for justice, "defines homicide as the killing of a human being—not a good man, a black man or a white man—not a rich man or a poor man, a villain or a hero, but a human being. And you cannot take a human life without justification, no matter who you are, without being brought to trial for it and having a jury decide whether you were justified or not."

Sherman ended with his plea: "In view of the damaging evidence we have produced, I cannot ask you for anything but a verdict of murder in the first degree."

ON SATURDAY AFTERNOON, September 29, Walter Ward's thirty-second birthday, the jury concluded its deliberations. It took them three hours and four separate votes before they reached a unanimous verdict.

There was a scramble of spectators into the courtroom when word of the verdict was announced. The defense attorneys took their seats, alongside a smiling Walter Ward. Beryl Ward stayed in the small anteroom, perhaps unable to face a guilty verdict. Justice Wagner, in an optimistic moment, warned the gallery before the jury returned. "When the verdict is announced," he said, "we want no demonstration in the court. Absolute silence must prevail."

Jury foreman Charles Schiller announced their decision to a silent, breathless courtroom: "Not guilty!"

Loud applause burst out in the back of the gallery and spread forward quickly as the spectators ignored Justice Wagner's early directive. With a widening smile, Ward reached out to his attorneys, shaking Campbell's hand and then Mills's, who, according to reports, looked dazed with relief, tears welling up in his eyes. Ward then proceeded to the jury box and shook the hands of the twelve men who'd acquitted him.

When a reporter asked Ward what he had to say, Ward simply replied, "Right now, I have this to say: I am going to my wife." Ward then moved through the courtroom chaos of spectators eager to shake his hand and congratulate him. In the anteroom, he met Beryl and his brother Ralph. "Thank God!" Beryl shouted as she hugged her husband, looking as if she might faint with the news.

Police escorted the Wards to a secret exit that led to the roof. Once there, they walked across the roof to another entrance that took them down a flight of stairs and to an elevator that carried them to the first floor. Outside on the sidewalk, more spectators cheered as the Wards waved and posed for the press photographers before ducking into a limousine. It was reported that the Wards would gather in New York City to celebrate Walter's birthday and his acquittal. It was also reported that George Ward, who had been staying in New Jersey during the trial, returned to New York that afternoon once he learned of his son's fate.

"I am always satisfied with the verdict of a jury," Sherman told reporters before leaving the courthouse. It was a brief and sedate response.

Senator Elwood Rabenold, who had been by Ward's side from the very beginning, dismissed a reporter's question. "You can see for yourself how we feel about it," he said.

Isaac Mills, teary-eyed and relieved, had a word for the New York *Daily News* reporter. "I hope your people are satisfied," he remarked. "You have your trial. You were right in your contention."[13]

Ward and Beryl would take a vacation at a local country club, where Ward and his father, George, planned many rounds of golf. "I'm going to knock those white pills around and do nothing else for a week," he told reporters. Before the couple left, Walter sent a large bouquet of American Beauty roses to the women at the insurance-company office in White Plains who'd encouraged him each morning by waving out their windows as he left his jail cell and entered the courthouse.[14]

It was reported the day after the verdict was announced that William Mundia, who offered sensational testimony at the grand jury about his relationship with Ward and was the subject of the defense attorneys' outrage at how Sherman was conducting his investigation, attempted suicide while held in the Manhattan jail. He was once again taken to Bellevue Hospital.[15]

It was also reported that the inquiry and trial had cost nearly $100,000, leading some to criticize the entire investigation. The *Brooklyn Daily Eagle* reported on one "Westchester official" who saw the verdict as a vindication of the way District Attorney Weeks had handled the case and Justice Seeger's dismissal of the indictment back in January 1923. "He found there was no evidence to substantiate the charge of murder against Ward," the official stated. "Then the Democrats stepped in hoping to win a few votes by having a Democratic Attorney General prosecute Ward."[16]

IN HAVERHILL, AN *Evening Gazette* reporter went to Grove Street to get the Peterses' reactions. "I expected all the while that they would let him go," Inez said, "and I'm not surprised. Where would my boy be if he had done it? He would have been electrocuted long ago and there would have been nothing said about it." Inez had only praise for Sherman and Chambers for the way they prosecuted the case. She expressed relief that she was able to bring Ward to trial.

"I let New York know what he was and I let them know that he couldn't kill my son without at least being tried for it." She added, "I'm glad this crime is on Ward's shoulders instead of mine. I can hold my head up and people can't talk about me when I go by on the street."[17] Outwardly, Inez displayed a certain resolve about Ward's acquittal, though we can imagine that those nightmares of Clarence still haunted her in the months and years that followed.

Epilogue

Careless People

Two months after a jury acquitted Walter Ward of first-degree murder, George Ward announced plans to sell the family company. In mid-December 1923, 51 percent of the company's shareholders voted in favor of an acquisition by United Bakeries. We might think the scandal and trial tainted the Ward Bakery brand and the company had suffered. But in fact, profits for 1923 were good, and sales were strong. By the end of the year, the company was worth $35 million.[1] Still, the scent of scandal hovered over the company president and his two sons.

The sale of the bakery was significant not only for its timing but also for who made the offer: George Ward's nephew William Ward, president of United Bakeries. William's father, Robert, had built the Ward Bakery Company along with George. Robert had commissioned the designs for those gleaming white bread factories. But when Robert died suddenly in 1915 and George ascended to company president, putting both his sons in senior management positions, William left to start his own bakery, a move that directly competed with George. William's return and takeover in the weeks after Walter's trial hinted at lingering family infighting over the management of the company. By February 1924 the deal was finalized with a purchase price of two hundred dollars per share, making George Ward, and his two sons, even wealthier men.[2]

We don't know how William forced George's hand in selling the company, if in fact he did. But we can get a clue to the animosity that simmered behind the deal a few months after the sale was completed. A key stipulation of the sale required that George, Walter, and Ralph would have nothing to do with the new company. As one news report described it, the three men were eliminated from the company.[3] William wasted little time announcing his return and erasing the legacy of George and Walter Ward.

"I have come back to my father's company," William declared in a public letter published as a full-page ad in major newspapers across the country, exactly two years since the start of the Ward scandal. Reclaiming the bakery in his father's name, William recounted the history of the company and his own involvement in its early success. But the letter was noticeably silent about William's now-famous cousins and uncle. From 1915, William wrote, "until February 1924, the management of the Company was in the hands of a different Ward family," adding, "Now, its management is returned to Robert Boyd Ward's family, and I have come back to the Ward Baking Company to carry on the work he started." William couldn't even mention George's name, nor acknowledge the growth of the company during his uncle's nine years as president.[4]

The newly merged companies would form the largest bakery in the country, with nineteen factories in thirteen cities and worth an estimated $75 million, around $1.3 billion in today's currency. The merger ignited fears of a bread monopoly and prompted several government antitrust lawsuits and investigations. Undaunted, William Ward continued to buy smaller bakeries through the 1920s, consolidating his brands and expanding their reach. The company produced some of the most iconic American baked goods of the twentieth century, including Wonder Bread—which it turned into a national brand in 1925 after purchasing the Indiana bakery that made it—and, in 1930, created a simple cream-filled yellow snack cake called the "Twinkie."[5]

NOT LONG AFTER the sale of the company, George and his wife Donna moved to the family estate outside Havana, Cuba, in the Anglo-American suburb Country Club Park. The *Miami Herald* described the neighborhood as "one of the finest and most exclusive close-in subdivisions of Havana," noting how the estates, with their "spacious lawns and gardens," were near the yacht club, the polo field, golf courses, and the National Casino.[6] George Ward had an interest in starting a new business venture in dairy farming. Undoubtedly, he followed the hordes of businessmen and American tourists who were descending upon Havana in the 1920s, buying up property and starting businesses. Prohibition was nowhere to be found in Cuba. American exiles opened bars, nightclubs, and casinos and built large hotels to welcome the caravan of tourists arriving on ships from Key West, New York, and New Orleans. Cubans were also prospering on the wealthy Americans who were eager to shed the burdens of Prohibition in a city where gambling was legal and music, dancing, and drinking were not difficult to find.

"The unreality is everywhere," observed American novelist Waldo Frank about his trip to Havana in 1926, noting the moral freedoms that simmered within the culturally diverse capital. "Many worlds mingled," he wrote, "as if in a dream."[7] George and Donna enjoyed the dream of Havana, staying in the city for nearly two decades. When George died in 1940, *The New York Times* described him as a "pioneer in the expansion of the baking industry" but said nothing about his son's scandal nor his own part in it.[8]

WALTER AND BERYL sold their home in Sutton Manor and moved to an apartment building on Manhattan's Upper West Side near Central Park. The building had a cadre of full-time doormen, who, we might suspect, gave Beryl and Walter a sense of privacy and protection. Ward had taken his experience with those bread delivery trucks and started his own company producing electric vehicles. He named the company the awkward-sounding Electruck, which was headquartered in a brick factory on West Forty-Sixth Street, not far from the underworld haunts of the Tenderloin between Times Square and the Hudson River. For two and half years both Walter and Beryl remained out of the headlines.[9]

Until, that is, May 1926 when Walter went missing.

The Wards had just returned to New York in late April from a trip to Havana. Ten days later, police found Walter's touring car abandoned near the train station in Trenton, New Jersey. Its windshield had been smashed with a large rock, which lay on the front seat. Inside, papers advertising Electruck and clothing were strewn about. Local authorities were at a loss to explain what happened to Ward. The shattered windshield suggested foul play. They dragged a nearby creek, searching for Ward's body, but came up with nothing.

Ralph Ward, who in 1924 took over as president of Drake Baking Company, expressed concerns about his brother's life. "He has always had a fear of that old gang," he told reporters, referring to the blackmail gang of the past. He refused to confirm whether the family would be offering a reward for information about Walter's disappearance.[10]

Rumors in the press speculated that Ward owed nearly $125,000 in gambling debts. The bookies, who demanded their money, so the reports informed, told Ward to get the money from his father. It was a familiar story to anyone who had followed the Ward-Peters case. Almost too familiar. Yet again the Wards appeared entangled in a mystery of money and underworld threats. And again, the details remained elusive.

Beryl Ward stayed silent. The doorman at her building told reporters she had been too ill to be seen. There were reports that she had succumbed to a nervous breakdown on news of Walter's disappearance and was bedridden. To friends, she did express her dread of Ward's fate. "They have either killed him or kidnapped him or he is in mortal fear of death at the hands of the men he owed money," she said. He had nothing to hide, she added: "I knew all about his women and his gambling."[11]

For months, clues and speculation of Walter's whereabouts appeared in the press. Police in Trenton and Philadelphia searched the hospitals on the theory that Ward suffered a bout of amnesia. An exhausted carrier pigeon in Pennsylvania allegedly had a message signed WARD that detailed how Walter was held prisoner in a shack near the Delaware River. A police search along the river found nothing. Another report described how a bottle washed ashore on Long Island containing a note claiming Ward was being held captive on an island off Long Island Sound. This clue too proved false. Still other sightings found him in California and upstate New York living under an alias and having changed his appearance.[12]

John Ayres, from the New York Missing Persons Bureau, followed every lead he came across. He claimed he was having difficulty getting information from the Wards about Walter's travels but was convinced that Ward had not met some horrible, violent end. "You may be sure," Ayres told a journalist, "that when Ward turns up he will be very much alive."[13]

Ayres was right. After nearly nine months of speculation, Ward reappeared among the living, arriving in Havana with his father. George Ward traveled to New Orleans in January 1927 to retrieve his son. What Walter had been doing in New Orleans and for how long remains a mystery. When journalists called to George Ward's home in Country Club Park, servants confirmed that Walter had in fact arrived in the city but offered no more information.[14]

Aside from a few trips to New Orleans and accompanying his father's body back to New York in 1940, Walter Ward remained in Cuba. He would eventually suffer acute emphysema and need treatment at the Anglo-American Hospital. On May 22, 1946, Walter Ward died at the age of fifty-two, exactly twenty-two years to the day since he'd publicly declared he shot Clarence Peters.[15]

IT WAS LIKELY that Ward's disappearance in 1926 had something to do with an impending civil lawsuit filed against him by Inez and Elbridge Peters for $75,000 in damages. In fact, the case was set to begin in federal court in New York a few weeks after Ward went missing.

Officers were unable to serve Ward with a subpoena to testify in the case, dragging the proceedings out for several months and prolonging the start of the trial.

It was not until February 1927, just a month after Ward appeared in Havana, that the trial eventually began. Allan Campbell once again represented Ward and once again enumerated Clarence Peters's many delinquencies, arguing that Ward had been the victim of a gang of blackmailers that included Peters.

Inez and Elbridge encountered new hurdles with each step of the case. Not only had Ward eluded a subpoena, but George Werner, who was no longer sheriff, also avoided subpoena servers, taking a seemingly sudden vacation out of state. When Peters's lawyer requested the former coroner Edward Fitzgerald's inquest report, which included Ward's comment about shooting Peters, he found all the coroner files about the case had gone missing from the DA's office. Even today, requests for the coroner's report and Peters's autopsy turned up nothing in the county medical examiner's archives.

Lacking key testimony and evidence, the jury remained deadlocked, and the lawsuit was eventually dismissed. There had been reports that the Peterses would try the case again, but there is no evidence they ever did. For Inez and Elbridge, who had sat through so many court proceedings and attorney meetings over the past five years, we can imagine their bitter resignation of never holding Walter Ward accountable for their son's death.[16]

In the 1930 census the Peterses lived on Ford Street in Haverhill, another cramped apartment that cost sixteen dollars a month in rent. After years of illness, Elbridge died in 1934 at the age of fifty-two, leaving Inez to care for their three youngest sons, Kenneth, eighteen, Merton, sixteen, and Raymond, nine. By 1940, Inez and Raymond, the only child remaining at home, had moved again, to a small house on School Street. Inez worked part-time as a salesperson in a dry goods store, earning about $370 a year. She would continue with odd jobs and remain in Haverhill until her death in January 1967 at the age of eighty-six.[17]

In September 1927, having not seen Walter for a year and a half, Beryl Ward boarded a train to Reno, Nevada, to petition for a divorce. In New York in the 1920s, one could file for divorce only on the grounds of adultery, and even then, it had to be proven through a lengthy court process. Reno became famous for its "divorce colony," as the state offered quick divorces after only a three-month residency. Once out west, Beryl remained "incognito" according to reports, hiding out at a local "dude ranch," which were increasingly catering to wealthy women seeking privacy as they lingered in the dry desert heat waiting for their divorces to be finalized.[18]

In her petition, Beryl claimed infidelity, nonsupport, and desertion. Details of the infidelity were not made public. By the end of November, the judge granted the divorce, and Beryl returned to New York. A week later she married W. Lysle Alderson, a Wall Street broker, who had only recently divorced as well.[19]

On her return from Reno, Beryl gave her last interview. "I believe there is still a chance for happiness for me," she said. She then wished to clarify her reticence about talking with the press during the case.

"My silence was entirely voluntary. I felt too deeply and suffered too much to give it voice. Even now that I have consented to speak," she added, "I prefer to ignore certain events of the past. I prefer to talk about the future." With respect to her ex-husband, Beryl claimed she had "no grievance against him," nor felt a need to forgive him. Rather she wished to wipe clean her entire memory of him.

"I intend to forget Walter Ward completely," she declared. "He has my best wishes, but he is out of my life forever." It was a stark statement from a woman who had become the image of the devoted wife and mother through the sixteen-month investigation and the trial. "I want nothing from him, whatever," she continued. "I have not seen him in eighteen months and I have no desire to do so. All I know of him is what I hear, that he is in Cuba or somewhere down there."

And then, wishing to clear up a key fact of Walter's defense about the murder, Beryl made a shocking admission. "I positively was not with Walter Ward on the night he was said to have shot Clarence Peters."[20]

On a number of occasions, Beryl had testified that she had in fact been at the Sutton Manor home when her husband returned around 4:30 in the morning on May 16. Her claim had been crucial to Walter's alibi. None of the reports provided any more details about this stunning admission, if she offered any. It was the last word from her as she exited the public stage once and for all, leaving us with only more uncertainty about what actually happened to Clarence Peters, while also reminding us how so much of Ward's defense rested on fiction.

There is little public record of Beryl's life after her return from Reno. She successfully managed to undo the notoriety and found a private life again. By 1930, she and Alderson were living at the posh Fifth Avenue Hotel near Washington Square in Greenwich Village where apartments rented for two hundred dollars a month. Her daughter, Betty, married in 1938, and Beryl and Lysle were in attendance. Son Willard studied aviation and at twenty-one left college to join the air force in the months before the United States entered World War II. In November 1942, Willard was killed in a training accident in Britain. In 1940 Beryl petitioned and was granted a divorce from Lysle citing cruel and abusive treatment. She never remarried. The 1950 census finds her living alone in Scarsdale, New York. She died in August 1974 on Cape Cod, Massachusetts, at the age of eighty-three.[21]

One hundred years after Peters's murder, the questions remain. What was the relationship between Ward and Peters? If blackmail was in fact behind the murder, what was so dire a secret that it would drive Ward to kill? Combing through hundreds of pages of detective reports, thousands of newspaper articles, and dozens of remaining court documents offers few clues that would convincingly explain how Peters met his death.

The one story about the murder that persists is the statement Walter Ward's attorneys concocted in the days after the murder. By the time of the trial, that statement grew in importance and became its own version of truth about the murder, despite its many improbabilities and uncertainties.

There are threads of clues that, taken together, can build a theory of the crime. Those who have explored the case have usually concluded that queer sexual blackmail was at the heart of the murder. In his book *Sexual Blackmail: A Modern History,* Angus McLaren included the Ward–Peters case in his chapter on homosexual blackmail. While acknowledging the "vague" reports of the crime in the press, McLaren supported the theory that the blackmailers were extorting money from George Ward, threatening to expose "the immoral acts . . . and disgrace of his son." A now-defunct true-crime podcast aired an episode entitled "The Twinkie Murder" and made a similar claim about the simmering queer relationship between Walter and Clarence as the cause of the murder.[22] Certainly queerness had been a constant possibility in the investigation from the earliest inquiries to the claims by William Mundia to the grand jury in August 1923—even if his testimony appeared highly dubious. We can hear the erasure of queer undertones in Mills's closing statement when he again pulled out the photograph of Beryl and the children and highlighted the respectability and wholesomeness of Walter Ward. How could Walter be involved in such immoral acts when he has such a lovely family, Mills implied.

Suppose Clarence had been hitchhiking his way back to Haverhill in May 1922, as Inez believed, and at some point met Walter. Suppose these two strangers engaged in a sexual encounter in Ward's car, parked along one of the many secluded dirt roads in the shadows of the Kensico Reservoir—well-known for evening outings by couples wishing privacy. Afterward, Peters may have asked for money, something to get him back home, and Ward may have refused. Peters may have threatened him, and Ward may have reacted violently.

Perhaps after the encounter, Ward panicked and grew violent— a reaction that would, in the following years, be called *homosexual panic.* We know that Ernest Stolz, Ward's neighbor, described him as a "quick tempered, nervy fellow, who, when driven to the wall would fight."

Was Ward pushed to the wall in his encounter with Peters? Is this why he said, "I couldn't do anything else," as Fifi Ziegler had testified to what she heard on the morning after the murder?

Of course the more compelling question of the case is why Ward came forward at all. As there were no identifying papers found on Peters, was Ward hoping that Peters's name would remain a secret and never be made public? And, once it was, did he feel a need to make a statement to authorities? The only reason to come forward was for fear that Clarence Peters's name would somehow lead investigators to Walter Ward.

Perhaps Ward really was being blackmailed. He clearly needed money in the spring of 1922, but for what we don't know. Were his gambling debts ballooning faster than he could pay them? Had he been set up by those racetrack con men in the summer of 1921, giving Ward leads on races only to then turn on him when those bets lost? Was he, perhaps, protecting someone else in the family from blackmail threats, such as his father, George, who was well-known in the cabarets and nightclubs near Times Square?

Perhaps Walter was being blackmailed for the incident from 1916 in Pittsburgh when he allegedly raped Martha Kendall in her apartment after trying to kidnap her. While her suit had been settled out of court, perhaps rumors of it lingered. Had that case reemerged in the summer of 1921 as Ward was enjoying his reinvented life as a bachelor on the Upper West Side, winning big at the racetrack and hosting parties filled with women and gin just like in his younger days?

Was this scheme a family fight between George and his nephew William, who clearly had little love for the takeover of his father's company by his uncle and cousins? Perhaps William, well known for his aggressive business tactics, was behind the scandal to expose the family secrets.

Or, perhaps Ward was the blackmailer, as Cunningham had suggested and James Clark had hinted during his interview with the *New York American*. Had Peters been one of the men he used to lure wealthy men into compromising situations? Had he concocted a scheme to exploit his father for thousands of dollars? Or had the blackmailers been using rumors of what the press called Walter's "immoral acts" to extort money from George? And what did Nathan Rosenzweig's sister mean when, in her rage at the sound of Ward's name, she told reporters the wealthy baker lured "innocent boys away from their innocence"?

We are left to speculate, read between the lines, pull together known facts and come up with our own theories—because that is as close as we can get to the truth of what happened to Clarence Peters. While we can certainly point to the acquittal as a conclusion to the case, the jury verdict reflected more the weaknesses of Sherman's prosecution than the strength of Ward's defense. The verdict may feel like closure, but it leaves so many questions unanswered, giving the story about the murder that Ward and his attorneys concocted even more implausibility.

It is hard not to see the Ward-Peters case in a more famous story of underworld crime and murder set in the summer of 1922: F. Scott Fitzgerald's *The Great Gatsby.* We know that Fitzgerald was an avid reader of the daily press, and as he and his wife, Zelda, settled into their Long Island home in the fall of 1922, he would have known about the murder and the ongoing investigation into the enigmatic Walter Ward as he was working on the early drafts of his novel. We could imagine how easily the youthful and attractive Walter and Beryl would have fit in at one of Gatsby's parties at his estate in the fictional town of East Egg, Long Island. While there were of course any number of underworld bootleggers who could have inspired the character of Gatsby, can we not see details of the wealthy and mysterious baker's son, who loved gambling and parties and finely tailored suits simmering just behind the iconic character of Jay Gatsby? When party guests gossip about Gatsby's background in one scene in the novel, three women tell the novel's narrator, Nick Carraway, in hushed tones, "I think he killed a man."[23]

But it is perhaps more apt to see Walter and Beryl Ward in the figures of Tom and Daisy Buchanan, whose marriage teeters between carelessness and revulsion. Tom is a brutish figure, racist and sexist, with little concern for moral codes. Carraway describes Tom's personality precisely through his physicality: "It was a body capable of enormous leverage—a cruel body."[24] Tom's affair with Myrtle Wilson, who lives with her husband George amid the "valley of ashes," a large scrap heap on the road to New York City, embodies the class tensions of the story as much as it illuminates Tom's appalling moral character. Daisy, Tom's attractive socialite wife, could be a mirror to Beryl Ward, smiling for the press and devoted to her husband—at least in public.

Scholars have debated the inspiration for the novel, trying to track down the real-life facts for Fitzgerald's fictional world. Often they point to the mysterious murder that happened in the fall of 1922 when the bodies of Edward Hall, an Episcopal priest, and Eleanor Mills, a member of the church choir who was having an affair with Hall, were found in a field near Somerset, New Jersey. Like Peters's, the bodies were strangely composed, laid side by side, facing the sky. Hall had a single gunshot to his head, while Mills suffered three gunshots, also to the head. At his feet police found Hall's calling card and strewn between the bodies pieces of torn-up love letters they had written each other. Their murder became a shocking national story, an illicit affair that ended in such a mysterious tragedy. News accounts of the crime often ran side by side with those detailing the ongoing investigation into the Ward-Peters case. The *Daily News* took on the Hall-Mills mystery with the same fervor it showed Clarence Peters's murder. "With the success obtained by THE NEWS in the fight to bring Walter Ward to trial," one reader declared in the Voice of the People column in September 1923, "it is little wonder that your readers are hoping you decide to take up the fight for a reopening of the Hall-Mills tragedy."[25] But despite months of investigations by the police and journalists and a failed 1926 prosecution of three relatives of Hall's wife, the case remains unsolved.[26]

The scholar Sarah Churchwell has noted that Fitzgerald's novel is not "in any meaningful way based on a true story." Instead, she argues, "it might be better regarded as an untrue story, one that took a myriad of facts and unmade them" into what has become an iconic American story of the Jazz Age.[27] Fitzgerald's novel absorbed and reimagined the sensibilities of the times.

In their review of *The Great Gatsby*, *Collier's* magazine described it as a "queer mixture of beauty and pain, courage and cruelty." It also noted something more intriguing. "If you had lived on western Long Island," the reviewer noted, "or in Westchester County, N.Y. or just outside Chicago or San Francisco or any other sizable city, you will recognize everything in *The Great Gatsby*." The reference was clear to anyone reading the daily newspapers and the increasingly entertaining headlines about scandals and crimes among the monied classes. But, the reviewer noted, Fitzgerald's novel gives us something more. "The newspaper tells him what happened, but it never makes it clear enough," he writes. "The reader wants to know *why* it happened. He wants to know how in thunder such a thing could happen."[28]

THAT, OF COURSE, is what art can offer—a certain truth that is often elusive in real life. As much as we can sift through the many known facts of the Ward-Peters case, there remains an uncertainty to the story where money and privilege protected the Wards' secret, while leaving Inez and Elbridge alone in their poverty and grief, burdened by an unrealized justice for their son's death. Gatsby ends up dead, floating in the pool he never used in life. His murder was a case of mistaken identity by George Wilson, who shot Gatsby and himself, wrongly believing the millionaire had run down and killed his wife, Myrtle, with his automobile. It was instead Daisy who drunkenly and carelessly hit Myrtle, but she and husband Tom leave the novel with little consequence for their actions and little justice for Myrtle, left there to die on the side of the road. Fitzgerald's novel lacks a moral center, which perhaps is the point. "They were careless people, Tom and Daisy," Fitzgerald writes near the end of the novel, which could also describe Walter and Beryl. "They smashed up things and creatures and then retreated back into their money or their vast carelessness, or whatever it was that kept them together, and let other people clean up the mess they had made."[29]

Acknowledgments

There are many people who helped make this book possible.

Once again it has been a great pleasure to work with the smart and talented people at Counterpoint. Dan Smetanka has always asked the right questions with the right balance of serious curiosity and humor. Dan López offered brilliant and thoughtful edits on the manuscript which improved it immensely. I am in debt to Jordan Koluch for her copyediting expertise both on the writing and those complicated footnotes. Farjana Yasmin's cover design and Laura Berry's book design captured the era and style of the book perfectly. And, of course, all the work of Megan Fishmann and Andrea Córdova and the entire publicity team in getting this book into the world.

My extraordinary agent Deirdre Mullane was supportive of this book from the start, and her encouragement and advice guided this entire process from idea to final manuscript. Her talents as an agent are only matched by her skills as a baker.

Julie Mostov, Dean of Liberal Studies at New York University, made possible a semester leave that gave me unfettered time to complete the manuscript.

Jackie Graziano at the Westchester County Archives was generous in accommodating my research needs even as COVID made in-person research limited. She went out of her way in trying to find court records that helped me fill in the many pieces of this story.

Kim Hazlett and Eileen Karsten at Lake Forest College provided vital archive support in the Joseph Patterson papers. They generously digitized files at a time when the archive was closed to the public, allowing me access to crucial Patterson correspondence.

Staff at the Bobst Library at New York University, the New York Public Library, and the New York State Archives provided valuable assistance at various stages of my research.

Justin Peavey was immensely generous in sharing his research into his family history and the case. Our conversations and email exchanges helped me better tell the story of the Peters family, and give clarity to many of the mysteries of the case.

My writing group partners, Carley Moore and Lynn Melnick, were extraordinary throughout this entire project. Without their feedback and encouragement in the early stages, and continued feedback through the writing, the manuscript would probably never have been completed.

Janet Burstein (1933–2022), who had been a mentor and friend for over thirty years, continued to challenge me in the research and writing of this book. Her intellectual curiosity was a force even in the final months. I would have been a much lesser writer and scholar without my conversations with her over the years.

Scott Gerace has been such a great friend throughout this project, knowing exactly when and where to take me out for a drink and to talk about the writing—or distract me from it.

Other friends and colleagues who have listened to me talk about the research and writing and offered their own insights: Kate Caulkin, Allen Ellenzweig, Ifeona Fulani, Peter Nickowitz, Patrick McCreedy, Suzanne Menghraj, and Jen Meyer.

My parents, Jack (1935–2020) and Gloria, who have supported my work in so many ways over the years.

My husband, Greg Salvatori, who shares my love of a good mystery, patiently supported me in this writing process, through COVID, and grief, and other difficulties that came our way as I worked on the book. He encouraged me at each step and reminded me about joy and pleasure and living in the present even as I was immersed in the past.

A Note on Sources

Most of the primary sources related to the investigation, including court filings and transcripts, DA correspondence, and detective reports are held in the Walter Ward Papers at the Westchester County Archives. These documents, while offering some information, are notably limited. There is no extant record of the coroner's inquest or autopsy report of Clarence Peters. There are also no extant documents related to Attorney General Sherman's investigation, nor an extant transcript of the 1923 trial. Testimony at the various hearings and the 1923 trial was gathered from remaining court records and public reporting.

Notes

Prologue: A Lonely Road

1. Duncan N. Rose, p. 5B [handwritten], line 85, Enumeration District 195, White Plains, Westchester County, New York Census of Population, *Fourteenth Census of the United States*, 1920 (National Archives Microfilm Publications T625, 2076 rolls) Records of the Bureau of the Census, Record Group 29; Duncan N. Rose, p. 5A [handwritten], line 43, Enumeration District 60-395, White Plains, Westchester County, New York Census of Population, *Fifteenth Census of the United States*, 1930 (National Archives Microfilm Publications T626, 2667 rolls) Records of the Bureau of the Census; Duncan N. Rose, June 5, 1917, Westchester County, New York, *World War I Selective Service System Draft Registration Cards, 1917–1918* (Family History Library M1509, 4582 rolls); Duncan N. Rose, January 16, 1918, *New York State Marriage Index, 1881–1967*, New York State Department of Health.
2. Joseph Cowan, "State's Blows Rip Ward Yarn," New York *Daily News*, September 19, 1923, 3.
3. *The Investigation Before the Attorney General, of the Circumstances Surrounding the Death of Clarence E. Peters: Stenographer's Transcript of Testimony*, April 1923, Walter Ward Papers, Westchester County Archive; "Ward Admits Taking Poison; Blackmail Mystery Deepens," *The New York Times*, May 24, 1922, 1.
4. Detective report, New York, June 28, 1922, Walter Ward Papers, Westchester County Archives.
5. Cowan, "State's Blows Rip Ward Yarn."
6. Simon A. Cole, *Suspect Identities: A History of Fingerprinting and Criminal Identification* (Cambridge, MA: Harvard University Press, 2001).

Kensico

1. David Soll, *Empire of Water: An Environmental and Political History of New York City Water Supply* (Ithaca, NY: Cornell University Press, 2013), 48.
2. Soll, *Empire of Water*, 50; Robert Marchant, *Westchester: History of an Iconic Suburb* (Jefferson, NC: McFarland & Company, Inc., Publishers, 2018), 81.

3. *Evidence List*, n.d., District Attorney, Walter Ward Papers, Westchester County Archives.
4. "Women's Dainty Kerchief Clew in Man's Murder," New York *Daily News*, May 17, 1922, 3.
5. Cowan, "State's Blows Rip Ward Yarn," 4.
6. "Former Coroner Dies Suddenly," *The Yonkers Herald*, September 11, 1931, 20; "Republican Nominees," *The Yonkers Statesman*, October 7, 1921, 4; "Proposed New Westchester County Charter," *The Yonkers Statesman*, October 23, 1925, 10.
7. *The Investigation Before the Attorney General.*
8. "Ward Admits Taking Poison"; *The Investigation Before the Attorney General.*

Penniless Sailor

1. "Be Independent With a Chevrolet," advertisement, *New York American*, July 1, 1923; Roger Panetta, ed., *Westchester: The American Suburb* (New York: Fordham University Press, 2006), 46; James J. Flink, "Three Stages of American Automobile Consciousness," *American Quarterly* 24, no. 4 (October 1972): 456.
2. Marchant, *Westchester*; "The Automobile and Crime," *Commercial Appeal* (Memphis, Tennessee), December 5, 1923, 6.
3. "Dice and Cards Found on Victim of Murder," *The New York Herald*, May 17, 1922, 26; "Woman's Dainty Kerchief Clew in Man's Murder," 3; "Slain Youth's Body Identified by Scars," *The New York Times*, May 20, 1922, 7.
4. "Haverhill Boy Victim of Mysterious Murder," *Haverhill Evening Gazette*, May 19, 1922, 1.
5. "Haverhill Youth Is Reported Murdered," *The Boston Globe*, May 19, 1922, 19.
6. "Sherriff Anticipates a Surprise for Public in the Chappaqua Mystery," *The Yonkers Herald*, May 20, 1922, 1.
7. "Mistaken for Robber, Killed by Autoist," *The New York Times*, May 21, 1922, 13.
8. "Mistaken for Robber."
9. "Haverhill Boy Victim of Mysterious Murder."
10. "Whole County Mourns Death of Rye's Prominent Citizen Long Active in Public Life," *The Daily Times* (Mamaroneck, New York), October 23, 1931, 1; "Mr. Sutherland Denies Any Break with Ward," *The Yonkers Herald*, June 17, 1920, 1.
11. "Sheriff Anticipates a Surprise for Public."

Majestic

1. "Majestic: Largest, Speediest Ship on the Seas," *The Evening World*, May 15, 1922, 20.
2. "World's Largest Liner," *The Liverpool Daily Post and the Liverpool Mercury*, May 8, 1922, 9; Cabin Liners (website), accessed October 10, 2023, cabinliners.weebly.com.
3. "World's Largest Liner."
4. "Crowds Flee as Majestic Bores Gap in Her Pier," New York *Daily News*, May 17, 1922, 2; "Biggest Liner Here with World Record," *The New York Times*, May 17, 1922, 3.
5. "Ward Studies at Penn," *The Philadelphia Inquirer*, May 30, 1922, 2; "Ward's Confession Fails to Solve Death Mystery," *Haverhill Evening Gazette*, May 23, 1922, 10.
6. Aaron Bobrow-Strain, "White bread bio-politics: purity, health, and the triumph of industrial baking," *Cultural Geographies* 15, no. 1 (January 2008): 20.
7. "Introduces Treasure of Colonial League" *Hartford Courant*, May 27, 1915, 18.
8. "Not One Cent for Blackmail," *The Boston Globe,* May 23, 1922, 12.

A Dime-Store Novel

1. "Efficiency and Honesty Proven," *The Daily Times* (Mamaroneck, New York), November 1, 1917, 2.
2. George Houston, "Peters Never Met Ward Before His Death," *Haverhill Evening Gazette*, June 7, 1922, 1.
3. "Allan Campbell, 78, Dies; Attorney for 54 Years," *Mount Vernon Argus*, February 18, 1957, 2; "E.M. Rabenold, Retired Lawyer," *The Philadelphia Inquirer*, July 7, 1970, 22; "Isaac N. Mills Dies; Was Noted Jurist," *The New York Times*, July 15, 1929, 16.
4. Detective report, Ward Family, n.d., Walter Ward Papers, Westchester County Archives.
5. Frederick E. Weeks deposition, November 1922, Walter Ward Papers, Westchester County Archives.
6. "Frederick E. Weeks, Ex-D.A. Dies at 75 in White Plains," *The Herald Statesman* (Yonkers, New York), September 28, 1946, 1; Gene Fowler, *The Great Mouthpiece: A Life Story of William J. Fallon* (New York: Grosset & Dunlap, 1931), 94.

7. "Ward's Confession Fails to Solve Death Mystery"; "Mystery Beauty if Believed Involved," *The Washington Times*, May 24, 1922, 1.
8. "Hear Ward Traded Cars After Killing," *New-York Tribune*, May 30, 1922, 1.
9. "Paid $30,000 Ere He Killed Peters," *The Boston Globe*, May 23, 1922, 1.
10. "Son of Millionaire Baker Killed Armed Man Who Demanded $75,000," *The Evening World*, May 22, 1922, 1; "Blackmail Victim Confesses," *The Boston Globe*, May 22, 1922, 1; "Millionaire Victim of Blackmail Plot Confesses He Killed Clarence Peters," *Haverhill Evening Gazette*, May 22, 1922, 1; "Blackmail Death a Mystery," New York *Daily News*, May 23, 1922. 1; Detective report, Ward Family, n.d.
11. "Justice Seeger Dies Aged 86 at Newburgh," *Mount Vernon Argus*, July 18, 1945, 2.
12. *The Investigation Before the Attorney General.*
13. "New Rochelle City Official Confesses That He Is Slayer of Clarence Peters," *The Yonkers Herald*, May 22, 1922, 1.
14. "Son of Millionaire Baker Killed Man," 2.
15. "Ward Tortured for 2 Months; Secrecy Veils Power of Gang" *New York American*, May 23, 1922, 3; "Millionaire Admits He Killed Head of Alleged Blackmail Ring," New York *Daily News*, May 23, 1922, 2.
16. "Ward Tortured for 2 Months."
17. "Hear Ward Traded Cars After Killing," 10.

Shadow Men

1. "Women the Prey of Blackmailers," *The New York Herald*, March 14, 1920, 24; "Extortion Ring Is Rounded Up," *The Charlotte News*, February 15, 1922, 5; "Police Hunt Oregon Blackmailer," *The Alaska Daily Empire*, January 13, 1921, 1; "'The Shadow' Shoots and Fades Away," *The Oregon Daily Journal*, January 14, 1921, 1; "Blackmail Trap for the Wealthy," *The Bedford Daily Democrat*, June 7, 1918, 3; "Police Posed as Spooners," *The Barre Daily Times*, April 11, 1922, 2.
2. "How Blackmailers Mulct Women," *Springfield News-Sun*, February 2, 1919, 29; "Murder Indictment Sends Ward to Jail," *The New York Herald*, June 16, 1922, 1; "Blackmail Trap for the Wealthy"; "Blackmail Plot of Vice Bared by Major," *Chicago Tribune*, January 17, 1918, 11; "A Billion Dollars a Year," *San Francisco Chronicle*, June 5, 1921, 4.
3. Chic Conwell, *The Professional Thief*, annotated and interpreted by Edwin Sutherland (Chicago: The University of Chicago Press, 1937).
4. Burton W. Peretti, *Nightclub City: Politics and Amusement in Manhattan*

(Philadelphia: University of Pennsylvania Press, 2007); Michael A. Lerner, *Dry Manhattan: Prohibition in New York City* (Cambridge, MA: Harvard University Press, 2007); "The Blackmailers," *Los Angeles Times*, December 10, 1921, 114.

5. "The Ponzi Lesson," *The New York Times*, August 14, 1920, 6.
6. "Blackmail," *The Boston Globe*, October 10, 1921, 10.
7. "Dapper Don, Con Man, Dies Behind Bars," New York *Daily News*, June 21, 1950, 196; "New York's Most Picturesque Swindler Caught at Last," *Pittsburgh Sun-Telegraph*, May 12, 1929, 83; "Why Broadway Gasps at the Underworld's Beau Brummel," *The Philadelphia Inquirer*, August 1, 1937, 102.
8. Robert Arthur Tourbillon, September 12, 1918, New York County, New York, *World War I Selective Service System Draft Registration Cards, 1917–1918* (Family History Library M1509, 4582 rolls); "New York's Most Picturesque Swindler"; "Blackmail Rich Men by White Slave Act," *The New York Times*, January 13, 1916, 1.
9. "Why Broadway Gasps"; Don Collins, June 29, 1939, number 96817, Sing Sing Prison, *Inmate Admission Registers, 1865–1971*, New York State Department of Correctional Services, Series B0143, New York State Archives.
10. "Government Aid to Blackmailers," *The New York Times*, January 14, 1916, 8; Angus McLaren, *Sexual Blackmail: A Modern History* (Cambridge, MA: Harvard University Press, 2002); "'Dapper Don' Sought as Master Mind of Rum-Running Plot," *The Philadelphia Inquirer*, December 18, 1921, 1.
11. "And Fools There Are," *Miami Herald*, December 27, 1920, 4.

Slipper City

1. "Body of Peters Arrives Home," *Haverhill Evening Gazette*, May 23, 1922, 2; "Peters Is Given Military Rites," *Haverhill Evening Gazette*, May 24, 1922, 1.
2. "Peters in No Plot, Father Feels Sure," *New York American*, May 24, 1922, 2; "Peters Had Appealed Reformatory Sentence," *The Boston Globe*, May 23, 1922, 12; "Arrested for the Boston Police," *The Boston Globe*, November 14, 1921; "Theft by Peters Led to His Swift Navy Dismissal," *New York American*, May 24, 1922, 2; "$50,000 Set as Ward's Bail," *The Evening World*, May 27, 1922, 2; Justin Peavey, in discussion with the author, December 15, 2022.
3. U.S. Department of Commerce, Bureau of the Census, *State*

Compendium: Massachusetts, (Washington, D.C.: Government Printing Office, 1924), www2.census.gov/library/publications/decennial/1920/state-compendium/06229686v20-25.pdf; Charles C. Chase, *The Haverhill Book* (Haverhill Chamber of Commerce, 1920); U.S. Bureau of Labor Statistics, *Labor Conditions in the Shoe Industry in Massachusetts, 1920–1924* (Washington, D.C.: Government Printing Office, 1925); Frederick James Allen, *The Shoe Industry* (New York: Henry Holt, 1922).

4. "Haverhill's Socialist Mayor at the South End," *The Boston Globe*, December 10, 1898, 3; "Socialism Beaten in Haverhill," *New-York Tribune*, December 5, 1900, 10.
5. Allen, *The Shoe Industry*; Mary H. Blewett, *Men, Women, and Work: Class, Gender, and Protest in the New England Shoe Industry, 1780–1910* (Champaign, IL: University of Illinois Press, 1988).
6. Elbridge O. Peters, p. 7B [handwritten], line 86, Enumeration District 0319, Haverhill Ward 5, Essex County, Massachusetts Census of Population, *Thirteenth Census of the United States*, 1910 (National Archives Microfilm Publications T624, 1178 rolls) Records of the Bureau of the Census, Record Group 29; Elbridge O. Peters, p. 5B [handwritten], line 57, Enumeration District 71, Haverhill Ward 5, Essex County, Massachusetts Census of Population, *Fourteenth Census of the United States*, 1920 (National Archives Microfilm Publications T625, 2076 rolls) Records of the Bureau of the Census, Record Group 29; William H. Hardy, p. 6, line 32, Enumeration District 0307, Haverhill Ward 6, Essex County, Massachusetts Census of the Population, *Twelfth Census of the United States*, 1900 (National Archives Microfilm Publications T623, 1854 rolls) Records of the Bureau of the Census; *Haverhill City Directory* (1921), 479; Viola May Peters, October 20, 1909, *Massachusetts Vital Records, 1841–1911*, New England Historic Genealogical Society; Justin Peavey, in discussion with the author.
7. Detective report, May/June 1922, June 9, 1922, Walter Ward Papers, Westchester County Archives.
8. "Father of Peters Calls Blackmail Story a Lie," *The Boston Globe*, May 23, 1922, 12.
9. Detective report, May/June 1922, June 18, 1922, Walter Ward Papers, Westchester County Archive; "Ex-Sailor Killed by Ward 12 Hours After He Got Here," *The New York Times*, May 31, 1922, 1.
10. "No Hint About Blackmailing in Missives" *New York American*, May 28, 1922, 3; "Father of Peters Calls Blackmail Story a Lie."
11. "Boston Lawyer Coming to Sift Ward Mystery," *New York American*, May 25, 1922, 2.

12. "Peters' Father Won't Comment on Son's Death," *Haverhill Evening Gazette*, May 24, 1922, 2.
13. "$1,000 Reward!" *New York American*, May 28, 1922, 3.

My Man

1. "Ward Admits Taking Poison."
2. "Give Up Ward Murder Guns; Grand Jury Action Near; New Mystery Note to Weeks," *Brooklyn Daily Eagle*, May 25, 1922, 1; "Ward's Habeas Corpus Writ Is Dismissed and He Goes Back to White Plains Jail," *The Evening World*, May 26, 1922, 1.
3. Detective report, May/June 1922, May 31, 1922, Walter Ward Papers, Westchester County Archive.
4. Marchant, *Westchester*, 67.
5. "Mystery Beauty if Believed Involved."
6. "Brooklyn Society, Miss Beryl Curtis a Fiancee," *Brooklyn Daily Eagle*, May 11, 1915, 7.
7. "Miss Beryl Curtis a Bride," *Times Union* (Brooklyn, New York), October 9, 1915, 3; "Wedded 'Midst Flowers," *The Chat* (Brooklyn, New York), October 16, 1915, 29; Beryl Curtis, p. 1A [handwritten], line 43, Enumeration District 769, Brooklyn Ward 26, Kings County, New York Census of Population, *Thirteenth Census of the United States*, 1910 (National Archives Microfilm Publications T624, 1178 rolls) Records of the Bureau of the Census, Record Group 29; N. Willard Curtis, August 23, 1919, *New York City Death Certificates*, New York City Department of Records & Information Services.
8. George S. Ward, p. 5A [handwritten], line 13, Enumeration District 0188, Sewickley Heights, Allegheny County, Pennsylvania Census of Population, *Thirteenth Census of the United States*, 1910 (National Archives Microfilm Publications T624, 1178 rolls) Records of the Bureau of the Census, Record Group 29; George S. Ward, p. 2A [handwritten], line 1, Enumeration District 464, Bronx Assembly District 8, Bronx County, New York Census of Population, *Fourteenth Census of the United States*, 1920 (National Archives Microfilm Publications T625, 2076 rolls) Records of the Bureau of the Census, Record Group 29; History, Sewickley Heights (website), sewickleyheightsboro.com.
9. Detective report, July/August 1922, July 28, 1922, Walter Ward Papers, Westchester County Archives.
10. Hugh Ward, January 5, 1916, Pennsylvania Death Certificates, Series 11.90, Records of the Pennsylvania Department of Health, Record

Group 11, Pennsylvania Historical and Museum Commission; "H. Malcolm Ward," *Pittsburgh Post-Gazette*, January 6, 1916, 2; "Mrs. Jessie Moore Ward," *The Sun* (New York, New York), August 31, 1916, 5; "Ward-Leslie," *The New York Times*, February 17, 1919, 13.

11. Walter Ward, June 5, 1917, Kings County, Brooklyn, New York, *World War I Selective Service System Draft Registration Cards, 1917–1918* (Family History Library M1509, 4582 rolls).
12. "State Troopers Undermine Ward Story of Killing," *Brooklyn Daily Eagle*, May 24, 1922, 1.
13. "Ward Faces Arrest if He Leaves State," *New York American*, May 25, 1922, 1; "Ward Must Prove Every Point in His Confession," *Haverhill Evening Gazette*, May 24, 1922, 1.
14. "Ward Admits Taking Poison"; "Ward Faces Arrest if He Leaves State."
15. "Ward Admits Taking Poison"; "State Troopers Undermine Ward's Story of Killing."
16. "Ward Rearrested," *The New York Times*, May 26, 1922, 1.
17. "Ex-Sailor Killed by Ward."
18. "Puzzle About Slayer Having Pistol," *New York American*, May 26, 1922, 2.

Untouched by Human Hands

1. "New Ward Baking Has Large Output," *The Wall Street Journal*, February 21, 1924, 11; "Ward Baking Company to Sell to Rival," *The Sun*, December 11, 1923, 2; *Bread Facts* (New York: Ward Bakery Company, 1920); "The Story of an American Business Success," *The Sun*, November 8, 1911, 5; "5,000 Will Strike in Ward Bakeries," *The New York Times*, April 30, 1923, 17.
2. Suzanne Spellen, "Walkabout: The Ward Bakery Company, the Snow-White Temple of Cleanliness," Brownstoner, April 7, 2015, brownstoner.com/history/walkabout-the-ward-bakery-company-the-snow-white-temple-of-cleanliness.
3. "The Story of an American Business Success."
4. "New Ward Baking Has Large Output."
5. Deborah Blum, *The Poison Squad: One Chemist's Single-Minded Crusade for Food Safety at the Turn of the Twentieth Century* (New York: Penguin Press, 2018).
6. "Ward Defends His Bread at Hearing," *The Boston Globe*, March 24, 1915, 5.

7. "Lederle Plans to Close All Unsanitary Bakeries," *Brooklyn Daily Eagle*, November 26, 1911, 9; "Cats Chase Rats over Bread Dough," *The Buffalo News*, November 15, 1911, 5; Aaron Bobrow-Strain, *White Bread: A Social History of the Store-Bought Loaf* (Boston: Beacon Press, 2012).
8. Bobrow-Strain, *White Bread*, 40.
9. "The Story of an American Business Success"; "Our Physician Guards Your Interests," *The Standard Union* (Brooklyn, New York), November 17, 1911, 6; "No Trouble Now to Buy Ward's Bread and Cakes," *The New York Herald*, September 5, 1919, 2.
10. Bobrow-Strain, "White bread bio-politics," 26.
11. F. C. Lane, "Robert Ward, Master Baker, Vice President of the Federal League," *Baseball Magazine*, 1915.
12. *Bread Facts*, 6.
13. Bobrow-Strain, *White Bread*; *Bread Facts*.
14. Stuart Bruce Kaufman, *A Vision of Unity: The History of the Bakery and Confectionery Workers International Union* (Kensington, MD: Bakery, Confectionery, and Tobacco Workers International Union, 1986), 67.
15. "Ward Co. Cuts Bread to 4 Cents Wholesale," *The New York Times*, May 7, 1915, 13; "Ward Co. Accused by Federal Board," *New-York Tribune*, December 16, 1917, 8.
16. "Strike of Bakers Lands Two in Jail," *Brooklyn Daily Eagle*, July 2, 1919, 5; "Ward Strikers in $100,000 Suit," *Times Union*, July 25, 1919, 1.
17. Kaufman, *A Vision of Unity*, 88.
18. Robert Peyton Wiggins, *The Federal League of Base Ball Clubs: The History of an Outlaw Major League, 1914–1915* (Jefferson, NC: McFarland & Company, Inc., Publishers, 2008), 110.

We Shall Have Nothing to Say

1. "Ward Rearrested on Court Order," New York *Daily News*, May 26, 1922, 2.
2. "Albert Seeger Dead; A Retired Justice, 86," *The New York Times*, June 17, 1945, 26; "Albert H. F. Seeger," Historical Society of the New York Courts, accessed November 10, 2023, history.nycourts.gov/biography/albert-h-f-seeger.
3. "Ward Rearrested, Dines with Sheriff but Sleeps in Jail," *The New York Times*, May 26, 1922, 1.
4. "Ward Rearrested on Court Order."
5. "Bail Is Accepted for Ward Witness," *The Washington Post*, June 11, 1922, 3.

6. "Ward Ordered Freed on Bail of $50,000," *Brooklyn Daily Eagle*, May 27, 1922, 1; "Declares Thaw Kidnapped Boy, Then Beat Him," *Bridgeport Times*, January 10, 1917, 11; Simon Baatz, *The Girl on the Velvet Swing: Sex, Murder, and Madness at the Dawn of the Twentieth Century* (New York: Mulholland Books, 2018).
7. "Ward Ordered Freed"; "Glass and Red Stains at Ward's Own Door," *New York American*, May 27, 1922, 3.
8. "Ward's Habeas Corpus Writ"; "$50,000 Set as Ward's Bail," 1.
9. "Ward Freed in $50,000 Bail," *New-York Tribune*, May 28, 1922, 1; "Ward Detectives Headed to Boston," *The New York Herald*, May 30, 1922, 20.
10. Ward Churchill, "The Pinkerton Detective Agency: Prefiguring the FBI," in *Race and Human Rights*, ed. Curtis Stokes (East Lansing, MI: Michigan State University Press, 2005); S. Paul O'Hara, *Inventing the Pinkertons; Or Spies, Sleuths, Mercenaries, and Thugs: Being a Story of the Nation's Most Famous (and Infamous) Detective Agency* (Baltimore: Johns Hopkins University Press, 2016).
11. Detective report, May/June 1922, June 1, 1922, Walter Ward Papers, Westchester County Archives.
12. Reprinted in "Ward Rearrested, Dines with Sheriff but Sleeps in Jail."

The World Is Full of Charlies and Jacks

1. Detective report, New York, n.d., Walter Ward Papers, Westchester County Archives.
2. Arne K. Lang, *Sports Betting and Bookmaking: An American History* (Lanham, MD: Rowman & Littlefield, 2016), 108.
3. "Declares He Heard Ward Threatened," *New York American*, May 25, 1922, 2.
4. Fowler, *The Great Mouthpiece*, 70.
5. Fowler, *The Great Mouthpiece*, 95.
6. "Ward Freed on $50,000 Bail."
7. "$500 Murder Offer Enters Ward Case," *The New York Times*, May 29, 1922, 1.
8. David R. Colburn, "Governor Alfred E. Smith and Penal Reform," *Political Science Quarterly* 91, no. 2. (Summer 1976): 316.
9. Rudolph W. Chamberlain, *There Is No Truce: A Life of Thomas Mott Osborne* (New York: Macmillan Co., 1935); Fowler, *The Great Mouthpiece.*
10. "Big Throng Hears Tribute to Osborne," *The New York Times*, January 18, 1916, 22.

11. "Thomas Mott Osborne," *Times Union*, January 27, 1916, 6.
12. "Attacks Osborne's Moral Character," *The New York Times*, December 14, 1915, 8.
13. Kathryn W. Kemp, "'The Dictograph Hears All': An Example of Surveillance Technology in the Progressive Era," *The Journal of the Gilded Age and Progressive Era* 6, no. 4 (October 2007): 409–30.
14. "Osborne Wins Fight on Felony Clause," *Brooklyn Daily Eagle*, April 18, 1916, 1.
15. Detective report, New York, June 2, 1922, Walter Ward Papers, Westchester County Archives.
16. Detective report, New York, June 2, 1922.
17. "Death Clew Sought in Ward's Own Home on 15 Day Old Crime," *The New York Herald*, June 1, 1922, 1.

Muzzle

1. "Charlie Ross, Pal of Ward Case Victim, Identified by the *News*," New York *Daily News*, May 27, 1922, 2; "Ward Threatened with New Blackmail as 'Ross' Flees," New York *Daily News*, May 29, 1922, 2.
2. Orville Tobey, September 12, 1918, Fairfield County, Connecticut, *World War I Selective Service System Draft Registration Cards, 1917–1918* (Family History Library M1509, 4582 rolls).
3. Unless otherwise noted, all details related to Tobey's experiences with Nat Ross and Joe Brown come from the court transcript: Court of General Sessions of the Peace, in and for the County of New York, *The People of the State of New York against Sam Dreyfus, Otherwise known as Joe Brown, Impleaded with Nathan Rosenschweig, Otherwise known as Nat Ross*, June 23, 1921, Walter Ward Papers, Westchester County Archive.
4. Conwell, *The Professional Thief*, 78–80.
5. "Held Him Up in Hotel," *The Washington Post*, October 29, 1915, 2; "Banker Gives $5,000 at Point of Pistol," *The New York Times*, October 29, 1915, 9.
6. Bryant Simon, "New York Avenue: The Life and Death of Gay Spaces in Atlantic City, New Jersey, 1920–1990," *Journal of Urban History* 28, no. 3 (March 2002): 303; "7 Seized at Shore in Blackmail Case," *The New York Times*, July 8, 1922, 2; "Boardwalk Blackmailers," *New-York Tribune*, July 11, 1922, 7; "Blackmailers Get Three Years in Prison," New York *Daily News*, February 8, 1922, 3.
7. "Charlie Ross, Pal of Ward Case Victim."

8. "Arrest of Ross May Solve Ward Blackmail Plot," *Chicago Tribune*, May 28, 1922, 4.
9. Orville Tobey, July 14, 1922, *U.S. Passport Applications, January 2, 1906–March 31, 1925*, National Archives and Records Administration, roll 2062.

Peters and the Wolf

1. "Peters Shared Secret Ward Clique's Weird Revels," *New York American*, May 29, 1922, 1.
2. "Peters Shared Secret Ward Clique's Weird Revels"; "The Wolf Holds Key to the Ward Tragedy," *New York American*, May 28, 1922, 1.
3. "Mobs in Tumult as Police Forbid 'Slave Market,'" New York *Daily News*, September 20, 1921, 2.
4. "Police Rout Women Who Feed Unemployed in Park," *New-York Tribune*, September 21, 1921, 4.
5. "The Drifter," *The New York Herald*, October 2, 1921, 26.
6. George W. Henry, *Sex Variants: A Study of Homosexual Patterns* (New York: Paul B. Hoeber, Inc., 1941), 474.
7. Henry, *Sex Variants*, 445.
8. Detective report, May/June 1922, June 6, 1922, Walter Ward Papers, Westchester County Archives.
9. "Peters Shared Secret Ward Clique's Weird Revels"; "The Wolf Holds Key."
10. "Peters' Parents Brand Story of Clark as False," *Haverhill Evening Gazette*, May 31, 1922, 1.
11. "Says Girl Offered $500 for Murder," *The New York Herald*, May 29, 1922, 4.
12. Detective report, May/June 1922, June 14, 1922, Walter Ward Papers, Westchester County Archives.
13. Detective report, Ward Family, June 27, 1922, Walter Ward Papers, Westchester County Archives.
14. Detective report, May/June 1922, June 14, 1922.
15. Detective report, New York, May 30, 1922, Walter Ward Papers, Westchester County Archives.
16. "Shady Cunningham Career Is Unfolded," *New York American*, June 3, 1922, 5.
17. Detective report, May/June 1922, June 6, 1922; detective report, May/June 1922, June 28, 1922, Walter Ward Papers, Westchester County Archives; detective report, July/August 1922, August 25, 1922, Walter Ward Papers, Westchester County Archives.

18. Detective report, July 1922, July 30, 1922, Walter Ward Papers, Westchester County Archives.
19. Detective report, July/August 1922, August 12, 1922, Walter Ward Papers, Westchester County Archives.
20. Detective report, May/June 1922, May 30, 1922, Walter Ward Papers, Westchester County Archives.
21. Detective report, May/June 1922, June 1, 1922.
22. Detective report, May/June 1922, May 31, 1922.

Ideal Sherlock Mystery

1. "Ward Case Stumps Sherlock Holmes," *The New York Herald*, June 25, 1922, 5; "Would Solve Peters' Case by Spiritism" *The Boston Globe*, June 25, 1922, 19; "Doyle Wants Spook Put on Ward Trail," *The New York Times*, June 25, 1922, 9.
2. "Doyle Shows Spirit Pictures of Dead," *The New York Times*, April 22, 1922, 1; "Finds No Spirit Flappers," *The New York Times*, April 20, 1922, 17.
3. "Dancing to Radio Music on Ocean Gains Vogue," New York *Daily News*, July 2, 1922, 83; "532 Summer Resorts to Have Radio Music," *San Francisco Examiner*, April 7, 1922, 6; "Dance to Airs Orchestra Sends Through the Air," *The Evening World*, March 10, 1922, 13; "Radio Music While You Shave Is Latest Here," *The Press-Courier* (Oxnard, California), March 26, 1922, 1; Frederick Lewis Allen, *Only Yesterday: An Informal History of the 1920s* (New York: Harper & Row, Publishers, 1931), 78.
4. "Strange Sounds Come from Ether as Marconi Tries to Reach Mars," *Times Union*, June 16, 1922, 1.
5. "Condemns Spiritualism," *The News Journal* (Wilmington, Delaware), May 8, 1922, 11; "Take Spiritualism Carefully," *Missoulian*, May 6, 1922, 4; "Local Writer Asks if Mind of Sir A. Conan Doyle Is Normal," *Lansing State Journal*, May 15, 1922, 16.
6. Christopher Sandford, *Houdini and Conan Doyle: The Great Magician and the Inventory of Sherlock Holmes* (London: Duckworth Books, 2011).
7. "How the Spooks Imposed on the Great 'Sherlock Holmes,'" *The Washington Times*, May 14, 1922, 55; "How I Make Just as Good Ghosts as Dr. Doyle," *The New York Herald*, May 7, 1922, 95.
8. "Prehistoric Film of Conan Doyle's Stumps Magicians," *The Evening World*, June 3, 1922, 3; Sandford, *Houdini and Conan Doyle.*
9. "Conan Doyle Tells How He Fooled Magicians," *Brooklyn Daily Eagle*, June 4, 1922, 64; Sandford, *Houdini and Conan Doyle.*

10. Harry Houdini, *A Magician Among the Spirits* (New York: Harper & Brothers, 1924), 270.
11. Houdini, *A Magician Among the Spirits*, 152–54.
12. "Houdini's Answers on Psychic Phenomena," *The Washington Times*, August 22, 1922, 3.

The Rat

1. *Hotel McAlpin* (New York: Norman Pierce Company, 1913) babel.hathitrust.org/cgi/pt?id=nnc2.ark:/13960/t6pz7sk3j&view=1up&seq=1.
2. Detective report, May/June 1922 June 1, 1922.
3. "Ward Witness Arrested," *New York American*, June 2, 1922, 1.
4. "Death Clew Sought in Ward's Own Home."
5. "Search Ward Home but Find No Clue to Death Mystery," *The New York Times*, June 1, 1922, 1.
6. "Search Ward Home," 2.
7. "Search Ward Home," 2.
8. "Death Clew Sought in Ward's Own Home."
9. "Tipster Clew in Ward Case Is Punctured," *New-York Tribune*, June 3, 1922, 1.
10. "Ward Witness Arrested."
11. "Ward Letter on Forger Suspect Called a 'Plant,'" *New-York Tribune*, June 13, 1922, 1.
12. "Revelation by New Witness in Ward Mystery Blows Up After a Searching Inquiry," *The Evening World*, June 2, 1922, 1.
13. "Twin Mysteries," *New-York Tribune*, June 2, 1922, 8.
14. "Revelation by New Witness"; "Pittsburgh Woman to Tell of Ward Blackmail Plot," New York *Daily News*, June 3, 1922, 2.
15. "Ward Witness Arrested;" detective report, June 2, 1922, Walter Ward Papers, Westchester County Archives.
16. "Revelation by New Witness."
17. "'Jimmy the Rat' Most Amazing Figure in Ward Case," *New York American*, June 3, 1922, 3.
18. "Revelation by New Witness"; "Ward Witness Arrested"; detective report, June 2, 1922.
19. "Cunningham Story Baffles Officials in Ward Mystery," *The New York Times*, June 3, 1922, 1.
20. "Ward Faces Cunningham; Rebuffs Him," *New-York Tribune*, June 6, 1922, 1; "Ward Ready to Tell All as Jury Opens Inquiry into Peters' Death," New York *Daily News*, June 6, 1922, 2.

21. "Ward Ready to Tell All."
22. "Cunningham Faces Ward, Says 'Hello!' but Is Repudiated," *The New York Times*, June 6, 1922, 1.
23. "Cunningham Faces Ward."
24. "Ward Faces Cunningham."

The Devil's Dance

1. "Heat Overcomes Governor Miller; Two Men Killed," New York *Daily News*, June 10, 1922, 27.
2. "Ex-Gov. Miller Dies in Hotel Here, Aged 84," New York *Daily News*, June 27, 1953, 53; Lerner, *Dry Manhattan*; "Harding Is Elected by Popular Majority of 6,000,000," *Times Union*, November 3, 1920, 1.
3. "Governor Goes into Ward Case, Rumor Insists," *Democrat and Chronicle* (Rochester, New York), June 12, 1922, 1; "Miller to Wedge in Ward Investigation," New York *Daily News*, June 12, 1922, 3.
4. "Ward to Face Jury Tuesday in Son's Case," *New-York Tribune*, June 11, 1922, 1.
5. "High Time," *The Evening World*, June 13, 1922, 26.
6. Phil Payne to Governor Nathan Miller, June 9, 1922, box 56, folder 200–339, Extraordinary Special and Trial Term of Supreme Court, Westchester County (Ward Case), Governor Alfred E. Smith Central Subject and Correspondence Files, New York State Archives; Governor Nathan Miller to Phil Payne, June 13, 1922, box 56, folder 200–339, Extraordinary Special and Trial Term of Supreme Court, Westchester County (Ward Case), Governor Alfred E. Smith Central Subject and Correspondence Files, New York State Archives.
7. "50 or More Dead in City's Worst Storm," *The New York Times*, June 11, 1922, 1.
8. "50 Or More Dead"; "Police Place Death List in Storm at 75 with Bodies of 47 Recovered," *The Evening World*, June 12, 1922, 1; "Storm of Fifteen Minutes Leaves a Wide Path of Wreckage in Its Wake," *The Yonkers Herald*, June 12, 1922, 1; "Fifty-Three Found Dead After Storm; Losses in Millions," *New-York Herald*, June 13, 1922, 1; "Remarks on Tornadoes," *The New York Times*, June 25, 1922, 106.
9. "Ralph Ward Defies Grand Jury; Faces Jail for Contempt," *The New York Times*, June 14, 1922, 1; "Tubbs Backs Ward Story of Shooting," *The New York Times*, July 4, 1922, 8; "Miller Drives Wedge into Ward Mystery," New York *Daily News*, June 12, 1922, 3.
10. "Tubbs Backs Ward Story of Shooting."

11. "J. Morschauser, Jurist, Dies at 84," *The New York Times*, November 4, 1947, 25; "He Humanized the Law," *Mount Vernon Argus*, November 4, 1947, 6.
12. "Mrs. Ward, Forced to Testify, Proves Evasive Witness," *The New York Times*, June 7, 1922, 1; "Mrs. Ward Says She Heard No Blackmail Plot," *New-York Tribune*, July 7, 1922, 4.
13. "Weeks Hopes to Indict Ward on Murder Charge," New York *Daily News*, June 13, 1922, 2.
14. "High Time"; "Millionaire Baker Well Guarded and Numerously Counseled in Pennsylvania," *The Boston Globe*, June 17, 1922, 3; "Bullet-Torn Shirt, Stained with Blood, Newest Ward Clue," *The New York Times*, June 18, 1922, 1; "G.S. Ward in Cleveland; Will Not Make Statement," *The Washington Post*, June 19, 1922, 3.
15. Detective report, July 1922, July 2, 1922, Walter Ward Papers, Westchester County Archives.
16. Detective report, May/June 1922, June 29, 1922, Walter Ward Papers, Westchester County Archives; "Mother-in-Law of Ward Warned to Take Flight," *Haverhill Evening Gazette*, July 7, 1922, 1.
17. Affidavit of Ralph D. Ward, July 18, 1922, Walter Ward Papers, Westchester County Archives.
18. "Affidavit of Ralph D. Ward, July 18, 1922; "Mrs. Ward Says She Heard No Blackmail Plot."
19. Detective report, Ward Family, July 10, 1922, Walter Ward Papers, Westchester County Archives.
20. "Ward Is Indicted in First Degree; Father Is Accused," *The New York Times*, June 16, 1922, 1.
21. "Ward Is Indicted in First Degree"; "Ward Indicted and Is Jailed; Brother Tells All to Judge," *New-York Tribune*, June 16, 1922, 1; "All Wards Involved," *Los Angeles Times*, June 16, 1922, 11.

Poinciana

1. Laura Wright, p. 4A [handwritten], line 16, Enumeration District 31-1864, New York, New York County, New York Census of Population, *Sixteenth Census of the United States*, 1940 (National Archives Microfilm Publications T627, 2669 rolls) Records of the Bureau of the Census.
2. Detective report, Ward Family, June 18, 1922, Walter Ward Papers, Westchester County Archives.
3. Detective report, Ward Family June 21, 1922, Walter Ward Papers, Westchester County Archives.

4. Detective report, Ward Family, June 18, 1922.
5. Appellate Division of the Supreme Court of New York, Third Department, *Ward Baking Company and Others, Appellants, v. Western Union Telegraph Company and Postal Telegraph & Cable Company*, Stenographer's Minutes of Attorney General Hearing, March 1923, Walter Ward Papers, Westchester County Archives.
6. "Ward and His Wife Living as Strangers," *New York American*, June 2, 1922, 2.
7. Detective report, Ward Family, June 15, 1922, Walter Ward Papers, Westchester County Archives.
8. "Ward Blackmailed Before over a Girl; $1,000 Hushed Case," *The New York Times*, May 30, 1922, 1; "Ward Victim in Previous Plot," *Los Angeles Times*, May 30, 1922, 5; "Pittsburgh Woman Denies She 'Blackmailed' Ward," *The Philadelphia Inquirer*, June 2, 1922, 3.
9. "Find Ward Case Woman Here," *Los Angeles Times*, June 1, 1922, 25.
10. "Jackson Disbarred on Clients' Charge," *The Pittsburgh Press*, March 10, 1921, 11.
11. "Introduces Treasure of Colonial League."
12. "Find Ward Case Woman Here," 25; "Pittsburgh Woman Denies She 'Blackmailed' Ward," 3.
13. Detective report, July 1922, July 5, 1922, Walter Ward Papers, Westchester County Archives; "Find Ward Case Woman Here."
14. "Ward Rented Flat in Wife's Absence, Received Women, Detectives Find," *New-York Tribune*, June 21, 1922, 1.
15. Detective report, September–November, October 15, 1922, Walter Ward Papers, Westchester County Archives.
16. Detective report, Ward Family, June 20, 1922, Walter Ward Papers, Westchester County Archives; "Trail of 'Peggy' in Ward Mystery Puzzles Sleuths," *The Evening World*, June 24, 1922, 3.
17. Detective report, Ward Family, June 22, 1922, Walter Ward Papers, Westchester County Archives.
18. "Ward Rented Flat in Wife's Absence."
19. "Ward's 'Love Nest' Revels Now Believed to Be Cause of Blackmail Conspiracy," *The Evening World*, June 21, 1922, 1.

A Perfectly Normal Prisoner

1. "Ralph Ward Eludes Probe; Jurors Vexed," *The New York Times*, June 15, 1922, 1; *The People of the State of New York vs. Walter S. Ward*, grand jury indictment, June 15, 1922, Walter Ward Papers, Westchester County Archives.

2. "Ward Is Indicted in First Degree."
3. "Everod Blankes, Frenzied with Jealousy, Shoots Frank Harris to Death in Third Street House," *Mount Vernon Argus*, February 18, 1922, 1.
4. "Ward Stays in Jail; Quick Trial Denied," *New-York Tribune*, June 17, 1922, 1; "3 Months in Jail Face Ward Before His Murder Trial," *The New York Times*, June 17, 1922, 1.
5. "Speedy Ward Trial Depends on His Father," *New-York Tribune*, June 20, 1922, 1; "Prosecutor Guards Ward Jury Minutes," *The New York Times*, June 29, 1922, 16.
6. "Speedy Ward Trial."
7. "Counsel for Ward Admits Existence of Family Skeleton," *The New York Times*, June 21, 1922, 1; "Trial of Ward Set for Week of July 20," New York *Daily News*, June 21, 1922, 3.
8. "Ward's Sister Subpoenaed Following Assertion She Knows of Blackmail Plot," *The Evening World*, June 19, 1922, 1.
9. "Weeks Says Court Won't Free Ward," *The New York Times*, July 6, 1922, 17.
10. "Ward Wins Liberty Under $50,000 Bond; Indictment Stands," *The New York Times*, July 12, 1922, 1.
11. "Decision Awaited for the Release of Ward," *The Yonkers Herald*, July 11, 1922, 1; "Ward Wins Liberty."
12. Justice Albert Seeger, *Opinion of Court on Motion to Dismiss Indictment*, Walter Ward Papers, Westchester County Archives.
13. "Great to Be Back on Job, Says Ward, Pale and Tired," *New-York Tribune*, July 13, 1922, 4.
14. "Mack Appears as Ward Prosecutor," *The New York Times*, July 15, 1922, 13; "Weeks Holds Up Curtis Statement for Ward Trial," *New-York Tribune*, July 15, 1922, 16.
15. "Court Drops Ward Conspiracy Hearing," *The New York Times*, July 20, 1922, 10.

Queenie of Haverhill

1. Testimony of Samuel Miller, *The People of the State of New York vs. Walter Ward*, August 14, 1923.
2. Detective report, July/August 1922, July 22, 1922, Water Ward Papers, Westchester County Archives; detective report, Boston, July 27, 1922, Water Ward Papers, Westchester County Archives.
3. Detective report, July/August 1922, July 23, 1922, Walter Ward Papers, Westchester County Archives.

4. "Peters Planned to Obtain Cash from Rich Man," *Haverhill Evening Gazette*, July 26, 1922, 1.
5. *William Mobley, Professor Bill Artist Bootblack shop, Haverhill*, black-and-white negative, Senter Digital Archive, Haverhill Public Library, haverhill.pastperfectonline.com/photo/6862F3C6-73CB-44D0-AABD-868044326262.
6. Detective report, May/June 1922, June 10, 1922, Walter Ward Papers, Westchester County Archives; "Ward Witness Is Found Here," *Los Angeles Times*, May 31, 1923, 22.
7. Detective report, Boston, July 19, 1922, Walter Ward Papers, Westchester County Archives; detective report, Boston, July 29, 1922, Walter Ward Papers, Westchester County Archives.
8. Detective report, Boston, July 12, 1922, Walter Ward Papers, Westchester County Archives.
9. Detective report, Boston, July 20, 1922, Walter Ward Papers, Westchester County Archives.
10. "Peters Planned to Obtain Cash from Rich Man"; "Scrap of Paper May Solve Ward Murder Case," *The Brooklyn Citizen*, July 26, 1922, 2; "Declare Ward's Victim Promised Them Money," *The New York Herald*, July 27, 1922, 7.
11. Harry Scott to Frederick Weeks, detective report, Boston, July 17, 1922, Walter Ward Papers, Westchester County Archives.
12. Detective report, Boston, July 19, 1922.
13. Detective report, Boston, July 27, 1922.
14. Detective report, Boston, August 8, 1922, Walter Ward Papers, Westchester County Archives; detective report, Boston, August 6, 1922, Walter Ward Papers, Westchester County Archives; detective report, Boston, August 3, 1922, Walter Ward Papers, Westchester County Archives.
15. Detective report, Boston, August 6, 1922.
16. Detective report, Boston, August 27, 1922, Walter Ward Papers, Westchester County Archives.

Housecleaning

1. Joseph Esser, September 12, 1918, Westchester County, Mount Vernon, New York, *World War I Selective Service System Draft Registration Cards, 1917–1918* (Family History Library M1509, 4582 rolls); "Esser Explains Issues in Talk Before 150 Republican Women," *The Yonkers Herald*, September 8, 1922, 1; "Ward Trial Made a Political Issue," *The New York Times*, September 8, 1922, 17.

2. "Ward Is Facing Fight of Life in Westchester," *New-York Tribune*, August 28, 1922, 3.
3. "Ward Trial Made a Political Issue"; "Ward Case to Be Issue in Westchester Politics," *The New York Herald*, August 7, 1922, 5; "Ward Mystery Factor in Revolt Against Boss of Westchester," *New-York Tribune*, August 7, 1922, 5.
4. "Esser, Candidate, Suffers Broken Rib," *The Herald Statesman*, September 13, 1922, 2; "Esser Visits Ward's City; Demands Trial," *The New York Times*, September 17, 1922, 10; "Stirs Up New Rochelle About Ward Case," *Mount Vernon Argus*, September 18, 1922, 3.
5. "Seek to Have Ward Released on Bail," *The New York Times*, June 26, 1922, 12; "Republicans Meet to Pick County Slate," *The Yonkers Statesman*, June 21, 1922, 1; "Speedy Ward Trial"; "Weeks Ignored Political Threat in Ward Mystery," New York *Daily News*, June 28, 1922, 4; "Can't Convict Him, Defense Stand," *The New York Herald*, June 22, 1922, 5.
6. "Resigned for His Son's Sake," *The Herald Statesman*, August 18, 1922, 3; "Taylor Unopposed for Bench," *The Yonkers Statesman*, August 15, 1922, 1; "Esser Explains Issues."
7. "Weeks Is Silent on Ward Case," *The New York Herald*, August 28, 1922, 3; "Ward Trial for Peters' Death in Discard, Belief," New York *Daily News*, August 24, 1922, 6; "Ward Case Row Drives Weeks from Politics," New York *Daily News*, August 13, 1922, 9.
8. "County Notes," *Mount Vernon Argus*, September 26, 1922, 10; "G.O.P. Organization in County Unscathed by Primary Result," *The Yonkers Statesman*, September 21, 1922, 2.
9. "Smith Assails Gov. Miller as Reactionary," *New-York Tribune*, October 6, 1922, 1; "Smith Sweeps the State, Wins by 375,000," *The New York Times*, November 8, 1922, 1; "Miller—'Smith, Brand of Government Chosen'; Smith—'I Am Grateful and Hope I Make Good,'" *The New York Times*, November 8, 1922, 4; Lerner, *Dry Manhattan*.
10. "Counsel for Ward Asks Early Trial," *The New York Times*, November 11, 1922, 11; "Try or Free Ward, Counsel Demands," *The New York Times*, November 14, 1922, 15; "Reserves Decision on Ward Dismissal," *The New York Times*, November 22, 1922, 12; "Dismissal of Ward Case Is Refused," *The New York Times*, November 24, 1922, 17.
11. "Pleas for Dismissal in Ward Murder Case," *The New York Times*, December 31, 1922, 4; "Dismiss Indictment of Murder Against Ward," *Haverhill Evening Gazette*, January 2, 1923, 1; "Court Frees Ward of Murder Charge," *The New York Times*, January 3, 1923, 1; "Ward Weighs Justice's Scales," New York *Daily News*, January 3, 1923, 2; "Ward Is

Freed, Court Quashes Death Charge," *New York American*, January 3, 1923, 3.

12. "Walter Ward, Rich Baker's Son, Freed of Murder," *Dayton Daily News*, January 2, 1923, 1; "Walter Ward Freed on Charge of Slaying," *Anaheim Bulletin*, January 3, 1923, 1; "Rich Baker's Son Is Freed of Murder Charges," *Detroit Free Press*, January 3, 1923, 1; "Ward Freed on the Charge of Murder," *Bangor Daily News*, January 3, 1923, 1; "Mysterious Shooting Case in New York Finally Dismissed," *The Alaska Daily Empire*, January 3, 1923, 1.
13. "An Expensive Mistake," *New-York Tribune*, January 4, 1923, 10.

Grief-Stricken Mothers

1. "Ward Inquiry Hums to Action," New York *Daily News*, January 8, 1922, 3.
2. Christopher M. Finan, *Alfred E. Smith: The Happy Warrior* (New York: Hill and Wang, 2002); Henry F. Pringle, "The Janitor's Boy," *The New Yorker*, March 5, 1927, 24.
3. "Smith Moved by Mother's Plea, Orders New Ward Case Inquiry," New York *Daily News*, January 7, 1923, 3; "Ask Smith to Act on the Ward Case," *The New York Times*, January 7, 1923, 1; "Ward Inquiry Hums to Action."
4. "Legislators Demand Ward Case Lid Lifting," New York *Daily News*, January 17, 1923, 3.
5. "The Still Small Voice," *The Jewell County Monitor* (Mankato, Kansas), March 9, 1923, 7.
6. All references to the letters come from box 56, folder 200–339, Extraordinary Special and Trial Term of Supreme Court, Westchester County (Ward Case), Governor Alfred E. Smith Central Subject and Correspondence Files, New York State Archives.

Voice of the People

1. "'Public Be ___' Attitude Adopted by Prosecutor in Ward Mystery," New York *Daily News*, January 12, 1923, 3.
2. "Justice 'Has a Heart,'" New York *Daily News*, January 4, 1923, 11.
3. "'Public Be ___' Attitude."
4. Biographical information on Patterson comes from several sources: Megan McKinney, *The Magnificent Medills: America's Royal Family of Journalism During a Century of Turbulent Splendor* (New York: HarperCollins,

2011); John Chapman, *Tell It to Sweeney: The Informal History of the New York Daily News* (New York: Doubleday, 1961); Simon Michael Bessie, *Jazz Journalism: The Story of the Tabloid Newspapers* (New York: E. P. Dutton & Company, 1938).

5. "Who We Are," New York *Daily News*, June 26, 1919, 5.
6. Joseph Patterson to Phil Payne, July 25, 1923, New York Daily News, 1919–1931, Publishing Enterprises, Joseph Medill Patterson Papers, Lake Forest College Archives and Special Collections.
7. Chapman, *Tell It to Sweeney*, 70.
8. Joe Pompeo, *Blood & Ink: The Scandalous Jazz Age Double Murder That Hooked America on True Crime* (New York: William Morrow, 2022).
9. The Inquiring Photographer, New York *Daily News*, January 11, 1923, 13.
10. Joseph Patterson to Phil Payne, February 5, 1923, New York *Daily News*, 1919–1931, Publishing Enterprises, Joseph Medill Patterson Papers, Lake Forest College Archives and Special Collections.
11. McKinney, *The Magnificent Medills*; Chapman, *Tell It to Sweeney.*
12. Allen, *Only Yesterday*, 81.
13. "Alder Blocks Ward Probe in Assembly," New York *Daily News*, February 27, 1923; "Committee Fights Ward Case Inquiry," New York *Daily News*, February 28, 1923, 12; "Ignore Ward-Peters Crime," *The New York Times*, March 6, 1923, 5.
14. "Gov. Smith, It's Your Move," New York *Daily News*, March 7, 1923, 13.
15. "The Ward Case Theory," The Voice of the People, New York *Daily News*, March 2, 1923, 11; "Law and Ward," The Voice of the People, New York *Daily News*, March 27, 1923, 13; "The Ward Case," The Voice of the People, New York *Daily News*, April 8, 1923, 11.
16. "Smith Orders Deep Ward Probe," New York *Daily News*, March 22, 1923, 2.
17. Phil Payne to Governor Al Smith, March 22, 1923, box 56, folder 200–339, Extraordinary Special and Trial Term of Supreme Court, Westchester County (Ward Case), Governor Alfred E. Smith Central Subject and Correspondence Files, New York State Archives.
18. "Ward Murder Case Inquiry to Be Open," *The New York Times*, April 1, 1923, 10.

False from Start to Finish

1. "Peters Inquiry Starts Tomorrow," *The Boston Globe*, April 1, 1923, 12; "Open Hearings Begin Monday in Peters Case," *Haverhilll Evening Gazette*, March 31, 1923, 1; "Ward Murder Case Inquiry to Be Open."

2. "Funeral of Sandor Sherman to Be Held This Afternoon," *Buffalo Morning Express*, November 2, 1913, 33; "Carl Sherman, Democratic Aide, Dies; Had Served as State Attorney General," *The New York Times*, July 18, 1956, 27; "Tell Insincerity of Hughes," *The Buffalo Enquirer*, October 31, 1916, 1.
3. "Buffalo Jewry Honored by Election of Carl Sherman as Attorney General," *Buffalo Jewish Review*, November 10, 1922, 1.
4. "Wilber W. Chambers, 62, Dies Suddenly While Visiting Friend," *The Standard-Star* (New Rochelle, New York), June 7, 1943, 1.
5. Allan Campbell's testimony comes from Appellate Division of the Supreme Court of New York, Third Department, *Ward Baking Company and Others, Appellants*, April 1923.
6. "Refuses to Give Up Blackmail Notes Received by Ward," *The New York Times*, April 3, 1923, 1; "Officials Welcomed Ward, and One Said He Did Just Right," *The New York Times*, April 4, 1923, 1; "Ward Lionized After Arrest, Counsel Says," *New-York Tribune*, April 4, 1923, 1; "Brother Won't Tell What Family Knows of Slaying by Ward," *The New York Times*, April 5, 1923, 1.
7. Elwood Rabenold's testimony: Appellate Division of the Supreme Court of New York, Third Department, *Ward Baking Company and Others, Appellants.*
8. Harry Green's and Eugene Roberts's testimony: Appellate Division of the Supreme Court of New York, Third Department, *Ward Baking Company and Others, Appellants.*
9. "Ward, Gone a Week, Was Found at Races," *The New York Times*, May 19, 1923, 6; Frank Cody's testimony: Appellate Division of the Supreme Court of New York, Third Department, *Ward Baking Company and Others, Appellants.*
10. "Doctors Re-enact Shooting of Peters," *The New York Times*, May 9, 1923, 21; "Course of Bullet Shows Ward Yarn False State Told," New York *Daily News*, May 9, 1923, 6.
11. "New Ward Witness Heard No Shooting," *The Boston Daily Globe*, April 29, 1923, 15; "2 New Witnesses Dispute Ward Tale of Peters Killing," *The New York Times*, April 29, 1923, 1.
12. "Re-enact Slaying of Clarence Peters," *The New York Times*, May 23, 1923, 14; "State Re-enacts Ward Killing at Scene of Tragedy," New York *Daily News*, May 23, 1923, 3; "State Sure Body of Ward Victim Carried to Road," New York *Daily News*, May 24, 1923, 3; "Use Revolver Test to Clear Mystery," *Los Angeles Times*, May 24, 1923, 12.
13. "Re-enact Slaying of Clarence Peters"; "Slaying of Peters Is Re-enacted;

Ward's Story Discredited," *Haverhill Evening Gazette*, May 23, 1923, 1; "State Re-Enacts Ward Killing"; "State Sure Body of Ward Victim Carried to Road."

14. "Brother Keeps Ward's Secret," *Los Angeles Times*, April 6, 1923, 16.
15. Ralph Ward's testimony: Appellate Division of the Supreme Court of New York, Third Department, *Ward Baking Company and Others, Appellants.*
16. "Re-enact Slaying of Clarence Peters"; George Zacharias's testimony: Appellate Division of the Supreme Court of New York, Third Department, *Ward Baking Company and Others, Appellants.*
17. "Ward, Gone a Week."
18. "Says Ward Agents Hid 3 Witnesses," *The New York Times*, April 27, 1923, 1.

Dirty Trick

1. Julia Harpman, "Ward Cash Buried Witnesses," New York *Daily News*, April 26, 1923, 3; Testimony of Samuel Miller, *The People of the State of New York vs. Walter Ward.*
2. Testimony of Samuel Miller, *The People of the State of New York vs. Walter Ward.*
3. Testimony of Samuel Miller, *The People of the State of New York vs. Walter Ward.*
4. Testimony of Samuel Miller, *The People of the State of New York vs. Walter Ward.*
5. *The People of the State of New York vs. Walter Ward.*
6. Testimony of Samuel Miller, *The People of the State of New York vs. Walter Ward.*
7. Harpman, "Ward Cash Buried Witnesses"; "Paid Witness Turn on Ward," New York *Daily News*, April 29, 1923, 2.
8. "Ward Hide and Seek Goes On," New York *Daily News*, April 27, 1923, 3.
9. Testimony of Samuel Miller, *The People of the State of New York vs. Walter Ward.*
10. Justin Peavey, in discussion with the author, March 12, 2023.

Five to One

1. Phil Payne to Joseph Patterson, April 13, 1923, New York Daily News, 1919–1931, Publishing Enterprises, Joseph Medill Patterson Papers,

Lake Forest College Archives and Special Collections; C. T. Corcoran, "Desire for Justice," New York *Daily News*, May 7, 1923, 11.

2. "How About It, Governor?" New York *Daily News*, May 7, 1923, 11; "On Being 'Unreasonable,'" New York *Daily News*, May 18, 1923, 15.
3. "What More Do You Want, Governor?" New York *Daily News*, May 25, 1923, 15.
4. "Smith Will Summon New Court and Jury to Hear Ward Case," *The New York Times*, May 26, 1923, 1; "Smith Orders New Ward Jury," New York *Daily News*, May 26, 1923, 3.
5. "Ward Case Judge to Be Named Monday," *Haverhill Evening Gazette*, May 26, 1923, 1.
6. "NEWS Created Tide That Inundated Ward Millions, Lawyer's Praise," New York *Daily News*, May 27, 1923, 4.
7. J. T. Evans, "Odds Favor Ward," New York *Daily News*, May 26, 1923, 11.

Let Us Have the Fish

1. "Walter Ward's Wife Fined for Speeding," *The New York Herald*, July 29, 1922, 3; "Walter S. Ward First Bumped by Law as Speeder," New York *Daily News*, June 2, 1923, 6.
2. "Mrs. Ward, Fighting Collapse, Sails for Rest in Bermuda," New York *Daily News*, March 4, 1923, 67; "Ward's Wife, Her Mother Exiles in Probe, He Charges," New York *Daily News*, May 10, 1923, 7; *The People of the State of New York vs. Walter S. Ward.*
3. Ralph Ward's testimony: Appellate Division of the Supreme Court of New York, Third Department, *Ward Baking Company and Others, Appellants*; *The People of the State of New York vs. Walter S. Ward.*
4. Julia Harpman, "Peters's Mother, Worn by Toil, Prays for Justice in Ward Case," New York *Daily News*, April 18, 1923, 3.
5. "Jury to Get Today Cables Ward Sent," *The New York Times*, June 26, 1923, 1.
6. All biographical information about Wagner comes from Pringle, "The Janitor's Boy"; J. Joseph Huthmacher, *Senator Robert F. Wagner and the Rise of Urban Liberalism* (New York: Atheneum Books, 1968).
7. Huthmacher, *Senator Robert F. Wagner and the Rise of Urban Liberalism.*
8. "Ward Loses Fight for His Messages," *The New York Times*, April 25, 1923, 23; "Ward Cables Near State Grasp," New York *Daily News*, April 25, 1923, 3.
9. "Ward Loses Fight for His Messages"; "Ward Cables Near State

Grasp"; Appellate Division of the Supreme Court of New York, Third Department, *Ward Baking Company and Others, Appellants*, June 19, 1923.

10. "Blackmail Cables Read to Ward Jury," *The New York Times*, June 30, 1923, 13.
11. Jean-François Fava-Verde, "Managing Privacy: Cryptography or Private Networks of Communication in the Nineteenth Century," *Technology and Culture* 61, no. 3 (July 2020): 789–814.
12. "Ward Asked $91,000 in Cable to Father," *The New York Times*, August 25, 1923, 1.
13. "Ward Grand Jurors Hear Code Messages," *The New York Times*, July 10, 1923, 22.
14. "Ward Asked $91,000."

Unprintable Practices

1. "Former Westchester County District Attorney Indicted," *The Yonkers Statesman*, July 12, 1923, 1.
2. "Jury Sought in Vain for Ward's Father," *The New York Times*, August 27, 1923, 13.
3. "Mother's Plea to Ward Jury," New York *Daily News*, July 25, 1923, 2; "Ward Jury Hears Mother of Peters," *The New York Times*, July 25, 1923, 8.
4. "Mystery Visits of Strangers to Ward Revealed," *New-York Tribune*, August 24, 1923, 4.
5. William Mundia, p. 1B [handwritten], line 93, Enumeration District 1229, Manhattan Assembly District 18, New York County, New York Census of Population, *Fourteenth Census of the United States*, 1920 (National Archives Microfilm Publications T625, 2076 rolls) Records of the Bureau of the Census, Record Group 29; William Mundia, September 9, 1918, New York County, New York, *World War I Selective Service System Draft Registration Cards, 1917–1918* (Family History Library M1509, 4582 rolls).
6. "New and Unheard Witness in Ward Shooting Disclosed When He Attempts Suicide in Cell," *The New York Times*, June 29, 1923, 1.
7. "Say 'Petting' Parties Drinking at Cabaret," *The Buffalo News*, March 17, 1923, 3; "Greenwich 'Queens' in Court," *The Kansas City Star*, January 24, 1923, 4; "Novelist Flays Drys, Exalting Our Flappers," New York *Daily News*, January 24, 1923, 18.
8. "Witness Says Ward Admitted Killing, Tried to Shoot Him," *The New York Times*, August 23, 1923, 1; "Mundia Describes Wild Ward Parties;

Minutes Published," *Brooklyn Daily Eagle*, August 23, 1923, 20; "Witness Bares What He Swears Is Ward Secret," *New-York Tribune*, August 23, 1923, 1.

9. George Chauncey Jr., "Christian Brotherhood or Sexual Perversion? Homosexual Identities and the Construction of Sexual Boundaries in the World War One Era," *Journal of Social History* 19, no. 2 (Winter 1985): 189–211.
10. C. V. Knightley to Henry Fielding, April 9, 1923, Walter Ward Papers, Westchester County Archives.
11. Thomas Keating, "A Moral Victory," New York *Daily News*, July 30, 1923, 11; Sumner Forsythe, "The Ward Indictment," New York *Daily News*, July 28, 1923, 9.
12. "A Mystery Under a Mystery," Topics of the Times, *The New York Times*, July 28, 1923, 6.
13. "Ward Reindicted, Held Without Bail, Goes to Prison Cell," *The New York Times*, July 27, 1923, 1; "Walter Ward Indicted for Murder; Slayer Goes to Trial September," New York *Daily News*, July 27, 1923.

Mousetrap

1. "President's Death Shocks Capital, Which Had Expected Recovery," *The New York Times*, August 3, 1923, 1; Allen, *Only Yesterday*, 134; NCC Staff, "Generations later, President Warren Harding's sudden death recalled," National Constitution Center, August 3, 2022, constitutioncenter.org/blog/after-90-years-president-warren-hardings-death-still-unsettled; "Governor Smith Shocked," *The New York Times*, August 3, 1923, 5.
2. *People of the State of New York vs. Walter Ward*, August 1, 1923, Walter Ward Papers, Westchester County Archives.
3. "An Open Letter to Justice Seeger," New York *Daily News*, August 3, 1923, 41.
4. "Call O'Neill to Aid Ward Prosecution," *The New York Times*, July 30, 1923, 4.
5. *The People of the State of New York vs. Walter Ward*, August 14, 1923; "Seeger Gives Ward Access to Minutes," *The New York Times*, August 15, 1923, 19.
6. "Witness Bares What He Swears Is Ward Secret."
7. "Ward Lawyer Hits Judge and State," *The New York Times*, August 31, 1923, 17.

8. "Court Rules Ward Must Stand Trial," *The New York Times*, September 7, 1923, 17; "Ward Must Stand Trial," New York *Daily News*, September 7, 1923, 3.
9. "Court Rules Ward Must Stand Trial"; "'Put Me to Work,' Asks Ward in Jail," *Hartford Courant*, July 29, 1923, 20; "Mousetraps for Justice," New York *Daily News*, September 7, 1923, 47.
10. Phil Payne to Joseph Patterson, August 30, 1923, New York Daily News, 1919–1931, Publishing Enterprises, Joseph Medill Patterson Papers, Lake Forest College Archives and Special Collections.

Fly into the Air Like Smoke

1. "Ward Story of Peters' Death Heard by Jury," *Haverhill Evening Gazette*, September 21, 1923, 1; "State Fails to Prove That Ward Owned Both Guns," *Brooklyn Daily Eagle*, September 21, 1923, 1.
2. "Ward Will Convict Himself of Murder, Trial Jury Is Told," *The New York Times*, September 18, 1923, 1.
3. "Chair for Ward, State Pleas," New York *Daily News*, September 18, 1923, 3.
4. "Chair for Ward, State Pleas"; "Ward Will Convict Himself."
5. "Witness Tells How He Found Peters' Body," *Haverhill Evening Gazette*, September 18, 1923, 1.
6. "Chair for Ward, State Pleas."
7. "Ward Shielding Someone Else Is New Theory," *Haverhill Evening Gazette*, September 19, 1922, 1.
8. "Testifies Peters Was Dropped by Navy for Theft," *Brooklyn Daily Eagle*, September 19, 1923, 1.
9. "State Fails to Prove."
10. "Call Ward Lawyer as State Witness to Identify Pistols," *The New York Times*, September 21, 1923, 1.
11. "Ward Jurors Hear Slayer's Wife and Mother of Victim," *The New York Times*, September 25, 1923, 1.
12. "Plot to Use Ward in Fleecing Father Told to Trial Jury," *The New York Times*, September 23, 1923, 1; "Ward Called a Blackmailer," New York *Daily News*, September 22, 1923, 3.
13. "Says Ward Tried to Blackmail Father," *The Boston Globe*, September 22, 1923, 1.
14. "Ward Defense Given Setback by Affidavit," *New York American*, September 23, 1923, 5.

His Story Is Still Unexplained

1. "Ward Story False, Mills Admits," *New York American*, September 19, 1923, 1.
2. "More Dramatic Incidents in Murder Trial Today, Mystery Deepens in Case," *Mount Vernon Argus*, September 21, 1923, 1; "State Fails to Prove"; "Crowds of Women Flock to Hear Ward Trial," *Olean Times Herald*, September 19, 1923, 13.
3. "2300 Letters Received by Mrs. Ward Since Murder Trial Opened," *Mount Vernon Argus*, September 27, 1923, 1.
4. "Mrs. Ward Keeps Secret," *New York American*, September 25, 1923, 1.
5. "Ward Jurors Hear Slayer's Wife."
6. "State Rests in Ward Trial," *Haverhill Evening Gazette*, September 25, 1923, 1.
7. "Mrs. Peters and Mrs. Ward Heard," *The Boston Globe*, September 26, 1923, 1.
8. "Ward Story False."
9. "Ward Defense Opens Today," *The Boston Globe*, September 25, 1923, 6.
10. "Ward Rest Case; Put in No Defense; Summing Up Begins," *Brooklyn Daily Eagle*, September 26, 1923, 1; "Ward Trial Halts; Defense Not Ready as State Ends Case," *The New York Times*, September 26, 1923, 1.
11. Comments from Mills's summation come from: Isaac N. Mills, *Address Delivered by the Honorable Isaac N. Mills, of the Westchester County Bar on September 26th, 1923 in Summing Up for the Defense to the Jury at the Trial of Walter S. Ward upon the Charge of Murder in the First Degree* (Mount Vernon, New York: privately printed, 1923).
12. Comments from Sherman's summation come from: "Sherman Asks Ward's Life," New York *Daily News*, September 28, 1923, 3; "Enact Killing Scene in Demand to Jury for Death of Ward," *The New York Times*, September 28, 1923, 1.
13. "Ward Acquitted of Murder," New York *Daily News*, September 29, 1923, 3; "Ward Is Acquitted; Verdict Applauded; Jury Out 3 hours," *The New York Times*, September 29, 1923, 1.
14. "Ward Begins Week of Golf with Father," *New-York Tribune*, September 30, 1923, 1; "Ward Sends Roses to Girls Who Waved Encouragement," *Brooklyn Daily Eagle*, September 30, 1923, 1.
15. "Walter Ward Gets Reception at Plant," *The Boston Globe*, September 30, 1923, 22.

16. "Westchester Sees Ward Trial Costing County $100,000," *Brooklyn Daily Eagle*, September 29, 1923, 2.
17. "Peters' Mother Expected Ward Would Go Free," *Haverhill Evening Gazette*, September 29, 1923, 1.

Epilogue: Careless People

1. "United Bakeries May Acquire Ward Chain," *The Buffalo News*, December 11, 1923, 34; "$75,000,000 Bread Merger Hinted by Ward Firm's Head," New York *Daily News*, December 16, 1923, 36.
2. "Ward and United Bakeries Merge," New York *Daily News*, December 18, 1923, 30; "51% of Holders of Ward Co. Stock Agree to Sale," *Brooklyn Daily Eagle*, December 17, 1923, 20.
3. "Changes in Ward Co. Following the Trial," *The Yonkers Herald*, May 22, 1924, 1.
4. "Why I Came Back to My Father's Company: A Statement by William B. Ward, New President of the Ward Baking Co.," *Brooklyn Daily Eagle*, May 23, 1924, 33.
5. "See Threat of Bread Monopoly in Ward Merger," *Brooklyn Daily Eagle*, February 15, 1924, 18; Ward Bakery Company, *Annual Report*, December 27, 1924.
6. "Havana Values Rising," *Miami Herald*, September 27, 1925, 82; Ada Ferrer, *Cuba: An American History* (New York: Scribner, 2021).
7. Waldo Frank, "Habana of the Cubans," *The New Republic*, June 23, 1926, 140–41.
8. "Geo. S. Ward Dies; Bakery Operator," *The New York Times*, September 4, 1940, 32.
9. "Police Fear Foul Play as Ward Disappears," New York *Daily News*, May 9, 1923, 2; Julia Harpman, "Ward Murder Fears Bared," New York *Daily News*, May 11, 1926, 3.
10. Harpman, "Ward Murder Fears Bared."
11. "Report Ward as Gambling Loser," *The Yonkers Herald*, May 14, 1923, 4.
12. "Report Ward as Gambling Loser"; "Walter Ward Father's Guest," *Wisconsin Rapids Daily Tribune*, January 17, 1927, 1; "W.S. Ward Found After 9 Months," *Evening Star* (Washington, D.C.), January 16, 1927, 1.
13. "Offer to Start New Life Turned Down by Ward," New York *Daily News*, May 19, 1926, 27.
14. "Walter Ward, Missing Rich Man Is Found," *Kenosha Evening News*, January 17, 1927, 2; "Walter S. Ward Found, Lost and Refound in Cuba," *Reading Times*, January 17, 1927, 1; "W.S. Ward Found."

15. "Walter S. Ward Dies in Havana," *The Standard-Star*, May 24, 1946, 1; American Foreign Service, "Report of the Death of An American Citizen," Walter Stevenson Ward, May 28, 1946, *Death Reports of U.S. Citizen Abroad, 1920–1962*, General Records of the Department of State, Record Group 59, box 1677, National Archives at College Park, Maryland.
16. "Ward Merely Hiding, Police Convinced," New York *Daily News*, May 17, 1926, 8; "Peters's Suit Begins Today Without Ward," New York *Daily News*, February 15, 1927, 3; "Peters' Record Hit in $75,000 Suit," *The Boston Globe*, February 17, 1927, 19; "Ward Jury Fails to Reach Verdict," *Times Union*, February 18, 1927, 73.
17. Elbridge O. Peters, p. 2B [handwritten], line 77, Enumeration District 68, Haverhill, Essex County, Massachusetts Census of Population, *Fifteenth Census of the United States*, 1930 (National Archives Microfilm Publications T626, 2667 rolls) Records of the Bureau of the Census; Inez Peters, p. 61A [handwritten], line 3, Enumeration District 5-112, Haverhill, Essex County, Massachusetts Census of Population, *Sixteenth Census of the United States*, 1940 (National Archives Microfilm Publications T627, 4643 rolls) Records of the Bureau of the Census; "Elbridge Oliver Peters," Find a Grave, accessed May 12, 2023, findagrave.com/memorial/100479037/elbridge-oliver-peters; Inez Peters, January 1967, *Social Security Death Index, Master File*, Social Security Administration.
18. "Son of Wealthy Baker Is Sued for Divorce," *Reno Gazette-Journal*, September 13, 1926, 8; Di Long, "Divorce in New York from 1850s to 1920s" (master's thesis, University of Georgia, 2013), getd.libs.uga.edu/pdfs/long_di_201312_ma.pdf.
19. "Infidelity Charged to Bakery King," *San Francisco Examiner*, September 14, 1927, 1; "Mrs. Beryl Curtis Ward Is Rewed at Doylestown," *The Morning Call* (Allentown, Pennsylvania), November 30, 1927, 1.
20. "Mrs. W.S. Ward Back from Reno to Forget Past," *New-York Tribune*, November 12, 1927, 3; "Mrs. Walter Ward Will Marry Again," *Daily Press* (Newport News, Virginia), November 13, 1927, 1.
21. "Lysle and Beryl Alderson," U.S. Census 1930; Beryl Alderson, p. 73 [handwritten], line 6, Enumeration District 60-369, Scarsdale, Westchester County, New York Census of Population, *Seventeenth Census of the United States*, 1950 (National Archives Microfilm Publications roll 135) Records of the Bureau of the Census, Record Group 29; "Walter S. Ward's Son Killed in Plane Accident in England," *The Standard-Star*, October 23, 1942, 1; Beryl Alderson, August 6, 1975, *Social Security Death Index, Master File*, Social Security Administration;

"Barnstable County Courthouse News," The Barnstable Patriot, March 14, 1940: 9.

22. McLaren, *Sexual Blackmail*, 134; "The Twinkie Murder," April 28, 21016, in *Blunt History*, podcast, MP3 audio, 39:35, podchaser.com/podcasts/blunt-history-podcast-498553/episodes/05-the-twinkie-murder-13355926.
23. F. Scott Fitzgerald, *The Great Gatsby* (New York: Scribner, 2018), 49.
24. Fitzgerald, *The Great Gatsby*, 7.
25. J. E. Canaday, "Hall-Mills Case," New York *Daily News*, September 23, 1923, 11.
26. Pompeo, *Blood & Ink*.
27. Sarah Churchwell, *Careless People: Murder, Mayhem, and the Invention of The Great Gatsby* (New York: Penguin Press, 2013), 291.
28. Grant Overton, "Have You Read" column found in "The Great Gatsby, to Silent-Film Version of Gatsby," Series 10: Scrapbooks, 1896–1935, F. Scott Fitzgerald Papers, 1897–1944, C0187, Manuscripts Division, Department of Special Collections, Princeton University Library.
29. Fitzgerald, *The Great Gatsby*, 178.

© Greg Salvatori

JAMES POLCHIN, PhD, is a writer, professor, and cultural historian. His book *Indecent Advances: A Hidden History of True Crime and Prejudice Before Stonewall* was an Edgar Award finalist and Macavity Award nominee and was named one of the Best True Crime Books of the Year by *CrimeReads*. His writing has appeared in *Slate*, *Time*, *HuffPost UK*, *CrimeReads*, *The Paris Review*, *Rolling Stone*, *NewNextNow*, and *The Gay and Lesbian Review Worldwide*. He is a clinical professor at New York University and previously taught at the Princeton Writing Program, Parsons School of Design, the New School, and the Creative Nonfiction Foundation. He lives in New York with his husband, the photographer Greg Salvatori, and a Labrador named Albert. You can follow him on X at @jamespolchin.